THE FIRST

****

NEW

****

NATION

****

BY SEYMOUR MARTIN LIPSET (IN CHRONOLOGICAL ORDER):

Agrarian Socialism
Union Democracy (with Martin Trow and James S. Coleman)
Social Mobility in Industrial Society (with Reinhard Bendix)
Prejudice and Society (with Earl Raab)
Political Man: The Social Bases of Politics
The First New Nation: The United States in Historical and Comparative Perspective
Estudiantes universitarios y politica en el tercer mundo
Revolution and Counterrevolution
The Politics of Unreason: Right-Wing Extremism in America 1790-1970 (with Earl Raab)
Group Life in America
Rebellion in the University
Professors, Unions, and American Higher Education (with Everett C. Ladd)
Academics, Politics, and the 1972 Election (with Everett C. Ladd)
The Divided Academy: Professors and Politics (with Everett C. Ladd)
Education and Politics at Harvard (with David Riesman)
Dialogues on American Politics (with Irving Louis Horowitz)

THE FIRST
NEW NATION

THE UNITED STATES IN
HISTORICAL AND
COMPARATIVE PERSPECTIVE

SEYMOUR MARTIN LIPSET

W. W. Norton & Company, Inc.

★ *New York*

To the memory of
WILLIAM LIPPMAN
(1894–1959)

First published as a Norton paperback 1979 by arrangement with
Basic Books, Inc.

Books That Live
The Norton imprint on a book means that in the publisher's
estimation it is a book not for a single season but for the years.
W. W. Norton & Company, Inc.

Library of Congress Cataloging in Publication Data
Lipset, Seymour Martin.
   The first new nation.
   Includes bibliographical references and index.
   1. United States—Civilization.   2. National
characteristics, American.   3. Comparative government.
I. Title.
E169.1.L546   1979   973   79-12263
ISBN 0-393-00911-4

1 2 3 4 5 6 7 8 9 0

Introduction to the Norton Edition

The First New Nation is a product of the early 1960s. Appearing in 1963, before the assassination of President Kennedy, it obviously did not deal with the sources and consequences of the prolonged series of political disasters and protest reactions which the United States faced from November 22, 1963 on. Those bygone almost bucolic days of the New Frontier, when America saw itself as the prosperous leader of the Free World, now seem like an almost ancient era.

There is little need to reiterate the dismal story of the subsequent decade-and-a-half of Vietnam, a country divided by mass protest, the growth of left- and right-wing extremism, Watergate, exposés of corruption and malfeasance in business and the intelligence agencies, the overthrow of two incumbent presidents, Johnson and Nixon, followed in office by two men perceived by much of the public as weak and inept, and finally during the seventies, serious recession succeeded by a run-away inflation.

Confidence in Institutions

These events, not surprisingly, resulted in a serious decline in confidence in most American institutions, which survey evidence dates as having begun in the late 1960s, leveling out at a much lower figure for the 1970s.[1] In 1965, Robert Lane, a political scientist at Yale University, published two articles in which he reported in some detail various polls

---

[1] For a review of the evidence on the poll data, see S. M. Lipset and William Schneider, *The Evaluation of Basic American Institutions, With Special Reference to Business* (New York: Macmillan, forthcoming).

dealing with American political institutions from the 1930s, when scientific polling began, down through the early 1960s. He found that on a number of different indicators, from a relative low point in the 1930s in the midst of the Great Depression, Americans had become increasingly positive about the operation of American society in general and about the political system in particular. By 1965 the great majority of those interviewed by various pollsters gave positive answers. In evaluating his results, Lane interpreted the growth of favorable replies as a function of affluence and higher education. As he noted, with the end of the Depression and with continuing prosperity on the one hand, and with an increase in the proportion of the population that had completed high school or had gone on to college on the other, more and more Americans said that they liked their society and believed that its political system was honest, effective, and responsive.[2]

The early 1960s, however, turned out to be a high-water mark in the history of the American public's attitudes toward their key institutions. The Vietnam involvement, the explosion of antiwar protest, and the rise of militant social movements concerned with the status of various minority groups—blacks, Hispanics, and particularly a non-minority group, women —seemingly changed the perception which Americans had of their country. Various pollsters registered a steady decline in the public's confidence in the country's institutions and in the people running them.[3]

The decline of confidence has been quite *general* in nature and not limited to political institutions. Louis Harris is probably the pollster most widely cited on trends in public confidence. In 1966, Harris asked for the first time a question about confidence in leaders of various institutions: "As far as people in charge of running [various institutions] are concerned, would you say you have a great deal of confidence, only some confidence, or hardly any confidence at all in them?" It has been argued that this question is phrased in such a way as to discourage positive responses, since the only positive response is "a great deal." Still, in 1966, the average percentage voicing "a great deal of confidence" in the leadership of fifteen different institutions was 41. Five years later, in 1971, the average percentage replying "a great deal" had fallen to 28.

---

[2] Robert E. Lane, "The Politics of Consensus in the Age of Affluence," *American Political Science Review*, 59 (1965), pp. 874–75 and "The Decline of Politics and Ideology in a Knowledgeable Society," *American Sociological Review*, 31 (1966), pp. 649–62.

[3] For a report on these see Lipset and Schneider, *op. cit.*

The important point is that confidence fell off in the leadership of *every* institution named by Harris. It appears that Americans became increasingly alienated from all the major institutions of society as the Vietnam war increasingly became a hopeless quagmire and as protest movements over the war and over minority rights disrupted the stability of the country. Thus, confidence in military leaders fell fastest between the 1966 and 1971 polls, from 67 percent expressing "a great deal of confidence" in 1966 to a mere 27 percent in 1971. Congress declined from 42 percent confidence to 19, while the Executive branch of the federal government fell from 41 to 23. Another public institution which was the focus of controversy during the late 1960s, education, suffered a considerable loss of confidence between 1966 and 1971, from 61 percent expressing "a great deal of confidence" in the people in charge of the educational system in 1966 to 37 percent in 1971.

Private institutions did not escape the prevailing trend of increasing alienation and cynicism. Harris asked Americans in both polls how much confidence they had in the leaders of "major companies." Business leaders declined in public esteem, from 55 to 27 percent, over the five-year period. Religious leaders also lost popularity, falling from 41 percent to 27. The leaders of two institutions which were not highly regarded to start with—the press and organized labor—declined even further, the press from 29 to 18 percent "high confidence" and labor leaders from 22 to 14. Two institutions which were highly regarded in 1966 continued to be so, relatively speaking in 1971: confidence in the leaders of medicine fell from 73 percent in 1966 to 61 percent in 1971, and in the leaders of science, from 56 percent to 46. Thus science and medicine, the two institutions most remote from the social turmoil of the late 1960s, showed the least decline in public confidence, although neither entirely escaped the prevailing trend. The point to be reiterated is the generality of the trend, the fact that it was not a period of declining confidence in business or political or religious or educational leadership, but a period of declining confidence in leadership generally—a dominant trend of alienation shared in varying degrees by all institutions.

The Harris poll has asked the "confidence in leaders" question in 1966 and 1971, as reported above, and then again in every year since 1971. Harris has inquired about ten of the same institutions using the same wording in every one of these ten surveys. The *average* percentage of the public voicing "a great deal of confidence" in leaders of these ten institutions fell from 46 in 1966 to 28 in 1971; since 1971, this average has varied erratically: 28 percent "high confidence" in 1972, 33 percent in

1973, 29 in 1974, 24 in 1975, 20 in 1976, 24 in February and 27 in November 1977, 26 in August 1978, and 23 in February 1979. It appears that the sizable decline of confidence following the Vietnam war and the period of protest began to reverse in the early 1970s with the end of the war and the reelection of President Nixon during a period of prosperity. The Watergate affair in 1973-1974 may have produced a new downturn, which, together with exposés of corruption in other institutions, resulted in an erosion of confidence from 1973 through 1976. Polls taken since Jimmy Carter took office in 1977 suggest higher levels of confidence in most institutions than were expressed at any time since Watergate, although confidence in the White House itself fell to new lows in the second half of 1978 and early 1979.

It appears that dramatic national crises such as the events of the late 1960s and the mid-1970s push confidence levels down. In the absence of such crises, as in the early 1970s and the first eighteen months of the Carter administration, there seems to be a natural tendency for the public to regain confidence as "good feelings" about the system resume. The public is inclined to believe that the system works unless they receive compelling evidence to the contrary. Still, what is most impressive about the public opinion findings is the extent to which Americans in the 1970s have remained much more dubious about their institutions than in the 1950s and early 1960s.

The downward trend in confidence from the mid-sixties on appears to correspond to a more general mood of increasing alienation in the American public, a reaction against "institutions," "leaders," and "power-holders" generally by a population which, though increasingly well-educated, feels increasingly powerless.[4] The negativism of the country in the late 1970s, however, does not appear to sustain the belief that alienation from major institutions, particularly government, labor and industry, will lead to radical protest. The growth of a new conservative mood reflected in the tax revolt, the steady increase in the proportion of those polled by various surveys who support conservative positions on various issues, and the gains made by conservative candidates in the 1978 primaries and elections clearly do not presage a rejection of American institutions by any important segment of the electorate.

The basic conservatism of the American people is also reflected in their very positive attitudes toward their economic system, but it should be

---

[4] See James D. Wright, *The Dissent of the Governed. Alienation and Democracy in America* (New York: Academic Press, 1976) and Vivien Hart, *Distrust and Democracy* (Cambridge: Cambridge University Press, 1978).

noted, not toward big business, to which they give a very low confidence rating. The United States, as we know, remains the only country in the developed world in which a socialist or social-democratic party has no representatives in its parliament. The polls also indicate relatively little backing for socialism as a concept and considerable continuing support for the idea of a "free enterprise" economic system. The public, it should be noted, is highly suspicious of, and critical of, what it views as the excessive power of big business, power which it feels is often misused in business's pursuit of "self-interest." To curb such abuses, majorities favor government regulation. They continue to oppose nationalization, possibly because they agree with Ralph Nader that "the only thing worse than having a car built by General Motors is to have one built by the government."[5]

Potomac Associates, which conducted a series of surveys from 1959 to 1976 of attitudes toward American institutions, reported in line with other studies that Americans have "cast a critical eye on various institutions within their society. . . . But they see themselves and their system in strongly positive terms, certainly a sign of health which pessimists would do well to recognize." Similarly, Harris, in interpreting the results of a poll taken in December 1978, noted that despite "the massive fall off in public confidence in most establishment institutions, fully 74 percent of Americans say they have a great deal of confidence in this country."[6] The level of confidence in the country did not vary much by occupation, or party affiliation. Self-identified liberals, however, were somewhat less positive (66 percent) than conservatives (80 percent).

The seeming contradiction between a low level of confidence in major American institutions, and considerable support for the American political, social and economic systems may be related to the fact that all through the tension-filled years of the late sixties and seventies, Americans, though worried about what was happening to their institutions and highly critical of most of their leaders, have felt positively about their own personal situations. Surveys taken by the Gallup Poll for Potomac Associates in 1959, 1964, 1971, 1972, 1974, and 1976 revealed that Americans tended to report their sense of personal well-being and their expectations for the future in much more positive terms than they did the state

---

[5] S. M. Lipset and William Schneider, "How's Business? What the Public Thinks," *Public Opinion*, 1 (July-August 1978), pp. 41–47 and "The Public View of Regulation," *Public Opinion*, 2 (January-February 1979), pp. 6–13.
[6] Francis E. Rourke, Lloyd Free and William Watts, *Trust and Confidence in The American System* (Washington, D.C.: Potomac Associates, 1976), pp. 26–27. Louis Harris, "Confidence in Country Is High—Contrasts with Confidence in the President," *ABC News-Harris Survey*, January 15, 1979, p. 1.

of the nation. As Watts and Free put it in their 1977 report: "Americans express a sharp dichotomy between views about their personal lives, which have remained uniformly positive and essentially unchanged over the years since 1959, and their far more sober view of the state of the nation than surfaced in 1971."[7] In a national survey taken by Yankelovich, Skelly and White in mid-winter 1974-75, the findings were comparable:

> Despite national economic and financial stress, the large majority of men and women report their *own* families are still doing well. A remarkable 83% report that their families are in good shape, but an equal number (79%) feel that things are going badly in the country. Undoubtedly this sense of family well-being is an important ballast in these times of uncertainty, and fortunately, this sense of family prevails among diverse income and age groups, and is shared by other family members as well.[8]

Similarly, in a national survey taken in February 1979, Gallup found that only 26 percent were "satisfied . . . with the way things are going in the U.S. at this time," while 69 percent expressed dissatisfaction. But when the same people were asked "In general, are you satisfied or dissatisfied with the way things are going in your own personal life?", over three-quarters (77 percent) replied satisfied, compared to only 21 percent dissatisfied.

Americans varied in the same way in their expectations for the future—pessimistic about the country, but again optimistic about themselves and their families—when asked by Potomac Associates to rank on a ten point ladder scale their estimate of their own life and the situation of the country five years ago, at the present time, and five years from now. In 1959 and 1964, the mean ratings for the present situation of the nation were slightly higher than for the past, while those for the future were much greater. From 1971 to 1976, the present was estimated as much below five years ago, while estimates for five years hence, while higher than for

---

[7] The reason Watts and Free mention 1971 as the first poll showing the dichotomy is that they did not poll between 1964 and 1971. Other surveys agree it began in the late 1960s. William Watts and Lloyd A. Free, *State of the Nation III* (Lexington, Mass.: Lexington Books, 1978), p. 204. See also Frank M. Andrews and Stephen B. Withey, *Social Indicators of Well-Being* (New York: Plenum Press, 1976), pp. 249–268.

[8] *The General Mills American Family Report 1974–75* (New York: Yankelovich, Skelly and White, 1975), p. 35. The 1979 Gallup Poll cited above is from George Gallup, "Public Pessimistic About Nation But Optimistic About Personal Lives," *The Gallup Poll*, March 29, 1979, pp. 1–6. See also George Gallup, "Americans Today Seem More Satisfied with Basic Aspects of Life than in '75," *The Gallup Poll*, June 1, 1978, pp. 2–3.

the present, were considerably under those anticipations made in 1959 and 1964.[9] Personal ratings, however, were quite different. The present was always judged as much better than a half decade earlier, while the future was consistently seen in even more optismistic terms than the present: "The great majority of Americans in mid-1976 felt they were doing well in their personal lives, exhibited a marked sense of personal progress, and were equally optimistic about the future."

Young people (18 to 29), the age group which contributed most to the protest waves of the late 60s and early 70s, turned out in 1976 to be the most optimistic for their personal futures: "The upward shift from the past to the present among them came to 1.5 steps on the ladder. . . . And the young were much more optimistic about the future: their present to future shift was a remarkable 2.2 steps on the ladder. . . ." It is especially interesting to note, in line with the empirical evidence about social changes to be discussed below, that "blacks in the latest [1976] survey had at least as much sense of progress from past to present as whites: the upward shift between past and present ratings amounted to 1.1 steps of the ladder among blacks, compared to 1.0 among whites. And they were much more optimistic about their personal futures, foreseeing an upward shift from present to future of 1.6 compared to 0.9 for whites. In sum, while rating their present position lower than that of whites, black Americans showed very marked feelings of progress and even greater optimism about the future."

Turning to the estimates of the national situation, however, Potomac Associates came up with a quite different picture, since in 1976 "more than one-half of the public (53 percent) thought the present situation was worse than five years ago, compared to less than the three out of ten (29 percent) who believed it was better, and 18 percent who felt it hadn't changed at all." A majority (52 percent), however, expected the national situation to be better five years from now, with blacks being the most optimistic.[10] In 1978, however, a somewhat different study by Albert and Susan Cantril which only used the "ladder" scale method to inquire about the state of the nation, found that anticipations for five years in the future were even lower than the evaluations of the present, which in turn were below those for five years ago. But as in the Potomac Associates polls, blacks were much more likely than whites to "see the nation as having made progress from the past to the present and are optimistic about progress in the future." Equally surprising is the fact that in 1978

---

[9] Watts and Free, *op. cit.*, pp. 4–6.
[10] *Ibid.*, pp. 4-6, 19-21.

low-income respondents were more likely than others to hold "the view that things will get better . . ."[11] The greater sense of optimism expressed by blacks as compared to whites about their personal futures, as well as for the state of the country, is perhaps the most surprising result of these surveys. It is reinforced by the findings of a national study of young blacks (ages 18 to 29) conducted in 1978 for *Ebony* magazine by the Roper Organization. As the report on this study in *Ebony* states, "This new breed of Blacks is optimistic about the future. Fully 89% of them say they will be *far* better off in terms of work and career ten years from now; another 32% feel they will be somewhat better off than they are today." Almost two-thirds "are sure they will earn more" than their parents. As *Ebony* describes their mood, "economically oriented, they are an optimistic, pragmatic, and materialistic group."[12]

This characteristic of American life in the late sixties and early seventies—severe criticism of institutions coupled with a high degree of satisfaction with personal situation and optimism for the future—goes far to explain another anomaly: that Americans are able to combine a high degree of criticism of major institutions and little confidence in their leaders with a strong attachment to the institutions and system as a whole. The fact that this long period of frustration has not resulted in a loss of legitimacy may account for the fact that increased conservatism, rather than leftist radicalism, is the popular reaction in the 1970s to the sense that things have been going badly. Americans want their traditional system(s) to work better, to behave the way they used to, rather than to fundamentally change them.

These developments suggest that the basic themes in this book have not been outmoded by the crises of the 1960s and 1970s. Fundamentally, the emphases on achievement values, linked to competition, and on equality of opportunity and respect, remain at the core of American values.[13] The protest movements which emerged in the sixties have, in fact, deepened the meaning of equality with respect to the situation of minorities and women. The "war on poverty" and successive efforts to enhance equality represent a response to the commitment in the American Creed to open the door of opportunity to all. Affirmative action programs attest to this, even though minorities and women are far from having achieved parity

---

[11] Albert H. and Susan D. Cantril, *Unemployment, Government and the American People. A National Opinion Survey* (Washington, D.C.: Public Research, 1978), pp. 16-17.

[12] "The New Generation: A Statistical Study," *Ebony*, 33 (August 1978), pp. 158-159.

[13] J. R. Pole, *The Pursuit of Equality in American History* (Berkeley: University of California Press, 1978).

with the dominant white male population.[14] My prediction in the first edition that immigration restrictions, which discriminated against persons from non-Nordic Protestant areas, would end has come true (p. 340). Although the evidence concerning trends in income inequality is subject to controversy among economists, when transfer payments are included in the income data it is clear that there has been a steady growth in the proportion of the total income received by the poorest fifth of the population. (See discussion on pp. 321–325).

Social Mobility

The data bearing on opportunity and income trends relate to findings that suggest that American society today is less rigid in terms of social advancement than it was in the past.[15] A *Scientific American* survey of the backgrounds of big-business executives (presidents, chairmen, and principal vice-presidents of the 600 largest U.S. nonfinancial corporations) found that as of 1964 the business elite had been opened to entry from below in a way that had never been true before in American history.

> Only 10.5 percent of the current generation of big business executives . . . are sons of wealthy families; as recently as 1950 the corresponding figure was 36.1 percent, and at the turn of the century, 45.6 percent. . . . Two-thirds of the 1900 generation had fathers who were heads of the same corporation or who were independent businessmen; less than half of the current generation had fathers so placed in American society. On the other hand, less than 10 percent of the 1900 generation had fathers who were employees; by 1964 this percentage had increased to nearly 30 percent.[16]

---

[14] For detailed documentation of the persistent pattern of the disproportionate benefits received by majority males, see *Social Indicators of Equality for Minorities and Women*, (Washington, D.C.: United States Commission on Civil Rights, 1978).

[15] S. M. Lipset, "Equality and Inequality," in R. K. Merton and R. Nisbet, eds., *Contemporary Social Problems* (New York: Harcourt, Brace and Jovanovich, 1976, 4th ed.), pp. 307–353.

[16] See *The Big Business Executive 1964: A Study of His Social and Educational Background*, a study sponsored by *Scientific American*, conducted by Market Statistics, Inc., of New York City, in collaboration with Dr. Mabel Newcomer. The study was designed to update Mabel Newcomer, *The Big Business Executive—The Factors that Made Him: 1900–1950* (New York: Columbia University Press, 1950). All comparisons in it are with materials in Dr. Newcomber's published work.

Surprisingly both to scholars in the field and to those radicals convinced that a mature capitalism would become increasingly immobile, particularly with respect to sharp jumps into the elite, the evidence indicates that the post-World War II period brought the greatest increase in the percentage of those from economically "poor" backgrounds who entered the top echelons of American business (the proportion rose from 12.1 percent in 1950 to 23.3 percent in 1964). There was a correspondingly great decline in the percentage from wealthy families (from 36.1 percent in 1950 to 10.5 percent in 1964). A number of the underlying structural trends that were expected to *limit* mobility appear to be responsible for this development: the replacement of the family-owned enterprise by the public corporation; the bureaucratization of American corporate life; the recruitment of management personnel from the ranks of college graduates; and the awarding of higher posts on the basis of a competitive-promotion process similar to that which operates in government bureaucracy. Because of the spread of higher education to the children of the working classes (almost one-third of whom now attend college), the ladder of bureaucratic success is increasingly open to those from poorer circumstances. Privileged family and class backgrounds continue to be enormous advantages in the quest for corporate success, but training and talent can make up for them in an increasing number of cases. These findings, drawn from observations of the backgrounds of the big-business elite, are reinforced by national surveys which indicate that opportunities "to enter high-status occupations appear to have improved in successive cohorts of U.S. men for at least the last 40 years, irrespective of those men's occupational origins."[17]

Other more broadly focused studies provide further evidence that there has been no hardening of class lines in American society. According to Stephan Thernstrom (who has played the leading role among historians both in doing research and in stimulating work on the part of others), a high rate of social mobility has continued over a 90-year period.[18]

Thernstrom notes that these findings challenge the often voiced belief that changes in American capitalism have created a permanent and growing class of the poor. In fact, all the available evidence points in the opposite direction. Statistical data from Poughkeepsie, New York in the 1840s,

---

[17] Robert M. Hauser et al., "Temporal Change in Occupational Mobility: Evidence for Men in the United States," *American Sociological Review*, 40 (June 1975), p. 280.

[18] Stephan Thernstrom, *The Other Bostonians: Poverty and Progress in the American Metropolis, 1880–1970* (Cambridge, Mass.: Harvard University Press, 1973).

Boston in five different samples from the 1880s to recent years, and Indianapolis in 1910, as well as from various surveys local and national after World War II, indicate that most of the sons of unskilled workers either moved up into the ranks of the skilled or found middle-class jobs of various kinds.

The conclusions are reinforced by comprehensive and methodologically sophisticated national sample surveys of the American population. An examination of the results of a number of surveys taken up to 1972 suggests that rates of social mobility have "been remarkably stable for more than half a century."[19] In evaluating the social implications of these findings, it should be noted that they were obtained by holding constant the changes over time in the occupational structure. Since the proportion of higher-status, higher-paying positions requiring more education and skill has been increasing steadily, there has in fact been an increase in the proportions of those securing a more rewarded position than their fathers. Hence, though relative opportunity has not increased, the absolute levels have, and this may affect the popular feeling about opportunity.

Speaking more generally to the issue of equality of opportunity, another set of studies by a group of Harvard sociologists and economists, led by Christopher Jencks, reanalyzed the data from a number of sources, seeking to specify the factors involved in occupational choice and earning capacity. These scholars, many of whom happen to be socialists politically, found that the results contradicted their anticipations:

> Poverty is not primarily hereditary. While children born into poverty have a higher-than-average chance of ending up poor, there is still an enormous amount of economic mobility from one generation to the next. Indeed, there is nearly as much economic inequality among brothers raised in the same homes as in the general population. This means that inequality is recreated anew in each generation, even among people who start life in essentially identical circumstances.

The researchers came to these conclusions by comparing the occupational status scores on the "Duncan scale" (which ranks occupations from 96 points to 0) of fathers, sons, and brothers with a random sample of unrelated individuals. They found that randomly selected individuals differed in occupational status by an average of 28 points, while brothers varied from each other by 23 points, and fathers from sons by 20 points. As they note, "there is nearly as much variation in status between brothers

---

[19] Hauser et al., *op. cit.*, p. 280.

as in the larger population. Family background is not, then, the primary determinant of status."[20]

But if fathers do have "some" effect on the occupations of their sons, a more recent analysis by Jencks of relationships over three generations indicates that

> paternal grandfathers have little or no direct effect on their grandson's life chances. Whether the father inherited his status, climbed up to it, or slid down to it seems to make little difference to the son's life chances. . . . The longer we make our time horizon, the more equal opportunity looks.[21]

Minorities and Women

The analysis of rates of opportunity is far from the whole story with respect to the underlying pattern of opportunity over time. It is important to recognize that in America occupational position has been differentially distributed among sex, ethnic, and racial groups.

The most recent study of the relative position of different ethnic groups in the United States indicates that among the non-Spanish-heritage white population, those of non-Anglo-Saxon, non-Protestant background have overcome and surpassed scions of those ethno-religious stocks who were here before them. Andrew Greeley summarizes his findings as follows:

> The most wealthy Americans are Jews, with an annual income of $13,340. Irish Catholics are in second place, some $900 behind the Jews, and Italian Catholics are third, a little less than $700 behind the Irish Catholics. German Catholics, Polish Catholics take fourth and fifth place, and Episcopalians and Presbyterians only then find sixth and seventh place on the income ladder. . . . At the bottom of the economic heap are the Scandinavian Protestants ($9,597), the American Protestants ($9,274), Irish Protestants ($9,147), and Baptists ($8,693). . . . In the American economic game, then, whether nationally or in Northern cities, Jews, the Irish, German and Italian Catholics are the big winners, and the Baptists, the Irish and "American" Protestants seem to be the big losers.

---

[20] Christopher Jencks et al., *Inequality: A Reassessment of the Effect of Family and Schooling in America* (New York: Basic Books, 1972), pp. 7–8, 179.
[21] Christopher Jencks, "The Effects of Grandparents on Their Grandchildren" (unpublished paper, Cambridge, Mass., Department of Sociology, Harvard University, January 30, 1975) pp. 15, 17.

In seeking to explain why the members of the more recent immigrant groups have done better economically than the descendants of old-stock Protestants, Greeley suggests that a phenomenon of "overthrust" or "overcompensation" is at work. The members of a less privileged, lower status group "that 'makes it' in American society does so with such tremendous energy and such tremendous 'need for achievement,' that they not only do as well as everyone else, but better because of the sheer, raw power of their elemental drive for respectability and success." Greeley goes on to ask, "May it be that in another generation or two, the effect may wear off, and the Catholic and Protestant and Jewish ethnic groups will have relatively similar levels of achievement—while the blacks and the Spanish-speaking profit from the 'overthrust' phenomenon?"[22]

But if whites, including working-class whites, experienced a fluid occupational class system in which the able and ambitious could rise, the reverse was true for blacks, prior to the mid-sixties. As Blau and Duncan indicate:

> Negroes are handicapped at every step in their attempt to achieve economic success, and these cumulative disadvantages are what produce the great inequalities of opportunities under which the Negro American suffers.

Education, which apparently opens all sorts of doors for whites, even for many of quite low social origin, had not worked in the same way for blacks:

> The difference in occupational status between Negroes and whites is twice as great for men who have graduated from high school or gone to college as for those who have completed no more than eight years of schooling. In short, the careers of well-educated Negroes lag even further behind those of comparable whites than do the careers of poorly educated Negroes. . . . Negroes, as an under-privileged group, must make greater sacrifices to remain in school, but they have less incentive than whites to make these sacrifices, which may well be a major reason why Negroes often exhibit little motivation to continue in school and advance their education.[23]

---

[22] Andrew M. Greeley, "Ethnicity, Denomination and Inequality," (unpublished paper, Center for the Study of American Pluralism, National Opinion Research Center, Chicago, Illinois, 1975), pp. 44–45, 51–52. Similar empirical findings from other surveys are reported in F. Thomas Jester (ed.), *Education, Income, and Human Behavior* (New York: McGraw-Hill, 1974).

[23] Peter Blau and Otis Dudley Duncan, *The American Occupational Structure* (New York: John Wiley & Sons, Inc., 1967), pp. 199–205, 404–406.

The Blau-Duncan conclusions were sustained by a reanalysis of the same data by Jencks and his associates, following a different methodological approach.[24]

But during the late 1960s the situation seemingly changed sharply for the better, particularly for younger and better educated blacks. An important factor in the improvement was the passage and subsequent enforcement, as a result of mass pressure from blacks and others, of the 1964 Civil Rights Act. In this new political context the impressive gains which blacks had been making in education enabled many of them to press on to higher levels of the occupational system. If median school years are used as an indicator, by the 1970s young blacks' formal educational attainment had come very close to that of whites. As of March 1977, "the median for whites was 12.6 school years completed and for blacks, 12.2 years."[25] By 1974, according to a U.S. Census Bureau report, the percentage of blacks entering college, 12.3, was *higher* than their proportion in the total population, 11.4. Black men in the professions formed 6.6 percent of all males, increased from 3.6 in 1962. Black women formed 10 percent of the female professionals, up from 7 in 1962.[26] A summary by Richard Freeman for the Brookings Institution points up the substantial changes in the labor market position of blacks in the past decade:

> The evidence that the labor market position of blacks underwent an unprecedented improvement in the 1960s is substantial and growing. . . . In some markets, such as that for female workers or young college graduates, discriminating differentials have effectively disappeared. In others, positions that were rarely filled by blacks, ranging from professional and managerial jobs in corporations to construction crafts to police and public employment beyond the laborer's level in the South, were effectively opened for the first time in history. On the other hand, certain important segments of the black labor force, notably older men who had missed out on the training, experience, and position on the seniority ladders as a result of past discrimination, experienced much more modest rates of relative economic advance. . . . In contrast to previous studies of the importance of education on income by race, the evidence for the late 1960's revealed a marked convergence in the returns to black

[24] Jencks et al., *op. cit.*, pp. 190–191, 217–218.
[25] Kopp Michelotti, "Educational Attainment of Workers, March, 1977," *Monthly Labor Review*, 100 (December 1977), p. 53.
[26] Stuart H. Garfinkle, "Occupations of Women and Black Workers, 1962–74," *Monthly Labor Review*, 98 (November 1975), p. 29.

and white male investments in schooling or in the impact of education on earnings, especially among the young.[27]

Similar results have also been reported by University of Wisconsin economist Stanley Masters and RAND economists James Smith and Finis Welch. The latter find that as blacks and whites become more similar in educational attainments, their earnings also become more comparable. From the end of World War II to 1975, the average income of black males moved up from half to nearly three-quarters of whites. Black women's earnings jumped from only one-third of whites' to practical equality. Blacks, however, continued to suffer more than whites from declines in the business cycle.[28] It is important to note that "younger blacks fare better compared with whites than their older counterparts," a finding which Smith and Welch conclude is now a result of the fact that younger blacks are more similar to whites in their labor marketable skills, and hence, as cohort analysis indicates, the improvement in black-white ratios should continue.[29]

Comparable changes in rates of social mobility also point up the improvement in the black situation. Thus a comparison of national surveys taken in March 1962 and March 1973 indicates that among all males, 20.3 percent of those who fathers held lower manual jobs had achieved upper white-collar positions in 1962, while 22.5 percent had moved up in 1973. Among black males, only 7.6 percent of those of lower-manual status background had secured an upper white-collar job in 1962; by 1973, however, the figure had climbed to 12.4 percent, much higher than a decade earlier, but still considerably behind that of whites.[30]

These changes, which resulted from a combination of improvements in the education of young blacks and a variety of political and judicial actions, have not of course made up for the deficiencies imposed by past

[27] Richard B. Freeman, "Changes in Job Market Discrimination and Black Economic Well-Being" (paper delivered at Notre Dame Civil Rights Conference, South Bend, Ind., on April 15–17, 1975), pp. 7–8.

[28] James P. Smith and Finis R. Welch, *Race Differences in Earnings: A Survey and New Evidence* (Santa Monica, Cal.: The RAND Corporation, 1978), and James P. Smith, *The Convergence in Racial Equality in Women's Wages* (Santa Monica, Cal.: The RAND Corporation, 1978). See also Stanley H. Masters, *Black-White Income Differentials* (New York: Acadmic Press, 1975), pp. 143–145.

[29] Smith and Welch, *op. cit.*, pp. 50–51.

[30] *Social Indicators 1976* (Washington, D.C.: U.S. Department of Commerce, Bureau of the Census, 1977), pp. 522, 525, 545.

discrimination, particularly among older people. Because of the relatively recent entrance of blacks into many companies which follow a "last-in/first-out" layoff policy, the position of black workers was far more sensitive to the business cycle than that of white workers.[31] Further, a much larger proportion of blacks than whites enter the labor market with major handicaps, derived from having been reared in poverty-stricken and/or broken homes.

The persistently inferior economic position of the black community as a whole shows up particularly with respect to family incomes. As of 1973 the ratio of black to white median family income was still only .58. A major reason for this discrepancy according to a 1975 U.S. Census Bureau report is that 35 percent of all black families are headed by women, as contrasted with 9.9 percent among whites. In both racial groups, female-headed families, which have grown greatly during the past decade, comprising one out of every seven families in 1977, have much lower incomes than those with an adult male present.[32] Thus the ratio of median income differences between the two races among male-headed families in 1973 was .72. Further major improvements in the ratio of black to white income have been recorded primarily for people under 35, not for older persons.

> The common thread running through each of the problem areas—family income and composition, the burden of poor backgrounds, and the lack of sharp progress among older black male workers—is that simply ending job market discrimination and guaranteeing equal employment opportunity will not achieve black/white parity in the foreseeable future.

Despite the considerable progress of certain segments of the black community, whites are still enormously advantaged by the presence of a racial minority which (together with other minority groups) handles a heavily disproportionate share of the less rewarded jobs and status positions.

It is important to recognize that the considerable progress made by younger and better-educated blacks in the last decade did not happen as a result of the "natural" operation of sociological and economic factors, as had occurred earlier with various white ethnic groups. In the case of blacks, discrimination had to be countered by political forces. Freeman indicates a close relationship between black progress and

---

[31] Freeman, *op. cit.*, p. 13.
[32] Beverly L. Johnson, "Women Who Head Families, 1970–1977: Their Numbers Rose, Income Lagged," *Monthly Labor Review*, 101 (February 1978), pp. 32–33, 36–37.

an index of anti-bias activity, E.E.O.C. [Equal Employment Opportunity Commission] spending per non-white workers. . . . Data on individual companies also suggest that governmental activities were effective, with companies facing, all else the same, greater federal pressure, increasing their employment of blacks. Qualitative evidence on company personnel practices also ties the changes to governmental action.[33]

Masters also concludes that much "of the improvement in the black economic position that took place in the late sixties appears to be the result of government and related antidiscriminatory activity associated with the 1964 Civil Rights Act."[34]

These conclusions are disputed, in part, by Smith and Welch, using national industry, rather than company, data. The evidence, as they interpret it, is ambiguous concerning the effect of affirmative action programs on the position of black males, but "the large expansion of black female employment in those industries most vulnerable to affirmative action pressures provides at least circumstantial evidence that the wages of black women may have been increased by these programs."[35]

A somewhat more complex analysis by Yale sociologist Paul Burstein, who factored in possible effects of attitude changes as well as of the Equal Employment Opportunity Commission activities, concludes that "the demand for labor, educational attainment, public attitudes, and EEO enforcement efforts all have a significant [independent] effect on the relative incomes of non-white men." But unlike Smith and Welch, Burstein finds the evidence demonstrating "a positive impact of EEO legislation" for women more ambiguous than for men.[36]

The occupational and economic status of women also improved considerably during the civil rights decade of the late 1960s and early 1970s. Between 1960 and 1970 the number of women in the labor force increased by 38 percent. The increase in the number working in skilled blue-collar jobs was most dramatic, jumping almost 80 percent, or "eight times the rate of increase for men in the skilled trades." Hedges and Bemis note: "With their legal rights to equal employment opportunity established,

---

[33] Freeman, *op. cit.*, pp. 14, 28.

[34] Stanley H. Masters, *Black-White Income Differentials* (New York: Academic Press, 1975), pp. 143–145.

[35] Smith, *op. cit.*, p. 41; Smith and Welch, *op. cit.*, pp. 47–50.

[36] Paul Burstein, "Equal Employment Opportunity Legislation and the Income of Women and Nonwhites," (unpublished paper, Department of Sociology, Yale University, August 1978), pp. 17, 21–23.

women were drawn to work that paid well. For those with a high school education, such jobs were most likely to be found in the skilled trades."[37]

Changes in the upper levels of the occupational structure, particularly in professional jobs, have been almost as striking. Between 1960 and 1970 the proportion of women entering the higher professions increased by 61 percent, much more than for men.

> In the broad category of professional occupations, women consti-
> tuted 40 percent of all employees in 1974, up from 36 percent in
> 1962. Rapid progress occurred in a number of the higher paying
> professions, among physicians and surgeons (6 to 10 percent), and
> lawyers and judges (3 to 7 percent). . . . Women have also made
> slow but steady gains in accounting, from 19 to 24 percent; in per-
> sonnel and labor relations work, from 27 to 35 percent; in college
> and university teaching, from 19 to 31 percent; and in drafting,
> from 4 to 8 percent.[38]

The improvement has been particularly notable in higher education. A detailed statistical study of first-job placements among new holders of Ph.D. degrees indicates that "earlier discrimination in teaching appoint-ments disappeared by 1973."[39] An independent analysis concluded that sex-related salary differentials, widely prevalent in academia, had been eliminated for new appointees by 1972. Among older established faculty, salary differentials between men and women still persist, but they have declined considerably. "In 1968-69, an average raise for women of more than $1000 across all ranks would have been required for equity in ac-cordance with the predictors of men salaries. The comparable figure in 1972-73 was $600."[40]

The improvement in the position of women in the higher professions is likely to continue, both because of government-enforced policies and because of a steady increase in the enrollment of women in professional training programs. Thus the proportion of women among recipients of the

[37] Janice N. Hedges and Stephen E. Bemis, "Sex Stereotyping: Its Decline in Skilled Trades," *Monthly Labor Review*, 97 (May 1974), p. 18.

[38] Garfinkle, *op. cit.*, p. 27.

[39] Allan M. Cartter and Wayne E. Ruhter, *The Disappearance of Sex Discrim-ination in First Job Placement of New Ph.D.'s* (Los Angeles: Higher Educa-tion Research Institute, 1975), p. 25.

[40] Alan E. Bayer and Helen S. Astin, "Sex Differentials in the Academic Reward System," *Science* (May 23, 1975), pp. 799, 800. See also Gary D. Brown, "Discrimination and Pay Disparities between White Men and Women," *Monthly Labor Review*, 101 (March 1978), pp. 17–22.

Ph.D. degree rose from 12 percent in 1967 to 18 percent in 1973.[41] The proportion of women enrolled in law schools rose from 5 percent in 1966 to 19 percent in 1974. In medicine it grew from 8 to 18 percent; in pharmacy, from 15 to 32 percent.[42]

The evidence regarding the change in the occupational position of women generally has been summed up by Bayer and Astin: "It is fair to say that substantial progress has been made since the anti-bias regulations have been in effect. It is equally clear, on the other hand, that neither the spirit nor the objectives inherent in the anti-bias regulations and laws have yet been fully achieved.[43]

Equality and Inequality: The Evidence

The concern for greater equality does not mean only equal opportunity; it also means equal reward, summed up in the description of the communist society as "from each according to his ability, to each according to his needs." No complex society, other than perhaps the *kibbutzim* (collective settlements) in Israel, which encompass over 100,000 people, has ever come close to approximating this objective. And though the mobility data reported by Blau and Duncan, and by Jencks and his associates, suggest the United States is beginning to approximate equal opportunity for white males, it is clear that such a situation occurs together with sharp inequalities in income and wealth. As Jencks notes:

> This implies that even if America could reduce inequalities in income to the point where they were no greater than those that now arise between one brother and another, the best-paid fifth of all male workers would still be making 500 percent more than the worst-paid fifth. We cannot, then, hope to eliminate, or even substantially reduce income inequality in America simply by providing children from all walks of life with equal opportunity. When people have had relatively equal opportunity, as brothers usually have, they still end up with very unequal incomes.[44]

The only solution Jencks sees to the problem of gaining greater income equality is government policies which "establish floors beneath which nobody's income is allowed to fall and ceilings above which it is not allowed

[41] Cartter and Ruhter, *op. cit.*, p. 8.
[42] John B. Parrish, "Women in Professional Training—An Update," *Monthly Labor Review*, 98 (November 1975), p. 49.
[43] Bayer and Astin, *op. cit.*, p. 801.
[44] Jencks et al., *op. cit.*, p. 220.

to rise." Although this proposal may appear quite radical, it is interesting to note that a leading Republican has asserted that "there is much in the new doctrine of equality of results that is solid"—to use the words of Paul McCracken, a member of President Eisenhower's Council of Economic Advisers from 1956 to 1959 and chairman of the same body for President Nixon from 1969 to 1972. McCracken, speaking to the American Business Council, noted approvingly that American society is concerned with finding an optimum balance between its traditional ideal of equality of opportunity and its growing commitment to greater equality of result.[45]

The gradual acceptance of the community's responsibility for upgrading the lives of the underprivileged in America constitutes an important shift in our values away from the primary, almost sole, focus on opportunity implied in the original achievement and Protestant orientations of the early republic, discussed in this book. Yet it may be argued that the initial emphasis on equality and an implied "classless society" in the Declaration of Independence strengthens the new trend toward using government power to eliminate "poverty."

In spite of McCracken's acceptance of much in the doctrine of "equality of results," it is also true that the great majority of Americans believe in the present pattern of income differentiation. In 1970 a public opinion survey asked Americans to suggest "a fair yearly salary" for various occupations ranging from "top management" to "lower skill"; the large majority of those interviewed suggested differentials nearly identical with existing patterns. Lee Rainwater reports that "respondents see equity in a system in which there is quite marked dispersion of income . . . [and] seem to have little complaint about the relative shares of different groups in the occupational hierarchy."[46]

Government policy has seemingly been committed to equalizing incomes somewhat beyond what would occur through the natural workings of the economy. Various policies have been used, ranging from the graduated income tax, which increases the tax percentage on higher income, to assorted income-transfer welfare programs, which give income directly to the less privileged. Such welfare policies, stimulated by the New Deal programs initiated in the 1930s, should have the effect of reducing the pattern of gross inequalities. While these programs attest to the continued significance of equality as a national value, more important in the long

[45] Paul W. McCracken, "The New Equality," *Michigan Business Review*, 26 (March 1974), pp. 2–7.
[46] Lee Rainwater, *What Money Buys: Inequality and the Social Meanings of Income* (New York: Basic Books, 1974), pp. 163–167.

run in affecting income distribution are changes in the occupational structure which serve to reduce the proportion of unskilled and low-paid jobs and to increase the proportion of jobs requiring higher education in the upper ranges of the income distribution. The spread of higher education to the point where close to half of all Americans of college age continue their education beyond high school attests to the extensiveness of this process.

Recent historical research has not only challenged the conventional wisdom about mobility rates, which assumed that the growth of large corporations would mean movement from greater to lesser equality of opportunity; it has also upset long-cherished notions about the direction of change in the distribution of income from the early nineteenth century on. The tentative conclusion which may be reached from a number of studies is that Jacksonian America—described by Tocqueville and others as an egalitarian social system (which, compared to Europe, it undoubtedly was)—was characterized by much more severe forms of social and economic inequality than the society of the 1970s. As historian Edward Pessen points out:

> The explanation, popular since Karl Marx's time, that it was industrialization that pauperized the masses, in the process transforming a relatively egalitarian social order, appears wanting. Vast disparities between urban rich and poor antedated industrialization [in America]. . . . Even Michael Harrington and Gabriel Kolko, whose estimates reveal the greatest amounts of [present-day] inequality, attribute percentages of income to the upper brackets that are far smaller than the upper one percent of New York City controlled in income in 1863 or in wealth in 1845.[47]

Most other pre-Civil War American cities resembled New York in these respects, and even in rural areas the pattern of property distribution was extremely unequal.[48]

---

[47] Edward Pessen, "The Egalitarian Myth and the American Social Reality: Wealth, Mobility, Morality in the 'Era of the Common Man,' " *The American Historical Review*, 76 (October 1971), pp. 989–1034; and *Riches, Class, and Power Before the Civil War* (Lexington, Mass.: D. C. Heath, 1973). Pessen cites many relevant recent historical works bearing on the intense forms of inequality in this period.

[48] Merle Curti, et al., *The Making of an American Community: A Case Study of Democracy in a Frontier County* (Stanford, Cal.: Stanford University Press, 1959).

Detailed analysis of the distribution of total personal income since 1929, by the foremost authority on the subject, Simon Kuznets, indicates that the proportion of the income going to the bottom sections of the population (the lowest fifth and lowest 5 percent) increased during the 1930s and 1940s, while the portion going to upper groups (the top fifth and top 5 percent) dropped considerably. Thus the proportions of the total family income received by the upper fifth fell from 54 percent in 1929 to 42.7 percent in 1951; the corresponding change for the top 5 percent was from 29.5 percent to 18.4 percent.[49] By 1970, according to the Organization for Economic Cooperation and Development, the proportion received by the top 5 percent of families had fallen to 14.4 percent.[50]

More refined analysis of the income distribution patterns suggests that the egalitarian trend may be even greater than the official government data indicate. Government welfare policies, combined with the American emphasis on individualism and the nuclear family, have led to a continuing increase in the number of separate households headed by those under 25, those 65 and older, and unmarried women—groups which in many other societies would live with relatives and would not be counted as independent family units in the income statistics. These three groups form a very large proportion of the lowest 20 percent of the income distribution.[51]

More recently, Kuznets has analyzed the impact of these changes on income distribution for the period 1947-1968. He finds that family units headed by women, persons over 65, or persons under 25 increased by 17.4 percent; they comprised fully two-thirds of the lowest fifth by 1968. Since old people constituted half of this group, a large proportion of it

---

[49] Simon Kuznets, "Income Distribution and Changes in Consumption," in H. S. Simpson (ed.), *The Changing American Population* (New York: Institute for Life Insurance, 1962), p. 30. See also Selma F. Goldsmith et al., "Size Distribution of Income Since the Mid-Thirties," *Review of Economics and Statistics*, 36 (February 1954), p. 20. For a contradictory interpretation which concludes that there has been little change in income distribution since 1910, see Gabriel Kolko, *Wealth and Power in America* (New York: Praeger, 1962), p. 13. Kolko's analysis, however, is based on data prepared by a private research group that have been rejected as too unreliable to be included in the *Historical Statistics of the United States* by a panel of the leading authorities of the subject in economics.

[50] OECD Secretariat, "Inequality in the Distribution of Personal Income" (Paper prepared for Seminar on Education, Inequality, and Life Chances, Paris, January 6–9, 1975), pp. 18, 20. Herman P. Miller *Income Distribution in the United States* (Washington, D.C.: U.S. Department of Commerce, 1966).

[51] Kuznets, *op. cit.*, pp. 36–36.

was not in the labor force. When these three groups are excluded from the income distribution, "the general level of the shares of the lowest fifth, and to a lesser extent of the second fifth, are raised perceptibly, while those of the [upper] 80-95 percent, and particularly of the top 5 percent group, are lowered—thus narrowing inequality significantly." Thus the share received by the bottom fifth rose from 5.8 percent after the war to 7.3 percent in 1968, while that of the upper 5 percent fell from 16 percent to 12.8 percent. In short, while the total income distribution among all families has been relatively stable, the distribution "among families with male heads aged 25-64 (what might be called 'standard' family units) showed a sustained movement of some magnitude through almost the whole period."

It may, of course, be argued that there is no equitable basis for excluding these units from a general analysis of trends toward greater or lesser equality. Kuznets answers such contentions by saying:

> One could argue that from the standpoints of productivity, equity, and welfare, the incomes of these units, on a per-person basis, should be lower than those in the "standard" family units. After all, young family heads are in their training period, may look forward to much higher returns that would compensate them later, and no equity or welfare considerations warrant claiming for them a per-person return as high as that which they themselves will secure later—so long as the current returns are minimally adequate otherwise. Old family heads, largely in their retirement period, do not contribute sufficiently to earn an income equal to that of prime members of the labor force; nor do they need such income for the purposes of further investment . . . or for utilizing the variety of new products. . . . It is thus permissible to argue that the income inequality contributed by the lower incomes of the young and old units represents no contribution to unwarranted earnings differentials.[52]

Controlling for the age factor, economist Morton Paglin also finds a significant steady 23 percent decline in income inequality from 1947 to 1972. In addition, Paglin calculated the impact of transfer payments such as "public housing, rent supplements, food stamps and food assistance, Medicaid, and social services . . ." on the income distribution. Including

[52] Simon Kuznets, "Demographic Aspects of the Distribution of Income Among Families: Recent Trends in the United States," in Willy Selle Kzerts (ed.), *Essays in Honour of Jan Tinbergen, Vol. 3, Econometrics and Economic Theory* (London: Macmillan, 1974), pp. 223–246.

these as income and controlling for age, he estimates that the poorest 20 percent of the population in fact received about 54 percent of what they would get if there were complete equality, as contrasted with the often quoted estimate of 27 percent, using traditional methods which do not control for age and do not include transfer payments as income.[53]

With respect to the way in which people *perceive* the distribution of income, it may be argued that the distribution of different kinds of *consumer goods*, those people use for immediate gratification, is more important in affecting their feelings about equity than the actual distribution of income as such. In this connection, it would appear that the distribution of consumer goods has tended to become more equitable as the size of national income has increased.[54]

In the United States the average per capita income has increased almost eightfold during the course of this century, and this dramatic growth has brought about a wide distribution of various social and economic benefits, greater than that in almost all other countries. The greater wealth of the United States also means that consumer goods such as education, automobiles and telephones are more evenly distributed than elsewhere.[55]

Sociologist Gideon Sjoberg has traced the implications of such developments historically in America. He suggests that the emergence of mass production during the twentieth century has caused such a redistribution of highly valued prestige symbols that the distinctions between social classes are much less immediately visible than they were in nineteenth-century America, or than they are in most other less affluent countries. Sjoberg argues that the status differences between many blue-collar workers and middle-class professionals have become less well-defined, since working-class families, like middle-class ones, have been able to buy goods that confer prestige on the purchaser—clothing, cars, television sets, and so on. Such improvements in style of life help to preserve the belief in the reality of the promise of equality. A person who can buy his own house, or a new car, may feel that he has moved up in the world even if he has not changed his occupational or relative income position.[56]

It has often been suggested that income trends, distribution of status-

---

[53] Morton Paglin, "The Measurement and Trend of Inequality: A Basic Revision," *American Economic Review*, 65 (September 1975), pp. 598–609.

[54] Gunnar Myrdal, *An International Economy* (New York: Harper and Row, 1956), p. 133.

[55] "Where the Grass Is Greener," *The Economist* (December 25, 1971), p. 15.

[56] Gideon Sjoberg, "Are Social Classes in America Becoming More Rigid?" *American Sociological Review*, 16 (December 1951), pp. 775–783. See the comparable analysis of David Potter, as discussed in this book on pp. 320–321.

enhancing consumer goods, and rates of mobility affect the extent to which a country is likely to experience intense class conflict, or polarized politics. Aspects of this thesis have been enunciated by a variety of contemporary sociological observers, as well as by Karl Marx and other nineteenth-century commentators.[57] A detailed effort to test some of the implications of these assumptions, particularly in the context of evaluating the political effects of social mobility, indicates that mobile individuals (up or down) are less likely to take strong class positions than the nonmobile. The political scientist James Barber concludes his study with the assertion: "The influence of mobility on the political system would seem . . . to be a moderating one: lending flexibility to the electoral process, reducing the stakes involved in elections, and diluting the class content of politics."[58]

The stress in this discussion on data supporting the continued vitality of egalitarian trends in American society does not imply that the United States even remotely approaches a state which can be described as egalitarian from any absolute point of view. This country, like all other nations maintaining some form of capitalism, has an enormous concentration of personal wealth in the hands of relatively few individuals. Even among white male Americans, equal opportunity does not exist, particularly with respect to the best paid positions. And in spite of considerable improvement in the last decade, the promise of equality remains a mockery for many mature blacks and women, as well as for members of some ethnic minorities, particularly American Indians and persons of Spanish origin.

Poverty, though concentrated among the minority groups, also affects a significant number of whites. It is particularly found among the aged, the uneducated and unskilled, migrant farm laborers, small farm operators (especially in the South), that large group with individual handicaps, (low IQ's, physical deformities, mental illness, or other chronic ailments), and families that do not have male heads. This last group, unfortunately, has been growing. "In 1976, 1 out of every 3 of these families was living below the officially defined poverty line." What is even more important is the fact that such families are more likely to have young children than husband-wife ones. In 1976, "52 percent of children under 18 in families headed by women were living below the poverty level. In contrast, about

---

[57] For a review of some of the literature on the subject, see James Alden Barber, Jr., *Social Mobility and Voting Behavior* (Chicago: Rand McNally, 1970), pp. 9–12, 264–266. See also Werner Sombart, "American Capitalism's Economic Rewards," in J. M. Laslett and S. M. Lipset, eds., *Failure of a Dream?* (Garden City, N.Y.: Anchor Press/Doubleday, 1974), pp. 593–608.
[58] Barber, *op. cit.*, p. 267.

8.3 percent of children in husband-wife families were living below the poverty level." While these families disproportionately are black, "the proportion of never-married mothers heading families has grown for both white and black women—a trend that seems likely to continue, at least for the next few years."[59]

Government efforts, in tandem with the emphasis on equality, are formally committed to ending discrimination and eliminating poverty. As yet, while such policies have resulted in a considerable decline in the numbers living in poverty, largely reflecting the effect of governmental income transference payments, they have been unable to remedy existing handicaps of low education, limited skill, incomplete families, and inadequate motivation. To a considerable degree also, the efforts to improve the lot of the underprivileged are limited or negated by economic declines that reduce opportunities and that press those who have advantages to resist opening more rewarded positions to new claimants. Thus the economic downturn of the mid-seventies disproportionately disadvantaged the traditional "outsiders"—blacks, women, those of Spanish origin, the less educated, and the less skilled. Efforts to further enhance the promise of equality clearly require both a high level of employment and economic growth.

Similar conclusions about a decline in inequality in the ownership of total wealth, as distinct from fungible (transferable or disposable) wealth, have been reached by Martin Feldstein. Estimates of the ownership of fungible wealth show no "reduction in concentration in the 1960s. Yet during this century the share of disposable income received by high income families has fallen considerably." The apparent explanation for this discrepancy is that the distribution of total wealth is quite different from fungible wealth. The former includes the assets of individuals in social security, private "pension and insurance rights, consumer durables, and the actual value of unemployment insurance, welfare, veterans' benefits, etc. All of these forms of wealth are distributed more equally than fungible wealth. . . . This difference implies that the concentration of total wealth has been decreasing during the past fifty years, an evaluation that is consistent with the more equal distribution of disposable income and the growing importance of estate taxes."[60]

Paglin also reports that some of the same considerations apply for the

---

[59] Johnson, *op. cit.*, pp. 32–33, 36–37.
[60] Martin Feldstein, "Social Security and the Distribution of Wealth," *Journal of the American Statistical Association*, 71 (December 1976), pp. 800–807.

distribution of wealth. Part of "wealth inequality" reflects the age structure and the social savings function rather than fundamental (lifetime)
inequality in the economic system. When controlling for age, he finds
that past uncontrolled measures had "overstated the degree of inter-family
inequality of wealth by about 52 percent."[61] Nevertheless, both income
and total wealth distribution remain highly skewed since, as Feldstein
notes, the "top one percent of families between 35 and 64 years old own
28.4 percent of the fungible wealth but only 18.9 percent of total wealth,
a fall of about one-third." But as indicated, the direction of change has
been toward more equality.

Attitudes Toward Equality

The movement toward greater equality is also reflected in the changing
attitudes of Americans toward the most visibly inferior segments of the
population, blacks and women. An examination William Schneider and I
made of the findings of over 100 opinion polls reveals that over the past
40 years there has been a vast improvement in American attitudes toward
blacks, other minorities, and women.[62] Many more Americans than ever
before are aware that these groups have suffered discrimination, and
minority claims to full equality are accepted much more widely than
in earlier eras. Most people say that further progress toward complete
equality should be made, and they endorse a variety of programs to this
end, including the Equal Rights Amendment and enforcement of anti-
discrimination legislation in jobs and other areas. Typical of such findings
are the trends reported by Gallup of surveys inquiring whether people
would vote for persons with varying types of backgrounds for President.
The proportion willing to do so for a woman rose from 31 percent in
1937 to 52 in 1955, to 66 in 1969 and 76 in July 1978. Those giving the
same response for a Jewish candidate increased from 46 in 1937 to 62 in
1958 and 82 in 1978. For a black nominee, the favorable percentages shot
up from 38 in 1958 to 54 in 1967 and 77 in 1978. But indicating perhaps
that, as noted in this book, Americans continue to harbor intense religious
feelings, those willing to vote for an atheist for president are still a

---

[61] Paglin, *op. cit.*, p. 50.
[62] S. M. Lipset and William Schneider, *From Discrimination to Affirmative
Action: Changing American Attitudes* (Washington, D.C.: American Enter-
prise Institute, in press). See also *A Study of Attitudes Toward Racial and
Religious Minorities*, prepared for the National Conference of Christians and
Jews (New York: Louis Harris and Associates, November 1978).

minority, although the size of that minority increased from 18 percent in 1958 to 40 in 1978.[63]

Voting for a black for President does not involve much change in personal behavior. It is, therefore, important to note that the proportion of whites reporting they have no objection to sending their children to schools in which half or more than half of the students are black or that they would not move "if blacks came to live in your neighborhood in large numbers" has also steadily increased. Among northern whites, objectors to children attending half-black schools have declined from 33 percent in 1963 to 23 in 1978, while the figures for predominantly black schools have fallen from 53 percent in 1963 to 28 in 1978. Southern whites, while more prejudiced than northerners, have also become much more liberal, moving from 78 percent opposed to their children going to half-black institutions in 1963 to 28 percent most recently. While 86 percent were against white children going to majority black schools in 1963, the proportion having such objections in 1978 had declined to less than half, 49 percent, in 1978. The proportion, nationally, of whites who say they would or might move "if blacks came to live next door" has fallen from 45 percent in 1963 to 13 percent in 1978, while the figures for those who would or might move if blacks "came in large numbers to your neighborhood" has declined from 78 percent to 51 percent over the same period. Southerners were somewhat more prejudiced on these questions than northerners, but, as of 1978, the variations by sections were not great.[64]

Perhaps the most severe test of white racial "liberalism" is attitudes toward intermarriage. As of mid-summer 1978, "disapproval continues to outweigh approval, 54 percent to 36 percent." But 10 years earlier, "the ratio was 72 percent to 20 percent."[65] Not surprisingly, these attitudes like others in this area correlated strikingly with education and age. The better educated and the younger a person, the more liberal he or she is. More than half the teenagers interviewed by Gallup approved of marriage between whites and blacks.

It must be noted, however, that most majority Americans are not willing to approve of certain kinds of "affirmative action" programs, particularly those which appear to give minorities or women special preference, i.e., job or educational quotas, or which involve compulsory integration

---

[63] George Gallup, "Present Time Is Good Time for Women, Minorities to Seek Top Political Office," *The Gallup Poll*, September 21, 1978, pp. 1–6.
[64] "A Question of Race. How Have Americans Changed?" *The Gallup Opinion Index*, Report No. 160 (November 1978), p. 25.
[65] *Ibid.*, p. 27.

in schools—busing—or housing. These suggest that an ambivalence or inconsistency about ways of dealing with racial inequality, in particular, still exists in the American mind.

American Values: Consensus and Conflict

Many of the inconsistencies point up a deep contradiction between two values that are at the core of the American creed—individualism and egalitarianism. Americans believe strongly in both values, and, as the discussion in this book suggests, the history of American social change reflects a shifting back and forth between these core values, as a period of concern with equality and social reform is typically followed by a period emphasizing individual achievement and upward mobility.

One consequence of this dualism in the American value system is that, as noted in the body of the book, political debate often takes the form of *one consensual value opposing the other.* Liberals and conservatives typically do not take alternative positions on issues of equality and freedom. Instead, each side appeals to one or the other core value, as liberals stress egalitarianism's primacy and the social injustice that flows from unfettered individualism, while conservatives enshrine individual freedom and the social need for mobility and achievement as values "endangered" by the collectivism inherent in liberal nostrums. Both sides treat as their natural constituency the entire American public. In this sense, liberals and conservatives are less *opponents* than they are *competitors*, like two department stores on the same block trying to draw the same customers by offering different versions of what everyone wants.

The contradiction between these core values has nowhere been more apparent than in racial attitudes. Gunnar Myrdal concluded that most Americans put their beliefs about race and their often inconsistent beliefs about equality and achievement into separate mental compartments: "few liberals . . . [are without] a well-furnished compartment of race prejudice," while those most "violently prejudiced against the Negro" also have "a whole compartment in . . . [their] valuation sphere housing the entire American Creed of liberty, equality, justice, and fair opportunity for everybody."[66]

Much of the progress in the early years of the civil rights movement was made by breaking down the "compartmentalization" of the American mind and forcing the public to see that the country's attitudes and institu-

---

[66] Gunnar Myrdal, *An American Dilemma* (New York: Harper and Row, 1944), p. xiv.

tions fell outrageously short of our egalitarian ideals. It is the egalitarian element in the American Creed that created the consensus behind the civil rights revolution of the past thirty years. But the more recent focus of the movement on substantive equality and "forced" integration has forced the country up against the individualistic, achievement-oriented element in the American Creed—and, as a result, the consensus has broken. The turning point can be dated from the "Watts riot" in Los Angeles in 1965, when black Americans demonstrated that they intended to press their claim for equality far beyond what white Americans were then willing to accept.

On every issue, the public opinion data show a "positive," pro-civil rights majority when only egalitarian questions are at stake but a "negative," anti-civil rights view when an issue also pushes up against basic notions of individualism. Thus, on the central issues involving racial discrimination and Jim Crow practices, American sentiment is powerfully *against discrimination*; trends on these issues have been consistently "liberal," and even the white South agrees with the national mood. The consensus breaks down, however, when compulsory integration is involved.

Similarly, most whites have endorsed the egalitarian *goals* of the civil rights movement while rejecting, repeatedly and consistently, the "collectivist" *tactics* of that movement. Most whites, and many blacks, continue to feel that it is better for disadvantaged groups to work through individual improvement and mobility than to press collective demands for all members of the group. Most Americans do approve of concrete federal programs to help the disadvantaged and to combat racial discrimination, even during the "tax revolt" of the late 1970s.[67] Given a choice, however, between government intervention to solve social problems and "leaving people on their own" to work out their problems for themselves, the public always chooses the latter option. This preference is particularly interesting in view of the fact that many of the achievements of the civil rights movements would not have been possible without the active intervention of the federal government, just as the widely approved reforms of the New Deal were brought about largely through an expansion of federal power.

Affirmative action policies have, of course, forced a sharp confrontation between egalitarian and individualistic values. White Americans look favorably upon "compensatory action," since compensation for past dis-

---

[67] S. M. Lipset and Earl Raab, "The Message of Proposition 13," *Commentary*, 66 (September 1978), pp. 42–46.

crimination is consistent with the egalitarian creed and essentially makes the conditions of competition "fairer" without violating the notion of a competitive system. But most Americans, including many blacks, oppose the notion of "preferential treatment," since such treatment precisely violates the notion of open and fair individual competition.[68]

In some measure, the distinction between "compensatory action" and "preferential treatment" parallels a distinction that many observers have drawn between "equality of opportunity" and "equality of results." Compensatory action is probably seen as a way to enhance equality of opportunity. Because blacks have been discriminated against in the past, it is fair to give them special consideration so that they will get a better break in the future. Preferential treatment, on the other hand, probably sounds to most whites like an effort to force equality of results by predetermining the outcome of the competitive process. Of course, the distinction between "opportunities" and "results" is a slippery one, and most situations are inherently ambiguous. For instance, admission to professional schools is probably seen by most whites as a reward for prior work and achievement—a *result* of the competitive process. But many liberals, blacks, and members of other minority groups would argue that admission merely provides "equality of opportunity" for disadvantaged groups to become professionals. Needless to say, admission to college or professional schools is *both* an opportunity for future success and a result of past achievement. Jobs also involve this inherent ambiguity, in that a job is both an opportunity and a reward.

It is a problem for legal opinion to determine how much weight is to be given to each of these points of view. But as far as public opinion is concerned, most whites and many blacks believe that race should be "considered" but not "preferred" in these ambiguous situations. My guess is that if significant further progress toward equality of results is to occur, it will take the form of what the British sociologist T.H. Marshall called the expansion of the idea of citizenship to include social rights—that every citizen can claim the right to a share in the prevailing material and cultural standards of the society; in other words, no one, even the runner who finished far back in the pack, will be condemned to a life of suffering and deprivation.

---

[68] S. M. Lipset and William Schneider, "The Bakke Case: How Would It Be Decided at the Bar of Public Opinion?," *Public Opinion* (March/April 1978), pp. 38–44 and Louis H. Bolce III and Susan H. Gray, "Blacks, Whites and 'Race Politics,'" *The Public Interest*, 54 (Winter 1979), pp. 76-93.

Values and Behavior

The First New Nation was not intended to be an exhaustive treatment of American society. As is evident to the reader, my principal intention was to explicate the nature and sources of basic values and to try to trace through some of the ways these values have affected behavior over time. Among the many important subjects not dealt with here is power relations. This, in turn, has meant that I have not discussed matters such as changes in the role of the state, and the power of business, labor and other institutions. Anyone concerned with what is happening to the United States may properly note that the enlargement of state power, the changing impact of the military, the increase in the proportion of the economy dominated by large corporations, many of which are multinational, the growth in the size and influence of academe and intellectuals generally, and the great change in the international role of the United States since 1940, all have more to do with determining and defining recent changes in the United States than its basic value system. I have no quarrel with such viewpoints, and would call attention to an excellent book by Charles Lindblom dealing with some of these issues.[69]

What continues to impress me, however, is how much of American behavior, after two centuries of national existence, can still be interpreted as derivative from its continued emphasis on equality and achievement. These interrelated values are linked to the formative political events which determined the national ideology, the social structure of a new society without a feudal status-bound past, and the fact the U.S. is the one country in the world dominated by the religious doctrines of Protestant "dissent"—the Methodists, Baptists and other sects. The teaching of these denominations called on people to follow their conscience, to be responsible for their own individual actions, with an unequivocal emphasis not to be found in those denominations which evolved from state churches (Catholics, Lutherans, Anglicans and Orthodox Christians). As noted in Chapter 4, the United States became the first nation in which religious groups were viewed as purely voluntary organizations, a view which served to strengthen the introduction of religious morality into politics. Although America, like other developed nations, has become more secularized, it is also still true that it remains the *most* religious nation, by far, among these countries, as reflected in the overwhelming proportion who report believing in God, in church attendance (controlling for Protestant and Catholic rates), and in taking religious beliefs seriously. Thus, the U.S. is the only country among thirteen surveyed in 1975-76 by the inter-

---

[69] *Politics and Markets* (New York: Basic Books, 1977).

national Gallup organization in which a majorty, 56 percent, said that "their religious beliefs are very important" to them, while an additional 30 percent said they were "fairly important." No other country can come close to the U.S. in commitments to religious beliefs. In most other countries, close to half or more said such beliefs were "not too important" or "not at all important."[70]

The combination of an emphasis on moralism and voluntarism, derivative from our Protestant sectarianism background, has sustained social movements to enforce that moralism, as may be seen in the large variety of such movements which have characterized American history. The strength of moralistic pressures may be seen most strikingly in reactions to foreign policy issues. There have been three uniquely American stances: conscientious objection to unjust wars, nonrecognition of "evil" foreign regimes, and the insistence that wars must end with the "unconditional surrender" of the Satanic enemy. Linked to Protestant sectarianism, conscientious objection to military service was until recently largely an American phenomenon.[71] To decry wars, to refuse to go, is at least as American as apple pie. Sol Tax of the University of Chicago, who attempted to compare the extent of antiwar activity throughout American history, concluded that as of 1968 the Vietnam war rated as our *fourth* "least popular" conflict with a foreign enemy.[72] Widespread opposition has existed to all American wars, with the possible exception of World War II, which began with a direct attack on United States soil. Large numbers refused to go along with the War of 1812, the Mexican War, the Civil War, and the Korean War. They took it as self-evident that they must obey their conscience rather than the dictates of their country's rulers.[73]

---

[70] *Social Indicators 1976*, op. cit., pp. 544, 555.

[71] It could also be found on a less widespread scale in other English-speaking countries, where, however, it has been less prevalent since a much smaller proportion adhere to the "dissenting" sects.

[72] Sol Tax, "War and the Draft," in Morton Fried, Marvin Harris, and Robert Murphy, eds., *War* (Garden City: Doubleday, The Natural History Press, 1968), pp. 199–203. Actually Tax concluded that there were seven wars out of twelve fought by the United States which were less popular than the Vietnam one. The twelve, however, include various Indian wars, the Civil War, and the Revolutionary War.

[73] Both abolitionists and others objected to fighting Mexico, and the Mexican army actually formed units manned by deserters from the United States forces. Frederick Mark, "Dissent in the Mexican War," in Samuel Eliot Morison, et al., *Dissent in Three American Wars* (Cambridge, Mass.: Harvard University Press, 1970), pp. 33–63; Edward S. Wallace, "Notes and Comment—Deserters in the Mexican War," *The Hispanic American Historical Review*, 15 (1935), p. 374.

The supporters of American wars invariably see them as moral crusades —to eliminate monarchical rule (the War of 1812) to defeat the Catholic forces of superstition (the Mexican War), to end slavery (the Civil War), to end colonialism in the Americas (the Spanish-American War), to make the world safe for democracy (World War I), and to resist totalitarian expansion (World War II, Korea, and Vietnam).[73] Unlike other countries we rarely see ourselves as merely defending our national interests. Since each war is a battle of good versus evil, the only acceptable outcome is "unconditional surrender" by the enemy.

George Kennan has written perceptively of the negative consequences of the "carrying-over into the affairs of states of the concepts of right and wrong." As he notes, when moralistic "indignation spills over into military context, it knows no bounds short of the reduction of the lawbreaker to the point of complete submissiveness—namely, unconditional surrender." Ironically, a moralistic "approach to world affairs, rooted as it unquestionably is in a desire to do away with war and violence, makes violence more enduring, more terrible, and more destructive to political stability than motives of national interest. A war fought in the name of high moral principle finds no early end short of some form of total domination."[74]

The stalemated struggle with Communism is, of course, a blow to this sense of a moralistic contest which must end with the defeat of Satan. America's initial reaction to Communism was one which implied no compromise. After each major Communist triumph—Russia, China, Cuba—we went through a period of refusing to "recognize" this unforgivable, hopefully temporary, victory of a wicked enemy. (This behavior contrasts with that of Anglican conservatives such as Churchill, or Catholic rightists such as DeGaulle or Franco, whose anti-Communism did not require "non-recognition.") Ultimately, the facts of power, and in the 1930s the rise of another even more belligerent enemy, Nazism, pressured the United States to deal with Communism. During World War II, we were even forced to ally ourselves with the Soviet Union and Communist partisan movements. Our initial reaction to this necessity is indicative of the way in which moralism affects the national purpose: the Soviet Union was quickly transformed into a beneficient, almost democratic state. Eddie Rickenbacker wrote in glowing terms in the *Reader's Digest* that the Soviet Union had practically become a capitalist society. Both Stalin and Tito were presented as "progressive" national leaders and heroes comparable to classic American figures. Franklin Roosevelt, for a time, allowed

---

[74] George Kennan, *Realities of American Foreign Policy* (Princeton: Princeton University Press, 1954), esp. pp. 3–50.

himself to see Stalin as a leader of anti-imperialist forces with whom the United States could cooperate in planning the post-war world, even against the French and British imperialists.

Subsequent Soviet behavior in Eastern Europe and Berlin during the latter years of the war and the early post-war years destroyed this effort to transform the image of Communism. The Communist victory in China, reinforced by the events of the Korean War, produced a reaction comparable to that directed against the Soviets after 1917. The United States refused to recognize evil in China (and later in Cuba). It engaged in an internal heresy hunt seeking to find and eliminate the traitors at home responsible for the inefficacy of our anti-Communist efforts abroad. The McCarthyite period, of course, coincided with a hot war against Communism, the Korean War, and thus also represented an effort to repress critics of the war, corresponding to previous waves of wartime repression.

The reaction to the Vietnamese War also reveals the extent to which the need for "moral" politics, particularly in foreign policy and in wartime, affects the behavior of Americans. For this conflict was the first war waged by the American political elite which was not presented as a political crusade designed to gain total victory. From the start, an unwillingness to get involved in a major war in Asia, a desire to avoid provoking Chinese and/or Soviet direct military intervention, and—not least—a fear that an anti-Communist crusade would reawaken a right-wing McCarthyist reaction led John F. Kennedy and Lyndon Johnson to underplay deliberately the anti-Communist ideological crusade as a justification for the war. It was defined as a limited war in which the United States would do as little as was required to prevent North Vietnam from taking over the South. There was almost no government-inspired propaganda designed to portray the repressive character of the North Vietnamese state. Pro-war journalists, seeking information about Communist atrocities or pictures such as those of the heads of village leaders on spikes, were actually denied them by the Defense Department to avoid inflaming public opinion. For some years after the anti-war movement reached mass proportions, Lyndon Johnson was quoted by intimates as worrying much more about right-wing "hawkish" opposition than that arising on his left.

Given the unwillingness of the government to motivate a crusading atmosphere, the obvious breakdown in the monolithic image of a totalitarian Communist empire in the wake of de-Stalinization in the Soviet Union—revolts and nationalist regimes in eastern Europe, and the Sino-Soviet split—and, finally, the inability of hundreds of thousands of U.S. troops to defeat the Viet Cong and the North Vietnamese, the rise of a moralistic mass opposition to the war was inevitable. An unengaged morality shifted to the side of the anti-war forces, and as the war was prolonged, it was inevitable that they would win.

Moralism and voluntarism, sustaining movements linked to egalitarian and achievement values, are also evident in the variety of movements and citizen's action and public interest groups, both on the left and right, which have informed the politics of the 60s and 70s.[75] The persistent conflict between these values continues. Policy programs stemming from each gain more support at different stages of the political cycle. As of 1979, a more conservative mood which supports achievement and individualist or competitive values appears regnant. But it follows on the heels of a liberal era in which efforts to foster egalitarianism were more dominant. And in spite of the fact that confidence in government as an agent of social reform has declined drastically in the 1970s, there is no evidence in the opinion polls that Americans have turned against the idea that government should support social welfare, provide needed services, help the disadvantaged and minorities, and protect citizens from economic and social adversity. The "tax revolt" of the late 70s is largely an expression of low confidence in the way government is managed—that is, concern with waste, corruption and inefficiency, as well as a general frustration with the abuses of power associated in the public mind with all powerful and self-interested institutions—government, labor unions, and big business.[76]

The struggle to combine the twin concerns for equality and liberty— the latter also involving some efforts strongly endorsed by liberals as well as conservatives to reduce the power of big institutions—continues and it is to be hoped will not slacken. For a free society must be a conflicted one, and America in the late 70s remains as divided as it ever has been.

SEYMOUR MARTIN LIPSET
Stanford, California

[75] See S. M. Lipset, "The Paradox of American Politics," *The Public Interest*, (Fall 1975), pp. 142–165.
[76] See Lipset and Raab, *op. cit.* and S. M. Lipset, "The Public Pulse: What Americans Really Think About Inflation," *Taxation and Spending*, 2 (April 1979), pp. 32–33.

Preface

In a real sense, this book pursues two substantive themes with which I have been concerned in previous writings—the problem of what was once known in the Marxist literature as "American exceptionalism" and the conditions for stable democracy.

In undertaking the study of a successful socialist movement in a Canadian province (*Agrarian Socialism*, 1950), I was initially interested in learning why Canada, seemingly so akin socially to the United States, was able to cast up a large socialist party when the United States could not. Many of the sociological explanations for the weakness of American socialism seemingly also applied to Canada. As the reader of *The First New Nation* will discover, sections of it still are concerned with the sources of structural variation between the two North American nations. The comparative sections of *Social Mobility in Industrial Society* (1959, with Reinhard Bendix) were similarly stimulated by an effort to test the thesis that political class consciousness was weak in the United States because the United States had a much higher rate of mass mobility than European nations. The research which sought to specify the extent of mass mobility (crossing the line between the manual working class and the nonmanual middle class) concluded that there were not significant differences between rates of mobility, as judged by these crude indicators, between industrialized Europe and America. (It should be noted, however, because many readers have ignored the caveat, that this book never contended that variations do not exist in rates of elite mobility, particularly among those occupational strata which require high levels of education.) Since the evidence with respect to mass mobility did not sustain the hypothesis, Reinhard Bendix and I turned to an analysis of the factors in American social structure which sustained the impression that mobility was higher in America. My subsequent work on values and the American class system presented here represents an elaboration of this work which I began with Bendix, and I acknowledge my indebtedness to him for helping me formulate my ideas on the subject.

My other two books, *Union Democracy* (1953, with Martin Trow and

James S. Coleman) and *Political Man* (1960), were addressed to analysis of the social conditions of stable democracy—the first on the level of private governments, the latter dealing with nation-states. In the present volume, I deal with both themes, the historical sources and the specific nature of the American social system, and the varying ways in which stable democracies, viewed comparatively, may occur. The last-named issue, dealt with in Part III, is of particular importance, since it should be clear that I am not holding up the American polity as an exportable model for all efforts at democracy. It should rather be recognized that the character of democratic polities may vary greatly, depending on various elements in the social structure of nations with which the political institutions must mesh. I think it particularly noteworthy that the two major English-speaking democracies, sometimes thought of as having similar political systems, differ considerably from each other politically as well as socially.

It is a foolish man who believes that he knows the sources of his ideas. I shall not pretend, therefore, to try to specify them here. In previous books, I have indicated some of those whom I regard as the most important influences on my intellectual development, and I will not repeat this discussion. I should indicate, however, that the general theoretical perspective and methodology of this book owes much to the classic work of Max Weber, who set standards for comparative and historical sociology which no one has even come close to emulating. With respect to the contents of this book, however, I think it appropriate to point out that much of my thinking about the relations of values to behavior in American society has been heavily influenced by Robert Merton's noted essay, "Social Structure and Anomie," and that my efforts to locate the analysis of given societies in a comparative and historical context have borrowed heavily from the work of Talcott Parsons. On the methodological side, Karl Deutsch has shown the way for those who seek to fully incorporate comparative historical and social analysis into systematic social science. Both he and Parsons, who have worked together on these problems, have shown the value to scholarship of men who are not afraid to present new, incomplete, and untested approaches for the rest of social science to elaborate or reject. Significant innovators in any field must be prepared to learn that they have been in error; these are the risks inherent in opening new perspectives on old problems.

Although a few parts of this book, particularly some of the materials in Part II, were initially written before the book was conceived as an entity, work on the book as such began in 1960 during the year I spent at Yale University as the Ford Visiting Research Professor of Political Science and Sociology. I would like to express my deep gratitude to the Yale Department of Political Science and particularly to its then-chairman, Robert Dahl for the luxury of a year free from all university duties combined with the opportunity to exchange ideas with a stimulating group of colleagues interested in many of the problems I was working on. On my return to Berkeley, the continuing research on this book was supported both financially and intellectually by the Training and Research Group on Comparative Development of the Institutes of Industrial Relations and International Studies of the University of California. This group operates with a grant of funds from the Carnegie Corporation. Composed of about ten men from the various social science departments, it is now chaired by Reinhard Bendix. I would like to thank the members of this group, particularly David Apter, David Landes, Franz Schurmann, and Neil Smelser, for detailed critical readings of sections of the book. In paying for various services which went into this work, I also made use of funds from a grant which I have from the Ford Foundation for the support of my "basic research."

My efforts to analyze behavior comparatively would be impossible without the help of many friends abroad who have given freely of their time to act as "research assistants" gathering data and, more important, as consultants furnishing me with ideas on developments in their own countries. I hope that it will be understood that they are in no way responsible for my interpretation of behavior in their countries. Among those who have taught me much are Frank Underhill and S. D. Clark in Canada, Tom Truman and Ronald Taft in Australia, Mark Abrams and C. A. R. Crosland in the United Kingdom, Michel Crozier and Mattei Dogan in France, and Otto Stammer and Ralf Dahrendorf in Germany. I would also like to express my particular indebtedness to my friend Stein Rokkan, who, though based at the Christen Michelsens Institute in Bergen, Norway, is perhaps as deserving of the title of *European* social scientist as anyone I know.

Three graduate research assistants, Ruth Ann Pitts, Arthur Goldberg, and Gene Bernardi, contributed much to helping locate research data. Daniel Bell of Columbia University and Irving Kristol of Basic Books have given generously of their time and stock of ideas. I must particularly thank the latter for his suggestion that I write a book about American society viewed comparatively. I should also like to acknowledge the generosity of William Nisbet Chambers, who let me see a prepublication draft of his book, *Political Parties in a New Nation* (since published by Oxford University Press, 1963). Chambers and I discovered, after each of us had written a draft of our books, that we were working on similar topics defined in comparable terms. This discovery came in time for us to exchange manuscripts and to take account of each other's work.

Some materials contained in this book have been presented on earlier occasions, either in print or at academic meetings. A summary of Part I was given as a paper at the Fifth World Congress of Sociology at Washington in September, 1962, and is scheduled to be published in the *Transactions* of that congress. Much of Chapter 3 uses materials presented in my chapter of a book edited by Leo Lowenthal and myself, *Culture and Social Character* (The Free Press, 1961); a brief preliminary statement of some of my analysis of American religion was published in the *Columbia University Forum* in 1959; and a previous discussion of the relationship of the characteristics of the American trade-union movement to the value system appeared in *Industrial Relations* (I, 1961–1962).

An early detailed analysis of the relationship of national values to the conditions for stable democracy, as presented in Part III, was given at a conference on "Internal War" sponsored by the Princeton University Center of International Studies in September, 1961. This version will appear in a volume of papers from that meeting which is being edited by Harry Eckstein and Klaus Knorr and will be published by The Free Press. A summary of the analysis of the value systems of the English-speaking democracies presented in the latter part of this book was given as the 1963 MacIver Award Lecture at the meetings of the Eastern Sociological Society in New York in April, 1963. This lecture was published in the August, 1963, issue of the *American Sociological Review*. An early version of one chapter of this book was written and published before the rest of it was outlined. This is Chapter 9, on party systems and representation, which appeared in the first issue of the *European Journal of Sociology*, in 1960. This paper was rewritten for inclusion here because it offers an example of comparative analysis bearing on problems discussed in the other chapters of Part III which employ variables other than the basic value system.

As all authors well know, the final housekeeping details of finishing a book, the editing, the checking of quotations and footnotes, the retyping of the completed manuscript, the reading and even revision of galleys can take a large proportion of the time necessary to complete a book. That these stages went much more quickly and efficiently than anticipated I owe to the staff of the Institute of International Studies of the University of California, particularly to Mrs. Cleo Stoker, the administrative assistant who runs the shop.

SEYMOUR MARTIN LIPSET
Institute of International Studies
University of California, Berkeley

Contents

Introduction to the Norton Edition   v

Preface   xli

Introduction   1

PART I
AMERICA AS A NEW NATION   13

1. Establishing National Authority   15

*The Crisis of Legitimacy and the Role
of the Charismatic Leader*   16

The Problem of National Unity   23

*Opposition Rights and the Establishment
of New Polities*   36

The Need for "Payoff"   45

2. Formulating a National Identity   61

The Need for Autonomy and Neutrality   62

The Role of the Intellectuals   66

Revolution as the Source of National Identity   74

Conclusion   90

PART II
STABILITY IN THE MIDST OF CHANGE   99

3. A Changing American Character?   101

The Unchanging American Character   106

*The Unchanging American Values and Their Connec-
tion with American Character*   110

*The Indequacy of a Materialistic Interpretation of
Change*   122

Conclusion   129

4. Religion and American Values 140

    All-Pervasiveness, a Consistent Characteristic of American Religion 141

    Secularity, a Persistent Trait of American Religion 151

    Voluntarism, the Source of Religious Strength 159

5. Trade Unions and the American Value System 170

    Social Structure: the Source of American Unionism 173

    Societal Values and the Union Movement 178

    Societal Values and Union Leadership 187

    The American Political System and the Union Movement 196

    Other Equalitarian Societies: Canada and Australia 199

    Conclusion 203

PART III
DEMOCRACY IN COMPARATIVE PERSPECTIVE

205

6. Values and Democratic Stability 207

    Value Patterns and a Democratic Polity 209

    The United States and Great Britain 213

    France and Germany 224

    Social Change and Political Stability 239

7. Value Differences, Absolute or Relative: The English-Speaking Democracies 248

    Values and the Democratic Process 268

8. Values, Social Character, and the Democratic Polity 274

    The Authoritarian versus the Democratic Personality 277

    The Inner-directed versus the Other-directed Personality 281

9. Party Systems and the Representation of Social Groups   286

    Social Structure and the Character of the Party System   289

    Social Structure and Electoral Systems   293

    Party Systems and the Bases of Social Cleavage   295

    Consequences of the Different Systems   307

    Conclusion   312

10. Epilogue: Some Personal Views on Equality, Inequality, and Comparative Social Science   318

    Inequality in America   321

    The Ever-Present Conflict between Equality and Inequality   340

    Comparative Analysis   343

Name Index   349

Subject Index   356

Introduction

There has been a quite extraordinary number of books published in recent years that seek to analyze American society. Among those most widely read and talked about have been the works of Vance Packard, especially *The Status Seekers; The Power Elite* by C. Wright Mills; *The Organization Man* by William H. Whyte; *The Lonely Crowd* by David Riesman; *Image of America* by R. L. Bruckberger; *America as a Civilization* by Max Lerner; and the *Self-Conscious Society* by Eric Larrabee. These and other works arrive at roughly two sorts of conclusions:

According to the first view, America suffers from elaborate corruption in business and labor, and in law enforcement practices; from a growing concentration of business power; from the influences of mass media run by entertainment tycoons who satisfy the lowest common denominator in popular taste; and from a wasteful expenditure of resources directed to the enhancement of social status.

According to the other view, America is an affluent, highly democratic society in which the distribution of income, of status symbols, and of opportunities for social mobility is becoming more even-handed all the time; in which tolerance for differences in culture, religion, and race is growing; and in which demand for the best in art, literature, and music is increasing.

This book tries, in part, to reconcile these two pictures. To look at America in a comparative and historical context is to point up the fact that such contrasts have distinguished American society through its history. The contrasts, moreover, are linked to two basic American values—equality and achievement. These values, though related, are not entirely compatible; each has given rise to reactions which threaten the other.

When I say that we value equality, I mean that we believe all persons must be given respect simply because they are human beings; we believe that the differences between high- and low-status people reflect accidental, and perhaps temporary, variations in social relationships. This

emphasis on equality was reflected in the introduction of universal suffrage in America long before it came in other nations; in the fairly
consistent and extensive support for a public school system so that all
might have a common educational background; and in the pervasive
antagonism to domination by any elite in culture, politics, or economics.

The value we have attributed to achievement is a corollary to our
belief in equality. For people to be equal, they need a chance to
become equal. Success, therefore, should be attainable by all, no matter
what the accidents of birth, class, or race. Achievement is a function
of equality of opportunity. That this emphasis on achievement must lead
to new inequalities of status and to the use of corrupt means to secure
and maintain high position is the ever recreated and renewed American
dilemma.

America's key values—equality and achievement—stem from our
revolutionary origins. The United States was the first major colony
successfully to revolt against colonial rule. In this sense, it was the first
"new nation." For this reason, to see how, in the course of American
history, its values took shape in institutions may help us to understand
some of the problems faced by the new nations emerging today on the
world scene. For the values which they must use to legitimate their
political structure, and which thus become part of their political institutions, are also revolutionary. Thus in addition to explaining "what makes
America tick," this book is designed to suggest how the sociologist's
analysis of value systems can contribute to the systematic study of the
development of a nation's institutions.

I do not mean to suggest that the new nations will necessarily re-
capitulate the American experience. Indeed, anxiety about the social
conditions that foster stable, non-authoritarian political relations in the
new nations of Asia and Africa has become a major preoccupation of
statesmen and academicians alike in the post-war era. A new field of
inquiry—the study of development—has emerged in economics, political
science, and sociology. Most scholarship in this area has understandably
devoted itself to a detailed examination of specific problems (e.g., economic growth) or of specific politico-geographical entities; however, I
feel that a general analysis of the relation between a nation's values
and its institutions can be of some utility. Studying fundamental
processes rather than any specific disorder may actually be the shortest
road to correct diagnosis and cure of a particular problem. (For example,
study of the laws of blood chemistry may turn out to be more useful

in the cure of mental illness than the development of *ad hoc* generalizations based on psychotherapeutic efforts.) Therefore, the last section of this book attempts to examine—by comparative analysis of nations at roughly similar levels of industrial development—some of the relations between a nation's values and the evolution of a stable polity that are suggested by the American example.

The three sections of this book deal with the role of values in a nation's evolution. However, each approaches this role from a different perspective. The first section, using America's first decades as a point of departure, identifies some of the problems of new nations arising from a break in the continuity of political legitimacy, and analyzes some of the consequences of a revolutionary birth for the creation of a national character and style. The second section traces how values derived from America's revolutionary origins have continued to influence the form and substance of American institutions in later years. The third section attempts to show by comparative analysis some ways through which a nation's values determine its political evolution.

Because each section approaches the role of values from a different perspective, its procedure is different. The first compares early America with today's emerging nations to discover problems common to them as new nations. The second concentrates on American history in later periods: religious institutions and trade unions have been selected for discussion in this section because they are critical cases. The third compares political development in several modern industrialized democracies, including the United States.

Talcott Parsons, perhaps the foremost contemporary exponent of the importance of value systems as causal factors, has explained and justified their systematic use as explanatory variables in these terms:

> That a system of value-orientations held in common by the members of a social system can serve as the main point of reference for analyzing structure and process in the social system itself may be regarded as a major tenet of modern sociological theory. Values in this sense are the commitments of individual persons to pursue and support certain *directions* or types of action for the collectivity as a system and hence derivatively for their own roles in the collectivity. Values are, for sociological purposes, deliberately defined at a level of generality higher than that of goals—they are *directions* of action rather than specific objectives, the latter depending on the particular character of the situation in which the

system is placed as well as on its values and its structure as a system.[1]

Karl Deutsch too has pointed to the social scientist's need for general variables to codify national experiences. He suggests that nations vary in their "wills" (a concept close to "central value systems") as a result of differing historical experiences:

> Will . . . may be described as the set of constraints acquired from the memories and past experiences of the system, and applied to the selection and treatment of items in its later intake, recall, or decisions. Any self-steering system . . . requires some operating preferences.[2]

The emphasis on values in this book does not, of course, negate other approaches, but is intended merely to demonstrate that values are one important source of variation among social systems.[3]

Talcott Parsons himself disavows the notion that an emphasis on values implies a monistic approach to social analysis:

---

[1] Talcott Parsons, *Structure and Process in Modern Societies* (Glencoe, Ill.: The Free Press, 1960), p. 172.

[2] Karl Deutsch, *Nationalism and Social Communication* (New York, John Wiley, 1953), p. 151. This book should be required reading for students of development.

[3] An excellent discussion of the general assumptions underlying the sociological analysis of the central value system of societies may be found in Edward Shils, "Centre and Periphery," in *The Logic of Personal Knowledge: Essays Presented to Michael Polanyi on His Seventieth Birthday* (London: Routledge & Kegan Paul, 1961), pp. 117–130.

Although many political analysts have attempted to relate various aspects of the polities of different nations to specific structural components of the value system, no one as yet has formulated a general theory in this area. Perhaps the closest approximation to this may be found in Harry Eckstein, *A Theory of Stable Democracy* (Princeton University Center for International Studies, 1961). Eckstein does not describe his approach as an effort to relate general values to political systems but rather writes of the need for "propositions relating governmental authority to other forms of social authority" (p. xiii). He tries to relate the stability of political systems to their congruence or lack of congruence with authority relations in non-political areas, e.g., family, school, religion, and so forth. Since authority relations are necessarily closely involved with the central value system, if they are not to be conceived as core components of that system, Eckstein is essentially engaged in what I would describe as value analysis.

It should be clear that using values as the initial point of reference for the structural analysis of social systems does not imply that they are the sole or even the most important *determinants* of particular structures and processes in such systems. . . . Beliefs and values are actualized, partially and imperfectly, in realistic situations of social interaction, and the outcomes are *always* co-determined by the values and the realistic exigencies; conversely . . . "interests" are by no means independent of the values which have been institutionalized in the relevant groups.[4]

Interestingly enough, Friedrich Engels—whose Marxist approach generally underplays the independent significance of values—recognized the force that values exert on political change. It may be worthwhile to cite a few of his descriptive comments on national polities:

It seems a law of historical development that the bourgeoisie can in no European country get hold of political power—at least for any length of time—in the same exclusive way in which the feudal aristocracy kept hold of it during the Middle Ages. Even in France, where feudalism was completely extinguished, the bourgeoisie as a whole has held full possession of the Government for very short periods only. . . . A durable reign of the bourgeoisie has been possible only in countries like America, where feudalism was unknown, and society at the very beginning started from a bourgeois basis. . . .

In England, the bourgeoisie never held undivided sway. . . . The English bourgeoisie are, up to the present day, so deeply penetrated by a sense of their social inferiority that they keep up, at their own expense and that of the nation, an ornamental caste of drones to represent that nation worthily at all State functions; and they consider themselves highly honored whenever one of themselves is found worthy of admission into this select and privileged body. . . .

Parliamentary government is a capital school for teaching respect for tradition; if the middle-class look with awe and veneration upon what Lord Manners playfully called "our old nobility," the mass of the working-people then looked up with respect and deference to what used to be designated as "their betters" the middle-class. . . .[5]

Furthermore, in accounting for the "rebellious" behavior of the French and German workers, as contrasted with the British, Engels (writing in

---

[4] Parsons, *Structure and Process in Modern Societies*, p. 173.

[5] Friedrich Engels, *Socialism, Utopian and Scientific* (Chicago: Charles H. Kerr and Co., 1912), pp. 37–43.

1892) stressed the strength of specific values, not class relationships. To keep the masses in line, once they are aware of their political rights, one must rely on *"moral means."* And England was more stable than various continental societies because it had not broken with traditional religion. "Religion must be kept alive for the people—that was the only and last means to save society from ruin. Unfortunately for themselves, they [the continental bourgeoisie] did not find this out until they had done their level best to break up religion forever."[6]

For Engels and other Marxists, of course, "juridical, philosophical, and religious ideas are the more or less *remote* offshoots of the economical relations prevailing in a given society." But these ideas account for variations in societies having the same "economical relations."[7] Such statements, while clearly outside the formal Marxist framework of analysis, may be viewed as attempts to analyze systematically variations *within* major historical epochs and to go beyond the *ad hoc* descriptions of most Marxists,

---

[6]*Loc. cit.* This is an area of considerable scholarly controversy. Elie Halévy in his classic *History of the English People in the Nineteenth Century* (London: Ernest Benn Ltd., 1961), also refers to the evangelical revival in the eighteenth century to explain "the extraordinary stability which English society was destined to enjoy throughout a period of revolutions and crises" (Vol. 1, p. 387). However, his causal analysis was somewhat different from that of Engels. He pointed out that the evangelical sects were largely middle-class movements, that the working class was not directly involved. The Nonconformist churches "gave the middle class distinctive beliefs, a distinctive religious organization and a self-respect which respected without envying the aristocracy" (Vol. 4, p. 337). "But by becoming the religion of the middle classes it had separated the latter, not only the upper middle, but the lower and the lowest middle class, from the common people and had deprived the latter of the leaders they required to wage the war against the rich which they wanted to lead. Deprived of leaders, the populace fell back into a state of incoherence, demoralization, and at last apathy" (Vol. 4, p. 395). Reinhard Bendix, however, suggests that religious revivalism did contribute to reducing the radicalism of the English workers. See his *Work and Authority in Industry* (New York: John Wiley, 1956), pp. 60–73. Most recently the English Marxist historian Eric Hobsbawn has argued that religious revivalism among English workers in the nineteenth century did not affect their radicalism. See his *Social Bandits and Primitive Rebels* (Glencoe, Ill.: The Free Press, 1959), pp. 126–149; while Gustav Rimlinger, "The Legitimation of Protest: A Comparative Study in Labor History," *Comparative Studies in Society and History*, 2 (1960), pp. 329–343, has attempted to show that it did so contribute.

[7] Engels, *Socialism, Utopian and Scientific*, p. 43. (Emphasis mine.)

or indeed of most economists concerned with "non-economic" factors.[8]

The approach to value analysis in this book assumes a perspective taken by Max Weber. Much of contemporary sociology has neglected his insight in explaining differences in national systems by specifying key historical events which set one process in motion in one country and a second in another. He, in fact, used the analogy of loaded dice: once the dice came up with a certain number they would tend to come up with the same number again.[9] In other words, historical events establish values and predispositions, and these in turn determine later events. In this way values become determinants of the direction of social change. Following the logic of Weber's analysis of the genesis of capitalism, we may argue that the existence of certain values is a prerequisite for some of the characteristics of contemporary America. Furthermore, these characteristics may become more pronounced as these values interact with material conditions.

By emphasizing the role of values in political evolution I am attempting to connect studies of historical change with basic assumptions in contemporary sociological theory. Seen in the light of Weber's methodology, the sociological emphasis on key values in a social system is an effort to relate the operation of the system to elements rooted in its history.[10] Within these historical "givens," furthermore, a certain body of theoretical propositions states what kind of system is operating, its relations with external systems, its internal relations, its tensions, its contradictions, and so on. Sometimes, if one utilizes a stable equilibrium model, one emphasizes the self-regulating and restorative mechanisms. For the purposes of this book, I have tried to think in terms of a dynamic (that is, moving or unstable) equilibrium model, which posits that a complex society is under constant pressure to adjust its institutions to its central value system, in order to

---

[8] Engels' emphasis on values may not be as "heretical" as it appears. Marx himself once stated, "We know that the institutions, manners and customs of the various countries must be considered, and we do not deny that there are countries, like England and America, . . . where the worker may attain his object by peaceful means." Quoted by Andrew Hacker, "Sociology and Ideology," in Max Black, ed., *The Social Theories of Talcott Parsons* (Englewood Cliffs, N.J., Prentice-Hall, 1961), p. 289. Hacker goes on to say that "It is remarks like this which turn scholarly heads gray."

[9] Max Weber, *The Methodology of the Social Sciences* (Glencoe, Ill.: The Free Press, 1949), pp. 182–185.

[10] For an excellent discussion of the relationship between the concerns of historical and social science, see David M. Potter, *People of Plenty* (Chicago: University of Chicago Press, 1954), esp. pp. 3–72.

alleviate strains created by changes in social relations; and which asserts that the failure to do so results in political disturbance.

The attempt to generalize about the development of social systems in this way has been questioned by some sociologists, e.g., Barrington Moore, Jr.,[11] C. Wright Mills,[12] and George Lichtheim.[13] Basically, these critics argue that all complex social systems must be analyzed primarily from a historical point of view. They feel that the analysis of the consequences of specific historical situations is a more adequate "explanation of the 'system' " than is the effort to specify the interrelated functions served by the system and its parts at any given time.

This criticism, that the efforts to formulate generalizations about systems necessarily conflicts with the analysis of historical processes, is unwarranted.[14] The attack aimed at sociological theory for ignoring the Marxian "principle of historical specification" has been discussed by Lewis Feuer, a student of both scientific methodology and Marxian thought. After pointing out that Marx never used the expression, "the principle of historical specification" (which Mills attributed to him), Feuer goes on to state:

> There is, to my mind, a bit of obscurantism in "the principle of historical specification" which, at the present time, obstructs the advance of social science. The principle rightly warns us to specify clearly the variables in our sociological laws; do not, for instance, enunciate as a law for all economic systems what may be true only of a competitive capitalist one. The principle has its obvious counterpart in physics. Kepler's laws, for instance, are laws for the motions of planets, not for masses in general. But Kepler's laws turned out to be special cases of the Newtonian Laws which did apply to all masses. And, in a similar sense, the laws of different societies might likewise be special cases of the operation of universal psychological and soci-

[11] Barrington Moore, Jr., "The New Scholasticism," *World Politics*, 6 (1953–54), pp. 122–138; also "Sociological Theory and Contemporary Politics," *American Journal of Sociology*, 61 (1954–55), pp. 107–115. See also his *Political Power and Social Theory: Six Studies* (Cambridge, Mass.: Harvard University Press, 1958).

[12] C. Wright Mills, *The Sociological Imagination* (New York: Oxford University Press, 1958).

[13] George Lichtheim, *Marxism* (London: Allen and Unwin, 1962), pp. xiii–xix.

[14] S. M. Lipset and Neil Smelser, "Change and Controversy in Recent American Sociology," *The British Journal of Sociology*, 12 (1961), pp. 41–51.

ological laws. To specify the historical structure would simply then be to state the social initial conditions which would bound the operation of the universal laws in the specific historical situation. We cannot indeed understand how one social system evolves into another without using some guiding laws of a common human nature; the revolt of men against their society's mores and values would be otherwise unintelligible.[15]

To be sure, since there are relatively few existing societies to compare, specific hypotheses about their evolution are less subject to verification than generalizations about, say, the development of individual persons, where many more cases can be compared. And because social systems are complex units, we must rely on historical case studies as our basic method for the study of national evolution. However, this does not rule out generalization altogether.[16] The historical case study approach need not concentrate solely on the unique. It can draw out generalizations that can apply to all similar cases, and can test and elaborate general hypotheses. Thus there is no necessary clash between developing general sociological hypotheses and taking historical specificity into account. "Much may be gained by using analytical concepts to guide our historical inquiry, and by using the results of historical inquiry to modify our concepts regarding present day problems."[17]

The analyst of societies must choose between a primarily historical or

---

[15] Lewis Feuer, "A Symposium on C. Wright Mills's 'The Sociological Imagination,'" *Berkeley Journal of Sociology* (University of California, Department of Sociology), 5 (1959), pp. 122–123.

[16] Another criticism that has been leveled at the sociologist's attempt to generalize by comparing the histories of several nations is that he must inevitably rely extensively on secondary authorities, without going back to the original sources. T. H. Marshall, one of the deans of British sociology, has justified this practice: "Nothing is more unreliable than the first-hand account of an eye-witness, nor more liable to deceive than diaries and correspondence whose authors thoroughly enjoyed writing them. And even the accounts of treasurers cannot always be accepted as representing the final and absolute truth. It is the business of historians to sift this miscellaneous collection of dubious authorities and to give to others the results of their careful professional assessment. And surely they will not rebuke the sociologist for putting faith in what historians write." *Sociology at the Crossroads and Others Essays* (London: Heinemann, 1963), pp. 36–37.

[17] Karl W. Deutsch, S. A. Burrell, R. A. Kann, M. Lee, Jr., M. Lichterman, R. E. Lindgren, F. L. Loewenheim, R. W. Van Wagenen, *Political Community and the North Atlantic Area* (Princeton, N.J.: Princeton University Press, 1957), p. 14.

a primarily comparative approach for a given piece of research. He must choose simply because each of these requires a different mode of generalization. But even if he chooses one approach, he cannot ignore the other. Without examining social relations in *different* countries, it is impossible to know to what extent a given factor actually has the effect attributed to it in a *single* country. For example, if it is true that the German *Ständestaat* (rigid status system) has contributed to the authoritarian pattern of German politics, why is it that similar status systems in Sweden and Switzerland are associated with very different political patterns?

Such an example suggests that comparisons may better enable the researcher to evaluate the effect of specific factors in the development of single national patterns. Three chapters in this book, " A Changing American Character?" "Religion and American Values," and "Trade Unions and the American Value System," use comparative materials in this way.

On the other hand, the analyst obviously cannot ignore specific historical events in attempting to assess what is common to the evolution of different nations. Chapter 6, "Values and Democratic Stability," attempts to show how the French and American revolutions have affected the value systems of these two countries so that they differ greatly from other countries with similar economic structures. And varying value systems, in turn, influence the political stability of the nations in question. "Party Systems and the Representation of Social Groups" (Chapter 9) shows even more clearly the necessity to focus on specific historical events in a comparative analysis, for the electoral systems in each of the countries described are themselves an important determinant of the degree to which the polities of the various countries are stable.

In the end the choice between a primarily historical or a primarily comparative approach is a matter of relative emphasis. If the analyst stresses an historical approach, he must use comparative materials to show to what degree his findings are specific to the country he is studying. If he selects an essentially comparative approach, he should employ historical detail to show how specific social conditions affect the operations of the general relationships he has discovered.

A general theory of social development can scarcely be formulated from the analyses presented in this book. Much more evidence and conceptual clarification are necessary before any such theory is possible. However, comparisons between America's development and that of other nations may silhouette some of the problems involved, for instance, in establishing a new nation. Consider the following:

One of the necessary conditions for a stable *democratic* polity is a clear distinction between the source of sovereignty and the agents of authority. In a nation which has broken sharply with the traditional sources of legitimacy, the dominant political ideologies are the products of a revolutionary mood, and hence are most often populist: they emphasize that sovereignty comes from the people. They will therefore also be tempted to emphasize that authority should be exercised by the people—which is almost never feasible. A populist source of the values which legitimate the authority structure is inherently unstable because in its purist sense it would promise the citizenry more direct control over the government than it could possibly have.

In democracies, the rights of the minority must be respected. Populism has a tendency to deny these rights, to assume that those whose values do not agree with the basic consensus of the society should be driven out. The populist source of the values which legitimate authority in post-revolutionary societies must be supplemented with a respect for the rule of law if a stable democracy is to result. But where the law lacks the support of old traditions, the institutionalization of a respect for the rule of law is difficult. The Founding Fathers consciously sought to inhibit such excesses by creating a system of constitutional checks and balances. America is particularly fortunate in that its long history of effective government and national growth has had the effect of legitimating constitutional government and, consequently, of making appeals to the people over the law increasingly less effective. In France today the rule of law has not been institutionalized to nearly the same degree, and populism remains as the principal source of, and threat to, the legitimacy that is granted agents of authority.

Only if we recognize that in the United States the difficulties encountered in making a distinction between the authority to establish government and the authority to govern almost resulted in a failure to create a nation, can we appreciate the tremendous problems faced by contemporary post-revolutionary societies with much more complicated and less advantageous conditions than ours. Clearly, the odds are against democracy in the new states of Africa and Asia. Many experts on these countries suggest that democracy may be a utopian short-term objective for such nations. Instead of speaking generally about democracy, it may be advisable to focus on the conditions which protect personal liberty, that is, on due process and the rule of law. Perhaps we should ask, as we look at new countries: under what circumstances is a post-revolutionary regime, or the government of a new state, compatible with the rule of law?

AMERICA
AS A NEW
NATION

PART 1

Establishing
National
Authority

★★

The United States may properly claim the title of the first new nation. It was the first major colony successfully to break away from colonial rule through revolution. It was, of course, followed within a few decades by most of the Spanish colonies in Central and South America. But while the United States exemplifies a new nation which successfully developed an industrial economy, a relatively integrated social structure (the race issue apart) and a stable democratic polity, most of the nations of Latin America do not. They remain underdeveloped economically, divided internally along racial, class, and (in some cases) linguistic lines, and have unstable polities, whether democratic or dictatorial. So perhaps the first new nation can contribute more than money to the latter-day ones; perhaps its development can give us some clues as to how revolutionary equalitarian and populist values may eventually become incorporated into a stable nonauthoritarian polity.

In this section I will examine the early period of America's history as a new nation, in an effort to elucidate through comparative analysis some of the problems and some of the developmental processes that are common to all new nations. And in so doing, I will also highlight some of the circumstances that were unique to American development, some of the conditions that made young America a particularly auspicious place to develop democratic institutions.

There is a tendency for older nations to view with impatience the internal turmoil of new ones, and to become especially alarmed at the

way oligarchical-dictatorial and revolutionary forces shake their tenuous foundations. Coupled with this is a tendency to expect them to
accomplish in a decade what other nations have taken a century or more
to do. A backward glance into our own past should destroy the notion
that the United States proceeded easily toward the establishment of democratic political institutions. In the period which saw the establishment of
political legitimacy and party government, it was touch and go whether
the complex balance of forces would swing in the direction of a one- or
two-party system, or even whether the nation would survive as an
entity. It took time to institutionalize values, beliefs, and practices, and
there were many incidents that revealed how fragile the commitments
to democracy and nationhood really were.

But it was from this crucible of confusion and conflict that values and
goals became defined, issues carved out, positions taken, in short *an
identity established.* For countries, like people, are not handed identities
at birth, but acquire them through the arduous process of "growing up,"
a process which is a notoriously painful affair.

Let us now turn to a more detailed examination of some of the
specific problems common to new nations.

The Crisis of Legitimacy and the Role of the Charismatic Leader

A basic problem faced by all new nations and post-revolutionary
societies is the crisis of legitimacy. The old order has been abolished and
with it the set of beliefs that justified its system of authority. The
imperialist ogre upon whom all ills were blamed has now disappeared, and
there has been a slackening of the great unifying force, nationalism, under
whose banner private, ethnic, sectional, and other differences were
submerged. The new system is in the process of being formed and so the
questions arise: To whom is loyalty owed? And why?

Legitimacy of any kind is derived from shared beliefs, that is, from
a consensus as to what constitutes proper allegiance. Such a consensus
develops slowly. In the words of Ernest Renan in a lecture in 1882:
"To have done great things together in the past, to wish to do more
of them, these are the essential conditions for being a people. . . . The
existence of a nation is a daily plebiscite."[1] In the early period of a

---

[1] Quoted in Frank H. Underhill, "A United Nation Is Not Enough," *The
Globe Magazine,* March 24, 1962, p. 5. For a more detailed discussion of the
relationship of legitimacy to democracy see S. M. Lipset, *Political Man: The
Social Bases of Politics* (Garden City, N.Y.: Doubleday, 1960), pp. 77–90.

nation's history, the results of this plebiscite are never a foregone conclusion.

According to Max Weber, there are basically three ways in which an authority may gain legitimacy, that is, an accepted "title to rule":

(1) It may gain legitimacy through *tradition,* through "always" having possessed it—the title held by monarchical societies is essentially of this type.

(2) *Rational-legal* authority exists when those in power are obeyed because of a popular acceptance of the appropriateness of the system of rules under which they have won and hold office.

(3) *Charismatic* authority rests upon faith in a leader who is believed to be endowed with great personal worth: this may come from God, as in the case of a religious prophet, or may simply arise from the display of extraordinary talents.

Old states possess traditional legitimacy, and this need not concern us further, beyond suggesting that new nations may sometimes be in a position to enhance their own legitimacy by incorporating the already existing legitimacy of subordinate centers or persons of authority. Thus, new nations which retain local rulers—for example dukes, counts, chiefs, clan heads, etc.—and create a larger national system of authority based on them, may be more stable than those which seek to destroy such local centers of authority. It can be argued that the case of Europe's most stable republican government, Switzerland, is to be explained as a consequence of the preservation of cantonal government and power, *i.e.,* as an extension of cantonal legitimacy. Contemporary Malaya is a recent example of an effort to foster national legitimacy by retaining traditional symbols of local rule.[2]

But where traditional legitimacy is absent, as it was in post-revolutionary America or France and in much of contemporary Asia and Africa, it can be developed only through reliance on legal and/or charismatic authority.

Legal domination, resting on the assumption that the created legal structure is an effective means of attaining group ends, is necessarily a weak source of authority in societies in which the law has been identified with the interests of an imperial exploiter. Charismatic au-

---

[2] A crisis of legitimacy may occur even when the traditional forms of rule are maintained, if the authority figures are subordinated to alien rulers. Beaumont noted this problem among Indian tribes during his visit to America with Tocqueville in the early 1830's. Gustave de Beaumont, *Marie, or Slavery in the United States* (Stanford, Calif.: Stanford University Press, 1958), especially p. 241.

thority, on the other hand, is well suited to the needs of newly developing nations. It requires neither time nor a rational set of rules, and is highly flexible. A charismatic leader plays several roles. He is first of all the symbol of the new nation, its hero who embodies in his person its values and aspirations. But more than merely symbolizing the new nation, he legitimizes the state, the new secular government, by endowing it with his "gift of grace." David Apter has shown how the government of Ghana gained diffuse legitimacy from the charisma of Nkrumah.[3] Charismatic authority can be seen as a mechanism of transition, an interim measure, which gets people to observe the requirements of the nation out of affection for the leader until they eventually learn to do it out of loyalty to the collectivity.[4]

Charismatic leadership, however, because it is so personalized, is extremely unstable. The source of authority is not something distinct from the various actions and agencies of authority, so that particular dissatisfaction can easily become generalized disaffection. The charismatic leader must therefore either make open criticism impermissible or he must transcend partisan conflict by playing the role of a constitutional monarch. Even where opposition to specific policies on an individual—or informal factional—basis may be tolerated, there cannot be an Opposition to him that is organized into a formal party with its own leader. But the difference between these options can have fateful consequences for the entire nation.

The early American Republic, like many of the new nations, was legitimized by *charisma*. We tend to forget today that, in his time, George Washington was idolized as much as many of the contemporary leaders of new states. As Marcus Cunliffe, the English author of a brilliant biography of the first President, points out:

> In the well-worn phrase of Henry Lee, he was *first in war, first in peace and first in the hearts of his countrymen*. . . . He was the prime native hero, a necessary creation for a new country. . . . Hence . . . the comment . . . made by the European traveler Paul Svinin, as early as 1815: "Every American considers it his sacred duty to have a likeness of Washington in his home, just as we have the images of God's saints." For America, he was originator and vindicator, both patron saint *and* defender of the faith, in a

[3] David Apter, *The Gold Coast in Transition* (Princeton, N.J.: Princeton University Press, 1955), p. 303.

[4] See Edward Shils, "The Concentration and Dispersion of Charisma," *World Politics*, 11 (1958), pp. 2–3; and Immanuel Wallerstein, *Africa, Politics of Independence* (New York: Vintage Books, 1961), pp. 85–102.

curiously timeless fashion, as if he were Charlemagne, Saint Joan and Napoleon Bonaparte telescoped into one person. . . .[5]

And:

[T]he dying Roman emperor Vespasian is supposed to have murmured: "Alas, I think I am about to become a god." . . . George Washington . . . might with justice have thought the same thing as he lay on his deathbed at Mount Vernon in 1799. Babies were being christened after him as early as 1775, and while he was still President, his countrymen paid to see him in waxwork effigy. To his admirers he was "godlike Washington," and his detractors complained to one another that he was looked upon as a "demi-god" whom it was treasonable to criticize. "O Washington!" declared Ezra Stiles of Yale (in a sermon of 1783). "How I do love thy name! How have I often adored and blessed thy God, for creating and forming thee the great ornament of human kind!" . . .

His contemporaries vied in their tributes—all intended to express the idea that there was something superhuman about George Washington. . . .

Some of his countrymen—notably John Adams—were a little irked by the Washington cult. They felt that adulation had gone too far—as in the suggestion that God had denied Washington children of his own so that he might assume paternity for the whole nation. But even Adams was prepared to defend Washington as a native product against all challengers from other lands, with the proviso that Washington's virtues were America's virtues, rather than vice versa.[6]

---

[5] Marcus Cunliffe, *George Washington, Man and Monument* (New York: Mentor Books, 1960), pp. 20–21. "A legendary figure from the Revolution on, Washington reached the final stages of his apotheosis with the adoption of the Constitution and the establishment of the new government. . . . Sedgwick wrote . . . 'Today I dined with the President and as usual the company was as grave as at a funeral. All the time at table the silence more nearly resembled the gravity of . . . worship than the cheerfulness of convivial meeting' . . . [I]f the operations of the government had reflected the atmosphere which surrounded Washington, monarchy would have been only a little way ahead." Joseph Charles, *The Origins of the American Party System* (New York: Harper Torchbooks, 1961), pp. 38–39.

[6] Cunliffe, *George Washington*, pp. 15–16, 22. "In America . . . do not look . . . for monuments raised to the memory of illustrious men. I know that this people has its heroes: but no where have I seen their statues. To Washington alone are there busts, inscriptions, column; this is because Washington, in America, *is not a man but a God*." Beaumont, *Marie*, p. 106.

Washington's role as the charismatic leader under whose guidance democratic political institutions could grow was not an unwitting one:

> America's primary requirement, as he saw it, was confidence. *Crescit eundo*—She grows as she goes—could well have been the Union's official motto. In the words of his Farewell Address, "time and habit are at least as necessary to fix the true character of government as of other human institutions. . . .
>
> "With me . . . a predominant motive has been, to endeavor to gain time for our country to settle and mature its yet recent institutions, and to progress without interruption to that degree of strength and consistency, which is necessary to give it, humanly speaking, the command of its own fortunes."[7]

Like latter-day leaders of new states, Washington was under pressure from those close to him actually to become an autocrat. However, he recognized that his most important contribution to the new state was to give it time to establish what we now call a rational-legal system of authority, a government of men under law. He permitted the members of his cabinet to form hostile factions under the leadership of Hamilton and Jefferson, even though he personally disliked the views of Jeffersonians.[8] Before leaving office in 1797, he brought together Hamilton and Madison (leader of the Jeffersonians) to prepare drafts for his Farewell Address. And in the final sentence of the address he expressed the hope that his words "may be productive of some partial benefit, some occasional good; that they may now and then recur to moderate the fury of party spirit."[9]

Washington wished to retire after one term in office, but the conflict between his two principal collaborators would not permit it. And on the urging of many, including Hamilton and Jefferson, he agreed to serve another term—thereby unwittingly permitting the further peaceful extension of party conflict while he was still President, though, of

---

[7] Cunliffe, *George Washington*, pp. 136, 149–150.

[8] By commanding the respect of both factional leaders he was able to act as a unifying symbol. "Both Hamilton and Jefferson respected the President and believed they were loyal to him and to their different ideas of the Union. In his presence they did not squabble. Their grievances were at one another, not at Washington. . . . If Washington was a somewhat remote figure . . . he was not a fool or a weakling." *Ibid.*, p. 141.

[9] *Ibid.*, p. 147.

course, he bitterly regretted the emergence of such parties. This turned out to be a crucial decision, since during his second administration, the country was torn apart by opposing opinions of the French Revolution, and between pro-British and pro-French sentiments.[10]

There seems little question that Washington was treated like a charismatic leader. But his refusal to take full advantage of his potential charisma—he withdrew from the presidency while seemingly in good health—doubtless pushed the society faster toward a legal-rational system of authority than would have been the case had he taken over the charismatic role *in toto* and identified himself with the laws and the spirit of the nation. This particular halfway type of charismatic leadership had a critical stabilizing effect on the society's evolution. Of particular importance in this regard is the fact that the first succession conflict between John Adams and Jefferson took place while Washington still held office, enabling him to set a precedent as the first head of a modern state to turn over office to a duly elected successor. If he had continued in office until his death, it is quite possible that subsequent presidential successions would not have occurred so easily.

The charismatic aspects of Washington's appeal were consciously used by political leaders as a means of assuring the identity of the young nation. In 1800, shortly after Washington's death, the then British Ambassador to the United States analyzed the functions of tributes to Washington in a report to the Foreign Office:

> The leading men in the United States appear to be of the opinion that these ceremonies tend to elevate the spirit of the people, and contribute to the formation of a *national character*, which they consider as much wanting in this country. And assuredly, if self-opinion is (as perhaps it is) an essential ingredient in that *character* which promotes the prosperity and dignity of a nation, the Americans will be the gainers by the periodical recital of the feats of their Revolutionary War, and the repetition of the praises of Washington. The hyperbolical amplifications, the Panegyricks in question have an evident effect especially among the younger part of the com-

---

[10] The Hamiltonian Federalists, on the whole, viewed the terror of the French Revolution with horror and were pro-British; the Jeffersonian Republicans, as they were to be called, were pro-Revolutionary and pro-French. During this second term, also, Washington became increasingly a partisan of Federalist politics, and was attacked by various Republican papers and speakers, although usually in mild terms.

munity, in fomenting the growth of that vanity, which to the feelings of a stranger had already arrived at a sufficient height.[11]

The "near-apotheosis" of Washington characterized almost all that was written and said about him for the first few generations of the new nation. As Cunliffe points out:

> Washington, up to about the Civil War, was so venerated that no biographer would dream of criticizing him. On the contrary, biographers vied in finding new ways of praising him. "He was as fortunate as great and good," said Aaron Bancroft. For Peleg Sprague, Washington was "The Patriot Hero of our Revolution, the Christian Statesman of our Republic, great in goodness, and good in greatness." Edward Everett did not hesitate to pronounce Washington, "of all men that ever lived, THE GREATEST OF GOOD MEN AND THE BEST OF GREAT MEN" . . . . The American public demanded to be told of a Washington who was a "human angil"—spotless, pious, dauntless.[12]

The importance of Washington's role for the institutionalization of legal-rational authority in the early United States can be summarized as follows:

1. His prestige was so great that he commanded the loyalty of the leaders of the different factions as well as the general populace. Thus, in a political entity marked by much cleavage he, in his own person, provided a basis for unity.

2. He was strongly committed to the principles of constitutional government and exercised a paternal guidance upon those involved in developing the machinery of government.

---

[11] Quoted in Charles, *The Origins of the American Party System*, p. 52. (Emphasis in original.) Writing in the 1830's, the English liberal Harriet Martineau described Washington's halo in terms similar to those of Beaumont, cited earlier: "Washington's influence is a topic which no one is ever hardy enough to approach, in way of measurement or specification. Within the compass of his name lies more than other words can tell of his power over men. It is Washington, the man, not the President, whose name is lovingly spoken, whose picture smiles benignly in every inhabited nook of his congregation of republics. It is even Washington, the man, not the President, whose name is sacred above all others, to men of all political parties." Harriet Martineau, *Society in America* (Garden City, N.Y.: Doubleday Anchor Books, 1962), p. 82.

[12] Marcus Cunliffe, Introduction to Mason L. Weems, *The Life of Washington* (Cambridge, Mass.: The Belknap Press of Harvard University Press, 1962), pp. xliv–xlv.

3. He stayed in power long enough to permit the crystallization of factions into embryonic parties.

4. He set a precedent as to how the problem of succession should be managed, by voluntarily retiring from office.

In most new nations the charismatic leader has tended to fulfill only the first of these tasks, acting as a symbol which represents and prolongs the feeling of unity developed prior to the achievement of independence.[13] The neglect of the other three important aspects of Washington's role results in "charismatic personalities . . . [who do] not ordinarily build . . . the institutions which are indispensable for carrying on the life of a political society"[14]—personalities whose disappearance raises again, as did the achievement of independence, the difficult problem of maintaining national unity among a conglomeration of groups and interests.

The Problem of National Unity

One of the problems shared by all new nations is that of creating a feeling of national unity among diverse elements. "The parochialism of the constituent segments of the societies of the new states has been commonly observed. The sense of membership in the nation, which is more or less coterminous with the population residing within the boundaries of the new states, is still very rudimentary and very frail."[15] This tendency toward parochialism is common because the boundaries of new national communities are artificial, in the sense that they follow those "established by the imperial power rather than those coincident with precolonial socio-political groups."[16] Myron Weiner suggests the urgency

---

[13] "Whereas a seemingly cohesive national force pressed the imperial power for concessions, a grant of independence or self-government will bring separatist forces into the open. The integrative energies generated by the struggle for independence cannot be depended upon to survive after independence is won." Donald S. Rothchild, *Toward Unity in Africa* (Washington: Public Affairs Press, 1960), p. 2.

[14] Edward Shils, "Political Development in the New States," *Comparative Studies in Society and History*, 2 (1960), p. 288.

[15] *Ibid.*, p. 283.

[16] James S. Coleman, "Nationalism in Tropical Africa," in John H. Kautsky, ed., *Political Change in Underdeveloped Countries* (New York: John Wiley, 1962), p. 189. "Little attention was paid in the original partition of Africa or in its re-partition after the First World War to effective social groupings; so that people who had traditionally enjoyed a certain coherence found themselves divided between the territories of different colonial powers. The Somalis, divided between British, French and Italian Somaliland, as well as Ethiopia are a classic example; but the Ewes, distributed over the Gold Coast

of this issue when he reports with specific reference to South Asia that "the maintenance of national unity in the countries of South Asia is perhaps their most severe political problem."[17] In Africa too the "issues and problems of national unification are at the center of politics in the new and emergent societies."[18] A recent study by a group of scholars at MIT suggests that in order to create genuine stable new nations, "the first prerequisite is a sense of national unity, a political consensus. . . ." They go on to urge that "the issues of national unity represent basic constitutional problems. Only as they are resolved can a society develop its policy and create the means for grappling with social and economic problems of modernization."[19]

The problems of national unity and consensus alluded to by the various writers cited above are clearly more complex than those faced by the United States when it broke with Britain. Many African and Asian states are the home of numerous linguistic groups and tribal units, several of which have histories of bitter antagonism to each other.[20] India has been unable to resist demands that its internal state boundaries be drawn along linguistic lines, a development which can place severe strains on

and British and French Togoland and the Bacongo, split by the frontiers of French Moyen-Congo, the Belgian Congo and Portuguese Angola, are in a comparable situation. In these and other cases, nationalisms aiming at reuniting peoples whom European colonization divided have begun to assert themselves, making the pattern of African nationalism more complicated. . . . For the moment, the difficulties in the way of preserving unity in multi-national, multi-religious Nigeria seem considerable." Thomas Hodgkin, *Nationalism in Colonial Africa* (New York: New York University Press, 1957), pp. 22–23.

[17] Myron Weiner, "The Politics of South Asia," in Gabriel Almond and James S. Coleman, eds., *The Politics of Developing Areas* (Princeton, N.J.: Princeton University Press, 1960), p. 239.

[18] Coleman, "Nationalism in Tropical Africa," *op. cit.*, p. 367.

[19] Max F. Millikan and Donald L. M. Backmer, eds., *The Emerging Nations* (Boston: Little, Brown, 1961), pp. 76–78.

[20] "[T]here is no such thing as a single Indian or Indonesian language. Some ten or twelve major languages and hundreds of minor tongues and local dialects are spoken in India. Some thirty languages are spoken in the Republic of Indonesia. . . . [I]n Nigeria a population of approximately 34,000,000 speaks roughly 250 different languages, a situation that is not unusual in much of Africa and among the tribes in the interior of Southeast Asia and Latin America. In Australian-ruled Papua and New Guinea . . . 1,750,000 natives speak 500 different languages and dialects, no one language being used by more than 50,000 and some by only 300." John H. Kautsky (ed.), Introduction to *Political Change in Underdeveloped Countries* (New York: John Wiley, 1962), p. 34.

its ultimate national unity.[21] Pakistan is divided into two sections, which differ in language and in level of economic development. Indonesia has faced the difficulty of resolving differences between the Javanese and those living in the outer islands, as well as ethnic and religious cleavages. Burma has had at least five different separatist movements struggling for autonomy or independence. The West Indian Federation, in spite of a common language, has broken up. The various efforts to create a federated structure out of the successor states of the French African Empire have failed. This has been true also with respect to attempts to unite any two or more of the Arab nations. And the tragic story of the Congo presents the most extreme example of the difficulties inherent in winning the loyalty of areas and groups with diverse cultures and histories to a new political authority.[22]

Early American history presented similar problems and reactions. True, its Western European heritage "established certain common traditions in advance, facilitating the task of harmonizing differences of language, culture, religion, and politics."[23] Nevertheless, "throughout the colonial period, Americans had tended to assume that these differences of language, culture, and religion would prevent the growth of a common loyalty."[24]

Karl Deutsch and his associates point out that one of the essential

---

[21] For an analysis of the relationship between variations in knowledge of different languages and the statistical chances for the triumph of any single language as the national one, see Karl Deutsch, *Nationalism and Social Communication* (New York: John Wiley, 1953), especially pp. 97–126, 170–213.

[22] ". . . [N]ationalism becomes an infection radiating from the larger group to ethnic, religious, or racial subgroups, each in turn claiming for itself the prerogatives of national self-determination which the larger entity achieved. The division of British India along religious lines into the Indian Republic and Pakistan is one such example; and the 'chain reaction' of local nationalisms, largely based on linguistic identities, has continued to plague the Indian Republic to a marked degree ever since independence was attained in 1947. Similar developments can be found in other parts of newly independent Asian and African states. But it is still too early to know whether national integration will ultimately prevail over local or racial separation—as has been the case in this country, England, and France—or whether large parts of the non-Western world will suffer the fate of internal 'Balkanization' in the years to come." Harry J. Benda, "Revolution and Nationalism in the Non-Western World," in Warren S. Hunsberger, ed., *New Era in the Non-Western World* (Ithaca, N.Y.: Cornell University Press, 1957), pp. 42–43.

[23] Rothchild, *Toward Unity in Africa*, p. 6.

[24] Maldwyn Allen Jones, *American Immigration* (Chicago: University of Chicago Press, 1960), p. 40.

conditions for the amalgamation of small political units into a larger
one is the growth of "compatibility of the main values held by the
politically relevant strata of all participating units." They observe that
similarities in the values current in the colonies underwent "accelerated
change and development in the course of the American Revolution and
its aftermath."[25] And Maldwyn Jones points out:

> During the Revolutionary era the need to stress national unity some-
> times induced Americans to become forgetful of their diverse ethnic
> origins and to overlook the persistence of cultural differences. Par-
> ticularly was this so among men who were anxious that the young
> republic should not be fatally weakened by a denial of adequate
> powers to the federal government. Thus it was, that, in the *Fed-
> eralist Papers,* John Jay was moved to congratulate his countrymen
> on the fact that "Providence [had] been pleased to give this one
> connected country to one united people—a people descended from
> the same ancestors, speaking the same language, professing the
> same religion, attached to the same principles of government, very
> similar in their manners and customs. . . ."[26]

One of the processes by which the integration of political units often
proceeds is by the decline of "party divisions which reinforce the
boundaries between political units eligible for amalgamation, and the rise
in their stead of party divisions cutting across them."[27] Early America
possessed social bases for political cleavage which cut across the established political units, the states. After the revolution, equalitarian pressures—albeit in different forms—grew up in most states. In many of
them, demands emerged for broader voting rights and for greater
representation in the legislatures of rural and western counties. These
cleavages provided the basis for trans-state parties.

However, before parties based upon these cleavages could play a
role in unifying portions of the polity across state lines, interest groups
in the different states had to learn to see beyond the particular issues
with which they were concerned. They had to recognize that they had
something in common with other groups advocating different forms of
equality.

---

[25] Karl W. Deutsch, S. A. Burrell, R. A. Kann, M. Lee, Jr., M. Lichterman,
R. E. Lindgren, F. A. L. Loewenheim, R. W. Van Wagenen, *Political Community and the North Atlantic Area* (Princeton, N.J.: Princeton University
Press, 1957), p. 48.
[26] Jones, *American Immigration,* p. 39.
[27] Deutsch *et al., Political Community and the North Atlantic Area,* p. 76.

Many individuals resisted being herded; states and state leaders stressed their special identities and interests; and heterogeneities from regionalism to economic variety to religion, tossed up a multiplicity of opinions and interests. Although this very individualism and pluralism were eventually to stimulate the resort to party coordination, it was no easy matter to harness them at the onset.[28]

Above all, a political arena in which the individual rather than the state was the political unit had to be created. Nevertheless, in spite of working and fighting together in a seven-year struggle for independence, the best governmental structure which the Americans could devise was a loose federal union under the Articles of Confederation. This union lacked any national executive and, in effect, preserved most of the sovereignty and autonomy of each state.[29]

The pressure to establish a unified central authority in contemporary new states comes mainly from the nationalist intellectual elite who are concerned with creating an important arena of effective operation through which the new nation, and they, can demonstrate competence. The main instrument for such action has been the revolutionary party.

After 1783, a national party that unified interests across state lines was approximated by

the advocates of central authority, who set up the plans for a convention on federal authority, to be held in Philadelphia. . . . A small group of political leaders with a Continental vision and essentially a consciousness of the United States' *international* impotence, provided the matrix of the movement. . . . Indeed, an argument with great force—particularly since Washington was its incarnation—urged that our very survival in the Hobbesian jungle of world politics depended upon a reordering and strengthening of our national sovereignty.[30]

[28] William N. Chambers, *Parties in a New Nation* (New York: Oxford University Press, 1963), pp. 24–25.

[29] " 'The great and radical vice in the construction of the existing Confederation,' warned Alexander Hamilton, 'is in the principle of LEGISLATION for STATES or GOVERNMENTS, in their CORPORATE or COLLECTIVE CAPACITIES, and as contradistinguished from the INDIVIDUALS of which they consist.' He maintained that such a relationship divested the central government of sufficient energies with which to carry out its obligations under the Articles of Confederation. The result was a central government subordinate to and dependent upon regional compliance." Rothchild, *Toward Unity in Africa*, p. 5.

[30] John P. Roche, "The Founding Fathers: A Reform Caucus in Action," *The American Political Science Review*, 60 (1961), p. 801. (Emphasis in the original.)

Many of those who served as delegates in what became the Constitutional Convention had served in the Revolutionary Continental Congress. This experience "left a deep imprint on those connected with it . . . [since it had been] a continental war effort. If there is any one feature that most unites the future leading supporters of the Constitution, it was their close engagement with this continental aspect of the Revolution. . . ."[31]

> All of them had been united in an experience, and had formed commitments, which dissolved provincial boundaries; they had come to full public maturity in a setting which enabled ambition, public service, leadership, and self-fulfillment to be conceived for each in his way, with a grandeur of scope unknown to any previous generation.[32]

The future of this generation's careers was

> staked upon the national quality of the experience which had formed them. In a number of outstanding cases energy, initiative, talent, and ambition had combined with a conception of affairs which had grown immense in scope and promise by the close of the Revolution. There is every reason to think that a contraction of this scope, in the years that immediately followed, operated as a powerful challenge.[33]

John P. Roche has argued that there was no ideological rift within the Constitutional Convention because almost all the delegates belonged to the central government party. He suggests that the differences of opinion which did emerge were specific or tactical rather than ideological. That is, there was no conflict between "nationalists" versus "states-rightists" but rather an argument over representation, the small states versus the big states. "The Virginia Plan [which] envisioned a unitary national government effectively freed from and dominant over the states . . . may . . . be considered, in ideological terms, as the delegates'

---

[31] "A remarkably large number of these someday [advocates of a strong central government] . . . were in the Continental Army, served as diplomats or key administrative officers of the Confederation government, or, as members of Congress, played leading roles on those committees primarily responsible for the conduct of the war." Stanley Elkins and Eric McKitrick, "The Founding Fathers: Young Men of the Revolution," *Political Science Quarterly*, 76 (1961), p. 202.

[32] *Ibid.*, p. 203.

[33] *Ibid.*, pp. 205–206.

Utopia . . ."[34] However, "the delegates from the small states . . . [a]pparently realizing that under the Virginia Plan, Massachusetts, Virginia and Pennsylvania could virtually dominate the national government —and probably appreciating that to sell this program to the 'folks back home' would be impossible . . . dug in their heels and demanded time for a consideration of alternatives.[35] Out of this consideration came the New Jersey Plan, which according to standard analyses was an expression of the states-rightists' "reversion to the *status-quo* under the Articles of Confederation. . . ."[36] However, Roche suggests this was a political maneuver designed to gain support from those not represented at the Convention, rather than a defense of states' rights among the delegates.

> It is true that the New Jersey Plan put the states back into the institutional picture, but . . . to do so was a recognition of political reality rather than an affirmation of states' rights. A serious case can be made that the advocates of the New Jersey Plan, far from being ideological addicts of states' rights, intended to substitute for the Virginia Plan a system which would both retain strong national power and have a chance of adoption in the states. . . . In fact, [New Jersey delegate] Patterson's notes of his speech can easily be construed as an argument for attaining the substantive objectives of the Virginia Plan by a sound political route, *i.e.*, pouring the new wine in the old bottles. . . . In other words, the advocates of the New Jersey Plan concentrated their fire on what they held to be the political liabilities of the Virginia Plan—which were matters of institutional structure—rather than on the proposed scope of national authority.[37]

---

[34] "The lower house of the national legislature was to be elected directly by the people of the states with membership proportional to the population. The upper house was to be selected by the lower, and the two chambers would elect the executive and choose the judges. The national government would be thus cut completely loose from the states." Roche, "The Founding Fathers," *op. cit.*, pp. 804–805.

[35] *Loc. cit.*

[36] *Ibid.*, p. 806.

[37] "The critical fight was over representation of the states and once the Connecticut Compromise was adopted . . . the convention was over the hump. Madison, James Wilson, and Gouverneur Morris of New York . . . fought the compromise all the way in a last ditch effort to get a unitary state with parliamentary supremacy. But their allies deserted them and they demonstrated after their defeat the essentially opportunist character of their objections. . . . It nourishes an increased respect for Madison's devotion to the art of politics, to realize that this dogged fighter could sit down six months

This "group of extremely talented democratic politicians" were not "rhapsodic" about the final form of the Constitution, but they had

> refused to attempt the establishment of a strong, centralized sover-
> eignty on the principle of legislative supremacy for the excellent
> reason that the people would not accept it— *political realities* forced
> them to water down their objectives and they settled, like the good
> politicians they were, for half a loaf. . . . The result was a Constitu-
> tion which the people, in fact, by democratic processes, did accept,
> and a new and far better national government was established.[38]

The energy behind the "nationalistic" aims of the Constitutional Convention came from leaders of a young generation whose careers, having
been launched in the continental war effort of the Revolution, depended
upon the survival of a nationalistic outlook. In age and aspiration, they
resembled the leadership of many contemporary new states. On the
other hand, those opposed to a strong central American government, who
had little if any representation at the Constitutional Convention, came
from an older generation whose careers were not only state-centered but
had been formed prior to the Revolution.[39]

Following the war "the spirit of unity generated by the struggle for
independence . . . lapsed" and the older generation reverted to its old
provincial ways, the particularism and inertia of local authority.[40] With
the exception of Pennsylvania, this meant primarily that men far more
than measures, personal connections rather than party machines, played
the most significant role in the conduct of politics.[41]

In this respect, the difference between the anti-Federalists and the

---

later and prepare essays for The Federalist in contradiction to his basic
convictions about the true course the Convention should have taken." *Ibid.*,
pp. 806, 810.

[38] *Ibid.*, pp. 813, 815, 816. (Emphasis in the original.)

[39] Elkins and McKitrick, "The Founding Fathers," *op. cit.*, pp. 203–204. "Merrill Jensen has compiled two lists, with nine names in each, of the men he
considers to have been the leading spirits of the Federalists and Anti-
Federalists. . . . The age difference between these two groups is especially
striking. The Federalists were on the average ten to twelve years younger
than the Anti-Federalists. . . . This age differential takes on a special significance when it is related to the career profiles of the men concerned." *Ibid.*,
pp. 202–203.

[40] *Ibid.*, p. 206.

[41] Chambers, *Parties in a New Nation*, pp. 19–20.

"Continental" Federalists is suggestive of Hodgkins's classification of the structure of African parties into primitive and modern:

> Parties of the former type [primitive] are dominated by "personal-ities," who enjoy a superior social status, either as traditional rulers or members of ruling families, or as belonging to the higher ranks of the urban, professional elite (lawyers, doctors, etc.). . . . Their political machinery, central and local, is of a rudimentary kind. . . . They have little, if anything, in the way of a secretariat or full-time officials. . . . They depend for popular support less upon organization and propaganda than on habits of respect for traditional authority, or wealth and reputation. . . .
>
> Parties of the second type [modern] aim at . . . a much more elaborate structure. Since their chief claim and function is to represent the mass, they are committed to a form of organization that is (certainly on paper and to some extent in practice) highly democratic. . . . Parties of this type are able to achieve a much higher level of efficiency than the "parties of personalities"; . . . because they possess a continuously functioning central office. . . . Indeed, dependence upon professional politicians—*permanents*— "who naturally tend to form a class and assume a certain authority" for the running of the machine is one of the most distinctive features of the "mass" party. . . . It depends for its strength not on the backing of traditional authority but upon propaganda, designed to appeal particularly to the imagination of the young, to women, to the semi-urbanized and discontented; to those who are outside the local hierarchies, and interested in reform and change.[42]

---

[42] Hodgkin, *Nationalism in Colonial Africa*, pp. 156–159. If one accepts or overlooks the extreme nature of Merrill Jensen's view, an even closer parallel can be seen. In speaking of the "Federalists" he states: "They too could call conventions. They too could paint dark pictures of the times and blame the supposed woes of the country on the Articles of Confederation, as the radicals had blamed the British government before 1776. They too could, and did, adopt the radical theory of the sovereignty of the people; in the name of the people they engineered a conservative counter-revolution and erected a nationalistic government whose purpose in part was to thwart the will of 'the people' in whose name they acted. They too could use one name while pursuing a goal that was the opposite in fact. Thus, although [they were] 'nationalistic' they adopted the name 'Federalist' for it served to disguise the extent of the changes they desired. True, the government they created had a good many 'federal' features, but this was so because . . . [they] were political realists and had to compromise with the political reality of actual state sovereignty." Merrill Jensen, *The Articles of Confederation* (Madison: University of Wisconsin Press, 1940), p. 245.
Hodgkin in further describing the modern "mass" parties of Africa writes,

Early America differed from the nations in Africa in that there did not anywhere exist "modern" parties which a political leader could take as a model. These emerged as a result of needs in the American situation—some of which, however, parallel those which stimulate "modern" party organization in Africa and Asia today.

The continental "caucus" at the Constitutional Convention did not represent a full transition to a modern political party. Such a transition implies the growth of an organization that is rationally oriented toward vote-getting. It also implies that this organization is connected to a social base with common ideological interests. In contrast, the struggle for ratification was particular to each state. In some the upper classes were for it while in others they were against it, according to the peculiarities of politics in each. The "Constitutionalists" relied on old political techniques, including the manipulation of notables, cliques, and coteries to get ratification through.

However, insofar as the transition to modern parties implies the rational calculation of what policies are necessary to get votes, the Constitutional Convention did mark a step in this direction. First, it created an organ in which policies touching on the interests of persons in all of the states were to be debated. Secondly, it marked a movement away from the politics of notables and coteries who were deeply tied to the old political structure of state supremacy. By establishing the principle of rationally calculating how to marshal public support for national policy, it opened the door for policies that addressed themselves directly to specific interest groups in all states. It was only a step further for Hamilton to create a coherent fiscal program designed to mobilize interests on behalf of national power and economic development. His attempts to manage politics in the capital to get his plans through Congress, then, "brought strong responses across the country. In the process, what began as a *capital* faction soon assumed status as a *national* faction and then, finally, as the new *Federalist* party."[43]

The Federalist party organization could be described as parallel to those patron parties in Africa that are national but which represent a

---

"One common characteristic is the radical character of their professed aims, set out in elaborate written constitutions, in which western democratic and socialist ideas are blended with African nationalist doctrine. . . . Any African 'mass' party, if it wishes to gain popular support, must speak the language of modern radicalism." Hodgkin, *op. cit.*, pp. 161–162.

[43] Chambers, *Parties in a New Nation*, pp. 39–40. (Emphasis mine.)

linking of local notables rather than an organization designed to mobilize the common people.[44] The first "modern" party, in the sense that there was a "coordination in activity between leaders at the capital, and leaders, actives and popular followings in the states, counties, and towns,"[45] was to come with the crystallization of the Jeffersonian Democratic-Republican party. It is interesting to note that while the leaders of both parties were quite young in the first decade of the Republic, the liberal Jeffersonians were considerably younger than the more conservative Federalists. Chambers estimates that the average age of the Federalists at the time of the 1792 election was forty-four, while that of the embryonic Democratic-Republicans, including the "comparative oldsters," Jefferson (forty-nine), Clinton (fifty-three), and Burr (forty-six), was thirty-six.[46]

The Democratic-Republicans developed party organizations for some of the same reasons that leaders develop such organizations in Africa today. They were opposed to the established authorities whose policies largely dominated public affairs through the Federalist organization.[47] When the Jay treaty caused popular indignation, and provoked concern on the part of some merchants that the British would not pay their war debts, the Republicans took advantage of this disaffection to organize an opposition based on popular support. They appealed to social categories that cut across existing political boundaries, just as the African mass-based parties do.[48] In so doing, the Democratic-Republican party served

---

[44] Ruth Schacter, "Single-party Systems in West Africa," *American Political Science Review*, 55 (1961), p. 297.

[45] Chambers, *Parties in a New Nation*, p. 80.

[46] *Ibid.*, pp. 68–69.

[47] Schacter, "Single Party Systems . . . ," *op. cit.*, p. 295.

[48] Ruth Schacter describes the unifying functions of the African mass parties in this way: "While patron parties' leaders, once through this first simple phase of 'ethnic arithmetic,' generally stopped their calculations there [uniting local notables] the leaders of mass parties had taken that as a point of departure. They tried to use their party organizations in order to awaken a wider national sense of community. They appealed to particular categories existing within or cutting across ethnic groups—a technique suitable to recruiting in a mobile, changing society. Youth and women were of course two such categories which mass parties emphasized heavily. . . . They often appealed to rural underprivileged groups. . . . Finally, they appealed to those who earned money income for growing coffee, cocoa, peanuts or bananas, and had become restless with tradition. . . ." "Single Party Systems . . . ," *op. cit.*, p. 301. As this description of the nature of support for African mass parties emphasizes, while the power techniques used to unite the people of the different

as a means of uniting the citizens of the several states in national citizenship by mobilizing their common interests in the national arena.

However, as is well known, the evolution of national political parties could not erase differences in regional interests. Nor did the ratification of the Constitution serve to legitimate the new governmental structure, even though it provided a basis for national unity. Only with time, and after many attempts to thwart its powers, was the federal government finally able to achieve a high degree of political legitimacy. A number of Southern apologists after the Civil War, and more recently Arthur Schlesinger, Sr. (who definitely doesn't fall into that category), have documented the proposition that almost every state and every major political faction and interest group attempted, at one time or other between 1790 and 1860, to weaken the power of the national government or to break up the Union directly.[49]

There were many threats to secede in the first decade of national existence, and the threats came from both northern and southern states.[50] In 1798 two future presidents, Jefferson and Madison, sought the passage by a state legislature of nullification ordinances which proclaimed the right of each state to decide the extent of national authority to be tolerated within its boundaries. After leaving national office in 1801, various Federalist leaders sought in 1804, 1808, and 1812 to take the New England or northern states out of the Union.

Later, when the slavery issue became important, both abolitionists and defenders of slavery talked of destroying the Constitution and the Union. The activities of the Southerners are, of course, well known, but it is often forgotten that in the early period of the controversy, when the abolitionists despaired of eliminating slavery because of constitutional guarantees, the Constitution was described by some as a "slave-holders" document and Garrison called it "a covenant with death and an agreement with hell." [51]

---

sections in contemporary new nations and of the states in early America may be similar, the nature of the tradition that divides them is very different.
[49] See Arthur Schlesinger, Sr., *New Viewpoints in American History* (New York: Macmillan, 1922), pp. 220-240; Jefferson Davis, *The Rise and Fall of the Confederate Government* (New York: Collier Books, 1961), pp. 56-60.
[50] See Marshall Smelser, "The Federalist Period as an Age of Passion," *The American Quarterly*, 10 (1958), p. 393.
[51] W. L. Garrison, *The Words of Garrison* (Boston: Houghton, Mifflin, 1905), p. 25.

Because of their opposition to slavery, some northern states urged non-cooperation with the government during the Mexican War, perceived by them as a struggle to extend slave territory. There were, in fact, many deserters from the American Army during this war. It is "apparently the only case known in which a body of United States soldiers after deserting subsequently formed a distinct corps in the enemy's army. . . ."[52]

Various northern states during the 1850's passed laws—the so-called Personal Liberty Laws—which were designed to prevent the enforcement of federal legislation (the Fugitive Slave Law). New Jersey's legislature justified this position in 1852 by describing the Union as "a compact between the several States," while as late as 1859, Wisconsin, the state in which the Republican Party had been founded five years earlier, declared that the several states "which had formed the federal compact, being 'sovereign and independent,' had 'the unquestionable right to judge of its infractions' and to resort to 'positive defiance' of all unauthorized acts of the general government."[53]

Thus, in the early United States, as in contemporary new states, the achievement of national unity, and of respect for a national authority, was no easy task.

The possibility of secession remains one of the basic problems facing many new states in our century. Their unity immediately after gaining independence "is largely explained by the negative, anti-Western, anti-colonial content of non-Western nationalism. One need not be a prophet of doom to anticipate that this negative unity may in time, and perhaps before long, weaken, and that the newly independent non-Western nation-states may then find themselves confronted by some of the dissensions and antagonisms which nationalist aspirations have so often brought in their wake elsewhere."[54]

---

[52] Edward S. Wallace, "Notes and Comment—Deserters in the Mexican War," *The Hispanic American Historical Review*, 15 (1935), p. 374.

[53] Schlesinger, Sr., *New Viewpoints in American History*, p. 231.

[54] Benda, "Revolution and Nationalism . . . ," *op. cit.*, pp. 40–41. See also Coleman, "Nationalism in Tropical Africa," *op. cit.*, pp. 167–194. Coleman states that "until the recent decision to give the Southern Cameroons greater autonomy within the emergent Federation of Nigeria, Cameroonian nationalists were wavering between remaining an integral part of the Eastern Region of Nigeria, or seceding and joining with the nationalists in the French Cameroons in an endeavor to create a Kamerun nation based upon the artificial boundaries of the short-lived German Kamerun." (P. 189.)

Opposition Rights and the Establishment of New Polities

The issues involved in the emergence of legitimate national authority and a sense of national unity, and those which pertain to the establishment of democratic procedures, are clearly separate problems—although they are sometimes confused in discussing the politics of new nations. Democracy may be conceived of as a system of institutionalized opposition in which the people choose among alternative contenders for public office.[55] To create a stable, representative, decision-making process that provides a legitimate place for opposition, that recognizes the rights of those without power to advocate "error" and the overthrow of those in office, is extremely difficult in any polity. It is particularly problematic in new states which must be concerned also with the sheer problem of the survival of national authority itself.

In a recent Ghanese White Paper seeking to justify legislation and police actions which involved restrictions upon (and actual imprisonment of) opposition politicians, the Ghana government suggested that these actions were necessary because of plots, saboteurs, subversion, and threats of foreign intervention. The White Paper argues that "the strains experienced by an emergent country immediately after independence are certainly as great as, if not greater than, the strains experienced by a developed country in wartime."[56] According to Nkrumah, a new state "is still weakly expressed as a national unity," and its frail structure must be protected by "identifying the emergent nation with the party," that is, by denying the possibility of a legitimate opposition, since the latter would endanger the stability of the nation.[57]

---

[55] I have elaborated the concept of democracy in other writings. See my *Political Man*, pp. 45-47; Introduction to Robert Michels, *Political Parties* (New York: Collier Books, 1962), pp. 33–35; and S. M. Lipset, M. Trow and J. S. Coleman, *Union Democracy* (Glencoe, Ill.: The Free Press, 1956), pp. 405–412.

[56] Discussed and cited in Dennis Austin, "Strong Rule in Ghana," *The Listener*, 67 (1962) p. 156.

[57] Quoted in Austin, *loc. cit.* David Apter describes these problems as follows: "New nations are plagued with almost the entire range of political problems known to man. They are beset by an accumulation of immediate and often mundane tasks such as building up adequate medical, health, education, transport, and other services, as well as improvement of housing, food supplies and other basic necessities beyond the subsistence level." In trying to deal with these problems, and harassed by a populace hungry for some of the promised benefits, it is easy to see how debate, criticism, and opposition come to be

Restrictions on democratic rights and opposition parties are, of course, not unique to Ghana among the contemporary new states. In Africa, the only new state with more than one significant party is Nigeria, "and this is true only because it is a federal . . . [system] reflecting one-party domination in the regions."[58]

The early history of the United States reveals many of the same problems—and the resulting pressures to eliminate democratic rights— as do those of contemporary new states. During Washington's first administration, all important differences of opinion could be expressed within the government, since both Jefferson and Hamilton, the leaders of what were to become the two major parties, were the most influential members of the Cabinet. After Jefferson's withdrawal, at the end of Washington's first term, and the subsequent formation of an opposition party around 1797 the restraints on the tactics of both sides weakened greatly:

> Each was then exposed to a temptation which it had not had to face before. Secret societies, subversion, and defiance seemed the only course possible to many who disapproved of government policies. . . . From the point of view of the historian it does not matter whether force provoked subversion or subversion, force; the important thing for the development of parties is the way in

regarded by those trying to push through this revolution as stultifying anti-progressive influences that deter the attainment of goals and wreak havoc with the tenuous basis of consensus and authority. Because of these very factors, political opposition, according to Apter, needs a more limited and specialized role than is accorded it in stable, industrialized countries. See David Apter, "Some Reflections on the Role of a Political Opposition in New Nations," *Comparative Studies in Society and History*, 4 (1962), p. 154; see also Rupert Emerson, *From Empire to Nation* (Cambridge, Mass.: Harvard University Press, 1960), pp. 272–292.

[58] W. G. Runciman, "Charismatic Legitimacy and One-Party Rule in Ghana," *European Journal of Sociology*, forthcoming. David Apter has suggested that factors which determine the behavior of both governmental and opposition groups have worked against the development of legitimate oppositions in new states. The leaders of such states have monopolized national loyalties during the long struggle with the colonial power, and hence find it difficult to accept opposition from within the nation as anything but treason. Conversely, opposition groups and leaders have usually entered politics while taking part in the struggle against the colonial oppressor, and have developed a conception of opposition activity which identifies efforts to change a government with the need for an upset in the fundamental character of the polity. Apter, *loc. cit.*

which the attitudes of supporters and opponents of the Administration aggravated each other.[59]

Hamilton, the political genius behind the first incumbents, organized the first party to insure popular support for governmental policies. It was a "government party" on a national scale, as opposed to the previous state politicking. It was "a party of stability, dedicated to the idea that the first imperative for government in a new nation was that it must govern and sustain itself."[60] As such, the legitimate existence of organized opposition to it was contrary to its conception.

Opposition to its policies did not arise initially as a party matter but as individual protests both on the popular level and within the political elite. Opposition gradually crystallized, however, into a political movement around the leadership of Madison and Jefferson. Its adherents were maintaining "in effect, that the new polity should also [in addition to maintaining its stability] provide room for counteraction, for effective representation of interests and opinions that were slighted or discountenanced in the government party."[61]

> [T]he emerging Republicans were "going to the people" in a virtually unprecedented attempt not only to represent popular interests and concerns, but to monopolize popular opposition to those who held power. If they had their way, if their appeal to planters, farmers, and "mechanics" was broadened sufficiently to succeed, it would end by displacing the Federalists in power and substituting a new set of governors.[62]

The Federalists viewed such organized opposition in much the same light as many leader of the contemporary new states view their rivals:

> [T]he Federalists took an intolerant position regarding the opposition party, which seemed to be a race of marplots characterized by excessive ambition, unwholesome partisanship and a dangerous reliance upon the judgment of the voters. At best the Republicans often seemed governed by obstinacy, envy, malice or ambition. At worst they were seditious and treasonable. Federalist private correspondence was peppered with references to Republican disloyalty,

---

[59] Charles, *The Origins of the American Party System*, p. 42.

[60] Chambers, *Parties in a New Nation*, p. 65.

[61] *Loc. cit.*

[62] *Loc. cit.*

insincerity, intrigue and demagoguery. . . . The conclusion almost forced upon the reader of these and hundreds more of Federalist condemnations is that the *two-party system is immoral. . . . It became almost normal to consider opposition as seditious and, in extraordinary cases, as treasonable.*[63]

The strains endemic in the establishment of a new structure of authority were increased by the fact that the nation and the embryonic parties were divided in their sympathies for the two major contestants in the European war, Revolutionary France and Great Britain. Each side was convinced that the other had secret intentions to take the country into war in support of its favorite. The French terror was a particular evil to the Federalists, and they, like conservatives in other countries, were persuaded that French agents were conspiring with sympathetic Americans to overthrow the government here.[64] The Federalists were therefore opposed to any form of organized opposition. They were much more violent in their denunciations of the treasonable activities of the Republicans than were the Jeffersonians in return.[65] And given the tremendous moral indignation which characterized Federalist private opinions, it is not surprising that they attempted to repress their opponents.[66] The Alien and Sedition Acts passed in 1798 gave the President "the power to order out of the country any alien whom he thought dangerous to the public peace or whom he had reasonable grounds to suspect of plotting against the government" and left such aliens without recourse to the courts.[67] The Sedition Act "was intended to deal with citizens or aliens who too severely criticized the government. . . . In its final form it was made a high misdemeanor 'unlawfully to combine and conspire' in order to oppose the legal measures of the government . . . , [t]o publish a false or malicious writing against the

[63] Smelser, "The Federalist Period . . . ," *op. cit.*, pp. 394–395. (Emphasis mine.)
[64] John C. Miller, *Crisis in Freedom: The Alien and Sedition Acts* (Boston: Little, Brown, 1951), p. 14.
[65] Smelser, "The Federalist Period . . . ," *op. cit.*, pp. 397–398.
[66] In 1797, an unsuccessful attempt was made to convict a Republican Congressman of "seditious libel" for "unfounded calumnies against the unhappy government of the United States," an attempt which had the support of the Attorney-General. Leonard W. Levy, *Legacy of Suppression, Freedom of Speech and Press in Early American History* (Cambridge, Mass.: The Belknap Press of Harvard University Press, 1960), p. 241.
[67] See Miller, *Crisis in Freedom,* and James M. Smith, *Freedom's Fetters, The Alien and Sedition Laws and American Civil Liberties* (Ithaca, N. Y.: Cornell University Press, 1956).

government of the United States, the President, or Congress with the purpose of stirring up hatred or resistance against them. . . ."[68]

That the law was designed for partisan purposes was obvious. All those arrested and convicted under it were Republicans. Basically, Federalist officials and Federalist juries enforced the law against their political opponents.[69] These efforts to undermine democratic rights gave Jefferson and Madison a major issue, which historians believe played an important role in defeating the Federalists in 1800.[70]

Once defeated for the Presidency in 1800, the Federalists never were able to regain office on a national scale and virtually disappeared after 1814. The causes for the downfall of the Federalists are complex, and cannot be detailed here. However, one reason was undoubtedly their unwillingness or inability to learn how to perform as an opposition party in an egalitarian democracy. Some historians suggest that they failed basically because, as men convinced of their "natural" right to rule, they did not believe in parties which appealed to the people.[71]

---

[68] John Spencer Bassett, *The Federalist System* (New York: Harper & Bros., 1960), pp. 258–259.

[69] *Ibid.*, pp. 263–264. "All told, Federalist judges jailed and fined 70 men under the Sedition Act. . . . With few exceptions the trials were travesties of justice dominated by judges who saw treason behind every expression of Republican sentiments. Grand juries for bringing in the indictments and trial juries for rendering the monotonous verdict of guilty were handpicked by Federalist United States marshals in defiance of statutes prescribing orderly procedure. The presiding judges often ridiculed the defendants' lawyers and interrupted their presentations so outrageously that many threw up their hands and their cases, leaving the accused to the mercy of the court." Richard Hofstadter, William Miller, and Daniel Aaron, *The American Republic* (Englewood Cliffs, N. J.: Prentice-Hall, 1959), I, pp. 331–332. The Federalists not only persecuted Republican editors, but on a number of occasions Federalist mobs wrecked Jeffersonian papers and printing offices and beat up their editors. "[M]ost of the mobs of this period were composed of Federalists wearing the insignia of the black cockade." Miller, *Crisis in Freedom*, pp. 195–196.

[70] The Federalists "declared in effect that there were only two parties in the United States, Federalists and Jacobins: the one, the party of Americanism and constitutionalism, the other pledged to make the Republic a French province and to destroy the Constitution. Edmund Burke said that one could not indict a whole people; the Federalists implicitly indicted half a people—and thereby brought about their own downfall." Miller, *Crisis in Freedom*, p. 77.

[71] William O. Lynch, *Fifty Years of Party Warfare 1789–1837* (Indianapolis: Bobbs Merrill, 1931), pp. 122–123. While still in office, "the Federalist view [was] that their opponents were not the *other* party, but simply 'party' or 'faction'; not the 'opposition' who might one day justly inherit the reins of government." Cunliffe, *George Washington*, p. 151. "The party of Jefferson

The civil liberties record of the Jeffersonians, in office, is a better one than that of the Federalists. How much of this may be explained on the assumption that they believed more firmly in the virtues of democracy than their opponents, it is difficult to say. Certainly their years of opposition had led them to make many statements in favor of democratic rights, but oppositionists in other lands have forgotten such programs once in power and faced with "unscrupulous criticism." Perhaps more important is the fact that the Democratic-Republicans did believe in states' rights and did oppose using federal courts to try common-law crimes. Also, the federal judiciary remained for some time in the hands of Federalist judges, who presumably were loath to permit convictions of their political sympathizers for expression of belief. Finally, there was a difference in the nature of the opposition. The Federalists were fighting a growing party that could realistically hope for eventual victory; the Democratic-Republicans, when in office, were opposed by a rapidly declining party, whose very lack of faith in extending the scope of the democratic process was to undermine any chance it had of returning to office. Since the Federalists were committing political suicide, there was no need for the administration to find means to repress them. The existence of a real but declining opposition may, therefore, be regarded as being, under certain circumstances, a contribution to the institutionalization of democratic rights.

Yet it should be noted that on the level of state government, Demo-

---

and Madison was never recognized as a lawfully begotten party: even after Jefferson became President, to the Federalists he was still the leader of a 'faction' whose objective was the subversion of the Constitution." Miller, *Crisis in Freedom*, p. 11. One of the grievances which various Federalists expressed against the Jeffersonian Republicans "was that they went to some trouble to gain popularity, and disgraced themselves by seeking votes." Smelser, "The Federalist Period . . .," *op. cit.*, p. 395. "The first party—the Hamiltonian Federalists—was a party on the English model: a group of leaders associated loosely in a common policy expecting to command votes partly by their policy and partly by their influence. It failed to develop any rank and file organization and for this very reason its career as a national party was short-lived. Their Republican opponents, without control of the government and at most times before 1800 without a majority in Congress, were forced to make use of popular organization. Building upon Democratic Societies . . . , the Republicans developed a party in which the life came from local units. . . ." W. R. Brock, *The Character of American History* (New York: St. Martin's, 1960), p. 92.

For an analysis of the final decline of Federalism, see Shaw Livermore, Jr., *The Twilight of Federalism: The Disintegration of the Federalist Party 1815–1830* (Princeton, N.J.: Princeton University Press, 1962).

cratic-Republicans did use their power to crack down on Federalist opinion. "Jefferson was no advocate of a 'licentious' press; like Hamilton and Adams, he believed that the press ought to be restrained 'within the legal and wholesome limits of truth.' He differed from the Federalists chiefly in insisting that this restraint be imposed by the states rather than by the Federal government. . . ."[72] In 1803, Jefferson wrote to Governor McKean of Pennsylvania along the following lines:

> Jefferson cautioned the Democratic governor to keep confidential his remarks on the subject of libel prosecutions.The Federalists, he noted, having failed to destroy the freedom of the press "by their gag law, seem to have attacked it in an opposite form, that is by pushing its licentiousness and its lying to such a degree of prostitution as to deprive it of all credit." Jefferson was not without a suggestion for the melioration of the condition of the press: "I have long thought that a few prosecutions of the most eminent offenders would have a wholesome effect in restoring the intregrity of the presses."[73]

Where the Federalists controlled a state government, as in the case of Connecticut, and hence prevented the application of the Democratic doctrine that seditious libel was a state offense, Jefferson was not averse to inaugurating prosecutions in the federal courts. In 1806, six indictments were drawn against four Connecticut Federalist editors and two minis-

---

[72] Miller, *Crisis in Freedom*, p. 231. In December 1800, a Federalist editor "was fined two thousand, five hundred dollars in a Pennsylvania court for libeling a Republican. The amount of this fine was compared by distraught Federalists with the two-hundred-dollar fine imposed upon Abijah Adams for publishing a libel on the Massachusetts legislature and with the fines assessed by Federalist judges under the Sedition Act. 'What a difference there is between the chance of a Federalist among Jacobins, and of a Jacobin among Federalists!' they exclaimed. 'The boasted friends of liberty of the press inflict a tenfold more severe punishment, when their characters are canvassed.'" *Ibid.*, p. 229. In New York in 1803 Governor George Clinton, a friend of Jefferson, obtained an indictment for seditious libel against the editor of a Federalist journal, and the editor was convicted at a trial presided over by a Democratic Chief Justice, who was to become the next governor of New York. The judge charged the jury "that truth was not a defense against a charge of seditious libel, that its only duty was to find whether the defendant had in fact published the statement [that Jefferson had bribed an editor to denounce Washington] charged." Levy, *Legacy of Suppression*, pp. 297–298.

[73] *Ibid.*, p. 300. The state did indict a Federalist editor shortly thereafter.

ters on the charge of seditious libel on the President. The ministers were charged with committing the libel *in sermons*.[74]

Leonard Levy concludes his survey of freedom of speech and press in early American history by arguing that the Democrats, like the Federalists, did not believe in these freedoms when confronted with serious opposition. Each was prepared to use principled libertarian arguments when his "ox was being gored."[75] Perhaps the most ironic piece of evidence in this regard, indicating how fragile is a belief in "the rules of the game" in a new democracy, is an article by Tom Paine written for a New York newspaper in 1806, in which the great libertarian and convicted seditionist argued that "there is a difference between error and licentiousness," that "the term liberty of the press arose from a FACT, the abolition of the office of Imprimateur [sic], and that opinion has nothing to do with the case." Paine urged that the public authorities judge and punish "atrocious" statements.[76]

The various efforts by both Federalists and Democratic-Republicans to repress the rights of their opponents clearly indicate that in many ways our early political officials resembled those heads of new states in the twentieth century who view criticism of themselves as tantamount to an attack on the nation itself. Such behavior characterizes leaders of polities in which the concept of democratic succession to office has not been institutionalized. Thus, in many American trade unions today, national officers who hold effective power for life often interpret criticism as libelous and treasonable. To accept criticism as proper requires the prior accept-

---

[74] Jefferson claimed in 1809 that the prosecutions had been instituted without his knowledge, but Leonard Levy concludes that the historical record indicates that while they may have begun without his knowledge "he learned of them . . . nearly four months before they were scheduled for trial, and he approved of them until expediency dictated his disapproval some months later." *Ibid.*, pp. 302–305. Levy says that one of the "libels," the charge that Jefferson when young had tried to seduce a friend's wife, was demonstrably true and that when he learned that this was part of the case he saw to it that the charges were dropped.

[75] An earlier survey of Jefferson's relations with the press concludes: "[He] had lashed himself in a fine frenzy over the temporary sedition laws as a gag upon free speech and an attack upon a free press, yet would have the states permanently apply the same remedy; he had wished to reform journalism, but his idea of reformation was that of the character in Beaconsfield's novel of the agreeable man—'one that agrees with me.'" See W. C. Ford, "Jefferson and the Newspaper," *Records of the Columbia Historical Society*, (Washington: 1905), Vol. VIII, p. 110.

[76] Levy, *Legacy of Suppression*, pp. 307–308.

ance of the view that opposition and succession are normal, and that men may be loyal to the polity and yet disapprove of the particular set of incumbents. This view does not come easily to men who have themselves created a polity, and cannot, therefore, conceive of it functioning properly without them or in ways other than they think best.

Yet, though the behavior of members of both early American parties indicate that they, too, reacted to criticism as being damaging to the nation, it must also be recognized that both parties permitted a great deal of opposition, much more than is tolerated in most of the new states of Asia and Africa. In some part, this may reflect the fact that much as they disagreed, the heads of both groups had worked together to make the Revolution and establish the Constitution. They had known and trusted each other for some decades. In a real sense, the United States began with a small, highly educated political elite, the members of which recognized each other as belonging to the ruling club. Both Adams and Hamilton demonstrated this when, on different occasions, each put adherence to the rules of the game ahead of party advantage or personal feelings. The defeat of the Federalists in the elections of 1800 represented *the first occasion in modern politics in which an incumbent political party suffered an electoral defeat and simply turned over power to its opponents.* This acceptance of the rules of the electoral game has not occurred in many new states.

The decline of the Federalists after 1800 meant that the United States did not experience a real succession problem again until 1829, with the inauguration of Andrew Jackson. The Virginia Dynasty of Jefferson, Madison, and Monroe governed the country for twenty-four years, each President succeeding the other without real difficulty. From 1809, when Madison took over from Jefferson, to 1829, when John Quincy Adams was succeeded by Jackson, each President was followed in office by his chief cabinet officer, the Secretary of State. And a national two-party system did not emerge anew until the 1830's, when Jackson's opponents united in the Whig party.

In effect, the country was dominated on the national level for close to three decades by a loosely structured one-party system. Although the analogy may appear far-fetched, in a certain sense the political system resembled that which has grown up in recent decades in Mexico, and perhaps in some other underdeveloped countries. Interest groups and sectional concerns led to serious divisions within the country—over the purchase of Louisiana, relations with the warring powers of Europe, the War of 1812, and the Missouri compromise of 1819 over slavery. Any of these issues could have resulted in the dissolution of effective national authority.

However, all of them were resolved, not so much at the ballot box as by negotiations conducted under the authority of the three great Virginians —men who carried with them the prestige stemming from their role in founding the nation, and from their leadership of the all-powerful Democratic-Republican party. On the national level, conservatives and radicals all came to belong to the same party, formally at least, and gave formal allegiance to the same liberal doctrines and leaders.[77]

Thomas Jefferson had anticipated the complete triumph of his party following the electoral defeat of Federalism, and looked forward to political divisions among those who believed in the "correct," that is, Republican, principles. And presumably so long as all effective participants in politics were on the "good" side, the temptation to repress criticism within the party would be less:

> I had always expected that when the Republicans should have put all things under their feet, they would schismatize among themselves. I always expected, too, that whatever names the parties might bear, the real division would be into moderate and ardent republicanism. *In this division there is no great danger.* . . . It is to be considered as apostasy only when they purchase the vote of federalists, with a participation in honor and power.[78]

The almost unchallenged rule of the Virginia Dynasty and the Democratic-Republican Party served to legitimate national authority and democratic rights. By the time the nation divided again into two broad warring factions which appealed for mass support, the country had existed for forty years, the Constitution had been glorified, and the authority of the courts had been accepted as definitive.

The Need for "Payoff"

All claims to a legitimate title to rule in new states must ultimately win acceptance through demonstrating effectiveness. The loyalty of the different groups to the system must be won through developing in them the

---

[77] "Almost every man called himself a Jeffersonian Republican in those days and political conflicts on a national scale were apt to be conflicts between personalities and not between principles or programs." George Dangerfield, *The Era of Good Feeling* (New York: Harcourt, Brace, 1952), p. xiii. See also Bradford Perkins, *Prologue to War* (Berkeley: University of California Press, 1961), pp. 33–45.

[78] Cited in Perkins, *op. cit.*, pp. 99–100. Jefferson made this statement in 1807 while still President. (Emphasis mine.)

conviction that this system is the best—or at least an excellent—way to accomplish their objectives. And even claims to legitimacy of a supernatural sort, such as "the gift of grace," are subjected on the part of the populace to a highly pragmatic test—that is, what is the payoff? For new states today, demonstrating effectiveness means one thing: economic development. Given the "revolution of rising expectations" that has swept the emerging nations, need for payoff in terms of economic goods and living standards is more important than ever.[79]

As most new states lack the traditional means for rapid economic growth, they have been led in recent years to introduce large-scale government planning and direct state intervention. Although such efforts concur with the socialist ideology, the desire to use the state to direct and speed up the processes of economic growth has deeper roots than ideological conviction. It rests upon the dual necessity to demonstrate effectiveness to the various groups within the polity, and to display national competence to the outside world. To a considerable degree the leaders seek development as part of their more general effort to overcome feelings of national inferiority, particularly vis-à-vis the former metropolitan ruler.

Similar processes were at work in the United States, even though after the Revolution many leaders, particularly Jefferson, opposed any aid to manufacturing or commerce. As one economic historian has put it:

> American industrial consciousness . . . received much of its early stimulus from the political storm and stress which preceded and led to the winning of independence. . . . American industrial consciousness grew out of the broad wave of political and economic resentment against England, but was mainly directed almost from the start toward the transfer of English skill and technique to this country. By 1830, it had succeeded, and American technology and industrial organization were by then comparable to those of England.[80]

---

[79] "A 'down payment' of tangible gains for a substantial part of the supporters of amalgamation [into a new state] soon after the event, if not earlier, seems almost necessary. This was accomplished by the land policies of Jefferson, and the fiscal policies of Hamilton. . . ." Deutsch, *et al.*, *Political Community and the North Atlantic Area*, p. 49.

[80] Samuel Rezneck, "The Rise and Early Development of Industrial Consciousness in the United States, 1760–1830," *Journal of Economic and Business History*, 4 (1932), pp. 784–785.

Pressure to develop domestic manufacturing followed shortly on the first effort at a national government, since the depression "which intervened between 1783 and 1787 produced a reawakening of manufacturing zeal. Patriotism . . . provided the impetus to it, while there was also a better appreciation of the fact that English superiority in technique could be overcome only by borrowing it. The new wave of industrial agitation rose to a rapid climax in the first years of the federal government. Manufactures, like the Constitution, were expected to strengthen the country and help it achieve true independence."[81]

Even Jefferson, the enthusiastic supporter of the physiocratic doctrine that agriculture was the only source of true wealth, felt compelled, when President, to modify his former objections to manufacturing. "As early as 1805 . . . [he] complained that his former views had been misunderstood. They were intended to apply only to the great cities of Europe and not to this country at the present time."[82]

In fact, in this period prior to the War of 1812, the Federalists and Republicans appear to have supported government aid to industrialization when in office, and to have pointed up some of its adverse effects when in opposition. The Republicans defended Jefferson's Embargo on the grounds that:

> It must be truly gratifying to every true American to witness the rapid introduction and progress of manufacturing establishments in the various parts of the United States. The Federalists . . . attacked the Embargo . . . from every angle. It was ruining the state's wealth, destroying agriculture and commerce to the advantage of manu-

---

[81] *Ibid.*, p. 788. As Secretary of the Treasury, Hamilton, although he owned no stock in the company, was practically the chief sponsor and manager of the New Jersey Society for Establishing Useful Manufactures, which from the beginning was dubbed the National Manufactory. "For several years after 1787 every industrial undertaking, whether public or private, was identified with the national interest and helped to stimulate and arouse industrial consciousness in the country." Tench Coxe, Assistant Secretary of the Treasury and Hamilton's chief aid, originated an ingenious scheme for raising capital which was adopted by Hamilton in his Report on Manufactures. "It became part of the program of The New Jersey Society . . . for which it was proposed to mobilize the newly funded national debt. The capital stock of the company was to be paid for in public debt certificates, on which it was believed, a loan could be raised at Amsterdam at less than 6 per cent." *Ibid.*, pp. 793–794.

[82] *Ibid.*, p. 799; see also V. L. Parrington, *Main Currents in American Thought* (New York: Harcourt, Brace, 1930), Vol. I, pp. 347–348.

factures, building up an aristocracy [and] corrupting the moral
life. . . .[83]

In evaluating early American economic development, it should be
recognized that there was *a great deal of government intervention and
even public investment in the economy so as to develop industry and
commerce.* As Carter Goodrich has pointed out in discussing such
activities: "The closest modern analogy, indeed, is to be found in the
current projects of so-called underdeveloped countries. . . . So much,
indeed, was done by public initiative that the distinguished economic
historian, G. S. Callender, declared that this country was at the time
an early and leading example of the 'modern tendency to extend the
activity of the state into industry.' "[84] On a national level, efforts were
made—stimulated by Albert Gallatin, Jefferson's Secretary of the Treasury—to foster direct federal support for companies building new transportation facilities; but with some minor exceptions, these proposals,
though advocated by Jefferson and Monroe, failed. The most important
federal measures directly supporting economic growth took the form
of investment in the Bank of the United States and, more important,
protective tariffs to encourage domestic industry against products manu-
factured in England.[85]

The failure of the effort to involve the federal government directly
in economic activities did not reflect the strength of business opposition
or of *laissez-faire* beliefs. "States' rights, state and sectional interests, and
a belief in the capacities of the several states seem to have played the
decisive role in the downfall of national planning. By contrast business
enterprise offered far less formidable competition."[86] As a consequence,
most governmental efforts occurred at the state level, and many states
felt it proper and necessary to use public funds to develop transportation
facilities, banking, manufactures, and the like.

State intervention on behalf of economic growth took various forms,
sometimes regulative, as in the setting up of inspection standards, and
sometimes directly encouraging, as in financial assistance from lotteries

---

[83] From "The Democrat," quoted in "Mercury," October 24, 1811, as cited in
Richard Purcell, *Connecticut in Transition, 1775–1881* (Washington: American Historical Association, 1918), p. 132.

[84] Carter Goodrich, "National Planning of Internal Improvements," *Political
Science Quarterly*, 63 (1948), p. 18.

[85] See Fred A. Shannon, *America's Economic Growth* (New York: Macmillan, 1940), pp. 187–201, for an exposition of United States protective
tariff policy.

[86] Goodrich, "National Planning of Internal Improvements," *op. cit.*, p. 39.

or in the form of bounties. A third method was the franchise, which amounted to a monopoly that protected a company from competition during its early growth. And not unimportant in many states was direct government investment in, or outright ownership of, various companies whose development was deemed necessary for economic growth or the public welfare.

The system of public inspection "set up categories of goods which could not be sold and thus placed in a privileged position those the state judged fit."[87] The government relaxed its laws against gambling to sanction lotteries, the proceeds of which were used to finance various state projects such as the building of bridges and roads, paper mills and glasshouses.[88] The bounty was used to some extent by the states to encourage individual enterprises,[89] though this technique fell into disuse in the early part of the nineteenth century.

The granting of franchises was particularly important in the construc-

---

[87] Oscar Handlin and M. F. Handlin, *Commonwealth: A Study of the Role of Government in the American Economy: Massachusetts, 1774–1861* (New York: New York University Press, 1947), p. 72. Merchants to far-off ports, responsible for wares they purchased from others, approved of these acts, which guaranteed quality and added the prestige of state approval to their goods. *Ibid.*, p. 67.

[88] "In 1780, a $200,000 lottery financed roads in Berkshire and Hampshire counties." Similar schemes were used to raise funds to build or repair bridges and "in 1782, . . . to build a paper mill in Milton, and in 1783, for a foundering glasshouse in Boston." *Ibid.*, p. 73.

[89] In Connecticut, Governor John Cotton Smith "inclined toward a policy of bounties and exemptions by the state, especially in the case of household manufactures, or those allied with agriculture. The Assembly of May, 1817 . . . exempted cotton and woolen factories from taxation for four years, and their employees from a poll tax or militia service." Purcell, *Connecticut in Transition*, p. 136.

In Massachusetts "[a]griculture secured the assistance of £4 for the head of each crop-destroying wolf. In 1786, 1788, and 1791 laws granted a bounty for the production of hemp [which benefited shipping] farmers who raised it, the rope-makers, and the merchants. A similar subsidy went to the manufacture of sailcloth, duck, and twine in Boston in 1788 and 1791 . . ."

Variations on the bounty were the state's "occasional loans to enterprises, such as that of £300 to Benjamin Shepard for the manufacture of cotton goods in Wrentham. It freed from taxation the Boston glasshouses and cotton factories in Worcester and Rehobeth and elsewhere for periods of from five to ten years. Breweries which turned out one hundred barrels annually received the identical concession to encourage the production of the healthful beverage, create a product for export, and supply a market for farmers. Salt and sugar works had the same advantage held out to them for a time." Handlin and Handlin, *Commonwealth*, p. 84.

tion of bridges, aqueducts, and mills, all of which interfered in some way with public waterways and fishing rights. The building of dams flooded adjacent lands and diverted water from natural channels.

> Without the state's tolerance, builders faced unlimited responsibility for damages. To encourage industry, the government generously dealt out such franchises. . . . All franchises included an element of privilege, permitting to a few, as special assistance in a worthwhile enterprise, what was forbidden to all.[90]

While applying the techniques of inspection, lotteries, bounties, and franchises, the states soon found the granting of charters to new corporations the most successful means of promoting economic development, for the "coercive power of assessment . . . gave the corporation a more efficient fund-raising mechanism."[91] Consequently, the states' most important promotional policy became that of chartering business corporations. "After . . . [the Revolution] charter policy gradually established itself as one of the primary concerns of American state governments and expanded steadily through the pre-Civil War epoch."[92]

The granting of bank charters was closely linked with developments in transportation. "This was due to an established legislative practice which frequently incorporated into bank charters requirements for assisting

---

[90] *Ibid.*, pp. 76–78.

[91] *Ibid.*, p. 105. Between 1792 and 1800 there were twenty-three incorporations granted for bridge construction. "Charters for bridges . . . all contained the essential power to levy assessments and the lucrative franchise to take toll. In return the legislature imposed well-defined conditions: completion in a limited period, and construction in accordance with specified plans, the slightest change in which needed the consent of the General Court. . . . The patron state, having set up these rules, was, however, indulgent in administration. When the original tolls seemed insufficient to sustain dividends it often made gifts of land, raised the rates, extended the building time and the duration of the franchise.

"The urge for improvement also led to considerable canal building. The inland communities valued better water communications to bring farmers nearer markets and to facilitate transportation of lumber. Merchants [also] sought easier navigation on the great interstate rivers." *Ibid.*, pp. 113–115.

[92] Louis Hartz, *Economic Policy and Democratic Thought: Pennsylvania, 1776–1860* (Cambridge, Mass.: Harvard University Press, 1948), p. 38. "Between 1790 and 1860, apart from incorporations under general laws, the Pennsylvania legislature granted 2,333 charters for business purposes. . . . Well over half of the business charters granted by special act of the legislature from 1790 to 1860 were concerned with transportation." *Loc. cit.*

specified transportation companies. Such assistance usually took the form of stock subscriptions, loans, or outright grants of money."[93]

> Most of the early corporations were for religious or charitable organizations or for road, bridge, canal, bank and insurance companies. . . . In all some 557 manufacturing companies were incorporated in eight states between 1800 and 1823, Massachusetts and New York being far in the lead. . . . Before 1860 nearly all the states had general incorporation statutes.[94]

Direct government financing of economic activities which required large sums of capital occurred in many states. During the first thirty or forty years of the nineteenth century, the states created a funded debt of more than two hundred million dollars, "a larger debt than that created by any government for purely industrial purposes."[95] Internal improvements, particularly turnpikes and canals, constituted the most general area of direct state intervention. Virginia, Maryland, New York, Pennsylvania, Massachusetts, South Carolina, Georgia, Kentucky, Tennessee, Indiana, Illinois, and Michigan were among the states which used their financial resources for such purposes.[96] Railroads also were built with government support in many states. And many banks were formed with governmental help. "Almost from the first introduction of banks into this country, it became a common practice for the State governments to invest revenue in bank stock."[97]

---

[93] It reached its apogee in the charter granted to the Second Bank in 1835 which called for stock subscriptions ". . . amounting to $675,000 for 10 transportation companies and provided for grants of financial assistance to 12 others, totaling $139,000." *Ibid.*, pp. 46–47. "Banks were [also] compelled to lend sums to the state, usually in amounts up to 5% of capital stock at 5% if requests for such loans were made. The charter granted to the Bank of Pennsylvania, the first state bank to be incorporated, required it to lend to the state $500,000 at interest not to exceed 6% for the purpose of establishing a loan office for the assistance of farmers. The revenue to be derived from both the bonus and the loan policies became especially attractive during the thirties when monetary needs for construction of public works rocketed, and there is little doubt that the banking overexpansion of that period is in some measure traceable to them." *Ibid.*, p. 55.

[94] Shannon, *America's Economic Growth*, p. 210.

[95] G. S. Callender, "The Early Transportation and Banking Enterprises of the States in Relation to the Growth of Corporations," *Quarterly Journal of Economics*, 17 (1902), p. 114.

[96] *Ibid.*, pp. 112–113.

[97] *Ibid.*, pp. 113–114.

In Pennsylvania, a state under one-party Democratic control for the first thirty-five years of the nineteenth century, there was considerable direct government intervention in the form of public ownership of transportation facilities and banks. The state encouraged the growth of credit facilities by investing heavily in bank stocks between 1800 and 1815. Similarly, a number of turnpike, canal, and navigation companies were owned jointly by the state and private investors. With the coming of railroads, Pennsylvania added railway stock to the list of companies in which it had investments. Local governments, counties, and cities invested even more heavily than did the state in such businesses. "Total municipal and county investments between 1840 and 1853 were estimated at fourteen million dollars—over twice the state investment at its 1843 peak."[98] Direct public ownership occurred as well in many of these areas. Thus Pennsylvania built and owned the first railways along the main line.[99]

For the first forty years of Pennsylvania's existence as a state within the Union, there was little argument over the propriety or even necessity of direct state participation in ownership as a means of facilitating economic development. In effect, as in many contemporary new nations, Pennsylvania and other American states followed a policy of government investment in areas basic to economic growth where private efforts seemed inadequate. The *doctrine of "laissez-faire" became dominant only after the growth of large corporations and private investment funds reduced the pressures for public funds.*

The record of Virginia was similar to that of Pennsylvania. In 1816 it established a Fund for Internal Improvements and a Board of Public Works which played an important role in creating various enterprises up to the Civil War. The Board shared ownership with private investors of various canals, turnpikes, railroads, and banks. Some railroads such as the Blue Ridge and the Covington and Ohio were built totally with state funds. By 1860, the Fund held assets of forty million dollars.[100]

In Georgia, the state invested in a number of banks; for example, it owned two-fifths of the stock of the Bank of the State (1815), half the capital of the Bank of Darien (1818), and many others. It also held stock in many turnpike companies, and in the few canal ventures. Perhaps the largest form of state investment in Georgia was in railroads. The Western

---

[98] Hartz, *Economic Policy and Democratic Thought*, p. 88.
[99] *Ibid.*, p. 145.
[100] Carter Goodrich, "The Virginia System of Mixed Enterprise," *Political Science Quarterly*, 64 (1949), pp. 355–387.

and Atlantic was built entirely with state funds, while the Atlantic and Gulf was primarily owned by the state and two cities. All told, between 1835 and 1860 public investment in railroads amounted to almost thirteen million dollars, more than the total of private investment.[101]

A similar situation existed in New York where the outstanding example of direct intervention was the construction and operation of the Erie and Champlain canals. The story of how this project was originally financed through the state's sale of canal stock to small investors, and the working people's Bank for Savings, is a fascinating one.[102] Of even greater interest is the indirect facilitation of economic development which grew out of investment made by local banks in which the toll revenues of the Canal Fund were deposited.[103] "The Canal Fund became a development bank less by design than by dint of circumstances."[104] Only after several attempts to remove their deposits from banks without sufficient notice created difficulties did the Commissioner of the Canal Fund realize the heavy reliance of local economies on these publicly controlled deposits. Agricultural and salt manufacturing interests as well as the completion of the Tonawanda Railroad depended upon them.[105] During the railroad building era, many lines were built in New York with large state and city investments.[106]

Local governments, especially cities, also played a major role in foster-

---

[101] On these activities see Milton S. Heath, *Constructive Liberalism: The Role of the State in Economic Development in Georgia to 1860* (Cambridge, Mass.: Harvard University Press, 1954). For a similar story in Missouri, see James N. Primm, *Economic Policy in the Development of a Western State: Missouri 1820–1860* (Cambridge, Mass.: Harvard University Press, 1954).

[102] Only in the later stages, when the project was obviously headed for successful completion, was the stock absorbed by wealthy New Yorkers and English capitalists. See Nathan Miller, *The Enterprise of a Free People: Aspects of Economic Development in New York State during the Canal Period 1792–1838* (Ithaca, N.Y.: Cornell University Press, 1962).

[103] "Little did the comptroller realize when he negotiated with the banks in 1826 that he was taking the first step in the creation of a mechanism which would introduce the revenues of the Canal Fund into the channels of business, so that eventually their influence in the economy would be felt from one end of the state to the other." *Ibid.*, p. 116.

[104] *Ibid.*, p. 263.

[105] *Ibid.*, pp. 146–151. Of interest also are the Canal Commissioners' deliberate programs for alleviating the economic panics of 1834 and 1837 and the crisis after the great fire of 1835.

[106] Henry Pierce, *Railroads of New York: A Study of Government Aid, 1826–1875* (Cambridge, Mass.: Harvard University Press, 1953).

ing economic development. To elaborate further on their activities is not necessary here. It may be noted, however, that Cincinnati owned a major railroad, while Baltimore was an extremely important investor in the Baltimore and Ohio and other lines.[107] In New York state 315 municipalities were involved in the construction of railroad lines.[108] In Pennsylvania, cities and counties contributed far more to railway construction than did the state.[109] "The major portion of the stock issued by Missouri's state aided railroads in the 1850's was sold to counties and municipalities."[110]

The story of state and local investment in early economic development in the United States clearly justifies the conclusion that government in this period played a role corresponding to that envisaged in most new nations today. The need for large sums of investment capital in a new and as yet undeveloped economy could only be met domestically from government sources. And given the commitment and need of new states to develop economically, the American political leaders found the arguments to justify state intervention, even if they were different from those popular today. A reviewer of various recent works by economic historians dealing with economic development on the state and local level summarizes the conclusions to be drawn from these studies:

> [These studies suggest] a new view of American capitalism in its formative years. . . . [T]he elected official replaced the individual enterpriser as the key figure in the release of capitalist energy; the public treasury, rather than private saving, became the major source of venture capital; and community purpose outweighed personal ambition in the selection of large goals for local economies. "Mixed" enterprise was the customary organization for important innovations, and government everywhere undertook the role put on it by the people, that of planner, promoter, investor, and regulator.[111]

---

[107] See Carter Goodrich, "Local Government Planning of Internal Improvements," *Political Science Quarterly*, 56 (1951), pp. 411–445; and Carter Goodrich and Harvey Segal, "Baltimore's Aid to Railroads: A Study in the Municipal Planning of Internal Improvements," *Journal of Economic History*, 13 (1953), pp. 2–35.

[108] Pierce, *Railroads of New York*.

[109] Hartz, *Economic Policy and Democratic Thought*, p. 86.

[110] Primm, *Economic Policy in the Development of a Western State*, p. 106. For Iowa see Earl S. Beard, "Local Aid to Railroads in Iowa," *Iowa Journal of History*, 50 (1952), pp. 1–34.

[111] Robert A. Lively, "The American System: A Review Article," *The Business History Review*, 29 (1955), p. 81.

Rapid economic growth during this formative period in our economy benefited not only from assistance by the states themselves, but perhaps even more from the massive foreign capital furnished the new nation by outside investors, particularly British. There is a definite parallel between the dependence of contemporary new nations on external funds and the conditions which facilitated development here:[112]

> England was the principal source of loans to American enterprise, both directly . . . through the purchase by Englishmen of stock in American banks or railways, as well as indirectly through the purchase by English investors of American State bonds, the proceeds of which in large measure were employed in the furtherance of "internal improvements."[113]

The dependence of American expansion on foreign capital was to be seen in all areas of economic development: trade, internal improvements, banking, agriculture, and industry. Jenks has summarized the story:

> [The wholesale merchants of the Yankee drygoods houses, who handled the import trade at the Atlantic ports in the antebellum period] could not trade adequately with their own capital. The[se] Yankee firms depended to a large extent in their buying upon credits which came, directly or indirectly, from such firms as Barings themselves.

---

[112] "By 1805 the coupons paid through Barings [Bros., London] represented a nominal capital of £5,747,283. This sum included, besides the unpaid debt of the United States abroad, at least seven million dollars in the stock of the First Bank of the United States. As the debt, foreign and domestic, was paid off British holdings diminished. The extinction of the Bank in 1811 and the War of 1812 reduced to £1,500,000 the amount upon which Barings paid dividends. . . .

"A more progressive movement set in after the war. In 1817 and 1818 temporary loans of bullion were made to the Second Bank of the United States. They became the basis of a permanent investment in the stock of that institution which in 1820 amounted to nearly three million dollars. Another million was added to this amount by 1828, and the total was doubled during the next three years. Out of 300,000 shares in private hands in July, 1831, 79,159 were held abroad by 466 shareholders. . . . Meanwhile part of the American public debt had returned abroad. Fourteen million dollars of it were owned by British investors in 1828, five millions by other European creditors." Leland Hamilton Jenks, *The Migration of British Capital to 1875* (New York: Alfred A. Knopf, 1927), p. 66.

[113] W. B. Smith and A. H. Cole, *Fluctuations in American Business, 1790–1860* (Cambridge, Mass.: Harvard University Press, 1935), p. 42.

. . . promoter-politicians, who perceived the advantages, whether public or private, which could accrue from the building of highways, canals and railroads, turned to foreign capital, filtered thru the public treasuries for support. . . . State-owned and state-constructed the Erie Canal was financed by the issue of New York state bonds. Something over seven million dollars' worth were sold between 1817 and 1825, and they passed almost at once into the hands of Englishmen.

Before 1836 over ninety million dollars had been invested in canals and railways in the North, of which more than half was a charge upon public credit. The bulk of this capital had been procured from England.

. . . British capital which promoted transportation and westward expansion indirectly financed industry as well. American merchants and banks could draw credits for objects unspecified, and these were available in the United States for the expansion of industry. . . . *It will not be far wrong to estimate the total quantity of British capital invested in the United States during the thirties as approximately equal to the indebtedness incurred by the several states.*[114]

It should be noted that the willingness of English holders of capital to invest heavily in American economic development was not unrelated to the governmental policies which fostered the growth of industry. Government sponsorship was fostered by the need for large sums of capital, since both domestic and foreign investors were often not willing to expend the large sums necessary for speculative and unknown ventures in distant lands.

The only securities that could do this were public securities, or the securities of corporations which were guaranteed or assisted by the government. . . . Accordingly, we find that English foreign investments in the early part of the nineteenth century were made chiefly in public securities. The stock and bonds of private corporations formed in foreign countries, unless endorsed by the government, played but a very small part on the London stock market until after the middle of the century.[115]

---

[114] Jenks, *The Migration of British Capital to 1875*, pp. 68, 73, 75, 77, 85. (Emphasis mine.) See also Frank Thistlethwaite, *The Great Experiment* (New York: Cambridge University Press, 1955), pp. 71–78.

[115] Callender, "The Early Transportation and Banking Enterprises . . . ," *op. cit.*, pp. 152–153.

And the legislation which gave corporations various governmental protections, referred to earlier, fostered the trans-Atlantic migration of capital.

> [T]he fact that the privileges of incorporation were much more easily acquired in America than in England in the first half of the [nineteenth] century gave certain types of American industry readier access to nonindustrial savings and indeed, it was sometimes said, gave them readier access even to English "blind capital" than English industrialists themselves enjoyed.[116]

But if the activities of state governments and foreign investors contributed to economic growth, the rapidity of that development must also be credited to a particularly productive, symbiotic relationship between economic growth and the American value system. The existence of a set of values that enshrined "the good life" as one of hard, continuous work, frugality, self-disciplined living, and individual initiative provided the necessary ideological framework for making use of foreign capital for long-range industrial development.[117] Also, the weakness of aristocratic traditions meant that the United States was free to develop a dominant economic class of merchants and manufacturers whose passion for the accumulation of wealth was unfettered by values that deprecated hard work and the concentration of capital. The rationale for concentrating national resources and energies on such pursuits violated the anti-urban, agrarian utopia of the Jeffersonians, but it was defended on nationalistic grounds. The prospect of spiritual and economic domination at the hands of European manufacturers was viewed as especially degrading since this group was presided over by a "devilish class of aristocrats" to whom were attributed all kinds of corruptions, from immoral leisure to extravagance and intellectual cunning:

> Convinced, on the whole, of an identity between moral and material progress, these industrialists, while not averse to profits, were

---

[116] H. J. Habakkuk, *American and British Technology in the Nineteenth Century* (New York: Cambridge University Press, 1962), p. 71.

[117] These two factors, the Protestant Ethic and foreign investment, can be viewed as functional substitutes for present day socialist ideology and foreign aid. Incidentally, it is becoming increasingly common to see Marxism, Communism, or Socialism fulfilling in the twentieth century what the Protestant Ethic did for Western Europe and North America in the eighteenth and nineteenth centuries—that is, fostering motivation for work and economic development.

conscious of making a patriotic contribution and of trying to establish a pattern in manufacturing for the nation. . . .

The rising tide of nationalism stimulated by the American Revolution and the War of 1812 made it popular to justify American manufacturing on the ground of economic independence. Such pleas for a national economic independence, however, usually pointed to the horrifying alternative of a moral and spiritual as well as economic prostration at the feet of the manufacturers of Europe. Though these public pronouncements may have functioned consciously as convenient rationalizations of economic interest . . . the same ideas appeared again and again in their private letters and journals, when they had no need for propaganda. To them European manufacturing, on the whole, not only seemed degrading to character; it was presided over by a devilish class of aristocrats. . . .

Belief in the existence of a conspiratorial European devil led also to the patriotic contrast of honestly made American manufactures with reputedly fraudulent European goods.[118]

Foreign visitors to the United States were struck, from its earliest days, with the greater emphasis on materialism here, on economic gain, as contrasted to that present in Europe, including even Britain. A detailed analysis of the writings of English travelers in America from the end of the Revolution to the age of Jackson sums up the evidence:

At this period, the Americans already had the reputation for being a money-loving and money-getting people. So universal was this belief that it is with surprise that we see any denial of it. . . . [T]he enterprise of the Americans could not be charitably attributed to a dread of future want, nor did it seem to most Englishmen that they were consciously actuated by a "desire to obtain distinction by means of wealth". . . . Flint said that it was security of property and the high profits on capital that tended to promote this disposition. Fowler attributed the eagerness to accumulate to the fact that in the absence of titles and all acknowledged distinctions in rank, wealth constituted the primary basis of contrast between individuals. At any rate, this trait became to foreigners an integral part of the American nature.[119]

Given the absence of a traditional aristocratic class, and the withdrawal into Canada of many of those who most sympathized with such

---

[118] Charles L. Sanford, *The Quest for Paradise: Europe and the American Moral Imagination* (Urbana: University of Illinois Press, 1961), pp. 158–163.
[119] Jane L. Mesick, *The English Traveller in America, 1785–1835* (New York: Columbia University Press, 1922), pp. 309–310.

a societal model, the entrepreneur became a cultural hero—and rapid growth followed. Canada, on the other hand, though possessing many of the same material conditions as the United States, did not develop as rapidly or as strongly. The combination of foreign rule and a different class model apparently had negative effects on its potentialities for development. And the new states of nineteenth century Latin America, led by traditional Catholic oligarchies drawn mainly from the landed aristocracy, were even more backward economically. They retained many of the pre-industrial values of the Iberian Peninsula. Latin America lacked a dynamic business class, a Protestant work ethos, and an ideological commitment to economic modernization.

The emergence of a functioning polity in the first half-century of American independence was accompanied by rapid economic growth and territorial expansion.[120]

The United States gradually acquired legitimacy as a result of being *effective*. There was no question that the new nation worked, that its economy had "taken off," to use Walt Rostow's image.[121] Henry Adams, in his great history of the early years of the republic, saw these economic developments as crucial in guaranteeing the survival of the country as a viable unit:

---

[120] "Beginning with the Louisiana Purchase, the United States entered upon an era of growth which, within less than two generations, pushed her borders to the Pacific Ocean. This startling expansion came by stages, to be sure, but it was always championed by the popular party of the day; first by the Republicans, then by Democrats. The conservative party, Federalist or Whig, consistently opposed the acquisition of new territory. . . . From the beginning, however, the opponents of American expansion were running counter to popular feeling. The sentiment of the country was 'expansionist.' . . . [T]he real cause of the War of 1812 lay not in anything the British had or had not done, but rather in the aggressive temper of the War Hawks, who, backed by their frontier constituents, coveted new lands from Canada to Florida." John R. Bodo, *The Protestant Clergy and Public Issues 1812–1848* (Princeton, N.J.: Princeton University Press, 1954), p. 193. (See also p. 205 for documentation of the conservative opposition to the expansionist wars.)

[121] "In 1784, a traveller tells us the exports from the United States amounted to $4,000,000, the imports to $18,000,000; by 1790, the former had increased to $6,000,000 while the imports were now valued at $17,260,000. An examination of Bristad's statistics reveals the fact that, beginning with 1791, the export trade increased steadily. By 1816 it had reached $81,920,452, in spite of two setbacks during the Long Embargo and the second war with Great Britain. In 1825, according to Harriet Martineau, the exports represented a value of $3,000,000 more than the imports, which were estimated at $96,-000,000; while by 1835, the imports were $126,000,000 as against $104,-000,000 in exports." Mesick, *The English Traveller in America*, p. 183.

The results of the sixteen years [1800–1816], considered only in the economical development of the Union, were decisive. Although population increased more rapidly than was usual in human experience, wealth accumulated faster. . . .

These sixteen years set at rest the natural doubts that had attended the nation's birth. . . . Every serious difficulty which seemed alarming to the people of the Union in 1800 had been removed or sunk from notice in 1816. . . . This result was not the only or even the chief proof that economical progress was to be at least as rapid in the future. . . . The continent lay before them, like an uncovered ore-bed. They could see, and they even could calculate with reasonable accuracy the wealth it could be made to yield.[122]

It is important to recognize that a basic condition for acquiring legitimacy in a new state is effectiveness, particularly in the economic sphere. In return for support, the populace demands from its leaders rewards, some symbolic in content, such as national heroes and prestige, and others, perhaps more important, of a tangible nature. This is true today; it was true in America a hundred and fifty years ago. As Denis Brogan has well said:

The first and almost the last rule is that the rulers must deliver the goods, that they must share some of the winnings of the game with their clients, with the great mass of the American people, and that these winnings must be absolutely more than any rival system can plausibly promise. I have used the word "clients" advisedly, for the rulers of America have not the advantage of some of their European brethren, the advantage of a patina of age.[123]

---

[122] Henry Adams, *History of the United States During the Administration of James Madison* (New York: Albert and Charles Boni, 1930), Book IX, pp. 172–173. An analysis of the writings of foreign travelers before the Civil War reveals that most of them then described "the essential pattern of modern mass production." Summary of unpublished paper by Marvin Fisher, "The Uniqueness of American Industrialization, as Reported by European Observers, 1830–1860"; discussed by Eric Larrabee, "The Doctrine of Mass Production," in Robert Spiller and Eric Larrabee, eds., *American Perspectives* (Cambridge, Mass.: Harvard University Press, 1961), p. 207.

[123] D. W. Brogan, *American Themes* (London: Hamish Hamilton, 1948), p. 37.

Formulating
a National
Identity

2

★★★

In addition to laying the institutional framework for a stable polity, there was the task of proving to the populace that the system could establish America as a nation. But by what standards was its growth toward nationhood to be judged? We have seen that gaining economic independence was one of them. But even here there was little agreement as to what economic course the nation should follow. As Chambers points out:

> There was, indeed, irony in the economic position of both parties. The general ideological theme of the Federalists was conservative and traditionalist, whereas new parties in later emerging nations have been radically innovative and anti-traditionalist. On the other hand, Federalist economic policy was highly innovative and modernist, emphasizing government action toward an advanced, industrial capitalist society—again, however, contrary to the often anti-capitalist attitudes of new nations in the twentieth century. The Republicans were post-Enlightenment and anti-traditionalist in political ideology, but still largely wedded to agrarian economic conceptions in a pre-industrial economy—conceptions that the American nation with its already comparatively prosperous agricultural economy could afford, but which stood in sharp contrast to the intense drives for industrialization in new nations today.[1]

[1] William N. Chambers, *Parties in a New Nation* (New York: Oxford University Press, 1963), p. 102.

The Federalist and the Democratic-Republican economic policies only appear contradictory to their political ideologies in the light of comparisons with new nations today. When viewed within their own context, each of their political and economic ideologies forms a coherent but different kind of nationalism. On the one hand, the Federalists were saying that America as a nation should be just as powerful as England. In so doing they accepted her economic as well as some of her political standards of nationhood. On the other hand, the Democratic-Republicans were saying that America as a nation was already, in its own way, just as good as England. They therefore lauded and sought to maximize what was unique both in American political ideals and in the American economy.

The Federalists' and the Democratic-Republicans' views represented two poles of an ambivalence toward the Mother Country that is characteristic of all new nations. The need to dissociate themselves from any deep identification with their former imperialist ruler, or with any major foreign power, is characteristic of all new states. All new nations must establish their own identities. But along with a self-conscious effort to establish a separate identity, which usually leads to a rejection of all things associated with the Mother Country, there continues to exist a deep-rooted admiration for its culture and values. So that on the one hand, the former colonial power is hated as an evil imperialist exploiter or "monarchical" conspirator, and on the other hand, it is emulated and admired as the representative of a superior civilization.

The Need for Autonomy and Neutrality

Perhaps a consideration of this ambivalence will lead to a better understanding of the positions taken by "new" nations relative to those international crises in which the "old" nations are involved. In the contemporary world, we have witnessed the rise of "neutralism" as the dominant tendency among the new nations of Asia and Africa. This concept of non-alignment has proved frustrating to the contenders in the Cold War who see the struggle as one between freedom and tyranny. They cannot understand why nations which have just won their own independence can be so blind to an international struggle involving the issue of freedom. And the new nations' tactics of selling their support to the highest bidder by playing the non-Communist bloc off against the Communists is regarded as a highhanded display of blatant self-interest.

Placing the issue in these terms ignores the fact that nations are inherently egotistical, and that they act in terms of what they believe will enhance national growth and survival.

The United States, in the early years of its independence, exhibited a similar equivocalness. It began life as a unified nation about the same time that Britain and France started their almost twenty-five-year-long conflict stemming from the French Revolution. The behavior of the United States toward these nations was often inconsistent. The leaders of both American factions, the Republicans and the Federalists, desired above all else to keep the young nation out of the war.[2] But each faction had a specific bias to its "neutrality."

In 1793, when France declared war against England, the latter strongly urged the United States to declare its neutrality. At this point, Jefferson firmly opposed any declaration of neutrality, arguing that the President did not have the power to do so.[3] Hamilton, on the other hand, "was

---

[2] "[H]owever much the members of Washington's cabinet may have disagreed on most questions, they were all thoroughly convinced that the United States must avoid war as long as possible, whatever the cost. They differed widely in their views on the best way of doing this; so widely, in fact, that each member at times thought his opponents insincere in their protestations of neutrality. If even an impartial observer chanced to read only certain portions of the works of either man he might get the impression that Jefferson would have welcomed war with England or that Hamilton was ready for a rupture with France. . . . Washington was the only member of the Executive Department in 1793 who approached . . . [the] point of true neutrality. If he had a preference there is no record of his having expressed it. With Jefferson and Hamilton it was a question of honestly trying to maintain an actual neutrality in spite of those predilections that were often expressed by each, within the inner circle of his friends. Jefferson was convinced that the fate of the American experiment was bound up with the success of the French. . . . Hamilton . . . wished to preserve the neutrality of his country although he was as partial to England as Jefferson was to France." Charles M. Thomas, *American Neutrality in 1793* (New York: Columbia University Press, 1933), pp. 14–18.

[3] *Ibid.*, pp. 35–37. The argument revolved around an existent treaty with France, that of 1778. Hamilton argued that the treaty "should be suspended or nullified. He based his contention on the principle that the treaty which had been negotiated with the French monarchy was no longer binding, since the French had altered their form of government by the establishment of a republic. Jefferson replied . . . that the treaty was 'not between the United States and Louis Capet, but between the two nations of America and France; and the nations remaining in existence, though both of them have since changed their forms of government,' the treaty was not annulled by such changes." Here Jefferson applied "his theory of the sanctity of international

strongly in favor of the issuance of such a proclamation."[4] Five years later, in 1798, when the French ordered the confiscation of all American ships bound for England and closed French ports to any American ships that had visited an English port, the Federalists assumed a belligerent stance, passed legislation creating a standing army, increased armaments, and enacted the Alien and Sedition Acts designed to repress criticism of the government in time of crisis, while the Jeffersonians discovered the virtues of neutrality.

Despite these ideological differences, however, the leaders of both factions throughout this period were determined to keep out of the war. Hamilton, though bitterly anti-French, worked to restrain his Federalist friends from going to war with France. During the subsequent Democratic-Republican administration, Jefferson stubbornly ignored British provocations; and the United States, by declaring an embargo and ordering its ships not to go into war ports, did everything possible to keep clear of the conflict.

War did, of course, finally come in 1812. The pressure for American entry into war did not come so much from the specific annoyances imposed by Britain, but rather reflected the growth of nationalist sentiment, particularly among the new western states.[5] Indeed, the weakness of the United States in this war was due to the lack of

---

agreements under all circumstances save 'impossibility' or 'self-destruction,' and asserted that in this case the obligations could be claimed, at worst, merely to be 'dangerous'. . . . They were not dangerous [however], since France had made no demand that the United States join in the war. . . .

"Monroe . . . writing to Jefferson, announced himself an advocate of peace 'against every invitation to war.' He would ignore . . . the insults and irritations of Britain and Spain. He would wish to help France in any way short of war. But 'to expose ourselves to their fury (i. e., the provocations of European nations) would be as imprudent' as for a man in health to expose himself to a lunatic. 'To preserve peace will no doubt be difficult, but by accomplishing it, we show our wisdom and magnanimity. . . .' On the other hand, he could not conceive upon what principle the right to issue the neutrality proclamation was claimed." Stuart Gerry Brown, *The First Republicans* (Syracuse, N. Y.: Syracuse University Press, 1954), pp. 96–98.

[4] Thomas, *American Neutrality in 1793*, p. 38.

[5] The westerners wanted to press the Indian farther west, and ultimately to secure Canada, both as a means of reducing Indian strength and of enlarging American territory. To many, the continued presence of British rule on North American soil meant that the Revolution was not complete. See D. R. Anderson, "The Insurgents of 1811," *Annual Report of the American Historical Association*, 1911 (Washington: 1913), Vol I, pp. 173–174; and Julius W. Platt, *The Expansionists of 1812* (New York; Macmillan, 1925), pp. 133–153.

unanimity behind the war effort,[6] and it showed the danger of taking a new nation into war before effective national unity had occurred.

All in all, it can be said that American foreign policy during these first couple of decades was essentially expediential. It threatened war at one time or the other with both sides, and it sought to capitalize on the weaknesses of both sides by taking their territories in America (Louisiana, Florida, and Canada). Ideological alignment with the French Republic, ancestral solidarity with Britain, opposition to the conquest of all Europe by Napoleon—these played little role in determining our ultimate policy. It can even be said that in order to "liberate" Canada, we finally ended the period in alliance with the tyrant who had destroyed the French Republic and sought to subordinate all of Europe and Britain to his will!

Basically, our early foreign policy followed the principles laid down in the *Federalist,* in a section written by Alexander Hamilton. He insisted that permanent peace between the nations was a utopian goal, that all nations are and must be self-interested in their foreign policy, and that America should remain out of overseas conflicts that do not touch on its direct interests and should "aim at an ascendant in the system of American affairs." These principles were to appear anew in Washington's Farewell Address of 1796,[7] written in large part by Hamilton, and finally in the Monroe Doctrine of 1823, in which John Quincy Adams ". . . was personally a power . . . in laying down uncompromisingly" its three dicta which included the principle of Abstention. This policy of ". . . Abstention from the 'ordinary' vicissitudes and 'ordinary' combinations and collisions of European politics and wars" made possible the justification of a policy concerned with establishing the United States' manifest political destiny in its own hemisphere.

> Sensing America's advantage from Europe's distress [John Quincy Adams] peaceably broke through the paper trammels of Old World imperialism in the empty western stretches of North America. Diplomatically he carried the ball of American Empire . . . across

---

[6] In their remaining New England strongholds, the Federalist merchants "were able to convince themselves that Jefferson and Madison were sold to France. . . . The Federalist members of Congress issued an Address to their constituents . . . which declared the war to be unnecessary and inexpedient." Henry Adams, *History of the United States During the Administration of James Madison* (New York: Albert and Charles Boni, 1930), Book V, pp. 399–401.

[7] For an elaboration of the forces affecting early American policy see Felix Gilbert, *To the Farewell Address: Ideas of Early American Foreign Policy* (Princeton, N. J.: Princeton University Press, 1961), especially pp. 111–136.

the boreal plains over the Rocky Mountains down through the continuous woods that veiled the Oregon, to establish republican sovereignty impregnably on the Pacific Coast beyond the reach of further European colonization.[8]

The "neutralism" of early American foreign policy, like that of many contemporary new states, was of extreme importance in reducing some of the internal tensions which might serve to break down a weak authority structure. Many Republicans would have refused to support a war against the French Republic in 1798. Although the Federalist party was near death in 1812, some of the states which it controlled in New England openly sabotaged the war effort. And the subsequent heavy immigration from all parts of Europe in the latter part of the nineteenth century reinforced these neutralist tendencies, since it gave rise to ethnic pressure groups that reacted sharply to American policies which affected their homelands. It is interesting to note that the one stable multi-national European state, Switzerland, has defended its historic neutralism on the grounds that any other policy would have made it impossible for the Swiss nation to survive, as a nation. The Swiss Minister of Foreign Affairs has argued that: "As a community composed of various ethnic, linguistic and denominational groups, the Confederation could not participate in European national and religious quarrels without running the risk of disintegration. Without neutrality, . . . Switzerland would hardly exist today."[9]

Though few of the new states are divided internally among ethnic groups which have national or cultural ties to external power blocs, they, like the young United States, have been divided as to whom they should be "neutral against." And many leaders of such states take the same position that Jefferson and Hamilton did in the 1790's. They may hope for the victory of one or the other side, or for a stalemate, but they feel that as a new nation, with the need to secure a legitimate structure of authority and rapid economic development, they must abstain from involvement in "foreign entanglements."

The Role of the Intellectuals

In the new states of the twentieth century, the intellectuals have been the innovators, the agents of social change. It is they who introduced the

[8] Samuel F. Bemis, *John Quincy Adams and the Foundations of American Foreign Policy* (New York: Alfred A. Knopf, 1949), pp. 567–568.
[9] Cited in F. E. Aschinger, "The United States and European Neutrals," *Swiss Review of World Affairs*, 12 (1962), p. 15.

ideas of nationhood, democracy, and equality to the populace. Not only do they bring new values into tradition-bound systems, but they head nationalist movements and are the leaders in the tactics of revolution. Thus they impose the ideas within which the nation may find its identity. As Edward Shils has put it:

> It was the intellectuals on whom, in the first instance, devolved the task of contending for their nations' right to exist, even to the extent of promulgating the very idea of the nation. The erosion of the conscience and self-confidence of the colonial powers was in considerable measure the product of agitational movements under intellectual leadership. The impregnation of their fellow-countrymen with some incipient sense of nationality and of national self-esteem was to a large extent the achievement of intellectuals, both secular and religious. . . .[10]

Shils suggests that because of the relatively small number of intellectuals in new states, "all persons with an *advanced modern education*" must be considered as falling within the intellectual class. And given the limited social need for creative artists and writers, university teachers, high ranking civil servants, and others, he argues that the legal profession has been the most important occupation open to those with higher education. The effort to apply "old country" law to colonies has led to a great deal of litigation. "The leisure time of the young lawyer was a fertile field in which much political activity grew. . . . [T]he legal profession supplied . . . many of the outstanding leaders of the nationalist movements during colonial times, and . . . the lawyer-intellectuals form . . . a vital part of the political elites of the new states."[11]

The nationalistic, revolutionary intellectuals are usually young men. They are often antagonistic toward the older generation, who are more closely identified with the *status quo* and who often do not share the young intellectuals' nationalistic vision because they are better established in local political and social hierarchies. The young intellectuals' more nationalistic philosophy may come from a more cosmopolitan perspective. Thus, in discussing the extremist national movements in Asia and Africa, Shils points out that they "drew inspiration and comfort from abroad [and] felt that their actions were one with a mighty surge all over the world. . . . *This sense of being a part of the larger world infused into the politics of the second [younger] generation the perma-*

---

[10] Edward Shils, "The Intellectuals in the Political Development of the New States" (mimeographed, 1962), pp. 3–4.

[11] *Ibid.*, pp. 14–15.

nently bedeviling tension between province and metropolis, and added, as it always does, the heat which arises from conflicting loyalties."[12]

Their political antagonism to the powers that be may also come from a sense of frustration because they have no place in the old society. Their new values do not coincide with those that would place them in honored positions in the old local hierarchies. These values are encapsulated in an ideology, and the ideology the intellectuals espouse is that of populism. "The people" are possessed of some kind of sacred mystique, and proximity to them endows the politician with esteem—and with legitimacy. "The people are a model and a standard; contact with them is good. Esteem and disesteem are meted out on the basis of 'closeness to the people' or distance from them. . . ."[13]

The nationalist intellectuals in new states are inclined to espouse populism because, either lacking connection with or being disaffected from the existing power hierarchies, their only source of power lies in the people. However, their populism is derived also from their ambivalence toward more developed nations. In attempting to establish a national identity, they feel they need to play up those elements that make their nation unique. They may try to overcome their own feeling of cultural inferiority by rejecting the premises of "culture" in the more developed countries and lauding the values in their own culture on some other grounds. These values are often seen to reside in the common people rather than in the upper classes who have been more frequently exposed to foreign cultures. Thus the cult of populism arises, the "belief in the creativity and in the superior moral worth of the ordinary people, of the uneducated and the unintellectual."[14]

Their populist ideology, however, does not lead the intellectuals to any real understanding or appreciation of, or even to an egalitarian attitude toward, the people. By definition, the intellectuals' backgrounds are very different from those of the people with whom they are concerned. Their life has been very different from that of the common man, so that their understanding of his ways can only be an idealized one. As a result,

> . . . despite this preoccupation with the "people" the populism of the intellectuals of underdeveloped countries does not necessarily bring with it either intimacy with the ordinary people, a concrete

---

[12] *Ibid.*, p. 27. (Emphasis mine.)

[13] *Ibid.*, p. 39.

[14] Edward Shils, "The Intellectuals and the Powers: Some Perspectives for Comparative Analysis," *Comparative Studies in Society and History*, 1 (1958), p. 20.

attachment to them or even a democratic attitude. It is compatible with them but it does not require them.

Populism can be the legitimating principle of oligarchic regimes, as well as of democratic regimes and of all the intermediate types. The people constitute the prospective good to be served by government policy.[15]

The intellectuals of the new states are not destined to become philosopher-kings. After independence, the emergence of mass politics sees the rise to prominence of politicians and administrators who tend to be more professional than intellectual. Having undergone the exhilarating experience of playing a major role in the creation of their nation, many intellectuals withdraw in disillusion from active politics.[16] The resulting tensions between them and the governing elite lead them to feel "spurned and disesteemed in the new state, for the coming of which they had worked and dreamed."[17]

If we turn from these generalizations about the new nations of our own century to the young United States, it is interesting to note the parallels. In both eras, the chief nationalist leaders were men who combined scholarship with action. They introduced the ideology of independence and equality and then campaigned on its behalf. In the early United States, the intellectuals played a major role in applying the doctrine of natural rights to the Americans' claims for independence. And not content to merely supply ideas, many took an important part in establishing the new nation itself.[18]

[15] Shils, "The Intellectuals in the Political Development . . . ," *op. cit.*, p. 41.

[16] Edward Shils, "Influence and Withdrawal: The Intellectuals in Indian Political Development," in Dwaine Marvick, ed., *Political Decision-makers* (New York: The Free Press, 1961), p. 30.

[17] Edward Shils, "Political Developments in the New States," *Comparative Studies in Society and History*, 2 (1960), p. 276. A similar process in the development of western revolutionary movements is described in Harry J. Benda, "Non-Western Intelligentsias as Political Elites," in John H. Kautsky, ed., *Political Change in Underdeveloped Countries* (New York: John Wiley, 1962), pp. 250–251; see also Harry J. Benda, "Intellectuals and Politics in Western History," *Bucknell Review*, 10 (1961), pp. 1–10.

[18] "The Constitutional Convention of 1787 has been called the first American brain trust. *At least thirty-one of the fifty-five members had been educated at colonial colleges* or at similar institutions abroad. Many, including Franklin, had become first-rate scholars and scientists by their own efforts. Two university presidents and three college professors sat in Independence Hall. . . . Many others had been 'schoolmasters.' " Merle Curti, *American Paradox: The Conflict of Thought and Action* (New Brunswick, N.J.: Rutgers University Press, 1956), pp. 15–16. (Emphasis mine.)

Richard Hofstadter has described the intellectuals' role as follows:

> When the United States began its national existence, the relation-
> ship between intellect and power was not a problem. The leaders
> *were* the intellectuals. . . . The Founding Fathers were sages,
> scientists, men of broad cultivation, many of them apt in classical
> learning, who used their wide reading in history, politics, and law
> to solve the exigent problems of their time.[19]

And as in the contemporary new states, many of these political intellectuals were also trained as lawyers. "Of the fifty-six signers of the
Declaration of Independence, twenty-five were 'lawyers'; of the fifty-
five members of the Constitutional Convention in Philadelphia, thirty-one
were 'lawyers'; in the first Congress, ten of the twenty-nine Senators
and seventeen of the sixty-five Representatives were 'lawyers.' "[20] Daniel
Boorstin, in citing these figures, makes a point similar to that of Shils
when he says that "this does not show the importance of a specialized
legal profession in the making of our nation," but rather "the vagueness
of the boundary between legal and all other knowledge in a fluid
America."[21]

America was more fortunate than contemporary new states in that the
European cultural values with which its intellectuals identified were not
very different from those held by the majority of the population. In
contemporary new nations, the young intellectuals are likely to be
alienated from their own society because they feel drawn to cultures
which speak a language foreign to most of the citizens of these societies.
The writer or scholar in a former part of the British or French empire
still seeks recognition from London or Paris.[22] But young America's intel-

---

[19] Richard Hofstadter, *Anti-Intellectualism in American Life* (New York:
Alfred A. Knopf, 1963), p. 145.

[20] Daniel J. Boorstin, *The Americans: The Colonial Experience* (New York:
Random House, 1958), p. 205.

[21] *Loc. cit.*

[22] See Immanuel Wallerstein, *Africa, Politics of Independence* (New York:
Vintage Books, 1961), p. 65, and Edward Shils, "Metropolis and Province in
the Intellectual Community," in V. M. Dandakar and N. V. Sovani, eds.,
Changing India (Bombay: Asia Publishing House, 1961), pp. 283–284. Shils
has described the situation generally: "[The Western intellectual outlook]
exercised an irresistible fascination on certain strata of the societies outside
the European centre, and the situation was not made any easier to bear by
the often explicit derogation of their own culture and society which its admirers encountered . . . in the works and attitudes of intellectuals of the foreign
culture to which they were attracted.

"This feeling of intellectual inferiority *vis-à-vis* the West still exists in the

lectuals, too, had a sense of cultural inferiority *vis-à-vis* the European metropolitan cultures. For eighteenth- and nineteenth-century American intellectuals, London and other European capitals were the centers which had to be impressed.[23] Only Europe's learning, literature, art, and higher education were viewed as good while America's—the product of "colonials and provincials"—were viewed as inferior.[24]

As has been already pointed out, such attitudes may foster anti-intellectualism and populism among nationalists in new nations. Some of the intellectuals in America have shown a soaring "belief in the creativity and in the superior moral worth of the ordinary people," just as do intellec-

underdeveloped countries, and indeed in almost all areas of the world outside the European centre. It survives in the Soviet Union, it was common in the United States in the nineteenth and early twentieth centuries, and is not entirely dead there. Among the more backward totalitarian countries and among the intellectuals of the pluralistic underdeveloped countries of Asia and Africa, it is very strong. The fascination by the Western intellectual outlook has, in the main, been strongest in those sections of the population which also have become fervently nationalistic. (These two conflicting attachments are very closely connected with each other.)" Edward Shils, "The Prospects for Intellectuals," *Soviet Survey*, No. 29 (1959), p. 86.

[23] A study of the reactions of American travelers in England in the first half century of American independence reports that "the leaders of American thought looked to the mellow and long-established cultural institutions of England with longing, and struggled to learn and to imitate. . . . [I]n education, art, and literature—American eyes were thus turned to the older orders. This was more true in literature than in almost any other aspect of cultural life." Robert E. Spiller, *The American in England During the First Half Century of Independence* (New York: Henry Holt, 1926), pp. 387–388. A study of American artists during this period makes the same point. Returning painters "brought home with them the belief that they were minor workmen who would never create great art. No deep intellectual conviction lay behind the American vernacular tradition." James T. Flexner, *The Light of Distant Skies, 1760–1835* (New York: Harcourt, Brace, 1954), pp. 64–65. See also Bradford Perkins, *Prologue to War* (Berkeley: University of California Press, 1961), p. 97.

[24] "Even now, when American intellectual life is at the height of its powers, large numbers of American intellectuals in all fields feel towards Britain— and especially towards Oxford, Cambridge and London—what Roman intellectuals in antiquity often felt toward Athens. Some sort of feeling of inferiority to a culture of greater refinement, greater subtlety, greater profundity, still persists—even among those who almost deliberately cultivate a populistic 'grass-roots' attitude. In the United States, too, provinciality is— despite the tremendous changes of fortune—still a wound. The intellectuals still struggle to escape its pain." Shils, "Metropolis and Province . . . ," *op. cit.*, p. 289.

tuals in latter-day new states.[25] Even Thomas Jefferson could write: "State a moral case to a ploughman and a professor. The former will decide it as well, and often better than the latter, because he has not been led astray by artificial rules."[26] And the great historian George Bancroft "rhapsodized over Jackson's unschooled mind" as an asset which would enable him to bring greater wisdom to the presidency than those who were "versed in books."[27]

But as is well known, the leadership of the intellectuals in new states

---

[25] Shils, "The Intellectuals and the Powers . . . ," *op. cit.*, p. 20. The great abolitionist political leader Charles Sumner revealed all the seeming inconsistencies of a politically involved intellectual from a "provincial" country. "He spent a good deal of his time abroad being embarrassed for his country and for his countrymen. . . . When compared with Great Britain, Sumner concluded, the United States was lamentably lacking in culture. . . . American colleges were shockingly deficient when compared to European universities. . . . By European standards, the professions in the United States were illtrained. . . . Even the use of language in the United States was slovenly, Sumner complained, when a great writer like Longfellow could in the middle of a beautiful poem 'commit that *Americanism—Side-Walk*.'" Yet at the same time, on his trip abroad "he had, apart from enjoying British society, only one purpose, to promote 'the diffusion of the writings of any American calculated to inspire respect . . . [for] liberal institutions.' [H]e secured the publication of the first serious article devoted to Emerson in a British periodical. . . ." And less than a decade after his youthful visit to England and Europe, Sumner was justifying his abolitionist politics and hopes with extreme populist statements. David Donald, *Charles Sumner, and the Coming of the Civil War* (New York: Alfred A. Knopf, 1960), pp. 59–60, 60–61, 180–182. (Emphasis in original.)

[26] Cited in Hofstadter, *Anti-Intellectualism in American Life*, p. 155.

[27] *Ibid.*, p. 159. "In all these [contemporary new] countries the intellectuals have developed anxiety about whether they have not allowed themselves to be corrupted by excessive permeation with the admired foreign culture. To identify themselves with the people, to praise the culture of the ordinary people as richer, truer, wiser, and more relevant than the foreign culture in which they had themselves been educated, has been a way out of this distress." Shils, "The Intellectuals and the Powers . . . ," *op. cit.*, pp. 20–21. The negative image of America fostered in the writings of many educated European conservatives is documented by Merle Curti, "The Reputation of America Overseas, 1776–1860," in his *Probing Our Past* (New York: Harper & Bros., 1955), pp. 191–218. American writers were extremely sensitive to such criticisms, especially to negative reviews in British journals. And some replied with populist answers: "In the bitter literary war, champions of America declared that if English letters could boast greater triumphs than the United States, at least there was no snobbish literary aristocracy in the new country. . . . Meantime a stout patriot insisted that if Americans were not yet capable of

does not survive the first revolutionary generation.[28] The change in American political life was associated with the rise of party politics.[29] The passions which emerged with the beginnings of partisan conflict in the late eighteenth and early nineteenth centuries were accompanied by the use of anti-intellectual imagery by both major factions. Jefferson, in particular, was attacked by Federalists as an ideologue whose dangerous politics reflected his preoccupations with ideas and abstract principles. And various liberals criticized the "learned and property-holding classes," suggesting that their learning might be used against the common people.[30] Finally the explicit anti-elitism of the Jacksonian movement, followed by the adoption of populist tactics by both major parties, meant that the intellectual could participate in politics only at his peril.[31]

The depreciation of abstract intellectual activities, of art for art's sake, of the contribution which intellectuals can make to political life, has also been stimulated in new states, both recent and past, by the commitment to practical economic and social development. The desire to catch up and surpass the former imperialist power has meant that "impractical pursuits" must be given low priority in the values both of politicians and of intellectuals themselves.[32]

---

writing books of theory, they contrived to anticipate in practice the contents of those produced abroad—several years before their appearance!" Curti, *op. cit.*, p. 200. See also Flexner, *The Light of Distant Skies*, pp. 231–234, 236.

[28] This stands in need of some qualifications. In new states there are obviously still many intellectuals working as technicians and civil servants in the government bureaucracy. The intellectuals have been rejected, however, as a major political stratum who wield influence as a "class."

[29] Dixon Ryan Fox, *The Decline of Aristocracy in the Politics of New York* (New York: Columbia University Press, 1919).

[30] Hofstadter, *Anti-Intellectualism in American Life*, p. 152.

[31] "The first truly powerful and widespread impulse to anti-intellectualism in American politics was, in fact, given by the Jacksonian movement. Its distrust for expertise, its dislike for centralization, its desire to uproot the entrenched classes, and its doctrine that important functions were simple enough to be performed by anyone, amounted to a repudiation not only of government by gentlemen which the nation had inherited from the eighteenth century, but also of the special value of the educated classes to civic life." *Ibid.*, pp. 155–156.

[32] Beaumont caught the spirit of this aspect of early American life: "Hardly was the American nation born when public and industrial life absorbed all its moral energy. . . . The Americans have too many political interests to trouble themselves with literary ones. . . .

"In America, the sciences are valued only for their applied uses. They study the useful arts but not the fine arts. . . .

"American literature is entirely lacking in good taste—that refined, subtle

As we have noted, intellectuals play an important role in most new nations in formulating the objectives and rationale of the struggle for independence. But after independence, leftist and populist ideologies, and an emphasis on practical pursuits as most useful in an "underdeveloped" society, press the intellectuals to withdraw from effective group participation in politics. And their concern with the "good opinion" of the elite of the former metropolitan power may even lead them to depreciate the achievements of the nation which they helped bring into being. For new nations are not only populist and pragmatic; they are also provincial. The resulting tension between the intellectuals and the dominant forces in the new nation may constitute a handicap in formulating an effective national self-image. Thus, all new nations face the problem of incorporating their intellectuals into their polities.

Revolution as the Source of National Identity

In most post-colonial nations, it is revolutionary ideas, not conservative ones, that are associated with the national image.[33] And ever since the

---

restraint, that delicate sentiment which results from the mixture of passion and cool judgment, enthusiasm and reason, spontaneity and design, which prevails in literary composition in Europe. To have elegance in taste, one must first have elegant customs. . . .

"Thus literature and the arts, instead of being invoked by the passions, come only to the aid of necessity. . . .

"And do not try to please . . . [Americans] by saying that the identity of language unites all the fine minds of England with those of America; they will reply that English literature has nothing whatever in common with American literature. . . .

"No one in America understands that completely intellectual life which sets itself up beyond the realm of the practical world and feeds on dreams, speculations, and abstractions; that nonobjective existence which shuns business affairs, for which meditation is a necessity, science a duty, literary creation a delightful pastime, and which, seizing upon the riches of antiquity and the treasures of today, taking a leaf from the laurels of Milton as from those of Virgil, makes the genius and glory of all the ages enhance its own richness." Gustave de Beaumont, *Marie, or Slavery in the United States* (Stanford, Calif.: Stanford University Press, 1958), pp. 107–115.

[33] Amitai Etzioni has argued that in Israel and most contemporary new states "left-of-center ideologies and groups have stronger political, economic and prestige positions than the right and liberal forces. . . . To be a Social Democrat in Israel—and the same holds for many of the newly developed countries—means to be in conformity with the majority of the politically

beginning of the modern era, revolutionary nationalism has tended to incorporate within itself supra-national ideas. As Karl Deutsch has put it:

> Behind the spreading of national consciousness there was at work perhaps a deeper change—a new *value* assigned to people *as they are,* or as they can become, with as much diversity of interlocking roles as will not destroy or stifle any of their personalities. After 1750 we find new and higher values assigned in certain advanced countries to children and women; to the poor and the sick; to slaves and peasants; to colored races and submerged nationalities. . . .
>
> National consciousness thus arises in an age that asserts birthrights for everybody, inborn, unalienable rights, first in the language of religion, then in the language of politics, and finally in terms involving economics and all society. . . .
>
> Once men formed a people, once they acquired many objective characteristics of nationality, they would become aware of what had happened. If this new awareness should come to them in the midst of a cultural and spiritual change, a change in the fundamental strategy of values, teaching them a new pride and a new confidence in what they were and in their own kind—or teaching them a hunger for this kind of pride and confidence not yet attained—then this new consciousness of nationality would become a potential center for patterns of individual and social behavior, and of political action.[34]

When Americans celebrate their national heritage on Independence Day, Memorial Day, or other holidays of this sort they dedicate themselves anew to a nation conceived as the living fulfillment of a political doctrine that enshrines a utopian conception of men's egalitarian and fraternal relations with one another. In linking national celebrations with political events and a political creed, the United States resembles such other post-revolutionary societies as France, the Soviet Union, or many of the new states. Nations whose authority stems from traditional legitimacy, on the other hand, tend to celebrate holidays linked with a religious tradition or a national military tradition, not with a political doctrine as such.

These differences in the sources of the national self-image should affect the character of political life, particularly in the early stages of the evolu-

---

conscious members of society." "Alternative Ways to Democracy: The Example of Israel," *Political Science Quarterly*, 74 (1959), pp. 213–214.
[34] Karl Deutsch, *Nationalism and Social Communication* (New York: John Wiley, 1953), pp. 153–155. (Emphasis in original.)

tion of systems of democratic authority.[35] In societies based on traditional legitimacy, there has been a congruence among a conservative respect for the existing pattern of social and political organization, national symbols, and the stratification system. Value consensus sustained these elements as an interrelated whole. When such societies developed economically, new classes were created, the bourgeoisie and the workers, who had no initial political rights and were subordinate to the old aristocracy and the monarchy. As these new classes became politically conscious, developing values based on their needs as socially inferior groups, they faced the problem of reconciling these new values with the dominant cultural norms that supported the political and social position of the old elites. In large measure, the general cultural norms strengthened conservative beliefs among *all* strata and reduced the strength of those factors making for left-wing predispositions. One finds generally that parties upholding traditional values not only retain the support of a large majority of the privileged strata, but that a considerable section of the depressed classes also retain their loyalty to the existing order. As Bagehot suggested in discussing England, where traditional class values have not been destroyed by revolution, habits of deference will help to maintain the polity.[36]

In newly independent societies there has often been a transition from a system dominated by traditionalist, usually aristocratic values, to one characterized by egalitarian populist concepts. These new value systems are variously referred to as "liberal," "democratic," or "leftist" in contrast to "elitist," "conservative," or "aristocratic." The elitist ideology takes for granted the desirability of the hierarchical ordering of society in which those who belong to the "naturally superior" strata exercise due authority and are given generalized respect. Social recognition rests on the sum of all the qualities of a person's status rather than on a given role he may be playing. In colonial situations, the native elites derive their status, or are protected in it, by virtue of their connection with the status and power of the foreign ruler. And with independence, the values of hierarchy, aris-

---

[35] A study of the American Tories in the Revolution concludes: "If there were any serious consequences to America from the silencing and expulsion of the Loyalists, they were certainly not social or, in the narrow sense, political consequences. Rather they were philosophical consequences: the Tories' organic conservatism represented a current of thought that failed to reappear in America after the Revolution. A substantial part of the whole spectrum of European social and political philosophy seemed to slip outside the American perspective." William H. Nelson, *The American Tory* (New York: Oxford University Press, 1961), pp. 189–190.

[36] Walter Bagehot, *The English Constitution* (London: Oxford University Press, 1928), p. 141.

tocracy, privilege, primogeniture, and (more recently) capitalism, all associated with the foreign imperialist power, are easily rejected.

Consequently, most struggles for independence have employed leftist ideologies, that of equality in revolutionary America, that of socialism in the contemporary new states. Man's status is to depend not upon inherited but upon achieved qualities; hence the system must be geared to abolish all forms of privilege and to reward achievement. The franchise is to be extended to everyone, the people being regarded as the source of power and authority; and various social reforms, such as economic development, the elimination of illiteracy, and the spread of education, are to reduce inequalities in status. We have seen how the need to legitimate the democratic goals of the American Revolution made mandatory a commitment sharply to improve the economic circumstances of the mass of the population, even though the struggle for independence was conceived by many of its leaders as primarily concerned with the issue of political independence. And in general, although many of those involved in a nationalist movement may have been conservatives on most matters other than that of foreign domination, the need to mobilize support against the ruling oligarchy forces even the conservative nationalists to use the leftist vocabulary of the time. Every revolutionary group proclaims "*all* men to be equal," to have "inalienable rights," or advocates a "classless society" and the elimination of minority rule in politics.

However, beneath this consistency of radical temper, there are profound differences in the ways in which various parties or strata interpret their revolutionary commitments. In the United States after the adoption of the Constitution, the conservative and socially privileged groups who had taken part in the anti-imperialist revolution continued to play a major, even dominant, role. This resembles the immediate post-independence political situation in Pakistan, Ceylon, Morocco, and others of the Arab states, where conservative elites have held the reins of government. Although formally committed to carrying out the social and humanitarian objectives of the nationalist revolution, the conservatives have attempted to resist the institutional elaboration of these goals. The American Federalists, though convinced advocates of views which were radical and republican by the standards of European states, sought to limit the application of egalitarian principles in such fields as property relations, religion, and the suffrage.[37] But as in most of the contemporary new states in which

---

[37] "The Federalists recoiled at the prejudice and violence of the masses, declaring that incompetence could not be trusted . . . [T]hey expressed open contempt. . . ." John Bassett, *The Federalist System* (New York: Harper & Bros., 1906), p. 295. The Federalists of New Jersey appealed in 1800 as the

conservatives have tried to defend traditionalist values after independence, the right-wing party soon lost office.

The defeat of the conservatives in the early political conflicts in new states usually results in a situation comparable to that in which "leftists" have established the nation. National identity and left-wing values are intertwined. The purpose of independence is perceived to be the creation of a new and more radical society than that which has existed. In the United States, the end of Federalism meant that henceforth all American political parties were to be egalitarian in overt ideology and populist in tone. The extension of adult suffrage solidified such sentiments. The dominant "one party," the Democratic-Republicans, ruled, as has been noted, without effective national opposition until the 1830's.[38] A historian of Pennsylvanian affairs explains this phenomenon in terms which apply, in large measure, to most other states:

> [T]he most acute students of Pennsylvania history agree that Democratic supremacy is to be explained largely in ideological terms. It was supported by the evocative power of certain dogmas which reversed the party allegiance . . . a power deriving in large measure from the early inception of virtual manhood suffrage. The mass base of political life in Pennsylvania meant that equalitarian slogans always had a profound, even mystical appeal there. The vaguest atmosphere of aristocracy was a decisive political handicap. . . .[39]

Although conservative groups in most new nations are deprived of the link with historic national values which they have in old states, there is at

party of " 'wealth and talent' . . . [asking] 'whether to continue our government in the hands of men opposed to untried theories and dangerous innovations and attached to the *existing order of things*—or whether we will abandon it to the direction of those whose conduct, whose writings, whose views are revolutionary.' It was the question whether the abler few should direct the many who were unstable, irrational and likely to be disorderly and destructive." Walter Fee, *The Transition from Aristocracy to Democracy in New Jersey, 1789–1827* (Somerville, N.J.: Somerset Press, 1933), p. 107. A Federalist broadside described their opponents as " 'the discontented—the ambitious—the unprincipled—and the disappointed of our countrymen,' " together with various kinds of foreigners. *Ibid.*, p. 111.

[38] In the elections of 1824 and 1828, all candidates for President were nominally members of the same party.

[39] Louis Hartz, *Economic Policy and Democratic Thought: Pennsylvania, 1776–1860* (Cambridge, Mass.: Harvard University Press, 1948), pp. 23–24; see also Philip S. Klein, *Pennsylvania Politics, 1817–1832* (Philadelphia: Historical Society of Pennsylvania, 1940).

least one traditional institution with which they may identify and whose popular strength they may seek to employ: religion. The leftist nationalist revolutionaries, in their desire to remake their society, often perceive traditional religion as one of the great obstacles; attitudes and values which are dysfunctional to efforts to modernize various institutions are usually associated with ancient religious beliefs and habits. And the efforts by the leaders of new states to challenge these beliefs and habits serve to bring them into conflict with the religious authorities.[40]

A look at the politics of contemporary new nations indicates that in many of them religion has formed the basis for conservative parties. Thus in Indonesia, two Moslem parties, Masjumi (Indonesian Moslem) and Nahdlatul-Ulama (Moslem Teachers) secured almost half (40 per cent) of the votes in the one election in that country.[41] These parties were subsequently dissolved by the Nationalist governing party. In India today, a conservative party, the Jana Sangh, has arisen to defend Hindu values. In Pakistan, the Moslem League, organized to foster Islamic principles and also the party which established the nation, lost power after Independence; but it remained as the major conservative group until parties were dissolved. Similarly in most of the Arab states, conservative politics and the Islamic religion have been closely intertwined. The situation is more complicated in most of the Negro African states, since there is no dominant national religion in many of them. In fact, where Christianity is strong, it faces the problem of being identified with the former colonial rulers. Islam has, however, formed the basis for conservative groupings in parts of Nigeria.

In the United States, the various efforts to sustain or create conservative parties in the early decades of the republic were closely tied to religion. The picture here, however, was clearly not one of religion versus irreligion, since the "dissenting sects," such as the Methodists, the Baptists, and the Catholics, all opposed the privileges of the established churches—the

---

[40] "The only reference to religion [in the Constitution] is contained in the provision that 'no religious Test shall ever be required as a Qualification to any Office or public Trust under the United States.' This omission, representing . . . the rationalistic tendency somewhat popular among the rather youthful public men who dominated the convention, roused a good deal of protest and the absence of any reference to divine authority was one of the points made against accepting the document." Roy F. Nichols, *Religion and American Democracy* (Baton Rouge: Louisiana State University Press, 1959), pp. 36–37.

[41] *A Review of Elections 1954–1958* (London: The Institute of Electoral Research, 1960), p. 67.

Congregationalists in New England, the Episcopalians in the South. The Democrats received considerable support from the former in their efforts to eliminate the tie between Church and State. Faced with the difficulty of combatting the political left on most social and political issues, the conservatives, whether religious or not, quickly saw the political potential of an identification with religious institutions and morality. Arthur Schlesinger, Jr., has well described their reactions:

> Federalism . . . mobilized religion to support its views of society. At the very start, many conservatives, with the discreet skepticism of eighteenth century gentlemen, considered religion indispensable to restrain the brute appetites of the lower orders but hardly necessary for the upper classes. As . . . the clergy loudly declared Jeffersonian deism to be a threat, not only to themselves, but to the foundations of social order, conservatism grew more ardent in its faith. In 1802 Hamilton, seeking desperately to rejuvenate the Federalist party, suggested the formation of a Christian Constitutional Society with the twofold purpose of promoting Christianity and the Constitution.[42]

With the growing strength of the Jeffersonians, dubbed irreligious Deists by their opponents, the religious conservatives, largely of Calvinist persuasions, banded together to form a number of moralistic organizations "to save men from folly, vice, and sin."[43] By winning men to the path of

---

[42] Arthur Schlesinger, Jr., *The Age of Jackson* (Boston: Little, Brown, 1946), p. 16. Tocqueville has pointed out how, in France, first the upper class and later the middle class returned to religion when they recognized that they needed it to stabilize a post-revolutionary society in which deference values no longer operated to sustain lower class loyalty. "The Revolution of 1792, when striking the upper classes, had cured them of their irreligiousness; it had taught them, if not the truth, at least the social usefulness of belief. This lesson was lost upon the middle class, which remained their political heir and their jealous rival; and the latter had even become more sceptical in proportion as the former seemed to become more religious. The Revolution of 1848 had just done on a small scale for our tradesmen what that of 1792 had done for the nobility: the same reverses, the same terrors, the same conversion. . . . The clergy had facilitated this conversion by . . . [professing] republican opinions, while at the same time it gave to long established interests the guarantee of its traditions, its customs, and its hierarchy." Alexis de Tocqueville, *The Recollections of Alexis de Tocqueville* (London: The Harvill Press, 1948), p. 120.
[43] Clifford S. Griffin, *Their Brothers' Keepers* (New Brunswick, N.J.: Rutgers University Press, 1960), p. 43.

righteousness, they would also guarantee their vote for Federalist principles.

Perhaps the first major example of this reaction was the temperance movement which developed in the early years of the nineteenth century. To a considerable extent this movement was dominated by members of the Federalist upper class and Congregationalist ministers. The downfall of the party and the disestablishment of the Church faced them with the need to explain their defeats. And they found their explanation in the low cultural level of the common man, his drunkenness and lack of education. The drive against alcohol became part of the "Puritan Counter-Reformation."[44] "The early temperance advocates of New England, for example, were so strongly Federalist in their political affiliations that Federalism and temperance became entangled in public thinking."[45]

> Early temperance efforts were combined with labors for morality in general. They arose not only to check drunkenness and other evils; but also to rescue the Federalist party from threatened destruction. . . . The Federalists reasoned that if they could wean men from profanity, vice, and inebriation, the former sinners would be amenable to changing their political allegiance.[46]

The left and the right in early America disagreed on the extent to which the United States was even to be viewed as a Christian nation. Thus, not only did the Jeffersonians seek to eliminate all forms of state support for the established churches; they went so far on the national level as to insist that the State was obligated to provide services for its citizens seven days a week—that, for instance, it could not deprive non-Christians of their right to receive mail on Sundays. In 1810, Congress passed a law providing for the Sunday delivery of the mails. The religious and political conservatives replied by agitation to support the Lord's Day. This issue was to remain alive for many decades. In 1825, Congress extended the provisions for Sunday mails. And in 1829, the Democratic

---

[44] John A. Krout, *The Origins of Prohibition* (New York: Alfred A. Knopf, 1925), pp. 83–100; David M. Ludlum, *Social Ferment in Vermont, 1791–1850* (New York: Columbia University Press, 1939), p. 65; Joseph Gusfield, "Status Conflicts and the Changing Ideologies of the American Temperance Movement," in David Pittman and Charles R. Snyder, eds., *Society, Culture, and Drinking Practices* (New York: John Wiley, 1962), pp. 105–106.

[45] Alice Tyler, *Freedom's Ferment* (Minneapolis: The University of Minnesota Press, 1944), p. 317.

[46] Griffin, *Their Brothers' Keepers*, pp. 36–37.

majority replied to the agitation against this law by endorsing the report of a Senate Committee which stated as a matter of national policy that religion and irreligion had equal rights, that laws setting aside Sunday as a special day of rest worked an injustice on non-Christians.[47]

Issues concerning the place of religion in society played a major role in structuring the revived two-party system which formed around supporters and opponents of Andrew Jackson. One of the first efforts to organize an anti-Jackson party, the Anti-Masonic party, which was to become one of the major constituent elements in the Whig party, sought to bring together those who favored an alliance between Church and State. And the Whig party took over this task:

> Battlegrounds shifted over time, but the lines drawn in the 1830's between the "Church and State party" and the "Jackson party" held fast. Struggles over Sunday laws, the sustained effort to open public assemblies with prayer, Jackson's refusal to act against Georgia for imprisoning missionaries to the Cherokees—on these and like issues, party differences were distinct, passionate, and enduring.[48]

The northern Whig spokesmen, like the Federalists before them, gave voice to the values of the dethroned Puritan Establishment. They argued that the State was a proper instrument to eradicate moral evils such as gambling and "grogselling." The religious sentiments that underlay the Federalist and Whig moralistic concerns may be seen in the activities of Lyman Beecher, who as a key figure in the Congregationalist Church also was involved successively in Federalist, Whig, and later Republican politics. He, like many others of the New England theocrats:

> sought to reestablish a clerically dominated social order by means of voluntary social and moral reform societies that would give the clergy an influential role in forming public opinion and molding public legislation. The many "benevolent societies" of the [Jacksonian] period, which sought to evangelize the unchurched, to save the heathen, to sober the drunkard, to rescue the wayward female, to purify the Sabbath, to end dueling, to inaugurate Sunday Schools,

---

[47] See John R. Bodo, *The Protestant Clergy and Public Issues 1812–1848* (Princeton, N. J.: Princeton University Press, 1954), pp. 39–43; Anson Phelps Stokes, *Church and State in the United States* (New York: Harper & Bros., 1950), Vol. II, pp. 12–20.

[48] Lee Benson, *The Concept of Jacksonian Democracy* (Princeton, N.J.: Princeton University Press, 1961), p. 196.

and to send freed slaves back to Africa . . . [were composed largely of] the ministers and leading laymen and women of the Congregational churches.[49]

The party struggle was clearly not between religion and irreligion, although apparently most free-thinkers and their organizations backed the Democrats while the very devout, particularly among the older once-established groups, backed the Whigs.[50] There was, however, considerable congruence between the Jacksonian concern for secular egalitarianism and the struggle against the domination of a theocracy in religion. As McLoughlin puts it: "Here was the essence of the quarrel between the Whigs and the Jacksonians: the fight against aristocracy and privilege in politics had a clear parallel in religion."[51]

While religious and moralistic issues do provide conservative parties in new nations with a popular appeal, they have not usually proven sufficiently strong to permit such parties to hold or win power democratically. Hence many of these parties also adhere to some variant of a socialist program. And the situation in the early United States was somewhat analogous. The Federalists had failed in their efforts to sustain a party which defended aspects of inequality, and their successors sought to learn from their errors.[52] When conservatism revived as a political force in the form of Whig opposition to Andrew Jackson, it had a distinctly "new look." In attacking Jackson, the tribune of the plebs, the new conservatives tried to fix the label of royalist and Tory on him; while it was the term Whig, the title of the opposition to Toryism and royal absolutism in Britain, that was taken by the American conservatives fighting "King Andrew."[53]

---

[49] William G. McLoughlin, Introduction to Charles G. Finney, *Lectures on the Revivals of Religion* (Cambridge, Mass.: Belknap Press of Harvard University Press, 1960), p. xviii.

[50] Benson, *The Concept of Jacksonian Democracy*, pp. 198–207.

[51] McLoughlin, Introduction to Finney, p. xix.

[52] Clinton Rossiter, *Conservatism in America* (New York: Vintage Books, 1962), pp. 117–119.

[53] "The historian of the Whig party in Pennsylvania recognizes that the weakness of the party was traceable mainly to a vague aristocratic reputation which it had, not to the specific points in its program. The Whigs themselves knew this. They tried to steal their opponents' equalitarian thunder by branding the Jacksonian administration itself as 'Federalist'—an epithet which, as Joseph Hopkinson bitterly said, was sufficient by itself to ruin political careers—and by claiming to be the true party of Jefferson." Hartz, *Economic Policy and Democratic Thought*, pp. 24–25.

Whig editor Horace Greeley "began publication of a paper called the

One of the major elements which went into forming the new Whig party was the Anti-Masonic party, an anti-elitist group which had emerged in the late 20's to fight the presumed influence of a Masonic cabal, of which Andrew Jackson was thought to be a member. The complete supremacy of egalitarian values in politics may be seen by the Whig behavior in the Presidential elections of 1840, incidentally the first such contest they were able to win:

> Harrison and Tyler were selected as the party candidates. . . . Webster was rejected on . . . [the] ground he was "aristocratic." This consideration showed how completely the old order had changed. The men of wealth well realized, now that liberty and equality had shown their power, that in enthusiastic profession of fraternity lay their only course of safety. Property rights were secure only when it was realized that in America property was honestly accessible to talent, however humble in its early circumstances. The Whigs found it useful to disavow as vehemently as they could any and all pretensions to a caste superiority in political life. . . .
>
> A fierce rivalry in simplicity sprang up between the parties. Charles Ogle, of Pennsylvania, made a speech in Congress arraigning President Van Buren as a sybarite, who drank Madeira wine, and had made a palace of the people's White House by his enormous expenditures for decoration. This speech, spread throughout the country, was the Whigs' most effective tract. . . . They circulated drawings of the President, pictured as the model of sartorial perfection, seated at his table heaped with massive gold and silver service. . . .
>
> When a Democratic paper in an ill-starred moment made a jest about the obscure Harrison, who, if left alone, would be content with his log cabin and hard cider, the Whigs realized that their opportunity had come. It mattered not that the general really was in fairly comfortable circumstances and had recently been drawing an annual stipend of six thousand dollars; he was to be the log-cabin candidate. It was observed that the Democrats should be discreet in choosing a vice-presidential candidate, for "Mr. Van Buren in consequence of his course of luxurious living to which he is addicted, may pass off any day without a moment's warning." Compare all this, exclaimed the outraged Whigs, with the severe simplicity of Harrison, the farmer of North Bend, whom visitors

Jeffersonian, a name considerably more representative of its humble readers than of its Hamiltonian benefactors." Robert G. Gunderson, *The Log-Cabin Campaign* (Lexington: University of Kentucky Press, 1957), p. 31.

had recently discovered flail in hand, threshing out his grain upon his barn floor.[54]

And in presenting their candidate for Governor in that year, the New York Whig Convention described him as "a true and worthy representative of Democrat-Republican principles, born in the forest of the noble Western region of our own State, trained among an industrious kindred to hardy toil and manual labor on the farm and in the manufactory—democratic in all his associations and sympathies. . . ."[55] Actually, many of the candidates in the Whig party were "gentlemen," men from some of the country's first families.[56] But in keeping with the democratic spirit of the times, they campaigned on a ticket of fraternity and equality, even appealing to class hatred against the elite.

It is important to place these events and doctrines in their historical context. American conservatives during the first half of the nineteenth century had come to recognize that, like it or not, they must operate within the context of a society in which egalitarian values were dominant, and in which both the rights of the people to govern, and of the able to succeed, must be accepted as inviolable. Many Whigs, to be sure, concentrated their egalitarian enthusiasm on the need to make opportunity possible, as distinct from an emphasis on actual equality in social relations. (Thus, Whig leaders such as William Seward in New York, Charles Sumner in Massachusetts, and Thaddeus Stevens in Pennsylvania gave vigorous support to the demand for a state-supported common school education, a demand which earlier had been espoused primarily by the radical Workingmen's parties.) But the important fact is that, for both the Democrats and Whigs, the aristocratic, monarchical, and oligarchic societies of Europe were anathema. Both looked upon the United States as a new social order which should be an example to the downtrodden of the rest of the world. Just as today competing parties in new states are almost automatically "socialist," so American political leaders in the first half-century of our existence were instinctively "democrats,"[57] believing

---

[54] Fox, *The Decline of Aristocracy* . . . , pp. 411–413. For a detailed description of the 1840 campaign, see Gunderson, *The Log-Cabin Campaign*.

[55] Benson, *The Concept of Jacksonian Democracy*, p. 251.

[56] Carl R. Fish, *The Rise of the Common Man 1830–1850* (New York: Macmillan, 1950), p. 165.

[57] For discussion of the predominant liberal ideology in America see Louis Hartz, *The Liberal Tradition in America: An Interpretation of American Political Thought Since the Revolution* (New York: Harcourt, Brace, 1955); and Rossiter, *Conservatism in America*.

that the United States had a special mission to perform in introducing a new form of political order to the world; some even felt that it had an obligation to give moral, financial, and other forms of support to European radicals fighting for republicanism and freedom.[58]

The significance of "leftism" as characterizing the core values in the American political tradition may be best perceived from the vantage point of comparative North American history, that is, from the contrast between Canada and the United States. For though American historians and political philosophers may debate how radical, liberal, leftist, or even conservative American politics has been, there is no doubt in the mind of Canadian historians. Looking at the divergent political history north and south of the border, Canadian historians see their nation as a descendant of the counterrevolution, and the United States as a product of the successful revolution. Once the die was cast, consisting of a triumphant revolution in the thirteen colonies and a failure to the north, an institutional framework was set. Consequent events tended to enforce "leftist" strength in the south and a "rightist" bias in the north.[59] The success of the revolutionary ideology, the defeat of the Tories, and the emigration of many of them north to Canada or across the ocean to Britain, all served to en-

---

[58] For an examination of one effort to press America to further democratic institutions in Europe see the discussion by Curti of "Young America," in *Probing Our Past,* pp. 219–245. This movement, started among Democratic Party intellectuals in the early 1850's, sought to get the United States to strongly support Kossuth and the Hungarian Revolution, as well as other similar European movements. Those involved in it saw the expansion of the American idea in Europe as an extension of the geographical expansion of America that had emerged from the Mexican War.

[59] Tocqueville provides a nice illustration of "casting the die" in the instance of extending electoral rights. "When a nation begins to modify the elective qualification, it may easily be foreseen sooner or later, that qualification will be entirely abolished. There is no more invariable rule in the history of society: the further electoral rights are extended, the greater is the need for extending them; for after each concession the strength of democracy increases, and its demands increase with its strength." He illustrates this process by pointing to Maryland: "The most democratic laws were consequently voted by the very men whose interests they impaired: . . . they [the men with vested interests] themselves accelerated the triumph of the new state of things; so that, by a singular change, the democratic impulse was found to be most irresistible in the very states where the aristocracy had the firmest hold. The state of Maryland, which had been founded by men of rank, was the first to proclaim universal suffrage and to introduce the most democratic forms into the whole of its government." Alexis de Tocqueville, *Democracy in America* (New York: Vintage Books, 1954), Vol. I, pp. 54, 58.

hance the strength of the forces favoring egalitarian democratic principles in the new nation, and to weaken conservative tendencies. On the other hand, the failure of Canada to have a revolution of its own, the immigration of conservative elements and the emigration of radical elements, and the success of colonial Toryism in erecting a conservative class structure all contributed to making Canada a more conservative and rigidly stratified society. Frank Underhill has pointed to some effects of the failure of the doctrines of the French and American revolutions to dominate in Canada:

> For this weakness of the Left in Canada, the ultimate explanation would seem to be that we never had an eighteenth century of our own. The intellectual life of our politics has not been periodically revived by fresh drafts from the invigorating fountain of eighteenth century Enlightenment. In Catholic French Canada the doctrines of the rights of man and of Liberty, Equality, Fraternity were rejected from the start, and to this day they have never penetrated, save surreptitiously or spasmodically. All effective liberal and radical [North American] democratic movements in the nineteenth century have had their roots in this fertile eighteenth-century soil. But our ancestors made the great refusal in the eighteenth century. In Canada we have no revolutionary tradition. . . .[60]

Another Canadian historian, A. R. M. Lower, has also emphasized the way in which the different results of the American Revolution affected the two nations which emerged from the British North American colonies:

> [C]olonial Toryism made its second attempt to erect on American soil a copy of the English social edifice. From one point of view this is the most significant thing about the loyalist movement; it withdrew a class concept of life from the south, moved it up north and gave it a second chance. . . . Canada in time came to be almost as wide a popular democracy as the United States itself: though a much more conservative one, for a country founded to preserve the old order against the new must necessarily be conservative.[61]

---

[60] Frank H. Underhill, *In Search of Canadian Liberalism* (Toronto: Macmillan, 1960), p. 12.
[61] A. R. M. Lower, *Colony to Nation: A History of Canada* (Toronto: Longmans, Green, 1946), pp. 114, 120.

The Canadian sociologist S. D. Clark has pointed to various other developments in the two nations which served to emphasize the variations in political and class values between them. He documents, for example, the change in religious behavior among the New England colonies. In Nova Scotia, part of New England before the Revolution, the victory of the English as a result of their control of the sea sharply affected the churches: "The institution which dominated in the life of the vast majority of Nova Scotians before 1775 was the Congregational Church and it came out almost solidly on the side of the Revolution." But with the failure of the revolutionists, many Congregationalist pastors fled south to American territory, and the Church of England ultimately became dominant in the province.[62]

In any evaluation of the consequences of establishing the new American nation through a revolution, it is important to remember that this revolution had its social and economic aspects as well as political. The English historian Frank Thistlethwaite has pointed up many of the changes that revolution wrought:

> . . . In the *élan* of their success the insurgents consolidated their control and in each of the new States proceeded to transform institutional life to fit their beliefs and interests.
>
> . . . The old colonial assemblies were transformed into virtually sovereign State legislatures more directly representing the interests of the mass of small farmers. Constituencies were reorganized to give a greater measure of equality to the back country. . . .
>
> They confiscated the Crown lands and most of the Tory estates, large and small, redistributing some of the land to small farmers and old soldiers. They abolished quit-rents, entails, primogeniture and titles of nobility. . . . Henceforward the aggregation of great estates, which remained a typical feature of American growth, had no longer as its sanction customary privilege with attendant duties, but property right. The change loosened the social bond between landlord and tenant; it increased the mobility of real estate and shifted the basis of proprietorship from social position to mere wealth. . . .
>
> The radicals also disestablished the Church of England where established. The new Episcopalian body, bereft of its ancient authority as the corporate, and indeed catholic, Church of a total society, was reduced to the somewhat anomalous position of being merely another independent sect, cherished among the conservative and

62 S. D. Clark, *Movements of Political Protest in Canada 1640–1840* (Toronto: University of Toronto Press, 1959), pp. 111–112.

well-to-do, but insignificant in the religious life of America as a whole.[63]

The cultural and institutional differences between the United States and Canada offer a useful basis from which to estimate the extent to which the revolutionary break from colonial rule, with its concomitant legitimation of various egalitarian ideologies and institutions as part of the national value system, has been a major determining factor in shaping the national ethos, as contrasted with the effects of such factors as an "open frontier," the absence of European feudalism and primogeniture, and so forth. Canada shares with the United States many of the same ecological conditions, but differs in the way its national identity was established. And though Canada is more similar to the United States in many ways than it is to Britain or other European nations, it also differs sharply from the United States in being a more conservative country culturally, and a more steeply stratified nation in terms of its society and polity.[64]

Conversely, American political and social history illustrates the effect of a nation operating within the context of a tradition in which liberal and egalitarian values are part of the definition of nationhood itself. The German sociologist Ralf Dahrendorf catches the essence of the relationship between the American value system and its revolutionary origins in his commentary on Richard Hofstadter's estimate of William Graham Sumner's conservative doctrines. Hofstadter says of the great nineteenth-century conservative American thinker: "we may wonder whether, in the entire history of thought, there was ever a conservatism so utterly progressive as this." Dahrendorf agrees with this as an evaluation of "conservatism" in America. And he goes on to suggest that our conservative values "are characterised by the desire to preserve progress rather than to preserve any particular state of affairs." And since all Americans are, ideologically speaking, descendants of revolutionaries, Americans both of the left and right remain utopian. It is probably the only *developed*

---

[63] Frank Thistlethwaite, *The Great Experiment* (New York: Cambridge University Press, 1955), pp. 38–41. The classic statement elaborating the radical character and consequences of the American Revolution is, of course, that of J. Franklin Jameson, *The American Revolution Considered as a Social Movement* (Princeton: Princeton University Press, 1926). This monograph, which appeared in 1925, was reevaluated in light of subsequent historical research; Frederick Tolles concludes: "Basically, the 'Jameson thesis' is still sound. . . ." See Tolles, "The American Revolution considered as a Social Movement: A Re-evaluation," *American Historical Review*, 60 (1954), pp. 1–12.

[64] These differences are discussed in more detail in Chapter 7.

country in the world "in which there are many who believe that Utopia can come true."[65]

Conclusion

All states that have recently gained independence are faced with two interrelated problems, legitimating the use of political power and establishing national identity. And if it is a democratic polity they seek to establish, they must develop institutional and normative constraints upon efforts to inhibit organized opposition or to deny civil liberties to individual critics of those in power.

This section has explored ways in which these problems were confronted in the early history of the United States. National identity was formed under the aegis, first of a charismatic authority figure, and later under the leadership of a dominant "left wing" or revolutionary party led successively by three Founding Fathers. The pressures in new nations to outlaw opposition movements were reduced in America by the rapid decline of the conservative opposition. The revolutionary, democratic values that thus became part of the national self-image, and the basis for its authority structure, gained legitimacy as they proved effective—that is, as the nation prospered.

The need to establish stable authority and a sense of identity led the leaders of the United States to resist efforts by "old states" to involve the young nation in their quarrels. But at the same time that Americans rejected "foreign entanglements," they clearly used the Old World as both a negative and a positive point of reference, rejecting its political and class structures as backward, but nevertheless viewing its cultural and economic achievements as worthy of emulation. The intellectuals in particular expressed this ambivalence, since they played a major role in establishing and defining the state; but they then found that the task of operating and even living in it required them to conform to vulgar populist and provincial values.

In specifying those processes in the evolution of the first new nation that are comparable to what has been taking place in the societies of Asia and Africa in our own time, I am relying upon analogy. It ought

---

[65] Ralf Dahrendorf, "European Sociology and the American Self-Image," *European Journal of Sociology*, 2 (1961), pp. 357, 364; see also Arthur Schlesinger, Sr., *New Viewpoints in American History* (New York: Macmillan, 1922).

to go without saying that: "We cannot assume that because conditions in one century led to certain effects, even roughly parallel conditions in another century would lead to similar effects. Neither can we be sure, of course, that the conditions were even roughly parallel."[66] It is fairly obvious that conditions in the early United States were quite different from those faced by most of the new nations of today. Many of the internal conditions that hamper the evolution of stable authority and a unifying sense of national identity in the new nations of the twentieth century were much less acute in the early United States. But the evidence suggests that despite its advantages, the United States came very close to failing in its effort to establish a unified legitimate authority. The first attempt to do so in 1783, following on Independence, was a failure. The second and successful effort was endangered by frequent threats of secession and the open flaunting of central authority until the Civil War. The advantages which the early United States possessed, as compared with most of the contemporary new states, then, only show more strongly how significant the similarities are.

There were other American advantages that should be mentioned. Although internal conflicts stemming from attitudes toward the French Revolution disrupted the young American polity, there was no worldwide totalitarian conspiracy seeking to upset political and economic development from within, and holding up an alternative model of seemingly successful economic growth through the use of authoritarian methods. Also the absence of rapid mass communication systems meant that Americans were relatively isolated, and hence did not immediately compare their conditions with those in the more developed countries. The United States did not so urgently face a "revolution of rising expectations" based on the knowledge that life is much better elsewhere. The accepted concepts of natural or appropriate rights did not include a justification of the lower classes' organized participation in the polity to gain higher income, welfare support from the state, and the like. And whatever the exaggeration in the effects frequently attributed to the existence of an open land frontier, there can be little doubt that it contributed to social stability.

Internal value cleavages, which frustrate contemporary new nations, were comparatively less significant in young America. Shils points out

---

[66] Karl W. Deutsch, S. A. Burrell, R. A. Kann, M. Lee, Jr., M. Lichterman, R. E. Lindgren, F. L. Loewenheim, R. W. Van Wagenen, *Political Community and the North Atlantic Area* (Princeton, N.J.: Princeton University Press, 1957), p. 11.

that in today's new nations "the parochialism of kinship, caste and locality makes it difficult to create stable and coherent nation-wide parties."[67] None of these parochialisms was as strong in the United States which was formed by a relatively homogeneous population with a common language, a relatively similar religious background (although denominational differences did cause some problems), and a common cultural and political tradition.

American social structure did not possess those great "gaps" which, in the contemporary new states, "conspire to separate the ordinary people from their government."[68] The culture with which the educated identified contrasted less strongly with that of the uneducated. The ideology in the name of which America made its revolution was less alien to prevailing modes of thought than some of today's revolutionary creeds. Perhaps most important, the class structure of America, even before the establishment of the new nation, came closer to meeting the conditions for a stable democracy than do those of the new nations of our time—or, indeed, than those of the Old World at that time. Writing shortly before Independence was finally attained, Crèvecoeur, though sympathetic to the Tory cause, pointed up the egalitarianism of American society:

> The rich and the poor are not so far removed from each other as they are in Europe. . . . A pleasing uniformity of decent competence appears throughout our habitations. . . . It must take some time ere he [the foreign traveler] can reconcile himself to our dictionary, which is but short in words of dignity, and names of honor. . . . Here man is as free as he ought to be; nor is this pleasing equality so transitory as many others are.[69]

The ability to work the institutions of a democratic nation requires sophistication both at the elite level and the level of the citizenry at large. And as Carl Bridenbaugh has well demonstrated, the America of revolutionary times was not a colonial backwater.[70] Philadelphia was the second largest English city—only London surpassed it in numbers. Philadelphia

---

[67] Edward Shils, "The Military in the Political Development of the New States" in John J. Johnson, *The Role of the Military in Underdeveloped Countries* (Princeton, N.J.: Princeton University Press, 1962), p. 14.

[68] *Ibid.*, p. 29.

[69] J. Hector St. John Crèvecoeur, *Letters from an American Farmer* (New York: Dolphin Books, n. d.), pp. 46–47.

[70] Carl Bridenbaugh, *Rebels and Gentlemen, Philadelphia in the Age of Franklin* (New York: Reynal and Hitchcock, 1942).

and other colonial American capitals were centers of relatively high culture at this time: they had universities and learned societies, and their elite was in touch with, and contributed to, the intellectual and scientific life of Britain.

In this respect, the political traditions that the American colonists held in common, were of particular importance since they included the concept of the rule of law, and even of constitutionalism. Each colony operated under a charter which defined and limited governmental powers. Although colonial subjects, Americans were also Englishmen and were thus accustomed to the rights and privileges of Englishmen. Through their local governments they actually possessed more rights than did most of the residents of Britain itself. In a sense, even before independence, Americans met a basic condition for democratic government, the ability to operate its fundamental institutions.[71]

> It requires, not only efficient administration, but an independent judiciary with high professional standards and, in all branches of government, a scrupulous respect for rules, written and unwritten, governing the exercise of power. What these rules are must be known to more people than those who actually have the power supposed to be limited by these rules, and it must be possible to lodge effective complaints against those people who are suspected of breaking the rules. This means that there must be, in the broad sense, constitutional government.[72]

In many contemporary new nations, a potentially politically powerful military class, who have a patriotic, national outlook, may use the army to seize power if it becomes impatient with civilian leadership.[73] When the United States was seeking to establish a national authority, it was not bedeviled by such a class. The entire army in 1789 consisted of 672 men; and even after a decade of threats of war, there were only 3,429 soldiers in 1800. The potential military strength was, of course, much larger, for it included various state militia reserves. The latter, however, were simply the citizenry, and as long as the government had the loyalty of the general population, it had no need to fear its professional soldiers.[74]

---

[71] See John Plamenatz, *On Alien Rule and Self Government* (New York: Longman's, Green, 1960), pp. 47–48.

[72] *Ibid.*, p. 51.

[73] Shils, "The Military . . . ," *op. cit.*, p. 40.

[74] James R. Jacobs, *The Beginning of the U. S. Army, 1783–1812* (Princeton, N.J.: Princeton University Press, 1947); see also Deutsch, *et al.*, *Political Community and the North Atlantic Area*, p. 26.

Of great significance in facilitating America's development as a nation, both politically and economically, was the fact that the weight of ancient tradition which is present in almost all of the contemporary new states was largely absent. It was not only a new nation, it was a new society, much less bound to the customs and values of the past than any nation of Europe. Crèvecoeur well described the American as a "new man," the likes of which had never been seen before.[75]

Religion, of course, may be viewed as a "traditional" institution which played an important role in the United States. But in the first half-decade of the American Republic, as we have seen, the defenders of religious traditionalism were seriously weakened, as the various state churches— Anglican in the South and Congregationalist in New England—were gradually disestablished. Moreover, the new United States was particularly fortunate in the religious traditions which it did inherit. Calvinistic Puritanism, which was stronger in the colonies than in the mother country, was not as "uncongenial to modernity" as are some of the traditional beliefs inherited by new nations today. A positive orientation toward savings and hard work, and the strong motivation to achieve high positions that derives from this religious tradition, have been seen as causes of the remarkable economic expansion that made possible the legitimation of equalitarian values and democratic government. Max Weber, the most prominent exponent of the thesis that ascetic Protestantism played a major role in the development of capitalism in the Western world, argued that "one must never overlook that without the universal diffusion of these qualities and principles of a methodical way of life, qualities which were maintained through these [Calvinist] religious communities, capitalism, today, even in America, would not be what it is. . . ."[76] Calvinism's "insistence that one's works were signs of eternal grace or damnation" has been transformed into a secular emphasis upon achievement.[77]

---

[75] "What then is the American, this new man . . . ? He is an American, who leaving behind him all his ancient prejudices and manners, receives new ones from the new mode of life he has embraced. . . . He becomes an American by being received in the broad lap of our great *Alma Mater*. The American is a new man, who acts upon new principles; he must therefore entertain new ideas and form new opinions." Crèvecoeur, *Letters from an American Farmer*, pp. 49–50.

[76] Max Weber, "The Protestant Sects and the Spirit of Capitalism," in *Essays in Sociology*, translated by Hans Gerth and C. W. Mills (New York: Oxford University Press, 1946), pp. 309, 313.

[77] Robin Williams, *American Society* (New York: Alfred A. Knopf, 1957), p. 313.

Other Puritan influences on American development have perhaps not been sufficiently emphasized. As Richard Schlatter has pointed out in a recent summary of the researches on this subject, the Puritan tradition involved a respect for learning which led to the establishment of schools and universities on a scale that surpassed England.[78] The opportunities for learning thus created, and the pressures for widespread education that equalitarian values implied,[79] led to a wide distribution of literacy. The census of 1840 reported only 9 per cent of the white population twenty years old and over as illiterate.[80]

The Puritan tradition may also have made it easier to legitimize American democracy as the rule of law. Tocqueville saw the special need of an egalitarian and democratic society for a self-restraining value system that would inhibit the tyranny of the majority, a function supposedly once fulfilled in the European societies by a secure and sophisticated aristocratic elite. In a democracy only religion could play this role, and therefore the less coercive the political institutions of such a society, the more it has need for a system of common belief to help restrict the actions of the rulers and the electorate. As he put it:

> But the revolutionists of America are obliged to profess an ostensible respect for Christian morality and equity, which does not permit

---

[78] Richard Schlatter, "The Puritan Strain," in John Higham, ed., *The Reconstruction of American History* (New York: Harper & Bros., 1962), pp. 39–42. See also Bernard Bailyn, *Education in the Forming of American Society* (Chapel Hill: The University of North Carolina Press, 1960), for a discussion of the influence which the multiplication of numerous sects by the eve of the Revolution had upon the spread of education. The promotional and propagandizing possibilities of education made it an instrument of survival among competing sects. "Sectarian groups, without regard to the intellectual complexity of their doctrine or to their views on the value of learning to religion, became dynamic elements in the spread of education, spawning schools of all sorts, continuously, competitively in all their settlements; carrying education into the remote frontiers." Bailyn, pp. 40–41.

[79] "What strikes one most forcibly about the Puritans' efforts in education is the expectation of uniformity. Every family, without regard to its fortunes and the accomplishment of its head, and every town, without regard to its condition or resources, was expected to provide an equal minimum of education—for who, in what place, should be exempt from the essential work of life? . . . the quest for salvation . . . this was an occupation without limit, in the proper training for which all were expected to join equally, without regard to natural ability and worldly circumstance." Bailyn, *op. cit.*, p. 81.

[80] Bureau of the Census, *A Statistical Abstract Supplement, Historical Statistics of the U.S. Colonial Times to 1957* (Washington: 1957), p. 214. The census of 1840 was the first to report literacy.

them to violate wantonly the laws that oppose their designs; nor would they find it easy to surmount the scruples of their partisans even if they were able to get over their own. . . . Thus while the law permits Americans to do what they please, religion prevents them from conceiving, and forbids them to commit, what is rash or unjust.[81]

While Tocqueville pointed out that Catholicism was not necessarily incompatible with democratic or egalitarian values, since "it confounds all the distinctions of society at the foot of the same altar," he describes the "form of Christianity" in early America as "a democratic and republican religion."[82] It would indeed seem that the Calvinistic-Puritan tradition was particularly valuable in training men to the sort of self-restraint that Tocqueville felt was necessary for democracy. By making every man God's agent, ascetic Protestantism made each individual responsible for the state of morality in the society; and by making the congregation a disciplinary agent it helped to prevent any one individual from assuming that his brand of morality was better than others.[83]

Puritanism had been associated with the movement of the squirearchy for political recognition in England. As Trevelyan has put it:

> Under Elizabeth the increasing Puritanism of the squires introduced a new element. The fear and love of God began to strive with the fear and love of the Queen in the breast of the Parliament men. . . . Protestantism and Parliamentary privilege were already closely connected, before even the first Stuart came to trouble [the] still further seething waters [of Cromwell's rebellion].[84]

So that, as Schlatter has pointed out, the Puritan tradition implied a concern for "constitutionalism and limited government," as well as a belief "that they are a peculiar people, destined by Providence to live in a more perfect community than any known in the Old World. . . ."[85]

In establishing its identity, the new America quickly came to see itself, and to be perceived by others, as a radical society in which con-

---

[81] Tocqueville, *Democracy in America*, Vol. I, p. 316.

[82] *Ibid.*, p. 311.

[83] Williams, *American Society*, p. 312.

[84] G. M. Trevelyan, *History of England* (Garden City, N.Y.: Doubleday Anchor Books, 1954), Vol. II, pp. 143–144.

[85] Schlatter, "The Puritan Strain," *op. cit.*, p. 42.

servatism and traditionalism had no proper place. The religious traditions on which it drew stressed that it was to be different from European nations. But its really radical character derived from its revolutionary origins.

The political scientist Clinton Rossiter has described the effects of the revolution on the political ideologies of the nation in explaining why conservatism as a doctrine is weak in America:

> The reason the American Right is not Conservative today is that it has not been Conservative for more than a hundred years. . . .
> Conservatism first emerged to meet the challenge of democracy. In countries like England it was able to survive the rise of this new way of life by giving way a little at a time under its relentless pounding, but in America the triumph of democracy was too sudden and complete. It came to society as well as to politics; it came early in the history of the Republic and found the opposition only half dug in. . . . The result was a disaster for genuine, old-country Conservatism. Nowhere in the world did the progressive, optimistic, egalitarian mode of thinking invade so completely the mind of an entire people. Nowhere was the Right forced so abruptly into such an untenable position. If there is any single quality that the Right seems always and everywhere to cultivate, it is unquestioning patriotism, and this, in turn, calls for unquestioning devotion to the nation's ideals. The long-standing merger of "America" and "democracy" has meant that to profess Conservatism is to be something less than "one hundred per cent American"; indeed, it is to question the nation's destiny. Worse than that, this merger has doomed outspoken Conservatism to political failure.[86]

From Tocqueville and Martineau in the 1830's to Gunnar Myrdal in more recent times, foreign visitors have been impressed by the extent to which the values proclaimed in the Declaration of Independence have operated to prescribe social and political behavior. And the legitimacy which the American authority structure ultimately attained has been based on the assumption that as a nation it is dedicated to equality and to liberty, to the fulfillment of its original political objectives.

As Frank Thistlethwaite put it a few years ago:

> In the mid-twentieth century the American people still pursue their Revolutionary ideal: a Republic established in the belief that men of good will could voluntarily come together in the sanctuary of an

---

[86] Rossiter, *Conservatism in America,* pp. 201–202.

American wilderness to order their common affairs according to rational principles; a dedicated association in which men participate not by virtue of being born into it as heirs of immemorial custom, but by virtue of free choice, of the will to affirm certain sacred principles; a community of the uprooted, of migrants who have turned their back on the past in which they were born; . . . a society fluid and experimental, uncommitted to rigid values, cherishing freedom of will and choice and bestowing all the promise of the future on those with the manhood to reject the past.[87]

---

[87] Thistlethwaite, *The Great Experiment*, pp. 319–320.

STABILITY
IN THE MIDST
OF CHANGE

PART **II**

A Changing
American
Character?

3

★★

Two themes, equality and achievement, emerged from the interplay
between the Puritan tradition and the Revolutionary ethos in the early
formation of America's institutions. In this section the thesis is advanced
that the dynamic interaction of these two predominant values has been a
constant element in determining American institutions and behavior.
As we have seen, equalitarianism was an explicit part of the revolt
against the traditions of the Old World, while an emphasis upon success
and hard work had long been a part of the Protestant ethic. In addition,
the need to maximize talent in the new nation's search to "overtake"
the Old World placed an added premium on an individual's achievement,
regardless of his social station. The relatively few changes that Andrew
Jackson made in the civil service, despite his aggressive equalitarian ethos,
and the fact that his appointments were well-trained, highly educated
men, show that ability was valued along with equality in the young
republic.[1]

---

[1] See Erik M. Erikkson, "The Federal Civil Service Under President Jackson,"
Mississippi Valley Historical Review, 13 (1927), pp. 517–540. Erikkson demonstrates convincingly that Jackson did not inaugurate a spoils system, that
relatively few civil servants were fired after he took office. His conclusions
have been reiterated recently in a detailed analysis of the backgrounds of the
upper echelons of government under Jackson. Sidney Aronson agrees with
Erikkson that there was little turnover when Jackson took office. Both men
point to the fact that the changes introduced by Jefferson were about as great

The relationship between these themes of equality and success has been complex. On the one hand, the ideal of equal opportunity institutionalized the notion that success should be the goal of *all*, without reference to accidents of birth or class or color. On the other hand, in actual operation these two dominant values resulted in considerable conflict. While everyone was supposed to succeed, obviously certain persons were able to achieve greater success than others. The wealth of the nation was never distributed as equally as the political franchise. The tendency for the ideal of achievement to undermine the fact of equality, and to bring about a society with a distinct class character, has been checked by the recurrent victories of the forces of equality in the political order. Much of our political history, as Tocqueville noted, can be interpreted in terms of a struggle between proponents of democratic equality and would-be aristocracies of birth or wealth.[2]

In recent years, many social analysts have sought to show how the increasing industrialization, urbanization, and bureaucratization of American society have modified the values of equality and achievement. In both the 1930's and the 1950's American social scientists were certain that the country was undergoing major structural changes. In the 1930's they were sure that these changes were making status lines more rigid, that there was a movement away from achieved status back to ascribed status, and that the equalitarian ethic was threatened as a consequence.[3] Such typical writers of the 1950's as David Riesman and William H. Whyte contend that it is the achievement motive and the Protestant ethic of hard work that are dying: they think that the new society prefers security, emotional stability, and "getting along with others." Riesman posits a transformation of the American character structure from "inner direction" (i.e., responding to a fixed internal code of morality) to "other direction" (i.e., responding to demands of others in complex situations).[4] Whyte believes that values

---

as by Jackson. Aronson also demonstrates that Jackson's appointees were highly qualified men, that most of them were college graduates in an age when the total number of such graduates was insignificant. See Sidney Aronson, *Status and Kinship in the Higher Civil Service: The Administrations of John Adams, Thomas Jefferson and Andrew Jackson* (doctoral dissertation, Columbia University Department of Sociology, 1961).

[2] Alexis de Tocqueville, *Democracy in America* (New York: Vintage Books, 1955), Vol. I, pp. 185–186.

[3] These studies of the 1930's are discussed at the end of this chapter in more detail.

[4] David Riesman, *The Lonely Crowd* (New Haven, Conn.: Yale University Press, 1950).

themselves have changed. He argues that the old value system of the Protestant ethic, which he defines as the "pursuit of individual salvation through hard work, thrift, and competitive struggle," is being replaced by the "social ethic," whose basic tenets are a "belief in the group as the source of creativity; a belief in 'belongingness' as the ultimate need of the individual; and a belief in the application of science to achieve the belongingness."[5]

If the changes suggested by the critics of the 1930's or the 1950's were occurring in the drastic form indicated in their books, then America no longer could be said to possess the traits formed as a consequence of its origin as a new nation with a Protestant culture. As I read the historical record, however, it suggests that there is more continuity than change with respect to the main elements in the national value system. This does not mean that our society is basically static. Clearly, there have been great secular changes—industrialization, bureaucratization, and urbanization are real enough—and they have profoundly affected other aspects of the social structure. Many American sociologists have documented changes in work habits, leisure, personality, family patterns, and so forth. But this very concentration on the obvious social changes in a society that has spanned a continent in a century, that has moved from a predominantly rural culture as recently as 1870 to a metropolitan culture in the 1950's, has introduced a fundamental bias against looking at what has been relatively constant and unchanging.

Basic alterations of social character or values are rarely produced by change in the means of production, distribution, and exchange alone. Rather, as a society becomes more complex, its institutional arrangements make adjustments to new conditions within the framework of a dominant value system. In turn, the new institutional patterns may affect the socialization process which, from infancy upward, instills fundamental character traits. Through such a process, changes in the dominant value system develop slowly—or not at all. There are constant efforts to fit the "new" technological world into the social patterns of the old, familiar world.

In this section I examine the thesis that a fundamental change has occurred in American society by treating three topics, each of which has been widely discussed as reflecting important modifications in the basic value system. This chapter deals with the arguments and evidence of

---

[5] William H. Whyte, *The Organization Man* (New York: Simon & Schuster 1956).

changes in the basic predominant character traits of Americans as suggested by men like David Riesman and William Whyte. The following chapter, 4, examines the evidence of major changes in religious participation and belief, since many have argued that American religion, the institution most closely identified with values, is much different from what it was in the nineteenth century. And the last chapter of the section, 5, analyzes an institution which has become significant only in this century, and especially in the past three decades: the trade union. Trade unions are given special treatment because the growth of these "class" organizations has suggested to some that the United States is finally entering the era of working-class consciousness as a result of the hardening of class lines, and that we are witnessing the end of the emphases on achievement and equality.

In brief, I attempt in this section to present some of the evidence for my thesis that it is the basic value system, as solidified in the early days of the new nation, which can account for the kinds of changes that have taken place in the American character and in American institutions as these faced the need to adjust to the requirements of an urban, industrial, and bureaucratic society.

Marcus Cunliffe has remarked on the American tendency to assert that a wondrous opportunity has been ruined, "that a golden age has been tarnished, that the old ways have disappeared, or that they offer no useful guide to a newer generation."[6] He points out that, American belief to the contrary, there has been surprising continuity in American history as compared with the histories of European nations. This American propensity to feel that the country is going through a major change at any "present time" is related to an almost "inherent American tendency to believe that one has been cut off decisively from the past as if by a physical barrier." Cunliffe attributes this tendency to three main elements:

> First it is a consequence of the undeniable fact of continuous and rapid social change since the origins of settlement. This process has, understandably, revealed itself in regrets and neuroses as well as in pride and exuberance. Second, the tendency is rooted in the constant American determination to repudiate Europe—Europe equated with the Past, in contrast with America as the Future—and so to lose the Past altogether. Third, the tendency is a consequence of the American sense of a society which is uniquely free to choose its own destiny. The sense of mission, of dedication and of infinite possi-

---

[6] Marcus Cunliffe, "American Watersheds," *American Quarterly*, 13 (1961), pp. 479–494.

bility, in part a fact and in part an article of faith, has led to acute if temporary despairs, to suspicions of betrayal and the like, as well as to more positive and flamboyant results.[7]

In a sense, Cunliffe's analysis shows how some of the values we have seen arising from America's revolutionary origins continue to be a part of its image of itself. And perhaps more important, his observation that there has been more continuity in American history than in European history suggests that the values around which American institutions are built have not changed abruptly. Others have pointed out that America is an example of a country where social change does not have to destroy the fabric of society, precisely because it is based upon an ideological commitment to change.[8]

The thesis that the same basic values which arose in the American Revolution have shaped the society under changing geographical and economic conditions, has also been advanced by many historians. Thus Henry Nash Smith has sought to show how the rural frontier settlements established in the West on the Great Plains reflected not only the physical environment but also "the assumptions and aspirations of a whole society."[9] He has argued that revisions in the Homestead Act, which would have permitted large farms and a more economical use of arid land, were opposed by the new settlers because they believed in the ideal of the family farm. Walt Rostow suggests there is a "classic American style [which] . . . emerged distinctively toward the end of the seventeenth century as the imperatives and opportunities of a wild but ample land began to assert themselves over various transplanted autocratic attitudes and institutions which proved inappropriate to the colonial scene . . . [and] came fully to life . . . after the War of 1812." And he further contends that this style has not changed basically, since "the cast of American values and institutions and the tendency to adapt them by cumulative experiment rather than to change them radically has been progressively strengthened by the image of the gathering success of the American adventure."[10] Commager, writing of America in general, has said: "Circum-

---

[7] *Ibid.,* pp. 489–490.

[8] Daniel Bell, "The Theory of Mass Society," *Commentary,* 22 (1956), pp. 75–83.

[9] Henry Nash Smith, *Virgin Land: The American West as Symbol and Myth* (Cambridge, Mass.: Harvard University Press, 1950), p. 124; for a similar point see George W. Pierson, "The Frontier and American Institutions," *New England Quarterly,* 15 (1942), p. 253.

[10] W. W. Rostow, "The National Style," in Elting E. Morison, ed., *The American Style: Essays in Value and Performance* (New York: Harper & Bros., 1958), pp. 247, 259.

stances change profoundly, but the character of the American people has not changed greatly or the nature of the principles of conduct, public and private, to which they subscribe."[11] Three books dealing with American values, by Daniel Boorstin, Louis Hartz, and Ralph Gabriel, have each, in a different way, argued the effective continuity of the fundamental ideals of the society.[12]

The conclusions of these historians are affirmed also in a "lexicographic analysis of alleged American characteristics, ideals, and principles" reported in a myriad of books and articles dealing with "the American way." American history was divided for the purposes of the study into four periods, "Pre-Civil War (to 1865), Civil War to World War (1866–1917), World War to Depression (1918–1929), and Depression to present (1930–1940)." For each period a list of traits alleged by observers was recorded, and "when the lists for each of the four time periods were compared, no important difference between the traits mentioned by modern observers and those writing in the earlier periods of American history was discovered." Among the traits mentioned in all four periods were: "Belief in equality of all as a fact and as a right" and "uniformity and conformity."[13]

The Unchanging American Character

Foreign travelers' accounts of American life, manners, and character traits constitute a body of evidence with which to test the thesis that the American character has been transformed during the past century and a

---

[11] Henry Steele Commager, *Living Ideas in America* (New York: Harper & Bros., 1951), p. xviii. In the introduction to a collection of the writings of foreign observers, Commager reported also that "a real unity emerges from these heterogeneous selections . . . implicit in the material itself. . . . To the visitors of the seventeen-seventies and the nineteen-forties, America *meant* much the same thing. *America in Perspective* (New York: Random House, 1947), p. xvi. (Emphasis in original.)

[12] See Daniel Boorstin, *The Genius of American Politics* (Chicago: University of Chicago Press, 1953), and his *The Lost World of Thomas Jefferson* (New York: Holt, 1948); Louis M. Hartz, *The Liberal Tradition in America: An Interpretation of American Political Thought since the Revolution* (New York: Harcourt, Brace, 1955); and Ralph H. Gabriel, *The Course of American Democratic Thought* (New York: Ronald Press, 1956). Boorstin sees these values or basic premises as "naturalism." Hartz calls his version "liberalism," while Gabriel speaks of a "democratic faith" with three aspects.

[13] Lee Coleman, "What is America? A Study of Alleged American Traits," *Social Forces,* 19 (1941), pp. 492–499.

half. Their observations provide us with a kind of comparative mirror in which we can look at ourselves over time. It is important to note, therefore, that the type of behavior which Riesman and Whyte regard as distinctly modern, as reflecting the decline of the Protestant Ethic, was repeatedly reported by many of the nineteenth-century travelers as a peculiarly American trait in their day. Thus the English writer Harriet Martineau at times might be paraphrasing *The Lonely Crowd* in her description of the American of the 1830's:

> [Americans] may travel over the world, and find no society but their own which will submit to the restraint of perpetual caution, and reference to the opinions of others. They may travel over the whole world, and find no country but their own where the very children beware of getting into scrapes, and talk of the effect of actions upon people's minds; where the youth of society determine in silence what opinions they shall bring forward, and what avow only in the family circle; where women write miserable letters, almost universally, because it is a settled matter that it is unsafe to commit oneself on paper; and where elderly people seem to lack almost universally that faith in principles which inspires a free expression of them at any time, and under all circumstances. . . .
>
> There is fear of vulgarity, fear of responsibility; and above all, fear of singularity. . . . There is something little short of disgusting to the stranger who has been unused to witness such want of social confidence, in the caution which presents probably the strongest aspect of selfishness that he has ever seen. The Americans of the northern states are, from education and habit, as accustomed to the caution of which I speak, as to be unaware of its extent and singularity. . . .
>
> Few persons [Americans] really doubt this when the plain case is set down before them. They agree to it in church on Sundays, and in conversation by the fireside: and the reason why they are so backward as they are to act upon it in the world, is that habit and education are too strong for them. They have worn their chains so long that they feel them less than might be supposed.[14]

Harriet Martineau is only one observer of early American life, and not necessarily more reliable than others. But it is significant that her comments on American "other-directedness" and conformism do not flow, as do those of other nineteenth-century visitors who made com-

---

[14] Harriet Martineau, *Society in America* (New York: Saunders and Otlay, 1837), Vol. III, pp. 14–15, 17.

parable observations, from fear or dislike of democracy. Many upper-
class visitors, such as Tocqueville or Ostrogorski, saw here a threat to
genuine individuality and creativity in political and intellectual life, in
that democracy and equalitarianism give the masses access to elites, so that
the latter must be slaves to public opinion in order to survive. Harriet
Martineau, as a left-wing English liberal, did not come to America with
such fears or beliefs. She remained an ardent admirer of American
democracy, even though she ultimately decided that "the worship of
Opinion is, at this day, the established religion of the United States."[15]

The most celebrated post-Civil War nineteenth-century English visitor
to America, James Bryce, saw inherent in American society "self-distrust,
a despondency, a disposition to fall into line, to acquiesce in the dominant
opinion. . . ." This "tendency to acquiescence and submission" is not to
be "confounded with the tyranny of the majority. . . . [It] does not
imply any compulsion exerted by the majority," in the sense discussed
by Tocqueville. Rather Bryce, like Harriet Martineau fifty years earlier,
described what he felt to be a basic psychological trait of Americans,
their "fatalism," which involved a "loss of resisting power, a diminished
sense of personal responsibility, and of the duty to battle for one's own
opinions. . . ."[16]

Although Harriet Martineau and James Bryce stand out among nineteenth-century visitors in specifying that these other-directed traits were
deeply rooted in the *personalities* of many Americans, the general
behaviors that they and Tocqueville reported were mentioned by many
other foreign travelers. For example, a summary of the writings of
English travelers from 1785 to 1835 states that one important characteristic mentioned in a number of books "was the acute sensitiveness to
opinion that the average American revealed."[17] A German aristocrat, who
became a devotee of American democracy and a citizen of the country,
stated in the 1830's that "nothing can excite the contempt of an educated
European more than the continual fears and apprehensions in which even
the 'most enlightened citizens' of the United States seem to live with
regard to their next neighbors, lest their actions, principles, opinions and
beliefs should be condemned by their fellow creatures."[18] An interpreter

---

[15] *Ibid.*, p. 7.

[16] James Bryce, *The American Commonwealth* (New York: Macmillan,
1912), Vol. II, pp. 351–352.

[17] Jane L. Mesick, *The English Traveller in America 1785–1835* (New York:
Columbia University Press, 1922), p. 301.

[18] Francis J. Grund, *Aristocracy in America* (New York: Harper Torchbooks, 1959), p. 162; see also pp. 52 and 157 for further comments.

of nineteenth-century foreign opinion, John Graham Brooks, mentions various other writers who noted the unwillingness of Americans to be critical of each other. He quotes James Muirhead, the English editor of the *Baedeker* guide to the United States, as saying: "Americans invented the slang word 'kicker,' but so far as I could see their vocabulary is here miles ahead of their practice; they dream noble deeds, but do not do them; Englishmen 'kick' much better without having a name for it." Brooks suggested that it was the American "hesitation to face unpleasant facts rather than be disagreeable and pugnacious about them, after the genius of our English cousins, that calls out the criticism."[19]

The observation that the early Americans were cautious and sensitive has been made not only by foreign visitors but also, at different times, by Americans—as in fact many of the foreign authors report. In 1898, the American writer John Jay Chapman echoed Tocqueville's dictum of seventy years before, that he knew "of no country in which there is so little independence of mind and real freedom of discussion as in America." Chapman saw the general caution and desire to please as the source of many of the ills of his day:

> "Live and let live," says our genial prudence. Well enough, but mark the event. No one ever lost his social standing merely because of his offenses, but because of the talk about them. As free speech goes out the rascals come in.
>
> Speech is a great part of social life, but not the whole of it. Dress, bearing, expression, betray a man, customs show character, all these various utterances mingle and merge into the general tone which is the voice of a national temperament; private motive is lost in it.
>
> This tone penetrates and envelops everything in America. It is impossible to condemn it altogether. This desire to please, which has so much of the shopman's smile in it, graduates at one end of the scale into a general kindliness, into public benefactions, hospitals, and college foundations; at the other end it is seen melting into a desire to efface one's self rather than give offense, to hide rather than be noticed.
>
> In Europe, the men in the pit at the theatre stand up between the acts, face the house, and examine the audience at leisure. The American dares not do this. He cannot stand the isolation, nor the publicity. The American in a horse car can give his seat to a lady, but dares not raise his voice while the conductor tramps over his toes.[20]

---

[19] J. G. Brooks, *As Others See Us* (New York: Macmillan, 1908), p. 95.

[20] *The Selected Writings of John Jay Chapman*, Jacques Barzun, ed. (New York: Doubleday Anchor, 1959), p. 278.

Although these accounts by travelers and American essayists cannot be taken as conclusive proof of an unchanging American character, they do suggest that the hypothesis which sees the American character changing with respect to the traits "inner-" and "other-directedness" may be incorrect.

The Unchanging American Values and Their Connection with American Character

The foreign travelers were also impressed by the American insistence on equality in social relations, and on achievement in one's career. Indeed, many perceived an intimate connection between the other-directed behavior they witnessed and the prevalence of these values, such that the behavior could not be understood without reference to them. An analysis of the writings of hundreds of British travelers in America before the Civil War reports: "Most prominent of the many impressions that Britons took back with them [between 1836 and 1860] was the aggressive egalitarianism of the people."[21] If one studies the writings of such celebrated European visitors as Harriet Martineau, the Trollopes (both mother and son), Tocqueville, or James Bryce, it is easy to find many observations documenting this point.[22]

Baedeker's advice to any European planning to visit the United States in the late nineteenth or early twentieth century was that he "should, from the outset, reconcile himself to the absence of deference, or servility, on the part of those he considers his social inferiors."[23] A detailed examination of the comments of European visitors from 1890 to 1910 reports general agreement concerning the depth and character of American equalitarianism:

---

[21] Max Berger, *The British Traveller in America, 1836–1860* (New York: Columbia University Press, 1943), pp. 54–55.

[22] For some detailed citations and references see S. M. Lipset, "Stability in the Midst of Change," *The Social Welfare Forum, 1959* (New York: Columbia University Press, 1959), pp. 16–18. See also Commager, *America in Perspective*, pp. xvi–xvii.

[23] Quoted by Philip Burne-Jones, *Dollars and Democracy* (London: Sidney Appleton, 1904), p. 69. Burne-Jones agrees with Baedeker and tells his English readers to follow his good advice, because he who "doesn't do so . . . will probably live in a perpetual state of indignation and annoyance . . . [since Americans at every social level think] that they are really every bit as good as you are, in a country where all social distinctions are supposed to be non-existent."

> Whether they liked what they saw or not, most foreign observers did not doubt that America was a democratic society. . . . Different occupations of course, brought differences in prestige, but neither the occupation nor the prestige implied any fundamental difference in the value of individuals. . . . The similarity of conclusions based on diverse observations was simply another indication of the absence of sharp class differences. Even hostile visitors confirmed this judgment. . . . Some foreign observers found the arrogance of American workers intolerable.[24]

Even today this contrast between Europe and America with respect to patterns of equality in interpersonal relations among men of different social positions is striking. A comparison of writings of European visitors at the turn of this century with those made by British groups visiting here to study American industrial methods since World War II states that "the foreign descriptions of . . . America in 1890 and 1950 are remarkably similar. . . . The British teams [in the 1950's reported] . . . the same values . . . which impressed visitors a half century ago. Like them they found the American worker is more nearly the equal of other members of society than the European, with respect not only to his material prosperity, but also to . . . the attitudes of others toward him."[25] And this attitude is apparent at other levels of American society as well. As one commentator put it when describing the high-status Europeans who have come to America in recent years as political refugees from Nazism and Communism:

> With his deep sense of class and status, integration in American society is not easy for the émigré. The skilled engineer or physician who . . . finally establishes himself in his profession, discovers that

---

[24] Robert W. Smuts, *European Impressions of the American Worker* (New York: King's Crown Press, 1953), pp. 3–7. It is interesting to note the similarity between the complaints of presumably conservative upper-class Europeans of the 1890's who found "the arrogance of American workers intolerable" and the complaint of Frances Trollope in 1830 concerning that "coarse familiarity, untempered by any shadow of respect, which is assumed by the grossest and lowest in their intercourse with the highest and most refined," or that of her son Anthony who visited America in 1860 and objected that "the man to whose service one is entitled answers one with determined insolence." See Frances Trollope, *Domestic Manners of the Americans* (London: Whittaker, Treacher, 1832), p. 109, and Anthony Trollope, *North America* (New York: Alfred A. Knopf, 1951), p. 77.

[25] Smuts, *European Impressions of the American Worker*, p. 54.

he does not enjoy the same exalted status that he would have had in
the old country. I met several young Croatian doctors in the Los
Angeles area who were earning $25,000 to $35,000 a year, but still
felt declassed.[26]

American emphasis on equalitarianism as a dominant value is significant
in determining what to many of the Europeans were three closely related
processes: competition, status uncertainty, and conformity. Tocqueville,
for example, argued that equalitarianism maximizes competition among
the members of a society.[27] But if equalitarianism fosters competition for
status, the combination of the two values of equality and achievement
results, according to many of the travelers, in an amorphous social structure in which individuals are uncertain about their social position. In fact,
those travelers who were so impressed with the pervasive equalitarianism
of American society also suggested that, *precisely as a result of the
emphasis on equality and opportunity*, Americans were *more* status-
conscious than those who lived in the more aristocratic societies of
Europe. They believed, for example, that it was easier for the *nouveaux
riches* to be accepted in European high society than in American.
British travelers before the Civil War noted that Americans seemed to
love titles more than Englishmen. European observers, from Harriet
Martineau and Frances Trollope in the 1830's to James Bryce in the
1880's[28] and Denis Brogan in recent years, have pointed out that the
actual strength of equality as a dominant American value—with the
consequent lack of any well-defined deference structure linked to a
legitimate aristocratic tradition where the propriety of social rankings
is unquestioned—forces Americans to *emphasize* status background and
symbolism.[29] As Brogan has remarked, the American value system has

---

[26] Bogden Raditsa, "Clash of Two Immigrant Generations," *Commentary*, 25
(1958), p. 12.

[27] Tocqueville, *Democracy in America*, Vol. II, p. 146. See also Smuts, *European Impressions of the American Worker*, p. 13.

[28] For citations and references in the foreign travel literature, see Lipset,
"Stability in the Midst of Change," *op. cit.*, pp. 32–35.

[29] "It is only an apparent contradiction in terms to assert that the fundamental
democratic and egalitarian character of American life is demonstrated by the
ingenuity and persistence shown in inventing marks of difference and symbols
of superiority. In a truly class-conscious and caste-dominated society, the marks
of difference are universally recognized even if resented. In America they must
be stressed, or they might easily be forgotten, and they must be added to, as the
old standards of distinction cease to serve their purpose. Apart from the

formed "a society which, despite all efforts of school, advertising, clubs and the rest, makes the creation of effective social barriers difficult and their maintenance a perpetually repeated task. American social fences have to be continually repaired; in England they are like wild hedges, they grow if left alone."[30]

Status-striving and the resultant conformism have not been limited solely, or even primarily, to the more well-to-do classes in American society. Many of the early nineteenth-century travelers commented on the extent to which workers attempted to imitate middle-class styles of life. Smuts notes that visitors at the turn of this century were struck by "what they regarded as the spend-thrift pattern of the American worker's life"; Paul Bourget, a French observer, interpreted this behavior as reflecting "the profound feeling of equality [in America which] urges

---

simple economic criterion of conspicuous display, there are no generally accepted marks of social difference in America. And modern salesmanship makes clothes, cars, and personal adornment far more alike than was possible in the old days of belated styles and the Model T Ford. It is worth noting that the main stress of American class distinction is put on 'exclusiveness.' In a society without formal public recognition of difference in rank, with a poor and diminishing stock of reverence for hereditary eminence, and with a constant rise to the top of the economic system of new men amply provided with the only substitute for hereditary eminence, wealth, it becomes extremely difficult to make 'society' anything but the spare-time activities of the rich. It is characteristic that it is in cities whose days of economic advance are over, in Boston, Philadelphia, Charleston, that it has proved easiest to keep out the newcomers." Denis W. Brogan, *U. S. A.: An Outline of the Country, Its People and Institutions* (New York: Oxford University Press, 1941), pp. 116–117.
[30] Denis W. Brogan, *The English People* (London: Hamish Hamilton, 1943), p. 99. Gabriel Almond has commented in the same vein. "*In a sense America is a nation of parvenus.* A historically unique rate of immigration, social and geographic mobility has produced a people which has not had an opportunity to 'set,' to acquire the security and stability which come from familiar ties, associations, rights, and obligations. . . . In more stably stratified societies the individual tends to have a greater sense of 'location,' a broader and deeper identification with his social surroundings. [The American pattern, consequently,] leaves the individual somewhat doubtful as to his social legitimacy. . . ." *The American People and Foreign Policy* (New York: Harcourt, Brace, 1950), pp. 63–64. (Emphasis mine.)
An American historian, Rowland Berthoff, has also noted recently: "The evidence is already becoming plain that status striving is no latter-day degeneracy of Americans: rather . . . such insecurity was a by-product of excessive mobility." "The American Social Order: A Conservative Hypothesis," *American Historical Review*, 65 (1960), p. 512.

them to make a show." As Werner Sombart, the German sociologist and economist, put it, "since all are seeking success . . . everyone is forced into a struggle to beat every other individual; and a steeple-chase begins . . . that differs from all other races in that the goal is not fixed but constantly moves even further away from the runners." And in an equalitarian democracy "the universal striving for success [becomes a major cause of] . . . the worker's extravagance, for, as Münsterberg [a German psychologist] pointed out, the ability to spend was the only public sign of success at earning." [31] And lest it be thought that such concerns with conspicuous consumption emerged only in the Gilded Age of the 1890's as analyzed by Veblen, sixty years earlier a medical study of the "Influence of Trades, Professions, and Occupations, in the United States, in the Production of Disease," described and analyzed behavior in much the same terms:

> The population of the United States is beyond that of other coun-
> tries an anxious one. All classes are either striving after wealth, or
> endeavoring to keep up its appearance. From the principle of
> imitation which is implanted in all of us, sharpened perhaps by the
> existing equality of conditions, the poor follow as closely as they
> are able the habits and manner of living of the rich. . . . From these
> causes, and perhaps from the nature of our political institutions, and
> the effects arising from them, we are an anxious, care-worn people.[32]

While some Europeans explained American behavior that they found strange—the sensitivity, kindliness, concern for others' feelings, and moral

---

[31] Smuts, *European Impressions of the American Worker*, p. 13.

[32] Benjamin McCready, "On the Influence of Trades, Professions, and Occupations in the United States, in the Production of Disease," *Transactions
of the Medical Society of the State of New York* (1836–1837), III, pp.
146–147. It is interesting to note the congruence between this report and
Tocqueville's comments about the same period. He noted: "In America I saw
the freest and most enlightened men placed in the happiest circumstances that
the world affords; [yet] it seemed to me as if a cloud hung upon their brow,
and I thought them serious and almost sad, even in their pleasures.

"The chief reason for this contrast is that the former [the peasants in
Europe] do not think of the ills they endure, while the latter [the Americans]
are forever brooding over advantages they do not possess. It is strange to see
with what feverish ardor the Americans pursue their own welfare, and to
watch the vague dread that constantly torments them lest they should not
have chosen the shortest path that leads to it." Tocqueville, *Democracy in
America*, Vol. II, p. 144.

Riesman apparently overlooked this observation of Tocqueville's, since he
suggests that things have changed "since Tocqueville wrote . . . [in] that

meekness—by reference to the nature of political democracy or the over-bearing desire to make money, others saw these traits as consequences of the extreme emphasis on equality of opportunity, the basic American value which they properly regarded as unique. Many argued that this very emphasis on equality, and the constant challenging of any pretensions to permanent high status, has made Americans in all social positions extremely sensitive to the opinions of others, and causes status aspirants greater anxiety about the behavior and characteristics indicative of rank than is the case with their counterparts in more aristocratic societies. Discussing the writings of various travelers, John Graham Brooks states:

> One deeper reason why the English are blunt and abrupt about their rights . . . is because class lines are more sharply drawn there. Within these limits, one is likely to develop the habit of demanding his dues. He insists on his prerogatives all the more because they are narrowly defined. When an English writer (Jowett) says, "We are not nearly so much afraid of one another as you are in the States," he expressed this truth. In a democracy every one at least hopes to get on and up. This ascent depends not upon the favor of a class, but upon the good-will of the whole. This social whole has to be conciliated. It must be conciliated in both directions—at the top and at the bottom. To make one's self conspicuous and disagreeable, is to arouse enmities that block one's way.[33]

One may find an elaboration of this causal analysis among many writers at different periods. Thus Max Weber, after a visit to America in the early 1900's, noted the high degree of "submission to fashion in America, to a degree unknown in Germany" and explained it in terms of the lack of inherited class status.[34] Seven decades earlier another

---

the sphere of pleasure has itself become a sphere of cares." *The Lonely Crowd,* p. 148.

Herbert Spencer and Matthew Arnold made similar observations about work and play in post-Civil War America. Gabriel Almond cites Spencer as reporting that in America, "Exclusive devotion to work has the result that amusements cease to please; and when relaxation becomes imperative, life becomes dreary from lack of its sole interest—the interest in business," and states that Arnold felt that Americans "were extremely nervous because of excessive worry and overwork." Almond, *The American People and Foreign Policy,* pp. 34–35.

[33] Brooks, *As Others See Us,* p. 97.

[34] H. H. Gerth and C. Wright Mills, eds., *From Max Weber: Essays in Sociology* (New York: Oxford University Press, 1946), p. 188.

German, Francis Grund, who saw in American equality and democracy the hope of the world, nevertheless also believed that the ambiguous class structure made status-striving tantamount to conformity. He presents both sides of the picture in the following items:

> Society in America . . . is characterized by a spirit of exclusiveness and persecution unknown in any other country. Its gradations not being regulated according to rank and title, selfishness and conceit are its principal elements . . . What man is there in this city [New York] that dares to be independent, at the risk of being considered bad company? And who can venture to infringe upon a single rule of society?

> This habit of conforming to each other's opinions, and the penalty set upon every transgression of that kind, are sufficient to prevent a man from wearing a coat cut in a different fashion, or a shirt collar no longer *à la mode*, or, in fact, to do, say, or appear anything which could render him unpopular among a certain set. In no other place, I believe, is there such a stress laid upon "saving appearances."[35]

James Bryce, a half-century later, also linked conformity to the ambiguity of the status system, particularly as it affected the wealthy classes. He pointed out that it was precisely the emphasis on equality, and

---

[35] Grund, *Aristocracy in America*, pp. 52, 157. In describing the emerging America of pre-Civil War days, Dixon Wecter reports that "already in the making was that peculiarly American psychology—symbolized in the great caravans moving westward—of keeping up with one's neighbors, of regarding solitude and independence as a little eccentric, if not dangerous. In business and mechanics the most daring of innovators, the American was already developing that social and personal timidity, that love of conformity, which is the hallmark of the *parvenu*." *The Saga of American Society* (New York: Scribner's, 1937), p. 103; see also his comments on p. 314.

In an essay concerning early Kansas, written in 1910, the historian Carl Becker pointed to the interrelationship of intolerance, individualism, and equalitarianism in American behavior. He asserted that intolerance has been fundamental in the American character. American individualistic values, according to Becker, stress personal achievement, rather than eccentricity; conformity has always been a prerequisite to success. And he notes, as did many of the nineteenth-century foreign travelers, that Americans have tolerated different religions, but have been intolerant of irreligion. See Carl L. Becker, "Kansas," in his *Everyman His Own Historian* (New York: Appleton-Century-Crofts, 1935), pp. 1–28.

the absence of well-defined rules of deference, which made Americans so concerned with the behavior of others and seemingly more, rather than less, snobbish toward each other than were comparably placed Englishmen.

> It may seem a paradox to observe that a millionaire has a better and easier social career open to him in England, than in America. . . . In America, if his private character be bad, if he be mean or openly immoral, or personally vulgar, or dishonest, the best society may keep its doors closed against him. In England great wealth, skillfully employed, will more readily force these doors to open. . . . The existence of a system of artificial rank enables a stamp to be given to base metal in Europe which cannot be given in a thoroughly republican country.[36]

In comparing the reactions of Englishmen and Americans to criticism, James Muirhead (the editor of the American *Baedeker*) stated that "the Briton's indifference to criticism is linked to the fact of caste, that it frankly and even brutally asserts the essential inequality of man. . . . Social adaptability is not his [the Briton's] foible. He accepts the conventionality of his class and wears it as an impenetrable armor."[37]

A number of the foreign travelers, particularly those who visited America after the 1880's, were startled to find overt signs of anti-Semitism, such as placards barring Jews from upper-class resorts and social clubs which denied them membership.[38] But this, too, could be perceived as a consequence of the fact that "the very absence of titular distinction often causes the lines to be more clearly drawn; as Mr. Charles Dudley Warner says: 'Popular commingling in pleasure resorts is safe enough in aristocratic countries, but it will not answer in a republic.' "[39] The most recent effort by a sociologist, Howard Brotz, to account for the greater concern about close contact with Jews in America than in England, also suggests that "in a democracy snobbishness can be far more vicious than in an aristocracy."

---

[36] James Bryce, *The American Commonwealth*, Vol. II, p. 815.

[37] James Fullerton Muirhead, *America, the Land of Contrasts: A Briton's View of His American Kin* (London: Lemson, Wolffe, 1898), p. 91.

[38] Andrew J. Torrielli, *Italian Opinion on America as Revealed by Italian Travelers, 1850–1900* (Cambridge, Mass.: Harvard University Press, 1941), p. 99.

[39] Muirhead, *America, the Land of Contrasts*, p. 27.

Lacking that natural confirmation of superiority which political authority alone can give, the rich and particularly the new rich, feel threatened by mere contact with their inferiors. . . . Nothing could be more fantastic than this to an English lord living in the country in the midst, not of other peers, but of his tenants. His position is such that he is at ease in the presence of members of the lower classes and in associating with them in recreation. . . . It is this "democratic" attitude which, in the first instance, makes for an openness to social relations with Jews. One cannot be declassed, so to speak, by play activities.[40]

The intimate connection between other-directedness and equalitarian values perceived by these observers recalls the same connection noted by Plato in his theoretical analysis of democracy. In *The Republic* we find these words:

[In a democracy, the father] accustoms himself to become like his child and to fear his sons. . . . Metic [resident alien] is like citizen and citizen like metic, and stranger like both. . . . The schoolmaster fears and flatters his pupils. . . . The young act like their seniors, and compete with them in speech and action, while the old men condescend to the young and become triumphs of versatility and wit, imitating their juniors in order to avoid the appearance of being sour or despotic. . . . And the wonderful equality of law and . . . liberty prevails in the mutual relations of men and women . . . the main result of all these things, taken together, is that it makes the souls of the citizens so sensitive that they take offense and will not put up with the faintest suspicion of slavery [strong authority] that anyone may introduce.[41]

Plato's analysis points up the main question to which this chapter is addressed: Are the conformity and the sensitivity to others—"other directedness"—observed in the contemporary American character solely

---

[40] Howard Brotz, "The Position of the Jews in English Society," *Jewish Journal of Sociology*, 1 (1959), p. 97. Writing twenty years earlier Dixon Wecter also suggested that "the present anti-Semitism of Society—as expressed in visiting lists, club memberships, and personal attitudes is markedly keener in the United States than in England or France, where Rothschilds, for example, seem to find virtually no doors barred against them. It is probably an aspect of that insecurity, that timidity and conventionalism which looms so large in our social picture." *The Saga of American Society*, p. 152.

[41] Plato, *The Republic*, Ernest Rhys, ed. (London: J. M. Dent, 1935), pp. 200–226.

a function of the technology and social structure of a bureaucratic, industrialized, urban society, as Riesman and Whyte imply, or are they also to some considerable degree an expected consequence of a social system founded upon the values of equality and achievement? It seems that sociological theory, especially as expounded by Max Weber and Talcott Parsons, and much historical and comparative evidence, lend credence to the belief that the basic value system is at least a major, if not the pre-eminent, source of these traits.

As Plato noted, and as the foreign travelers testify, democratic man is deeply imbued with the desire to accommodate to others, which results in kindness and generosity in personal relations, and in a reluctance to offend. All books that are published are "exalted to the skies," teachers "admire their pupils," and flattery is general.[42] The travelers also bear out Plato's remarks about the socialization of children in a democracy. It appears that equalitarian principles were applied to child-rearing early in the history of the republic. Early British opinions of American children have a modern flavor:

> The independence and maturity of American children furnished another surprise for the British visitor. Children ripened early. . . . But such precosity, some visitors feared, was too often achieved at the loss of parental control. Combe claimed that discipline was lacking in the home, and children did what they pleased. Marryat corroborated this. . . . Children were not whipped here [as in England], but treated like rational beings.[43]

[42] Martineau, *Society in America*, Vol. III, pp. 63–64.
[43] Berger, *The British Traveller in America*, pp. 83–84. Dixon Wecter, who relied more on the French foreign visitors, detailed similar comments and reached the same conclusions: "Indeed without some mention of the dictatorship of the young, any chapter on American manners would be incomplete. No other country in the world has made so much of its children, or given them so free a hand in shaping its customs. . . . As early as Revolutionary times, French visitors in the more aristocratic households like the Schuylers', for example, reported that children were 'spoiled' and 'self willed.' Yet social precosity was one evident result of the attention paid them: Bayard describes the master of a country house near Winchester, Virginia, where, 'dinner hour having sounded, we sat down at a round table, his daughter, nine years old, doing the honors very gracefully in the absence of her mother.'" And Wecter goes on to report that throughout the nineteenth and twentieth centuries, "the surprise of visitors from abroad over the autocracy of our youth has never ceased." *The Saga of American Society*, pp. 191–192.

Harriet Martineau's description of child-rearing in the America of Andrew Jackson sounds like a commentary on the progressive other-directed parent of the mid-twentieth century:

> My [parent] friend observed that the only thing to be done [in child-rearing] is to avoid to the utmost the exercise of authority, and to make children friends from the very beginning. . . . They [the parents] do not lay aside their democratic principles in this relation, more than in others. . . . They watch and guard: they remove stumbling blocks: they manifest approbation and disapprobation: they express wishes, but, at the same time, study the wishes of their little people: they leave as much as possible to natural retribution: they impose no opinions, and quarrel with none: in short, they exercise the tenderest friendship without presuming upon it. . . . the children of Americans have the advantage of the best possible early discipline; that of activity and self-dependence.[44]

What struck the democratic Miss Martineau as progressive was interpreted quite differently by Anthony Trollope, who visited this country in 1860: "I must protest that American babies are an unhappy race. They eat and drink as they please; they are never punished; they are never banished, snubbed, and kept in the background as children are kept with us."[45] And forty years later, another English visitor, typical of the many who described American child-parent relations during a century and a half, tells us that nowhere else, as in America, "is the child so constantly in evidence; nowhere are his wishes so carefully consulted; nowhere is he allowed to make his mark so strongly on society. . . . The theory of the equality of man is rampant in the nursery. . . . You will actually hear an American mother say of a child of two or three years of age: 'I can't *induce* him to do this. . . .' "[46]

---

[44] Martineau, *Society in America*, pp. 168, 177. See also Arthur W. Calhoun, *A Social History of the American Family from Colonial Times to the Present* (Cleveland: The Arthur H. Clark Co., 1918), Vol. II, pp. 63–64. For a thorough documentation of child-centeredness in the nineteenth-century American family, see Anne L. Kuhn, *The Mother's Role in Childhood Education: New England Concepts, 1830–1860* (New Haven, Conn.: Yale University Press, 1947).

[45] Anthony Trollope, *North America*, p. 142; for similar comments see also J. S. Buckingham, *America: Historical, Statistic, and Descriptive* (New York: Harper & Bros., 1841), pp. 362–363; J. Boardman, *America and the Americans* (London: Longman, Rees, Orme, Brown, Green and Longman, 1833), p. 156; Brooks, *As Others See Us*, pp. 48–50.

[46] Muirhead, *America, The Land of Contrasts*, pp. 67–68. (Emphasis in original.)

If these reports from the middle and late nineteenth century are reminiscent of contemporary views, it is still more amazing to find, in a systematic summary of English travelers' opinion *in the last part of the eighteenth and early years of the nineteenth centuries,* that the emphasis on equality and democracy had *already* created the distinctive American child-oriented family which astonished the later visitors:

> A close connection was made by the stranger between the re-publican form of government and the unlimited liberty which was allowed the younger generation. . . . They were rarely punished at home, and strict discipline was not tolerated in the schools. . . . It was feared that respect for elders or for any other form of authority would soon be eliminated from American life. . . . As he could not be punished in the school, he learned to regard his teacher as an inferior and to disregard all law and order.[47]

Equality was thus perceived by many of the foreign travelers as affecting the socialization of the child not only within the family but in the school as well. The German psychologist Hugo Münsterberg joins the late-eighteenth-century visitors in complaining, over a century later in 1900, that "the feeling of equality will crop up where nature designed none, as for instance between youth and mature years. . . . Parents even make it a principle to implore and persuade their children, holding it to be a mistake to compel or punish them; and they believe that the schools should be conducted in the same spirit."[48] Various visitors were struck by the extent to which the schools did carry out this objective. The following description by an Englishman of schools in the New York area in 1833 sounds particularly modern:

> The pupils are entirely independent of their teacher. No correction, no coercion, no manner of restraint is permitted to be used. . . . Parents also have as little control over their offspring at home, as the master has at school. . . . Corporal punishment has almost dis-

---

[47] Mesick, *The English Traveller in America,* pp. 83–84. A detailed summary of the opinion of foreign travelers concerning the indulgent, child-centered, pre-Civil War family may be found in "The Emancipation of Childhood," in Calhoun, *A Social History of the American Family,* Vol. II, pp. 50–77. Calhoun also tells us that the freedom of children was "attributed . . . to the spirit of republicanism. . . . All men are sovereigns. Personality is exalted; and the political status overflows and democratizes family institutions." *Ibid.,* p. 53.

[48] Hugo Münsterberg, *The Americans* (New York: McClure, Phillips, 1904), p. 28.

appeared from American day-schools; and a teacher, who should now give recourse at such means of enforcing instruction, would meet with reprehension from the parents and perhaps retaliation from his scholars.[49]

Tocqueville also found examples of the American's mistrust of authority "even in the schools," where he marveled that "the children in their games are wont to submit to rules which they have themselves established."[50]

The educational policies which have become linked with the name of John Dewey and labeled "progressive education" actually began in a number of school systems around the country long before Dewey wrote on the subject: "To name but one example, the lower schools of St. Louis had adopted a system intended to develop spontaneously the inventive and intellectual faculties of the children by the use of games and with no formal teaching of ideas, no matter how practical."[51]

The Inadequacy of a Materialistic Interpretation of Change

Many of the foreign observers referred to above explained the other-directedness and status-seeking of Americans by the prevalence of the twin values of equality and achievement. Character and behavior were thus explained by values. They pointed out that the ethic of equality not only pervaded status relations but that it influenced the principal spheres of socialization, the family, and the school, as well.

Both Whyte's and Riesman's arguments, in contrast, explain character and values by reference to the supposed demands of a certain type of economy and its unique organization. The economy, in order to be productive, requires certain types of individuals, and requires that they hold certain values. In the final analysis, theirs is a purely materialistic interpretation of social phenomena and is open to the criticisms to which such interpretations are susceptible.

The inadequacy of such an explanation of change in values and social character is best demonstrated by comparative analysis. British and Swedish societies, for example, have for many decades possessed occupational structures similar to that of America. Britain, in fact, reached

---

[49] Isaac Fidler, *Observations in Professions, Literature, Manners and Emigration, in the United States and Canada, Made During a Residence There in 1832* (New York: J. and J. Harper, 1833), pp. 40–41.

[50] Tocqueville, *Democracy in America*, Vol. I, p. 198.

[51] Torrielli, *Italian Opinion on America*, p. 115.

the stage of an advanced industrial society, thoroughly urbanized, where the majority of the population worked for big business or government, long before any other nation. The occupational profiles of Sweden, Germany, and the United States have been similar for decades. If the causal connection between technology and social character were direct, then the patterns described as typical of "other-direction" or "the organization man" should have occurred in Great Britain prior to their occurrence in the United States, and should now be found to predominate in other European nations. Yet "other-direction" and the "social ethic" appear to be pre-eminently American traits. In Europe, one sees the continued, even though declining, strength of deferential norms, enjoining conformity to class standards of behavior.

Thus, comparative analysis strikingly suggests that the derivation of social character almost exclusively from the traits associated with occupational or population profiles is invalid. So important an element in a social system as social character must be deeply affected by the dominant value system. For the value system is perhaps the most enduring part of what we think of as society, or a social system. Comparative history shows that nations may still present striking differences, even when their technological, demographic, or political patterns are similar. Thus it is necessary to work out the implications of the value system within a given material setting—while always observing, of course, the gradual, cumulative effect that technological change has upon values.

In attempting to determine how American values have been intertwined with the profound changes that have taken place in American society, it is not sufficient to point out that American values are peculiarly congenial to change. Although equality and achievement have reinforced each other over the course of American history, they have never been entirely compatible either. Many of the changes that have taken place in family structure, education, religion, and "culture," as America has become a "modern" society, have manifested themselves in a constant conflict between the democratic equalitarianism, proclaimed as a national ideal in the basic documents of the American Revolution, and the strong emphasis on competition, success, and the acquisition of status—the achievement orientation—which is also deeply embedded in our national value system.

Richard Hofstadter has urged the recurring pattern of value *conflict* and *continuity* in commenting on papers presented at a conference on changes in American society:

Culturally and anthropologically, human societies are cast in a great variety of molds, but once a society has been cast in its mold— Mr. Rostow is right that our mold as a nation was established by the early nineteenth century—the number of ways in which, short of dire calamity, it will alter its pattern are rather limited. I find it helpful also to point to another principle upon which Mr. Rostow has remarked—the frequency with which commentators find societies having certain paradox polarities in them. . . . We may find in this something functional; that is, *Societies have a need to find ways of checking their own tendencies. In these polarities there may be something of a clue to social systems.* . . .

Mr. Kluckhohn's report contains some evidence that we have already passed the peak of this shift about which I have been speaking. I find some additional evidence myself in the growing revolt of middle-class parents against those practices in our education that seem to sacrifice individualism and creativity for adjustment and group values. Granted the initial polarities of the success ethic, which is one of the molds in which our society is cast, this ethic must in some way give rise, sooner or later, to a reaction. . . . I do not think that we must be persuaded that our system of values has ceased to operate.[52]

The analyses of American history and culture in the nineteenth and twentieth centuries, by both foreign and native interpreters, often differ according to whether they stress democracy and equality, or capitalism and achievement. Generally, conservatives have found fault with the decline of individuality and the pampering of children, and have seen both as manifestations of democracy and equality; while liberals have noted, with dismay, tendencies toward inequality and aristocracy, and have blamed them upon the growth of big business. These contrary political philosophies have also characterized the interpretation of American culture that predominates at any given period. Arthur Schlesinger, Sr., has even tried to measure the systematic characteristic duration of the "epochs of radicalism and conservatism [that] have followed each other in alternating order" in American history.[53]

A cursory examination of the numerous differences between the con-

---

[52] Richard Hofstadter, "Commentary: Have There Been Discernible Shifts in Values During the Past Generation?" in Elting E. Morison, ed., *The American Style: Essays in Value and Performance* (New York: Harper & Bros., 1958), p. 357. (Emphasis mine.)

[53] Arthur M. Schlesinger, Sr., *New Viewpoints in American History* (New York: Macmillan, 1922), p. 123.

clusions of American social scientists in the 1930's and in the 1950's shows the way in which interpretations of American culture vary with social conditions. Writers of the 1930's amassed evidence of the decline of equalitarianism and the effect of this on a variety of institutions. Karen Horney in *The Neurotic Personality of Our Time,* for example, named anxiety over chances of economic success as the curse of what she, with many of her contemporaries, regarded as a completely pecuniary, achievement-oriented culture dominated by the giant corporations. Such analysts as Robert S. Lynd, and W. L. Warner all agreed that the egalitarian emphasis in American democracy was declining sharply under the growth of the large-scale corporation, monopoly capitalism, and economic competition.[54] They asserted categorically that mobility had decreased, and Warner predicted the development of rigid status lines based on family background.

Twenty years later, these interpretations are almost unanimously rejected. Warner himself in one of his most recent works, shows that chances of rising into the top echelons of the largest corporations are *greater* than they were in the 1920's.[55] As indicated earlier in this chapter, typical writers of the 1950's are concerned that the emphasis on achievement in American society may be dying out.

In large measure, the difference between writers of the two decades reflects the contrast between the economic circumstances of the times. The depression of the 1930's inclined intellectuals toward an equalitarian radicalism, which condemned capitalism and achievement orientation as the source of evils. Even a conservative like Warner was led to emphasize the growth of inequality and the restriction of opportunity. The prosperity of the 1950's, however, renewed the legitimacy of many conservative institutions and values, and discredited some of the innovations of the previous decades. The social analyses of the 1950's, even those written by men who still considered themselves liberals or socialists, involved at least a critique of the radical excesses of the former period, if not a critique of equalitarian values themselves. Perhaps the similarity in attitudes between the analysts of the 1950's and many of the foreign travelers of the last century is due to the fact that most of the European

---

[54] Robert S. Lynd, *Knowledge for What?* (Princeton, N.J.: Princeton University Press; 1940), p. 75; Harold Laski, *The American Democracy* (New York: Viking Press, 1948); W. L. Warner and Paul S. Lunt, *The Social Life of a Modern Community* (New Haven, Conn.: Yale University Press, 1941).
[55] W. L. Warner and J. C. Abegglen, *Occupational Mobility in American Business and Industry* (Minneapolis: University of Minnesota Press, 1953).

visitors have been conservatives, or members of the elite of much more aristocratic societies, and the modern Americans reflect the post-war revival of conservative values.

While Riesman and Whyte would deny that their works contain conservative value preferences, and insist that they are simply analyzing changes, it seems fairly evident that like the more elitist travelers of the nineteenth century, they deplore many of the dominant trends. They point to the spread of progressive education, with its disbelief in rewards for hard work, as illustrating the decay of the Protestant ethic, and they assume, as a result of this, a decline in the opportunity for developing creativity. Whyte points to the shift in scientific research from individual to group projects, which in his opinion are less creative. Neither Riesman nor Whyte explicitly asserts that there is more conformity now than in the past, for the reason that men have always conformed to the values of the day; but both argue that contemporary values and personality traits emphasize accommodation to others, while the declining Protestant ethic and the inner-directed character structure stressed conformity to a fixed rule of conduct rather than to the fluctuating actions and moods of others.[56]

This reaction against the apparent decline of the Protestant ethic of

---

[56] It is ironic to note that most contemporary discussions which employ Weber's concept of the Protestant ethic to typify a certain type of behavior, which is then contrasted with other-directed behavior, ignore the fact that, to Weber, one of the significant components distinguishing ascetic Protestantism, and particularly Calvinism, from other religious ethics was precisely its use of the need to conform to the judgment of others as a means of enforcing discipline: "The member of the sect (or conventicle) had to have qualities of a certain kind in order to enter the community circle. . . . In order to hold his own in this circle, the member had to *prove* repeatedly that he was endowed with these qualities. . . . According to all experience there is no stronger means of breeding traits than through the necessity of holding one's own in the circle of one's associates. . . . The Puritan sects put the most powerful individual interest of social self-esteem in the service of this breeding of traits . . . to repeat, it is not the ethical *doctrine* of a religion, but that form of ethical conduct upon which *premiums* are placed that matters. . . . The premiums were placed upon 'proving' oneself before God in the sense of attaining salvation—which is found in *all* Puritan denominations—and 'proving' oneself before men in the sense of socially holding one's own within the Puritan sects." A key difference between the Puritans and the Lutherans and Catholics, in Weber's judgment, lies in this extensive use of an appeal to "social self-esteem" or the power of group opinion by the former, and imposing religious discipline "through authoritarian means" and punishing or placing premiums on "concrete individual acts," by the latter. Gerth and Mills, eds., *From Max Weber*, pp. 320–321.

achievement and hard work, which has become a dominant theme among the intellectual middle class of the 1950's and early 1960's, should be viewed as the counterpart of the concern with the seeming breakdown of equality which moved comparable groups in the 1930's. The differences in the concerns of the two periods illustrate the important point that although the equalitarian ethos of the American Revolution and the achievement orientation of the Protestant ethic are mutually supporting, they also involve normative conflict. Complete commitment to equality involves rejecting some of the implications of valuing achievement; and the opposite is also true. Thus, when the equalitarianism of left or liberal politics is dominant, there is a reaction against achievement, and when the values of achievement prevail in a conservative political and economic atmosphere, men tend to depreciate some of the consequences of equality, such as the influence of popular taste on culture.

The supremacy of equalitarian values and liberal politics in the 1930's was reflected in the school system in the triumph of progressive education, a cause always associated with left-of-center leaders and ideologies; in industry, by the introduction of the human relations approach as an attempt to "keep the worker happy"; and in the society at large by efforts toward a general redistribution of goods and services. Social scientists and others interested in family structure criticized the supposedly typical middle-class family as too authoritarian and rigid in its treatment of children, suggesting that, in contrast to the more democratic and affectionate working-class family, it bred "authoritarian" and "neurotic" personalities. Popular psychology saw the "competitive personality" of our time as the source of many personal and social evils. Historians pictured the creators of American industry as "robber barons" and as irresponsible exploiters of American resources.

This equalitarian liberalism was perhaps strongest in the school system, where educators carried the ideal of equal treatment to a point where even intellectual differences were ignored. Special encouragement of the gifted child was regarded as an unfair privilege that inflicted psychic punishment on the less gifted: personality adjustment for *all* became the objective. In New York City, Fiorello La Guardia, the militant progressive mayor, abolished Townsend Harris High School—a special school for gifted boys in which four years of work was completed in three—on the grounds that the very existence of such a school was undemocratic, because it conferred special privileges on a minority.

In the prosperous 1950's and 1960's, these tendencies have been almost completely reversed. Big business and business careers once more have become legitimate. The Republicans held office in the 1950's, and centrists rather than liberals dominate the revived Democratic Party of the 1960's. Although Keynesian economics has remained official government policy, and is still supported by most economists, some leading members of that profession have emerged who oppose almost all government intervention.[57] Studies of the social structure of the family have reversed the findings of the 1930's, suggesting that it is the working-class family that is more likely to be a source of "authoritarian" personality traits. Vulgarizations of the theses of Riesman and Whyte have been published in many magazines and are cited at P.T.A. meetings all over the country, where outraged middle-class parents demand a return to "old-fashioned" methods of teaching, in which hard work is rewarded and the gifted receive special attention.[58] Many middle-class parents have placed their children in private schools. While the rapid growth of private schools in large part stems from the increasing prosperity of the country, it also reflects the desire of middle-class parents that their children receive an elite education.

The political battle between the reactions stemming from the pre-war depression and those reflecting the post-war prosperity, between equality and achievement, has been most conspicuously joined today in the debate over schools. As the "progressive educationalists" begin to counter-attack, they appeal specifically to the values of equality and democracy. A speech by Professor A. Harry Passow of Columbia University Teachers' College attacked a proposal to create twenty-five elite high schools for gifted children in the following terms: "It is a perversion of democracy to set aside certain youngsters and give them privileges which automatically set them apart as an elite group of society. It goes against the basic idea of American education, which is to give all children an equal opportunity for the best possible education."[59]

---

[57] For example, Milton Friedman of the University of Chicago even advocates that the entire educational system from elementary school on up be placed under private ownership, since only through economic competition can we be assured of securing the best system.

[58] It should be noted again that the available evidence does not confirm the assumptions that educational standards have declined, as judged by the records and abilities of entering college freshmen over a thirty-year period. In addition, more teenagers are learning Greek and Latin and foreign languages now than in 1900, largely as a result of the great spread of educational facilities, though it is true that the *proportion* of students studying classical tongues has declined greatly.

[59] See "Plan of Schools for 'Elite' Scored," *The New York Times*, March 25, 1958, p. 25.

A leading expert, who has testified before Congressional committees for the past twenty years or more concerning the need for educational research, once reported that when a committee was discussing research on underprivileged or mentally deficient children, the Democrats on the committee would exhibit great interest; but when the committee turned to the question of the gifted child, the Republicans perked up and the Democrats sat back. The two parties did not, of course, oppose each other formally on these questions, since both favored research on all questions; but Republicans were simply more interested in *achievement*, or the problem of the gifted child, while Democrats were more interested in *equality*, or the problem of the underprivileged.

To stress the coincidence of these differing interpretations of American social trends with the political and economic cycle is not to suggest that they are simply ideological reflections of material conditions or of the climate of opinion. Most of them have pointed out genuine aspects of the culture, and in so doing have improved our understanding of the functions of different institutions and values. Both strands, the equalitarian and the achievement-oriented, remain strong, but changing conditions sometimes fortify one at the expense of the other, or alter the internal content of each. Thus opportunity, as measured by the chances of success in building up a major enterprise of one's own, has given way to opportunity measured by advancement in the bureaucratic elites.[60] The politics of liberalism and equality have fostered institutional changes, such as the constant spread of public education and of training facilities within corporations, which have increased opportunities for advancement.

Conclusion

This chapter essentially has urged that a materialistic interpretation of American society sharply underestimates the extent to which basic national values, once institutionalized, give shape to the consequences of

---

[60] It should be noted, however, that the desire and the number of attempts to start one's own small business certainly do not seem to have abated in this country, unless past rates were fantastically high. Survey studies indicate that the majority of American workers have thought of going into business, and that a fifth of them actually have once owned a small business. Conversely, of those in small businesses, 20 per cent have previously been manual workers. S. M. Lipset and R. Bendix, *Social Mobility in Industrial Society* (Berkeley: University of California Press, 1959), p. 102.

technological and economic change.[61] Clearly, many nations may be described as urbanized, industrialized, and capitalist, but they vary considerably in their status systems, their political institutions, parent-child relations, and so forth. The absence of a feudal past, with a concomitant emphasis on equality of manners and of opportunity, has played a major role in differentiating American behavior from that of other nations.

On the other hand, it may be argued that the entire Western world has been moving in the American direction in their patterns of class relationships, family structure, and "other-directedness," and that America, which was democratic and equalitarian before industrialization, has merely led the way in these patterns. Thus, at any given time, the differences between America and much of Europe may have remained constant, but this difference might have represented little more than a time lag.

If one compares the America of the 1960's with the America of the 1880's or the 1830's one would undoubtedly note changes in the direction suggested by Riesman. The vast majority of early- and mid-nineteenth-century Americans were self-employed and lived on farms or in small towns, while today most people are employees and live in cities. This change alone has many consequences along the lines suggested by *The Lonely Crowd:*

> We can contrast the small grocer who must please his individual patrons, perhaps by a "counter-side manner," with the chain-store employee who must please both the patrons and his co-workers. . . .

---

[61] In this discussion I have not been concerned with the truth of Riesman's description of the changes in technology and in the nature of the economy. One must be warned, however, against overestimating the drastic and far-reaching nature of these changes. For example, the common image of professional occupation is that they are increasingly embedded in bureaucratic structures, while they were formerly free of such structures. While this may be true of some professions, it is not true of others. Daniel Calhoun, in his recent study of American civil engineers, argues: "When a twentieth-century writer describes the earlier engineer as 'free and named on his own shingle,' he was slipping into a romantic notion of nineteenth-century society. This notion applies not to the typical nineteenth-century engineer, but to the exceptional or cantankerous individual. Almost as soon as American internal improvements became extensive enough to give the civil engineer much employment, the engineer became an organization man, a respectable member of a bureaucracy." See Daniel Hoven Calhoun, *The American Civil Engineer: Origins and Conflict* (Cambridge, Mass.: Technology Press, 1960), pp. 194–195. Calhoun's reference is to C. Wright Mills' description of the engineer in *White Collar.* But when Riesman speaks of the inner-directed man as "wanting to build a bridge, to run a railroad," (*The Lonely Crowd*, p. 120), he presumably has the image of the engineer in the back of his mind.

> The colleague, like the peer-grouper, is the very person with whom one engages in competition for the *scarce commodity of approval* and the very person to whom one looks for guidance as to what is desirable.[62]

The entrepreneur becomes an "other-directed person [who] gives up the one-face policy of the inner-directed man for a multiface policy that he sets in secrecy and varies with each set of encounters."[63] An employee has less freedom and motivation to be individualistic than does the self-employed. Farm and small-town dwellers know each other as total human beings rather than as actors in specific relations, and are presumably less motivated to exhibit status-seeking or to seek the good opinion of those whom they have known all their lives and who are "significant others" in a variety of limited contexts.[64] Residents of small communities are judged by their total background and personal history and by any specific set of

---

[62] P. 140. (Emphasis mine.)

[63] *Ibid.*, p. 147.

[64] However, it should be noted that an early history of the state of Illinois, written by a man who pioneered in the state, reports that the desire to be admired by others at the major social event of the week, Sunday church services, played an important role in stimulating general ambition: "For this advancement in civilization, the young people were much indebted to their practice of attending church on Sundays. Here they were regularly brought together at stated times; and their meeting, if it affected no better end, at least accustomed them to admire and wish to be admired. Each one wanted to make as good a figure as he could; and to that end came to meeting well-dressed and clean. . . . With pride of dress came ambition, industry, the desire of knowledge, and a love of decency. It has been said that civilization is a forced state of mind, to which [man] is stimulated by a desire to gratify artificial wants. . . ." Thomas Ford, *History of Illinois* (Chicago: S. C. Griggs, 1854), pp. 95–96.

In contrast, Albert Blumenthal emphasized that "putting on a front" in order to lay claim to a higher social status than one is entitled to is usually unsuccessful in a small town. He stated, "He who would indulge in pretense in Mineville must be very cautious lest he be wasting his time or be making himself a target for scorn, ridicule, or amusement. To be sure, a certain amount of bluffing can be done since, after all, persons have some privacy, even in Mineville. But this bluffing must not be of a sort that easily can be uncovered, for the people have little patience with pretenders. Persons long in the community know that there is scant use for them to 'put on front' of the more obvious sort such as by the wearing of fine clothes or the purchasing of a costly automobile. . . . By a ferreting-out process the people soon discover whether or not a newcomer 'has anything to be stuck up about.'" *Small-Town Stuff* (Chicago: University of Chicago Press, 1932), pp. 104–105.

acts. As many sociological studies of such communities have revealed, they tend to have a relatively static status system, permitting much less social mobility than that occurring in large cities. Consequently, the resident of the small town tends to be somewhat like the citizens of more rigidly stratified European states. The awareness of the relative permanence of status position reduces the anxiety to win the good opinion of others that exists where status is less stable.

There can be little question that Riesman and Whyte are right also in showing how bureaucratization and urbanization *reinforce* those social mechanisms which breed other-directedness. Success in a bureaucracy, and in the proliferating service occupations of modern society, depends primarily on the ability to get along well with others.

But it cannot be stressed too often that these mechanisms operate within the context of an historic American value-system and status structure that had also generated such traits in a non-bureaucratic and non-urban society. Other-direction, or, to put it less dramatically, sensitivity to the judgments of others, is an epiphenomenon of the American equalitarian ethos, of the opportunities for rapid status mobility, *and* of the general growth of an urban, bureaucratic society.[65] The increasing complexity introduced by industrialization and urbanization makes adherence to a rigid normative code obsolete, because such a code cannot be used as a guide to the great variety of situations confronting modern, bureaucratic man. This Riesman and Whyte have well noted. However, the greater flexibility and need to adapt to others that are demanded by urban and bureaucratic life add to an already existing disposition to be concerned with the opinions of others, a disposition caused by equalitarianism and by the emphasis placed on social mobility.

Even despite the changes brought about by urbanization and bureau-

---

[65] In commenting on the analyses of various, more psychologically oriented, writers who preceded Riesman in describing "other-directed" character traits (which, however, they tended to explain psychologically rather than sociologically, that is, by the patterns of child-rearing in the modern American family rather than by the structural changes that seemingly underlie these changes in child-rearing), Gabriel Almond also points up the dual causal pattern. "De Tocqueville attributed it [American conformism] to competitiveness and the equality of conditions of the American people. It is, of course, both factors taken together. What Horney, Fromm and Mead have done is to trace this and other tendencies from aspects of the culture, to patterns of child rearing in the family, to adult behavior." Almond, *The American People and Foreign Policy*, p. 43.

cratization, Americans still appear to be quite achievement oriented when compared to persons from more status-bound nations. Foreign travelers are still struck by the individual American's striving to get ahead.[66] Indeed, there is some evidence that the higher valuation placed on social skills in present American socialization practices is precisely oriented toward upward social mobility in contemporary society. A study comparing British and American beliefs about socialization points out that while it places "getting along with others" as the most important aim of socialization, the American pattern differs from the British in that it aims "at a smoothly functioning individual, equipped for getting ahead with a varied armament of social skills."[67]

Some evidence that achievement still ranks high in the United States as compared to other nations may be seen in the data from a comparative study of the attitudes of school youth in five countries—the United States, Norway, West Germany, England, and France. Surprisingly, at least so far as concerns the expectations of the researchers, American children were less "other-directed" than those in the European countries, except Norway, as judged by their responses to the question: "Would you rather be the most popular person in your class or the one who gets the highest grades?" Among both ten-year-olds and fourteen-year-olds, Americans were more likely to prefer high grades to popularity than were German, English, and French youth.

Another indicator of the relatively high level of concern for academic achievement may be seen in the response to a question concerning anxi-

---

[66] Arvid Brodersen comments in this way on the beliefs of prominent foreign visitors about the typical value orientations of the American people: "[They] repeated the pattern of positive-negative reciprocity stressing notions such as 'hard-working,' 'active,' and 'energetic' as well as 'materialistic,' 'ambitious,' 'rush all the time.'" Arvid Brodersen, "Themes in the Interpretation of America by Prominent Visitors from Abroad," *The Annals of the American Academy of Political and Social Science,* 295 (1954), pp. 21–32. Comments by Indian students in America reflect the same traits. "They are constantly in a hurry to get done whatever they are doing and give very little thought to the meaning of what they are doing. They see only the material values in life— get more money, get more luxuries. . . . Most [Indian students] are captivated by the opportunities for an open class system with its ample chances to climb on the basis of ability and work with the widespread sharing of a high standard of living." Ruth Hill Useem and John Useem, "Images of the United States and Britain Held by Foreign Educated Indians," *The Annals of the American Academy of Political and Social Studies,* 295 (1954), pp. 73–82.
[67] Maurice L. Farber, "English and American Values in the Socialization Process," *Journal of Psychology,* 36 (1953), pp. 243–250.

Table I

Preference for Highest Grades Rather than Popularity among Students in Five Nations

	PER CENT PREFERRING HIGHEST GRADES		
Nation	10 year olds	14 year olds	Combined ages
Norway	86%	83%	85%
United States	82	63	73
West Germany	62	50	56
England	63	45	54
France	53	30	42

Source: George Gallup and Evan Hill, "Is European Education Better than Ours?" The Saturday Evening Post, 233 (Dec. 24, 1960), p. 70

ety over school examinations. American and French youth led in the proportion who reported worrying about exams (63 per cent); Norwegians were slightly less anxious as a group (60 per cent), while English and German students showed considerably less concern (48 and 28 per cent).[68]

Comparative evidence that achievement orientation and other-directedness may, in fact, be mutually reinforcing has been presented by David McClelland as a conclusion of his extensive comparative studies of the psychological processes which are related to economic development. He suggests that " 'other-directedness' is an essential feature of rapid economic development even in its early stages, rather than a special feature of advanced urban culture in the United States as Riesman suggests."[69] As he puts it:

[W]hat a modern society needs for successful development is flexibility in a man's role relationships. His entire network of relations to others should not be traditionally determined by his caste or even his occupational status. . . . The transition to the new order is certainly likely to be helped if people can learn to listen to what "other people" say is the right thing to do.[70]

[68] George Gallup and Evan Hill, "Is European Education Better than Ours?" *The Saturday Evening Post*, 233 (Dec. 24, 1960), p. 73.
[69] David C. McClelland, *The Achieving Society* (Princeton, N.J.: Van Nostrand, 1961), p. 192.
[70] *Ibid.*, p. 194.

An increase in other-directedness helps facilitate economic development by making individuals more receptive to "the opinion of the 'generalized other.' " It creates greater willingness to accept new norms or techniques, and it helps reduce particularistic ties, thus facilitating the operation of pure market criteria.

To test the hypothesis of the interrelationship of other-directedness and achievement orientation, McClelland analyzed children's readers from over thirty countries in 1925 and 1950 by coding the themes of the stories in terms of measures of other-directedness and achievement motivation. Countries were then classified as above or below the median score for other-directedness and achievement motivation in each period. Nations could be categorized as high on both dimensions, low on both, or high on one and low on the other. Looking then at the various countries and the extent to which they grew economically during the succeeding years (as indicated by growth in electric power), McClelland found that nations which were high on both factors greatly outperformed countries which were low on both, "whereas those that were high on one and low on the other showed an average gain somewhere in between."[71]

> It may come as something of a shock to realize that more could have been learned about the rate of future economic growth of a number of these countries in 1925 or 1950 by reading elementary school books than by studying such presumably more relevant matters as power politics, wars and depressions, economic statistics, or government policies governing international trade, taxation, or public finance. The reason apparently lies in the fact that the readers' reflect sufficiently accurately the motives and values of key groups of men in a country which *in the long run* determine the general drift of economic and political decisions and their effect on productivity. Economic and political policies are of course the means by which economic change is brought about, but whether policies will be implemented, or even decided on in the first place, appears to depend ultimately on the motives and values of men as we have succeeded in detecting them in the stories which they think it is right for their children to read.[72]

The two orientations of other-directedness and achievement motivation, therefore, may be viewed as mutually supportive, rather than, as Riesman and Whyte suggest, mutually contradictory.

---

[71] *Ibid.*, pp. 201–202.
[72] *Ibid.*, p. 202.

The concern with specifying how various structural changes have weakened the Protestant ethic or inner-directed traits in American life has led Riesman and others sometimes to ignore the beneficial consequences of these changes. Thus, I have pointed out elsewhere that while bureaucratization results in a heightened need to make personality adjustments to win the esteem of colleagues and supervisors, it also sets bounds to arbitrary power. By establishing rules of fair treatment, and by reducing the area of personal discretion in personnel policy, bureaucracy can reduce the fear of the employer or of the supervisor.[73] Trade unions, found most commonly under conditions of large industry, accurately reflect their member's desires when their policies involve more, rather than less, bureaucratization of factory life. (As an example of this, unions have sought seniority rules in hiring, firing, and promoting, which increase bureaucratization and reduce arbitrary power.)

Similarly, it may be urged that some of the consequences of bureaucratization reinforce, rather than weaken, strong work and achievement orientations, particularly—but not exclusively[74]—in the upper echelons of white-collar and executive life. The shift from the family-owned company to the management-run corporation, as Whyte pointed out, has made group activities and adjustment to group norms seem more important than before. But whatever else group dynamics in industry may be concerned with, it certainly provides an excellent way of getting men to work hard for the company. Traditionally, it has been a postulate of business management, and an empirical finding of industrial sociology, that men do not work as hard as they are able when the rewards of their work seem to be going to others. Holding other factors constant, no one works so hard as the head of an organization, or the self-employed or

---

[73] S. M. Lipset, *Political Man: The Social Bases of Politics* (Garden City, N.Y.: Doubleday, 1960), p. 414.

[74] In the midst of the greatest prosperity in history, the U.S. Census reported that in the summer of 1957, three and a half million workers had two jobs, with the second job averaging twelve hours per week. In Akron, Ohio, where many rubber workers were on a six-hour day and a five-day week, at relatively high pay, and where a sizable proportion of wives were employed, it was estimated that among the men "from one in seven down to one in five rubber workers holds a second full-time job. . . . In addition, something like 40 per cent engage in some sort of part-time outside work . . . the shorter day even with a higher pay scale, increases the number of men who obtain second jobs . . ." August Heckscher, "Time, Work and Leisure," *Political Research: Organization and Design* (PROD), 1 (1958), p. 156.

the creative professional who is directly rewarded for his labors. By extending the control of work to committees at different levels in the corporation, contemporary American business has found a means of inculcating into a large number of people a sense of responsibility for the whole organization. "Non-owners" now feel individually responsible, and the number of hard-working executives who never watch the clock, and who take work home with them, has been enormously enlarged. Thus, while other-direction may have increased, the motivation for competition and hard work remains, because the best are chosen to move up the bureaucratic hierarchy.

It is a peculiar paradox that the same structural processes may account for diverse and even sharply conflicting tendencies. Many analyses of American society have stressed the fact that individualism *and* conformism, creative innovation *and* dominance by low-level mass taste, are outgrowths of identical forces. For example, the pronounced spread of higher education and a high standard of living have caused an unprecedented increase in both the proportion of the population involved in genuinely creative, intellectual activities, and the influence by the populace on the major expressions of art, literature, and drama.[75] Alexis de Tocqueville was fully aware of these dual tendencies when he pointed out that "the same equality that renders him [The American] independent of each of his fellow citizens, taken severally, exposes him alone and unprotected to the influence of the greater number. . . . I very clearly discern two tendencies; one leading the mind of every man to untried thoughts, the other prohibiting him from thinking at all."[76]

Today, too, there are many trends making for an increase in autono-

---

[75] Daniel Miller and Guy Swanson state, in their detailed study of changes in the American family: "[W]e wish to urge that serious consideration be given to the possibility advanced here that bureaucratization has begun to provide a new level of security and comfort for Americans and a new sense of participation in a responsible moral community. As a consequence, we are less disposed than some commentators to see the growth of 'do-it-yourself' projects and of adult education and the apparent increase of interest in morality and religion as symptoms of a population withdrawing from a complicated and confusing world. Instead, we suggest that these may well signify the seizing of newly available opportunities for self-expression in the fine and practical arts, for the development of sophistication about leisure, and for a confronting of the problems of the relations of man to his fellows and to history." Daniel R. Miller and Guy E. Swanson, *The Changing American Parent* (New York: John Wiley, 1958), p. 212.

[76] Tocqueville, *Democracy in America*, Vol. I, p. 12.

mous behavior, in free choice. Various social scientists have recently begun to document these countervailing tendencies, a phenomenon that may reflect the ever-present cyclical pattern of social analysis. Rowland Berthoff points to the seeming "gradual decline since 1920 of those make-shift communities, the fraternal lodges," which were part of the associational pattern that impressed Tocqueville, and suggests that "the psychic energy that Americans formerly expended on maintaining the jerry-built framework of such 'institutions' as these has in our more assured institutional structure of recent years been freed, at least potentially, for the creation of more valuable kinds of 'culture.' " He also infers that "the recent popular success of books deploring the unworthiness of status striving indicates that Americans are throwing off this obsession and making it, as in other societies, including preindustrial America, merely one concern among many."[77] Robert Wood suggests, in the same vein, that "the pattern of inconspicuous consumption, the web of friendship, and the outgoing life that Whyte describes also have something of the flavor of a renaissance. Although 'keeping down with the Joneses' may indicate group tyranny, it is still better than keeping up with them. At least it displays disapproval of overt snobbishness. . . . While Whyte finds pressures for benevolent conformity, he also discovers brotherhood."[78] Daniel Bell has argued that the growth in education, among other factors, has reduced conformity. He comments that "one would be hard put to find today the 'conformity' *Main Street* exacted of Carol Kennicott thirty years ago. With rising educational levels, more individuals are able to indulge a wider variety of interests," such as serious music, good books, high-level FM radio, and the like.[79]

It may be fitting to conclude this chapter with the paradox formulated by Clyde Kluckhohn, who has suggested:

> Today's kind of "conformity" may actually be a step toward more genuine individuality in the United States. "Conformity" is less of a personal and psychological problem—less tinged wih anxiety and guilt. . . . If someone accepts outwardly the conventions of one's group, one may have greater psychic energy to develop and fulfill one's private potentialities as a unique person. I have encountered no

---

[77] Berthoff, *op. cit.*, p. 512.

[78] Robert Wood, *Suburbia: Its People and Their Politics* (Boston: Houghton Mifflin, 1959), p. 15.

[79] Bell, "The Theory of Mass Society," *op. cit.*, p. 82.

substantial evidence that this "conformity" is thoroughgoingly "inward."[80]

As status-seeking is the by-product of strong equalitarianism, so conformity and other-directedness may permit, or even demand, inner autonomy.

The institution most intimately connected with the value system is, of course, religion. And many have suggested that developments within the American church establishment have reflected the increase in "other-directed" traits. For example, the American's greater propensity to conform is alleged to explain why church membership is at an all-time high point; men increasingly join churches because it is the expected thing to do. I would question the extent to which change has occurred in American religious participation and belief. The next chapter, therefore, turns to an examination of the evidence supporting the assumptions that such major modifications have occurred, and seeks to account for some of the persistent traits in American religion by relating them to continuities in the essential values of the society.

---

[80] Clyde Kluckhohn, "Have There Been Discernible Shifts in American Values during the Past Generation?" in Elting E. Morison, ed., *The American Style: Essays in Value and Performance*, p. 187. This article is the best single summary and reference guide to the various empirical studies of changes in values in America.

Religion and
American
Values

4 ★★★

It is widely assumed that structural changes inherent in industrialization
and urbanization, with consequent bureaucratization and an increase in
"other directedness," have resulted in two major changes in American
religious practice and belief. First it is argued that many more people
outwardly adhere to formal religion and attend church than ever before;
and second, that this increase in formal practice does not reflect greater
religiosity—on the contrary, it is suggested that American religion itself
is now secularized, that it has increasingly adjusted to the sentiments of
the general society.

> It is variously noted that much of religion has become a matter of
> private ethical convictions; that the churches are active in secular
> affairs; that religious observances have been losing their super-
> natural or other-wordly character. It is said that religion in America
> tends to be religion at a very low temperature. . . .[1]

These trends in American religion have been related to the urbanization
and suburbanization of American society that have taken place in the
twentieth century. When the different Protestant sects were geographically isolated from each other, and when immigrant Catholics and Jews

[1] Robin Williams, *American Society* (New York: Alfred A. Knopf, 1957),
p. 344.

were segregated in urban slums, the differences in their fundamental beliefs were relatively unimportant. Those who professed one set of beliefs were insulated against encountering beliefs that contradicted them. Now that no group is really isolated, the different professions of faith in America exhibit "other-directed" traits by emphasizing what is common in their beliefs.[2] Will Herberg points out that the interfaith movement, which has been reasonably successful on a national level, consists of pruning the transcendental beliefs of all three religions to bring about greater harmony among them.[3]

Recent changes in American society may have accentuated these aspects of American religion much as they have reinforced "other-directed" traits in the American character. However, I would suggest that, as in the case of "character" traits discussed in the previous chapter, much of the historical record indicates that these aspects have always distinguished American religion from religion in other nations. American religion, like all other institutions, has made major adjustments in response to changes in the size and scope of the nation, but as the institution most intimately linked with values it has shown the tenacity exhibited by the value system itself.[4]

All-Pervasiveness, a Consistent Characteristic of American Religion

Widespread interest in religion is not a new aspect of American society. For almost a century, prominent European visitors who wrote on American life have been unanimous in remarking on the exceptional religiosity of the society. After his visit to America in 1830, Tocqueville commented: ". . . there is no country in the world where the Christian religion retains a greater influence over the souls of men than in America."[5] Martineau in 1834, Trollope in 1860, Bryce in 1883, and

---

[2] *Ibid.*, pp. 344–345.

[3] Will Herberg, *Protestant—Catholic—Jew: An Essay in American Religious Sociology* (Garden City, N.Y.: Doubleday, 1955), Chapter 10.

[4] Talcott Parsons presents essentially the same thesis: "Looked at by comparison with earlier forms, religion seems to have lost much. But . . . the losses are mainly the consequence of processes of structural differentiation in the society, which correspond to changes in the character of the religious values themselves." Talcott Parsons, *Structure and Process in Modern Societies* (Glencoe, Ill.: The Free Press, 1960), p. 320.

[5] Alexis de Tocqueville, *Democracy in America* (New York: Vintage Books, 1954), Vol. I, p. 314.

Weber in 1904, all arrived at similar conclusions.[6] Their accounts agree substantially with that of a historian's summary of the impressions of pre-Civil War English travelers who

> pointed to the fact that America, though still largely a primitive country, had as many churches as the British Isles, that religious assemblages were being held at one place or another practically all the time; that large donations were constantly being made for religious purposes. America, they concluded, was basically a very religious country. . . . Church services were always crowded on Sundays. . . . Church-going, reported Maxwell, was all the rage in New York. . . . the high percentage of males in the audience was in sharp contrast to their paucity at English services.[7]

Religious practitioners reached similar conclusions. Thus Robert Baird, an American Presbyterian minister who spent eight years in Europe between 1835 and 1843, wrote on his return home:

> In no other part of the world, perhaps, do the inhabitants attend church in a larger proportion than in the United States; certainly no part of the Continent of Europe can compare with them in that respect. The contrast between the two must strike anyone who, after having travelled much in the one, comes to see any of the cities of the other.[8]

Philip Schaff, a Swiss theologian who eventually emigrated to America, reported in similar terms to German Lutheran bodies. He witnessed much greater church attendance in New York and Brooklyn than in Berlin. He stated unequivocally: "There are in America probably more awakened souls, and more individual effort and self-sacrifice for religious purposes, proportionately, than in any other country, Scotland alone perhaps excepted."[9]

[6] Harriet Martineau, *Society in America* (New York: Saunders and Otlay, 1837), II, p. 317; Anthony Trollope, *North America* (New York: Alfred A. Knopf, 1951), p. 277; James Bryce, *The American Commonwealth* (New York: Macmillan, 1912), Vol. II, pp. 770, 778; H. H. Gerth and C. Wright Mills, ed., *From Max Weber: Essays in Sociology* (New York: Oxford University Press, 1946), pp. 302–303.

[7] Max Berger, *The British Traveller in America, 1836–1860* (New York: Columbia University Press, 1943), pp. 133–134.

[8] Robert Baird, *Religion in America* (New York: Harper & Bros., 1844), p. 188.

[9] Philip Schaff, *America: A Sketch of the Political, Social, and Religious Character of the United States of North America* (New York: C. Scribner, 1855), pp. 94, 118.

And a German liberal foe of religion, who found the prevalence of religious practice in America distasteful to his agnostic sentiments, testified to the same set of facts which he, like others, linked in a very materialistic fashion to the effects of the separation of church and state:

> Clergymen in America must . . . defend themselves to the last, like other businessmen; they must meet competition and build up a trade, and it's their own fault if their income is not large enough. Now is it clear why heaven and hell are moved to drive the people to the churches, and why attendance is more common here than anywhere else in the world?[10]

The statistical data which bear on the question also suggest that the increase in church affiliation in recent times is not as significant as has been claimed. The earliest quantitative estimates of religious adherence in America that I have been able to locate are those reported in *The American Almanac and Repository of Useful Knowledge* which was published regularly for some years beginning about 1830. These volumes reported detailed statistics for members *and adherents* of the various denominations. The membership data were taken from statements by the different church groups while the estimates of the number of adherents were derived from various unmentioned publications. In 1831 the total number of adherents listed was 12,136,953, in 1832 the total was 12,496,-953, and in 1837 it had risen to 14,585,000. Since in 1831 the total national population was 13,321,000 and in 1837 it was 15,843,000,[11] these data testify to an almost universal religious adherence by Americans in the 1830's, comparable to the results obtained by public opinion surveys in the past few decades which report that almost every American identifies with a given denomination.

In 1856 Robert Baird published statistical data which also differentiated

---

[10] Karl T. Griesinger, "Lebende Bilder aus Amerika" (1858), a section of which is translated in Oscar Handlin, ed., *This Was America* (Cambridge, Mass.: Harvard University Press, 1949), p. 261.

[11] For estimates of religious adherence see William G. Ouseley, *Remarks on the Statistics and Political Institutions of the United States* (Philadelphia: Carey and Lea, 1832), p. 207; *The American Almanac and Repository of Useful Knowledge for the Year 1833* (Boston: Gray and Bowen, 1832), p. 156; *The American Almanac and Repository of Useful Knowledge for the Year 1838* (Boston: Charles Bowen, 1837), p. 172. For population statistics see U.S. Bureau of the Census, *Historical Statistics of the United States, Colonial Times to 1957* (Washington: U.S. Government Printing Office, 1960), p. 7.

between members and "those under the influence of the evangelical denominations." The total identified with these groups was 17,763,000. (The total population of the country at the time was 26,500,000.) These figures do not include Catholics, Unitarians, Universalists, Mormons, Jews, and various other small, non-evangelical groups. Without describing how he obtained his estimate of over 17 million supporters of the evangelical groups, Baird states: "Accuracy in such a calculation is hardly to be expected, but I have taken the best data I could find, and doubt not that the estimate I have made is not much wide of the truth. Including all the evangelical 'Friends,' this estimate would fall but little short of eighteen million."[12]

While the obvious problems of reliability and validity involved in the use of American church membership statistics make it difficult to reach any conclusions, the available evidence does suggest that, from some time early in American history down to the present, the United States has experienced a continuous "boom" in religious adherence and belief.

These data and observations pose the problem of how to reconcile the estimates concerning the general commitment to religion in the first half of the nineteenth century with the various estimates reported in the *Year Book of American Churches* which indicate a steep rise in membership in religious groups, particularly in the twentieth century.[13] There are many methodological problems concerning the reliability of any historical estimates of church membership, since all of them are presumably based on voluntary replies of church officers to questionnaires, and it is difficult to find out how the reports for much of the nineteenth century were compiled.[14] To some considerable degree, however, the rapid growth

---

[12] Baird, *Religion in America* (1856 edition), pp. 530–532.

[13] Benson Y. Landis, ed., *Year Book of American Churches* (New York: National Council of the Churches of Christ in the U.S.A., 1961), p. 247.

[14] The lack of reliability of church membership data, even in recent times, has been pointed out in a critique of the statistics assembled by the *Year Book of American Churches,* which indicates considerable growth in church membership since 1940. Winthrop Hudson concludes that the supposed boom is "largely an illusion." Among the many problems with the statistics is the fact that increases often reflect reports from denominations which had never reported before, as well as peculiar and suspicious increases, the validity of which are never questioned. For example "when the Christ Unity Church was listed for the first time in the 1952 *Year Book* with 682,172 members, it alone accounted for more than one-third of the 1,842,515 gain reported that year. The following year, the American Carpatho-Russian Orthodox Greek Catholic Church and the Ukrainian Orthodox Church, each with

in reported membership after 1890 is a result of the considerable increase in the non-Protestant denominations, whose concept of a church member differed greatly from those of the Protestants. These groups, largely Catholic and Orthodox, reported as a member every person born in the faith, regardless of age or religious status, while most Protestant denominations all through the nineteenth century only considered as members those who had joined the church as adults, often after fulfilling a rigorous set of requirements.

The discrepancy between the travelers' reports that most Americans

---

75,000 members, were listed for the first time. The year after that, five bodies listed for the first time contributed 195,804 to the total increase in church membership." Winthrop S. Hudson, "Are Churches Really Booming?" *The Christian Century*, 72 (1955), p. 1494. A critique of the reliability of data indicating Catholic growth may be found in B. G. Mulvaney, "Catholic Population Revealed in Catholic Baptisms," *American Ecclesiastical Review*, 133 (1955), pp. 183–193. A number of large denominations simply report their membership in round figures, such as one million for the Greek Orthodox. Others have reported amazing differences from year to year such as "the Romanian Orthodox Church, which reported an increase in the 1952 *Year Book* from 390 to 50,000. What these figures mean can best be seen in terms of a single year's report. The greatest gain in church membership that has been reported was in 1952—3,604,124. For this year, nine bodies with a total membership of 335,528 were listed for the first time. The Russian Orthodox Church reported an increase of membership from 400,000 to 750,000; the Churches of Christ, an increase from 209,615 to 1,500,000; Christ Unity Science Church, from 682,172 to 1,112,123. (The following year the Christ Unity Science Church reported a further 469,163 increase, making a total gain of 1,581,286 for the three year period.) These items alone account for 2,405,864 of the 3,604,124 gain in church membership for the year. If one subtracts the reported gain in Roman Catholic membership [which is also very dubious], all other religious bodies are left with no increase in membership, to say nothing of keeping up with the increase in population." A further difficulty rests in the extensive geographical mobility in the United States which "may have resulted in . . . duplications of church membership, with many people joining a new church without removing their names from the roll of the old church. Some spot checks of membership have tended to confirm this conjecture." Hudson, *op. cit.*, p. 1495.

A detailed look at the data provided by the twelve largest affiliates of the National Council of Churches, who together account for 30 million of the 35 million affiliated to the Council, indicates that their membership, relative to total population, actually "declined" between 1940 and 1954, the period dealt with by Hudson. He concludes that far "from offering 'proof' of a boom in church membership, the statistics . . . show that the boom is largely a fiction." *Ibid.*, p. 1496.

attended church regularly and the relatively small proportion of the
population who actually belonged to a church may be accounted for by
the fact that *during this period most of those who attended churches
did not belong to a given denomination.* Baird, for example, described
the situation as of the 1840's in the following terms:

> Not only do persons who have not yet become members, by formal
> admission as such, attend our churches; they form a very large part
> of our congregations. In many cases they constitute two thirds, three
> fourths, or even more; this depending much on the length of the
> period during which the congregation has been organized, and
> hardly ever less than a half, even in the most highly-favoured
> churches. Nor do they attend only; they are cheerful supporters of
> the public worship, and are often found as liberal in contributing of
> their substance for the promotion of good objects, as the members
> of the church themselves, with whom they are intimately connected
> by the ordinary business of life, and by family ties. . . . The non-pro-
> fessing hearers of the Word, then, are to be considered as simply
> what we call them, members of the congregation, not of the
> church. . . .[15]

The reasons why men might attend church and support a given
denomination without becoming a member are not difficult to understand, given the conditions for membership which existed for most of
the nineteenth century:

> Certainly by modern standards, church membership was a strenuous
> affair. All evangelical sects required of communicants a personal
> experience of conversion and a consistent life. Two worship services
> and Sunday School on the Sabbath were customary. The Methodists
> invariably kept new converts on "probation" for many months.
> Wesley's followers also attended a weekly class meeting. . . . Lay-
> men of most denominations were responsible for a large amount of
> missionary and benevolent work. . . .[16]

Perhaps the most comprehensive attempt to specify the number of
"adherents" as distinct from "communicants" of the different Protestant
denominations is the study by H. K. Carroll, who was in charge of the

---

[15] Baird, *Religion in America*, p. 188.
[16] Timothy L. Smith, *Revivalism and Social Reform in Mid-Nineteenth
Century America* (New York: Abingdon Press, 1957), p. 18; Baird, *Religion
in America*, pp. 185–187.

Division of Churches for the 1890 U.S. Census.[17] His efforts led him to conclude that in 1890 with a population of 62,622,250, only 5 million people were *not* communicants or adherents. In percentage terms, he estimated that 92 per cent of the population in 1890 and 91 per cent in 1910 were linked to a denomination. These estimates are comparable to those suggested by Ouseley for the 1830's and by Baird for the 1840's and 1850's, and are similar to the results of public opinion surveys since the mid-1930's and to the 1957 U.S. Census Sample Survey of Religious Affiliation. And these statistical conclusions, of course, reiterate the almost unanimous comments made for close to a century and a half by various foreign travelers, who have never ceased to indicate their amazement at the rarity of atheists or anti-religious people in America.[18]

---

[17] He secured an estimate of the ratio of communicants to adherents by "a comparison between the census returns of the religious populations of various communions in Canada [where the Census asks each person his religious affiliation] with those which the denominations give themselves of communicants." H. K. Carroll, *The Religious Forces in the United States* (New York: The Christian Literature Co., 1893), p. xxxv. The average of Canadian Protestant adherents to communicants was 3.2. To be on the safe side, Carroll suggested, however, that this ratio was probably higher than in the United States since there were many smaller and obscure denominations here, and he concluded that he would be safe in assuming "that there are at least 2.5 adherents in the United States to each Protestant communicant." Relating reports on Protestant membership to this estimate, he derived a total estimate of 49,630,000 for the aggregate of Protestant communicants and adherents. He also determined the adherents and communicants for Catholic, Jewish, and other religious groups. Some similar procedures were employed by Dr. Carroll two decades later using 1910 materials. Carroll, *op. cit.* (1912 edition), pp. lxxi–lxxii. The ratio of communicants to adherents, however, had to be reduced from 2.5 to 2 in view of the large gain in actual church membership reported. In seeking to interpret the great gain in church memberships in the 1910 report, we must note that little, if any resulted from any significant growth in Protestant religious enthusiasm. Rather, as Dr. Carroll pointed out, the churches had changed their definition of a member. "All Churches receive children into that relation much earlier in life than formerly and there are other factors tending to reduce the ratio of adherents to communicants, particularly the relaxation of discipline. . . ." *Ibid.*, p. lxxxii.
[18] It is undoubtedly significant that the major change in the requirements for church membership among the traditionally evangelical denominations occurred within two or three years after the 1906 Census of Religion. This Census (gathered like previous ones through reports by church bodies of their membership) followed two decades of massive, largely non-Protestant, immigration. The difference between the Protestant and the Catholic-Greek Orthodox-Jewish concept of member resulted in a gross underestimate of the actual nu-

More precise historical data which belie the claim of drastic changes in religious practice are provided by the Census reports for the second half of the nineteenth century, which present the number of seats available in all American churches. These data indicate an increase in the ratio of church seats to population of from 62 to 69 per cent,[19] although the *Year Book of American Churches*, the most frequently quoted source on church affiliation in the United States, estimates a growth in membership between 1850 and 1900 of from 15 to 36 per cent of the total population. Since the 1850 population included two million slaves (almost one-seventh of the population), a group which on the whole lacked substantial church accommodations, it seems probable that the relatively small increase in available church facilities was added by the Negroes. All during the second half of the nineteenth century, the churches kept up with the tremendous population expansion in providing accommodations for almost the entire adult population.

Figures on number of clergymen in America from 1850 to 1950 also reveal a striking constancy. In each census year there has been approximately one clergyman for every 1,000 persons. In 1850 there were 1.16 clergymen per 1,000 population; by 1960, the figure had changed to 1.13. Actually, there has been *no effective change* in the ratio of clergy to total population during the past century, although the proportions of others in professional occupations increased sharply, a difference which is shown in Table II.

This lack of an increase in the proportion of ministers adds further support to the idea that there has been little change in the strength of institutionalized religion, although in itself it is not conclusive evidence. Certainly the ratio of parishioners to clergy may have changed, so that

---

merical strength of the Protestant groups. While the reasons advanced for the changes made by the various denominations in their membership standards did not allude to such competitive considerations, there can be little doubt that these played a role. The decision to admit children to membership simply added numbers. Other modifications in the requirements, however, made it much easier for adults to join, as may be seen in the example of the Methodists. The 1908 Conference of the Methodist Episcopal Church dropped the requirement that a new member must have "met for at least six months in class," and the further condition that he be "on trial" for six months "under the care of the leaders" for the simple obligation that he be "properly recommended." Franklin Hamlin Littell, *From State Church to Pluralism* (Garden City, N. Y.: Doubleday Anchor, 1962), p. 81.

[19] Unfortunately, the Census stopped reporting this datum so that we have no comparable figures for this century.

Table II

Number of Clergymen and Professionals Per 1,000 Population for Census Years 1900–1960

	Clergymen	Professionals
1900	1.22	14.2
1910	1.28	18.6
1920	1.20	20.6
1930	1.21	26.5
1940	1.09	26.2
1950	1.12	32.8
1960	1.13	40.3

Sources: Data for Clergy in G. Stigler, Trends in Employment in the Service Industries *(Princeton, N.J.: Princeton University Press, 1956), p. 108; data for professionals calculated from Alba M. Edwards,* Comparative Occupational Statistics for the United States, 1870 to 1940, *Bureau of the Census, 1943, and* Statistical Abstracts, 1952.

modern clergymen may serve more members than those of the past. However, arguing against this possibility is the fact that the proportion of ministers has failed to rise with the long-term increasing wealth of the American people. That a congregation's ability to pay for religion would be a factor is suggested by the sharp drop in the depression decade revealed in the above table.

Some of those who contend that religious adherence in American society has reached an all time high in recent times point to evidence, derived from public opinion surveys and the 1957 U.S. Sample Survey of Religious Affiliation conducted by the Census Bureau, which indicate that over 95 per cent of the population state a belief in God and declare an identification with some specific religious group. There are, of course, no comparable interview data for the nineteenth century except for the nearly unanimous reports by foreign travelers that almost everyone they spoke to expressed religious beliefs and commitments. It is possible, however, to contrast the answers given by undergraduates in American colleges before World War I and in 1952 to questionnaires concerning their religious beliefs.

In a study made in 1913, 927 students in nine colleges of "high rank" replied to questions concerning their belief in God. Eighty-seven per cent of the men and 93 per cent of the women reported belief.[20] The

―――――――――

[20] James H. Leuba, *The Belief in God and Immortality* (Chicago: Open Court Publishing Co., 1921), pp. 184–202.

same author received replies from 90 per cent of the students in "one college of high rank," of whom 70 per cent believed in immortality and after-life.[21] Four decades later, in 1952, a group of Cornell sociologists administered questionnaires to 4,585 students selected through statistical sampling procedures to be representative of *male* undergraduates at eleven colleges and universities. Twenty-four per cent of the men were atheists or agnostics.[22] Comparing the findings of these two studies suggests that at least for college students the supposed religious "revival" of the 1950's still has considerable distance to go before belief reaches a point comparable to that of 1913.[23]

Such statistical data as we have examined all argue against the thesis that religious practice in America in the mid-twentieth century is at its high point. Rather, one concludes from these data that, although there have been ebbs and flows in enthusiasm, basic long-term changes in formal religious affiliation and practice have not occurred, and the current high level of religious belief and observance existed in the past as well. As the foreign travelers noted in their books, Americans have been and continue to be a highly religious people. In fact, the one empirical generalization which does seem justified about American religion is that from the early nineteenth century down to the present, the United States has been among the most religious countries in the Christian world. Considerably lower proportions of religious responses (belief in God) are reported by pollsters for European countries than for the United States.[24] With respect to attendance, it is misleading to compare national rates because of the varying proportions of Catholics and Protestants (who manifest divergent church-going patterns) within populations. But American Protestants attend church more frequently than Protestants in Sweden, Denmark, Czechoslovakia (before the Communist coup), and Great Britain.[25]

---

[21] *Ibid.*, pp. 213–216.

[22] Philip E. Jacob, *Changing Values in College* (New York: Harper & Bros., 1957), p. 108. Universities differed: Almost one-third (32 per cent) of the Harvard College students do not believe in God as compared with 13 per cent of those at the University of Texas.

[23] Actually, such a conclusion—that there is less belief today than four decades ago—would not be warranted since the sampling methods and questions asked differed greatly.

[24] Leo Rosten, *A Guide to the Religions of America* (New York: Simon & Schuster, 1955), p. 247.

[25] Hadley Cantril, *Public Opinion 1935–1946* (Princeton, N. J.: Princeton University Press, 1951), p. 699.

Secularity, a Persistent Trait of American Religion

From the available evidence it is difficult to discern actual trends with respect to the secularization of religion. There does appear to have been a historic trend toward secularization but it does not seem to be as great as many have argued. The supporters of the thesis of increased seculari- zation would seem to minimize two somewhat contradictory but co- existent tendencies. First, they ignore the possibility that the supposedly modern, secularized religion may have characterized much of American behavior in previous periods. Second, they are inattentive to the fact that, now as in the past, a considerable number of Americans have a propensity to follow evangelical religions—and middle-class intellectuals tend to compare nineteenth century evangelical movements which they know from historical records with contemporary middle- and upper-class liberal religion, the form they are personally acquainted with. They forget that the religion of the better educated and more privileged has always tended to be more secularly oriented than that of the lower strata.

In the past three decades, as in the early nineteenth century, the more orthodox and fundamentalist denominations, e.g., the Southern Baptists, the Missouri Synod of the Lutheran Church, the Catholic Church, and the numerous small Pentecostal and fundamentalist sects, have had more success in recruiting members than the "established" denominations which belong to the National Council of Churches—much as in the nineteenth century the then revivalist Methodists and Baptists had much greater success than the older higher status and more secularized denominations such as the Episcopalians, Congregationalists, and Uni- tarians.[26]

There is no question that various denominations have become more secularized and less evangelical over time. But this change within specific denominations such as the Presbyterians and the Methodists in large part reflects the fact that their constituency has changed, from "out" groups to "in" groups. Concentrating on the history of a given Protestant denomination necessarily results in the misleading conclusion that there has been a sharp change from ascetic fervor to a more secularized reli- gious liberalism.

American religious denominations, like ethnic groups, have experienced collective upward mobility. In the early years of the Republic, the

---

[26] Hudson, "Are Churches Really Booming?" *op. cit.*, pp. 1495–1496.

Presbyterians were among the more depressed strata economically and socially, and their religious and political behavior reflected this fact.[27] They, however, soon became identified with the Congregationalists, the Quakers, the Unitarians, and the Episcopalians, as the churches of the more well-to-do and the urban middle classes. The Methodists and Baptists became the predominant religions of the constantly expanding frontier population and the urban working classes. With economic and population growth, the Methodists, too, gained proportionally in middle-class members, and the ministry, which had been largely uneducated, gradually became a seminary or university trained one, a phenomenon which tended to reduce their evangelical fervor and their appeal to the "displaced" strata. New sects arose to satisfy the need for religious enthusiasm. The upward mobility of the members of the older Protestant denominations was also facilitated by immigration from Europe, largely of Catholic and Lutheran background, followed by increasing numbers of Jews and adherents of the Greek Orthodox creed. Most recently, southern Negroes have moved into the cities. Since most of these immigrants and Negroes have occupied the lowest positions in the class structure, many white Protestant groups, particularly the Methodists who had been the predominant evangelical sect for much of the nineteenth century, necessarily improved their location on the status ladder. Thus, while the denominational affiliations of urban middle-class Americans may have changed from a statistical point of view, the pattern of American religion has remained fairly constant. Negro religious behavior resembles that of the nineteenth century lower status migrant white population. The Catholics have taken on the coloration of a fundamentalist orthodox religion comparable in tone and style, if not in theology, to the nineteenth-century evangelical Protestant sects. Recently, a leading French Dominican student of the American Church has complained that American Catholics resemble American Baptists more than they do Mexican or French Catholics. He comments that "one often has the impression that American Catholics are more Puritan than anybody else and that they are close to setting themselves up as the champions of Puritanism."[28]

The historic American pattern of a more secularized higher status

---

[27] Manning Dauer, *The Adams Federalists* (Baltimore: John Hopkins Press, 1953), pp. 28–29.

[28] R. L. Bruckberger, "The American Catholics as a Minority," in Thomas T. McAvoy, ed., *Roman Catholicism and the American Way of Life* (Notre Dame, Ind.: University of Notre Dame Press, 1960), pp. 45–47.

religion has been well described by Baltzell, who points out that, from the beginning of the nineteenth century, men often turned to the Episcopal Church as they became well-to-do. This was true for Presbyterian cotton planters in the South, for the upper-class Quakers of Philadelphia, and even for many old-family New England Unitarians and Congregationalists.[29] The secular motivations underlying such conversions were not a secret to their contemporaries. Foreign travelers also were well aware of the relationship between status-seeking and church membership.[30]

Many of the foreign observers also confessed their surprise to find that the system of competing denominations in the United States did not mean that the different groups rejected each other for adhering to "false creeds." An Italian Jesuit, Giovanni Grassi, who served for five years, 1812 to 1817, as President of Georgetown College before returning to Rome, commented in disturbed tones on these "other-directed" religious phenomena:

> Every sect there is held as good, every road as correct, and every error as the insignificant weakness of poor mortals. . . .
>
> Although how can one speak of sects? Those who describe themselves as members of one or another of the sects do not thereby profess an abiding adherence to the doctrines of the founders of the sect. . . . Thus the Anglicans of today no longer take much account of their thirty-nine articles, nor the Lutherans of the Confession of Augsburg, nor the Presbyterians of the teachings of Calvin or of Knox. . . .
>
> Among the peculiarities of America, not the most extreme is that of finding persons who live together for several years without knowing each other's religion. And many, when asked, do not answer, "I believe," but simply, "I was brought up in such a persuasion."[31]

Timothy Smith concludes from his detailed examination of the writings of many nineteenth-century ministerial foreign travelers that visit-

---

[29] E. Digby Baltzell, *Philadelphia Gentlemen. The Making of a National Upper Class* (Glencoe, Ill..: The Free Press, 1958), pp. 225–233. See also Dixon Wecter, *The Saga of American Society* (New York: Scribner's 1937), pp. 480–481.

[30] Schaff, *America*, pp. 154–155. See also Thomas C. Grattan, *Civilized America* (London: Bradbury and Evans, 1895), Vol. I, pp. 60–61.

[31] Giovanni Grassi, *Notizie varie sullo stato presente della republica degli Stati Uniti dell' America* (1819), section translated in Oscar Handlin, ed., *This Was America* (Cambridge, Mass.: Harvard University Press, 1949), pp. 147–148.

ing "Evangelicals were especially heartened to discover that the elimination of legal privilege [separation of church and state in America]
seemed to lessen sectarian rivalry."[32] He cites one English visitor in the
1830's who "noted with pleasure *the numerous exchanges of pulpits,
union prayer meetings and joint efforts in Bible Society, Sunday school,
and mission work.* She decided that the sectarian spirit of Europe's
churches arise not so much from 'conscientious scruples and differences
of opinion on government or doctrine' as from the fact that some had
endowments and some did not."[33] A leading French Calvinist pastor
who visited the United States two decades later confessed his surprise
at this phenomenon of mutual esteem among competing sects:

> We thought, until our visit to the United States, that the multiplicity
> of sects there, must, of necessity, present an obstacle to the progress
> of the spirit of brotherly love. We do not yet think that a diversity
> of communions is an efficacious means of developing among Chris-
> tians the principle of charity; but we are glad to acknowledge that
> our American brethren have combatted very effectually the at-
> tendant dangers. So far as we have been able to judge, there exists
> much harmony and good feeling, between all the evangelical de-
> nominations. The pastors and members of the various religious com-
> munities even among those most widely differing in church polity
> speak mutually of each other with much kindness and esteem.[34]

Tocqueville's companion on his visit to America, Gustave de Beaumont, was also struck by this behavior and confessed his puzzlement as to
how Americans could be fervent in their particular belief yet approve
of exchange of pulpits among ministers of different Protestant denominations:

> As a matter of fact, nothing is commoner in the United States than
> this indifference toward the nature of religions, which doesn't
> however eliminate the religious fervour of each for the cult he has
> chosen. Actually, this extreme tolerance on the one hand towards
> religions in general—on the other this considerable zeal of each
> individual for his own religion, is a phenomenon I can't yet explain

[32] Smith, *Revivalism and Social Reform in Mid-Nineteenth Century America*,
p. 37.
[33] *Ibid.*, p. 19. (Emphasis mine.)
[34] J. H. Grand Pierre, *A Parisian Pastor's Glance at America* (Boston: Gould
and Lincoln, 1854), pp. 63–64.

to myself. I would gladly know how a lively and sincere faith can get on with such a perfect toleration; how one can have equal respect for religions whose dogmas differ. . . .[35]

And Beaumont asked the same question about American religion in the 1830's that many have raised in recent years: "Would it not be from their outward show of religion that *there is more breadth than depth in it?*"[36]

Tocqueville himself commented that in no other country is Christianity "clothed with fewer forms, figures, and observances than in the United States, or where it presents more distinct, simple and general notions to the mind. Although the Christians of America are divided into a multitude of sects, they look upon their religion in the same light."[37] And in his private notes Tocqueville reported:

Go into the churches (I mean the Protestant ones), you will hear morality preached, of dogma not a word. Nothing which can at all shock the neighbour; nothing which can arouse the idea of dissent. . . . [Ministers preach to other denominations.] But, said I, how do these men and children, who are communicants of one sect, like hearing the minister of another? The infallible response is this: The different preachers, treating only the common ground of morality, cannot do each other any harm.[38]

His English contemporary, Harriet Martineau, who stated that almost everyone professed some form of Christian belief, perceptively added that people are not supposed to feel intensely about a particular religion:

One circumstance struck me throughout the country. Almost as often as the conversation between myself and any other person on religious subjects became intimate and earnest, I was met by the supposition that I was a convert. It was the same in other instances: wherever there was a strong interest in the Christian religion, conversion to a particular profession of it was confidentially supposed. This fact speaks volumes.[39]

---

[35] Quoted in George W. Pierson, *Tocqueville in America* (Garden City, N.Y.: Doubleday Anchor, 1959), p. 70.

[36] *Loc. cit.* (Emphasis mine.)

[37] Tocqueville, *Democracy in America*, Vol. II, p. 28.

[38] Pierson, *Tocqueville in America*, p. 100.

[39] Martineau, *Society in America*, Vol. II, p. 336.

In 1860 Anthony Trollope was struck by the fact that "the question of a man's religion is regarded in a free and easy way." He notes that fathers believe "that a young lad should go somewhere on a Sunday; but a sermon is a sermon. . . . Everybody is bound to have a religion, but it does not much matter what it is."[40] And in 1900, the German sociologist Max Weber was also impressed, during his visit, with the seeming secularization of religion and acceptance of religious diversity. He reported: "In the main, the congregations refused entirely to listen to the preaching of 'dogma' and to confessional distinctions. 'Ethics' alone could be offered. . . . Today the kind of denomination [to which one belongs] is rather irrelevant. It does not matter whether one be a Freemason, Christian Scientist, Adventist, Quaker, or what not."[41]

The foremost modern British scholar of America concludes his discussion of late nineteenth-century religious life:

> Religion became a matter of conduct, of good deeds, of works with only a vague background of faith. It became highly functional, highly pragmatic; it became a guarantee of success, moral and material. . . . Theological schools turned from theology to a form of anthropology—a moralistic and optimistic form, but anthropology all the same. That 'the proper study of mankind is man' was the evasion by which many American divines escaped the necessity for thought about God.[42]

Reports that American religion is much more secular than that found in other nations have been just as consistent as reports that it has relatively

---

[40] Trollope, *North America*, p. 278.

[41] Gerth and Mills, eds., *From Max Weber*, p. 307.

[42] Denis W. Brogan, *The American Character* (New York: Alfred A. Knopf, 1944), p. 102. Stow Persons states that "by the middle of the nineteenth century . . . the denominational pattern that had matured . . . conformed closely to the contours of American social life. Under no other ecclesiastical system could the expressions of the religious spirit have been expected to reflect so immediately the character and outlook of the parishioners. . . . the middle classes generally preferred a more sedate and formal worship in which traditional dogmas were wedded to the individualistic ethic of the Gospel of Wealth. Urban professionals and intellectuals who were sensitive to currents of opinion in the secular world were frequently drawn into that new phenomenon, the big city parish, centered on the resonant personality of a pulpit orator who blended the elements of an innocuous theology with discussion of current interests to produce a romantic individualism." "Religion and Modernity, 1865–1914," in J. W. Smith and L. Jamison, eds, *The Shaping of American Religion* (Princeton, N.J.: Princeton University Press, 1961), pp. 370–372.

more adherents. Secularity has long been cited as a persistent trait of American religion and cannot simply be attributed to an increase in socially motivated church-going in the past few decades.

However, secularity is not the only notable characteristic of American religion throughout its history. New sects have developed more readily here than anywhere else in the world.[43] For the most part, these are drawn from economically and socially depressed strata, and their theology reflects this fact, such as in the belief that wealth or ostentation is sinful or corrupting.[44] During the last Great Depression, when efforts to form significant protest political parties failed totally, the religious sectarians grew, while other religions declined or showed no change.[45]

Since all of these characteristics have made American religion unique throughout its history, they must be attributed to those features of American society that have consistently distinguished it from other cultures, rather than to recent changes. In each age, men have seen in the almost total allegiance to religion by Americans a further evidence of the conformist propensity of democratic man. Analysts, in the past as well as the present,[46] have also attributed the secular quality of American

---

[43] There are more than 200 Protestant denominations in the United States. "Democracy has not only permitted the continuance of all the divisions of Protestantism; it has also allowed, if not encouraged, the growth of new groups." H. Richard Niebuhr, "The Protestant Movement and Democracy in the United States," in J. W. Smith and L. Jamison, eds., *The Shaping of American Religion*, pp. 52–53. See pp. 25–26 for a classification of Protestant denominations in the United States based on the times of their origins.

[44] E. T. Clark, *The Small Sects in America* (New York: Abingdon-Cokesbury, 1949), p. 17. Stow Persons, in discussing Clark's account of the Millerite movement and its reaction to the anticipated day of the Second Coming, interestingly concludes that millenialism "cannot be explained as a product of poverty or persecution [but rather] represented a stubborn refusal to accept a modernist version of the historical process in which divine immanence was reconciled with events naturalistically conceived." He finds evidence of diffuse anxiety, rather than misery or tragedy, in Adventist literature. Stow Persons, "Religion and Modernity, 1865–1914," *op. cit.*, pp. 399–400.

[45] William W. Sweet, *The American Churches* (New York: Abingdon-Cokesbury, 1947), p. 73; A. T. Boisen, *Religion in Crisis and Custom* (New York: Harper & Bros., 1955), pp. 71–75; also Michael Argyle, *Religious Behavior* (Glencoe, Ill.: The Free Press, 1958), pp. 138–140.

[46] H. Richard Niebuhr, indulging in a kind of animistic thinking, attributes "other-directedness" to Protestant groups themselves. "Seeking to survive, thrown into competition for attention, membership, and economic support, not only with each other but with secular enterprises claiming the same resources, they appear to have adjusted themselves all too well to the wishes of the people. . . . If Protestantism in America has . . . accepted . . . the dogmas

religion to its relationship with democracy. Tocqueville felt that the emphasis upon morality, rather than transcendental beliefs, in American religion, was a result of the numerous sects and religions being given equal status before the law and in the eyes of men. He observed:

> [The sects] all differ in respect to the worship which is due to the Creator, but they all agree in respect to the duties which are due from man to man. Each sect adores the Deity in its own peculiar manner, but all sects preach the same moral law in the name of God. . . . Society has no future life to hope for or to fear; and provided the citizens profess a religion, the peculiar tenets of that religion are of little importance to its interests.[47]

In this respect, he does not differ too greatly from Herberg who says:

> Just as the three great religions are the basic subdivisions of the American people, so are the three great communions felt to be recognized expressions of the spiritual aspect of the American Way of Life. This underlying unity not only supplies limits within which their conflicts and tensions may operate and beyond which they cannot go—it also supplies the common content of the three communities.[48]

Each of these analyses implies that both the secular and the all-pervasive character of American religion is a result of its being viewed as part of the "American Way of Life." Tocqueville found that "the whole nation," "every rank of society," felt that religion was indispensable to the maintenance of republican institutions. And he believed that this was why, on the one hand, even those who did not "profess the doctrines of Christianity from sincere belief in them" did so hypocritically "because they fear[ed] to be suspected of unbelief"; and why, on the other hand, Christian morality rather than transcendental beliefs stood out in American religious attitudes.[49]

American Protestantism has concentrated on the moral rather than the contemplative, mystical, or communal and traditional elements of religion partially because of its Puritan roots. The contemplative and the mys-

---

of democratic faith, then indeed it has lost its independence, then it no longer challenges the social faith but is a passive representative of the culture." "The Protestant Movement and Democracy . . . ," *op. cit.*, pp. 57, 67.

[47] Tocqueville, *Democracy in America*, Vol. I, p. 314.

[48] Herberg, *Protestant—Catholic—Jew*, p. 247.

[49] Tocqueville, *Democracy in America*, Vol. I, pp. 315–316.

tical have not played a significant role in Protestantism in general, and in addition "the intellectual, theological element, though prominent in Puritan Christianity came with the growth of the churches of the common man and the triumph of pietism to be neglected in American religion":

> In the main drift of religion in America the theological and liturgical and mystical and contemplative move into the background; the hierarchical and communal give place to the individualistic, the traditional to the immediate, the authoritative to the freely decided, the appeal to the mind and the aesthetic sense to the appeal to the will, the awareness of the ultimate to the concern with the practical life. The penumbra of beyondness, absoluteness, and mystery fades away, and leaves—as the core of what Americans think religion to be—the moral.[50]

Voluntarism, the Source of Religious Strength

In seeking to explain the special character of American religion many of the foreign visitors singled out the effect of the separation of church and state, which resulted in American churches being voluntary organizations in which congregational self-government was the predominant form of church government. More specifically, the special quality of American religion has been linked to three elements in the American past: first, New England Puritanism infused certain ascetic values into the very concept of Protestantism—the Puritans' "Protestant ethic" lay close to the heart of most denominations, regardless of doctrinal differences; second, ideological emphases and institutional changes which flowed from the American Revolution led to forms of church organization analogous to popularly based institutions; and third, the fact that all sections of the United States were formed out of an unsettled frontier without any traditional class structure or significant aid or control from a central government meant that religious institutions had to be created almost completely from the resources of the local population, and hence closely reflected their specific religious needs and their secular values.

It is difficult to separate out the contributions of each of these, and of other factors. As in all complex structures, the various elements tend to interact continually. Thus, Puritanism has been credited with sup-

---

[50] William Lee Miller, "American Religion and American Political Attitudes," in J. W. Smith and L. Jamison, eds., *The Shaping of American Religion* (Princeton, N.J.: Princeton University Press, 1961), p. 94.

plying much of the motivation behind the Revolution.[51] Congregationalist pastors overwhelmingly backed the Revolution, while the hierarchically organized Episcopalians tended to be Tories. Congregationalism, with its stress on self-government within the church, contributed to secular self-government in the form of the New England town meeting. Comparative studies of frontier settlement in Canada, Latin America, and Australia have suggested that part of the democratic aspects of American frontier settlement reflected the American ethos and political system, not simply the needs of any new frontier society. In Canada, as will be detailed in Chapter 7, central authorities played a much greater role in settling and governing the frontier than was true in the United States. And in examining developments in American religion, it seems obvious that the ideology which flowed from the Revolution and the subsequent political triumph of the "left" in the early decades of the Republic led to the decisive decision in favor of "disestablishment." The withdrawal of government support from religion made American Protestantism unique in the Christian world. The United States became the first nation in which religious groups were viewed as purely voluntary associations. To exist, American churches had to compete in the marketplace for support. And conversely, membership in a given religious denomination was a voluntary act.

This emphasis on voluntary associations which struck Tocqueville and other foreign travelers as one of the distinctive American traits, and which was also supportive of political democracy, has been traced by some as essentially derivative from "voluntary religion." Sidney Mead points out that even the Episcopalians became consciously aware of the fact that with the end of the Revolution they could now exist only as "voluntary associations" (a term explicitly used in such an analysis by an Episcopalian minister). This meant they had to involve the laity in church government, and that a priest would have only as much influence as there was good opinion of his ability. As Mead says, "the acceptance of religious freedom and separation" came to mean that ministers had only "persuasive or political power."[52]

---

[51] The best treatment of the relationship of religion to the background of the Revolution is Carl Bridenbaugh, *Mitre and Sceptre* (New York: Oxford University Press, 1962.

[52] Sidney E. Mead, "The Rise of the Evangelical Conception of the Ministry in America (1607–1850)," in H. Richard Niebuhr and Daniel D. Williams, eds., *The Ministry in Historical Perspectives* (New York: Harper & Bros., 1956), pp. 214–215. An excellent, detailed analysis of the interrelationship between voluntary organizations and religious practice in the early United States may be found in Baird, *Religion in America*.

The end of religious Establishment and the growth of the sects meant that a new structure of moral authority had to be created to replace the once dominant link between Church and State. In New England, many Congregationalist ministers and laymen consciously recognized that they had to establish voluntary organizations to safeguard morality in a democratic society that deemphasized the links between Church and Government.[53] The early organization of local and national associations for domestic missionary work, for the distribution of Bibles, for temperance, for opposition to slavery, and for peace, was invariably undertaken by well-to-do religious people, and by ministers adhering to the historic New England denominations, who felt these were the only ways they could preserve and extend a moral society. Eventually a host of voluntary groups developed around the voluntary churches.

> The separation of Church and State, and other causes, have given rise to a new species of social organization, before unknown in history. . . . Then opened on the American world the new era of the Religious and Benevolent Society system, and summoned into the field an immense body of superior and highly-cultivated talent. . . .
>
> As to the right or wrong of these institutions, or as to whether they are good or bad, is not, in this place, a subject of inquiry; but simply the fact of their social importance, and their power. . . . And it happens, that these voluntary associations are so numerous, so great, so active and influential, that, as a whole, they now constitute the great school of public education, in the formation of those practical opinions, religious, social, and political, which lead the public mind and govern the country. . . .[54]

American Protestantism, although Calvinist in origin, fairly early in its history became Arminian. A large majority of the Calvinist denominations, as well as most of the non-Calvinist ones, came to accept the Arminian "doctrines of free will, free grace, and unlimited hope for the conversion of all men."[55] To maintain themselves after disestablishment, practically all the Protestant groups had become proselytizing churches. And the Calvinist belief in predestination "could hardly survive amidst

---

[53] See Clifford S. Griffin, *Their Brothers' Keepers* (New Brunswick, N.J.: Rutgers University Press, 1960), pp. 23–43, for a description of the organization of these societies.

[54] An American Gentleman (Calvin Colton), *A Voice from America to England* (London: Henry Colburn, 1839), pp. 87–88, 97.

[55] Smith, *Revivalism and Social Reform in Mid-Nineteenth Century America,* pp. 88–89.

the evangelists' earnest entreaties to 'come to Jesus.' "[56] American Protestantism, with its emphasis on the personal achievement of grace, reinforced the stress on personal achievement which was dominant in the secular value system. Both sets of values stressed individual responsibility, both rejected hereditary status. The two dominant denominations, the Methodists and the Baptists, which contained most Protestants, stressed religious doctrines that reinforced "anti-aristocratic tendencies."[57] Here again it is possible to suggest an interacting complex. An early nineteenth-century analyst of American religion argued that the reason that these denominations outgrew others was that the "disciplinary habits, the political opinions, and ideological tenets, both of the Baptists and Wesleyans, are more congenial to American democracy, than those of the better educated and more accomplished religious sects. . . . Hence—the political opinions of America having been before determined—those forms of religion best adapted to harmonize with them, were likely to prevail most. . . ."[58] To understand the character and strength of religion in America, it is therefore important to see its fundamental links with the prevalent secular values.

The fact of disestablishment, that is, the absence of a state church, served also to enhance the application of religious morality to politics. The existence of a state Church in Europe meant that "even 'sin,' in European culture had been institutionalized."

> There, an actual place had been made for it in life's crucial experience. It had been classified from time out of mind and given specific names; the reality of "lust," "avarice," and "oppression" had given rise to the most intricate of social arrangements, not for eliminating them, but for softening their impact and limiting their scope—for protecting the weak and defining the responsibilities of the strong. . . . All this may well have been in [Henry] James's mind when he exclaimed of America: "*no church.*"
>
> What, then, might be expected to happen if *sin* should suddenly become apparent, in a nation whose every individual was, at least symbolically, expected to stand on his own two feet? The reaction was altogether destructive. The sense of outrage was personal, the sense of *personal* guilt was crushing. The gentle American of mild vices was transformed into the bloody avenger.[59]

---

[56] *Ibid.*, p. 89.
[57] *Ibid.*, pp. 24–25.
[58] Calvin Colton, *A Voice from America to England*, pp. 69–70. Colton himself was an Episcopalian conservative and disliked these tendencies.
[59] Stanley Elkins, *Slavery* (Chicago: University of Chicago Press, 1959), p. 35.

The need to assuage the sense of personal responsibility has meant that Americans have been particularly wont to support movements for the elimination of evil by violent means if necessary. The movements for temperance and prohibition, for the abolition of slavery, for resistance to the growth of Catholicism, and most recently for the elimination of Communists, have all drawn their vigor from the stress developed within American society on personal responsibility for the struggle against evil.[60]

Certainly there has been an interplay between religious and democratic values from the beginning of the nation's history. The gradual identification of Enlightenment ideals with national identity in turn affected the content of our religious values. J. Franklin Jameson explains the amazingly rapid decline of Calvinist doctrine in America after the Revolution, and its replacement by Arminian religious beliefs, not only as a reflection of the doctrinal need of evangelical revivalistic religion, but also by the assumption that, "in a period when the special privileges of individuals were being called into question or being destroyed, there would naturally be less favor for that form of theology which was dominated by the doctrine of the especial election of a part of mankind, a growing favor for forms which seemed more distinctly to be based upon the idea of the natural equality of all men."[61]

The Arminian emphasis on the personal attainment of grace, perhaps even more than the Calvinist stress on the existence of an "elect," served as a religious parallel to the secular emphasis on equality of opportunity and achievement. This parallelism, and even mutual reinforcement, was noted by many nineteenth-century foreign visitors. Unlike the situation in many European countries, in which economic materialism was viewed by the social and religious establishments—that is, the traditional aristocracy and the church—as conducive to uncouth behavior and immorality, in the United States hard work and economic ambition have been perceived as the proper activity of a devout man. Schaff commented that the "acquisition of riches is to them [the Americans] only a help toward higher spiritual and moral ends."[62] The considerable sums, as well as

---

[60] I have discussed these aspects of American political life in another publication dealing with "Religion and Politics in America," in Robert Lee, ed., *Religion and Social Conflict* (New York: Oxford University Press, forthcoming).

[61] J. Franklin Jameson, *The American Revolution Considered as a Social Movement* (Princeton, N. J.: Princeton University Press, 1926), p. 157.

[62] Schaff, *America*, p. 259.

time, contributed to philanthropic works, which reached heights un-
dreamed of in Europe, have also been perceived as part of the interrelationship between religious and secular activities. The emphasis on
"voluntarism" in both areas has clearly been mutually reinforcing. For
much of the nineteenth century many voluntary activities, such as those
dealing with charity, education, and moral and social reform were closely
linked to religious concerns. Men were expected to be righteous, hard-
working, and ambitious. Righteousness was to be rewarded both in the
present and the hereafter, and the succesful had an obligation to engage
in good works and to share the bounty they had attained.

It is important to stress also that the strong commitment to a voluntaris-
tic denominational Protestantism reinforced the support for minority
rights even in the religious sphere itself. Although Sunday Blue Laws
continued for many decades after the Revolution, the rights of the
irreligious found considerable backing, as reflected in the insistence—
already noted—by the Democrats that the mails be delivered on Sundays.
In 1830—twenty years after the passage of the Sunday mails bill—a
Senate committee report, authored by a future Vice-President and endorsed by a majority of that House, stated explicitly that in the United
States religion and irreligion had equal rights, and that laws proclaiming
that the government should not provide services on Sunday would work
an injustice to irreligious people or non-Christians, and would constitute
a special favor for Christians as a group. The report, written by a
deeply religious active Baptist, stated these principles in unequivocal
terms:

> The Constitution regards the conscience of the Jew as sacred as
> that of the Christian, and gives no more authority to adopt a meas-
> ure affecting the conscience of a solitary individual than that of a
> whole community. . . . If Congress shall declare the first day of the
> week holy, it will not satisfy the Jew nor the Sabbatarian. It will
> dissatisfy both and, consequently convert neither. . . . It must be
> recollected that, in the earliest settlement of this country, the spirit
> of persecution, which drove the pilgrims from their native homes,
> was brought with them to their new habitations; and that some
> Christians were scourged and others put to death for no other crime
> than dissenting from the dogmas of their rulers.
>   . . . If a solemn act of legislation shall in *one* point define the God
> or point out to the citizen one religious duty, it may with equal
> propriety define *every* part of divine revelation and enforce *every*

religious obligation, even to the forms and ceremonies of worship; the endowment of the church, and the support of the clergy.

. . . It is the duty of this government to affirm to *all*—to the Jew or Gentile, Pagan, or Christian—the protection and advantages of our benignant institutions on *Sunday*, as well as every day of the week.[63]

Before the Civil War, successful struggles, often led by deeply believing Protestants, were waged in many areas to eliminate any relationship between state supported education and religion. By so doing, these Protestants acknowledged the rights of all, even of the completely irreligious. In 1853, in defending a ruling that prayers "could not be required as a part of the school exercises" in New York state, a devout State Superintendent of Schools wrote as follows:

[T]he position was early, distinctly, and almost universally taken by our statesmen, legislators, and prominent friends of education— men of the warmest religious zeal and belonging to every sect— that *religious education must be banished from the common school and consigned to the family and church*. . . . Accordingly, the instruction in our schools has been limited to that ordinarily included under the head of intellectual culture, and to the propagation of those principles of morality in which all sects, and *good men belonging to no sect,* can equally agree. . . .

Not only have the Episcopalian, the Presbyterian, the Baptist and the Methodist met on *common* and *neutral* ground in the school room, but with them the Unitarian, the Universalist, the Quaker and even *the denier of all creeds.*[64]

The fact that public officials could openly advocate that the federal and state governments must consider the rights of non-believers indicates the extent to which many believing Protestants of the first half century of the United States were able to tolerate religious variety. Only Catholicism, viewed by many American Protestants not as a different set of religious beliefs but as an alien conspiracy seeking to undermine the American Way of Life, was outside the pale.

---

[63] Richard Mentor Johnson, "Sunday Observance and the Mail," reprinted in George E. Probst, ed., *The Happy Republic* (New York: Harper Torchbooks, 1962), pp. 250–254. (Emphasis in original.)

[64] Cited in R. Freeman Butts, *The American Tradition in Religion and Education* (Boston: The Beacon Press, 1950), pp. 136–137. (Emphases are Butts's.)

Thus we may say, once again, that Tocqueville and other early foreign travelers "foresaw" trends in American religious institutions, just as they "foresaw" trends in the American character. These trends have become accentuated as the nation's values have adjusted to the vast changes that have taken place in the fabric of American society. The identification which Tocqueville observed between democratic ideals and an affirmation of religion seems even greater today.[65]

While the secular and all-pervasive character of American religion may stem from the intertwining of democratic and religious values, it is easier to show how the propensity to form sects is a product of the way democracy affected the structural position of religion in America. Perhaps this can best be seen by comparing the growth of religion in Canada and the United States. Religious sects have tended to develop, in both Canada and the United States, where rapid social change, the heavy shift of population to the frontier or the growing cities, and the consequent social mobility, have torn individuals from their traditional ties. However, the fact that religion is less explicitly separated from the "national community" in Canada has meant that sects have been less able to survive there than in the United States. In Canada:

> Political pressures have forced the community to come to the support of organized religion and such support has placed a definite limitation upon sectarian activity. With the collective weight of the community brought to bear upon them, the sects have been forced either to retreat behind a wall of isolation or build themselves into an integral part of the community, or else to seek denominational supports by aligning themselves with the state and with the traditional institutions of the community.[66]

Once the sects aligned themselves with the traditional institutions in the community, their differences became less important and they found it easier to unite. As a result the union of churches proceeded more rapidly in Canada than in the United States.

The "religious fecundity" of American Protestantism seems to be an outgrowth of the intertwining of the democratic value of free expression

---

[65] Evarts B. Greene, *Religion and the State* (Ithaca, N. Y.: Great Seal Books, 1959), p. 101.

[66] S. D. Clark, *The Developing Canadian Community* (Toronto: University of Toronto Press, 1962), p. 178.

of all political ideas with the Protestant stress on the obligation to follow individual conscience.[67] The norms of political tolerance and religious tolerance have been mutually reinforcing. The special pressure on churches to proselytize *and* to tolerate each other, brought about by "voluntarism," is reinforced by another particular trait of American society—its geographic, occupational, and class mobility. "This means that people have to be won over and over again as they move geographically and as they change their class orientations and find different aspirations for themselves."[68] With the massive shifting of populations that has characterized American history, neither individual churches or national denominations could remain satisfied with holding their own. Those denominations which did little proselytizing fell far behind in the competition for members and adherents. In the past as in the present, those who changed their circumstances have often been potential converts to another denomination. And the wide-spreading religious mobility from one sect to another, which has been stimulated by other forms of mobility, has meant that in all periods of American history a large proportion of the population has adhered to a denomination other than the one in which they were reared. It has been suggested that at least one consequence of this heterogeneity of the religious backgrounds of church members is the "ecumenical movement in which major groups recognize the legitimacy of each other."[69]

The fact that American religion is denominational has facilitated the development of religious groups which tend to serve only those parishioners who are roughly on the same social level in society. And the absence of multi-class religions (such as exist in countries where the church is established or represents the sole religion of the country) has meant that each "class" or ethnic religion could adapt its practices and

[67] See A. T. Mollegen, "Ethics of Protestantism" in F. Ernest Johnson, ed., *Patterns of Ethics in America Today* (New York: [Institute for Religious and Social Studies], Harper & Bros., 1960), p. 53. "Christians and non-Christians . . . have a claim to our consideration both of their criticism of our own position and of their positive programs which differ from ours. This is the Protestant support of the democratic forum of public opinions. . . . they do it . . . in order that Christians may know the shock of sincere Christians differing deeply and thus be humbled in their own positions even when they cannot in conscience change them." *Ibid.*, p. 59.

[68] Albert T. Rasmussen, "Contemporary Religious Appeals and Who Responds," in Jane C. Zahn, ed., *Religion and the Face of America* (Berkeley: University Extension, 1958), p. 4.

[69] *Loc. cit.*

specific beliefs to suit the needs of the group which it serves.[70] This has also meant that in this country religion could be either conservative or radical in its view of the class structure. No major social group has long been excluded from, or caused to be disaffected from, the "normal" religious life of the nation. Thus, denominationalism may have served to stabilize the polity.

By virtue of their need to survive, denominational religions have historically resisted state control over different aspects of cultural life and in so doing have supported democracy. Tocqueville pointed out that, because of the survival need, even American Catholics, laymen and clergy alike, adopted democratic and republican principles. And he says: "They constitute a minority, and all rights must be respected in order to insure to them the free exercise of their own privileges. These . . . causes induce them, even unconsciously, to adopt political doctrines which they would perhaps support with less zeal if they were pre-ponderant."[71] This explanation of Catholic support for democratic values could easily be extended to all the denominations in the society, since none of them is large enough to constitute a majority. Such religious support for democracy constitutes the background for *religious affiliation* being considered a part of the "American Way of Life."

The separation of the church and state has increasingly given religion *per se* a specific rather than a diffuse role in American society. The minister, the priest, and the rabbi, all deal in generalizations that extend beyond the confines of the church itself; but the members of the congregation do not necessarily carry these with them to their other activities, because they judge the religious leader in his specific role. Democracy's giving religion a specific role in American society—as Sunday Religion—may have, oddly enough, contributed to its all-pervasive and secular qualities. The only mention of religion on "weekdays" must be in terms of generally agreed upon morality which cannot be identified with the teachings of any given denomination. In so far as the secular and all-pervasive characteristics of American religion are a result of the emphasis on role specificity in American society, they have become accentuated with urbanization and industrialization. However, the consistency over time of foreign observers' remarks to the effect that American religion is unique in these characteristics shows that neither of them has grown simply as a result of these modern trends.

---

[70] See Niebuhr, "The Protestant Movement and Democracy . . . ," *op. cit.*, pp. 57–59; and Persons, "Religion and Modernity . . . , *op. cit.*, pp. 371–372.
[71] Tocqueville, *Democracy in America*, Vol. II, p. 312.

The emphasis upon equality, between religions as among men, which intensified after the American Revolution, gave the subsequent development of religious institutions in America its special character. Democratic and religious values have grown together. The results have been that, on the one hand, Americans see religion as essential to the support of the democratic institutions they cherish, and therefore feel that all Americans should profess some sort of religious faith; on the other hand, American denominations stress the ethical side of religion which they all have in common (and which is closely associated with other democratic values) rather than stressing transcendental beliefs wherein they differ. At the same time, democracy, by giving religious institutions a specific role in American society, has allowed them to proliferate, to adjust to peculiar needs, and to have a limited influence on their members' lives.

Thus the consistency with which both secularization and widespread adherence have distinguished American religion throughout its history is a result of the fact that democratic values have continued to influence the growth of religious institutions as the society has changed. In this respect, the persistent traits in American religion resemble the constant traits in the American character. They have continued to distinguish America from other countries, precisely because they have stemmed from the basic American values that have remained relatively stable as the economy, population, and society of the country have changed.

Trade Unions
and the American
Value System

5

★★★

Although many may argue with my stress on the continuity of the essential traits of American character and religion, few would question the thesis that our business institutions have reflected the constant emphasis in the American value system on individual achievement.[1] From the earliest comments of foreign travelers down to the present, men have identified a strong materialistic bent as being a characteristic American trait. The worship of the dollar, the desire to make a profit, the effort to get ahead through the accumulation of wealth, all have been credited to the egalitarian character of the society, that is, to the absence of aristocracy. As Tocqueville noted in his discussion of the consequences of a democracy's destruction of aristocracy: "They have swept away the privileges

---

[1] See Francis X. Sutton, Seymour E. Harris, Carl Kaysen, and James Tobin, *The American Business Creed* (Cambridge: Harvard University Press, 1956), p. 355, for a statement of the emphasis on achievement in business ideology as well as the strains produced by conflicting values. These authors state that "A basic stability . . . in many elements of business ideology is evident from the most cursory examination of past business pronouncements" (p. 385). They believe that this ideological stability has maintained itself in the face of changing social structure and values. A study of managerial ideologies (how to deal with workers), as distinct from business ideologies, however, points to changes inherent in increased size and bureaucratization. See Reinhard Bendix, *Work and Authority in Industry* (New York: John Wiley, 1956), pp. 254–340.

of some of their fellow creatures which stood in their way, but they have opened the door to universal competition."[2] And the study of the comments on American workers of various nineteenth-century foreign travelers cited earlier notes that most of these European writers, among whom were a number of socialists, concluded that "social and economic democracy in America, far from mitigating competition for social status, intensified it. . . ."[3]

American secular and religious values both have facilitated the "triumph of American capitalism," and have fostered status striving. The focus on equalitarianism and individual opportunity has also prevented the emergence of class consciousness among the lower classes. The absence of a socialist or labor party, and the historic weakness of American trade-unionism, appear to attest to the strength of values which depreciated a concern with class. The growth of a large trade-union movement during the 1930's, together with the greater political involvement of labor organizations in the Democratic party, suggested to some that the day—long predicted by many Marxists—was arriving in which the American working class would finally follow in the footsteps of its European brethren. Such changes in the structure of class relations seemed to these observers to reflect the decline of opportunity and the hardening of class lines. To them such changes could not occur without modification in the traditional value system, that is, without a decline in the stress on equality and achievement.

A close examination of the character of the American labor movement, however, suggests that it, like the church, may be perceived as reflecting the basic values of the larger society. Although unions, like all other American institutions, have changed in various ways congruent with the growth of an urban industrial civilization, the essential traits of American trade unions, as of business corporations, may still be derived from key elements in the American value system.

Since a large labor movement is of relatively recent vintage in American society, I shall not try to trace historical continuities in its behavior and structure. Rather, I shall attempt to specify how the character of American unions differs from those in other industrial countries, and to account for these differences by analyzing the relationship between labor movements and the social structures of these nations. In moving from a

---

[2] Alexis de Tocqueville, *Democracy in America* (New York: Vintage Books, 1959), Vol. II, p. 146.

[3] Robert W. Smuts, *European Impressions of the American Worker* (New York: King's Crown Press, 1953), p. 13.

more historical to a more comparative approach, I have purposely limited the scope of the comparison to those countries which most resemble the United States in economic and political organization.

The union movements compared are all located in industrially developed nations which have relatively stable democratic political systems. They are characterized by "the uninterrupted continuation of political democracy since World War I *and* the absence of a major political movement opposed to the democratic 'rules of the game.' "[4] They are also similar in the assumptions they make about the role of unions and the nature of industrial relations. The labor movements of these countries all assume, more or less, as Hugh Clegg has recently put it, that "unions must be independent both of the state and of management . . . , that only the unions can represent the industrial interests of workers . . . [and] that the ownership of industry is irrelevant to good industrial relations."[5] These nations are "the United States, Britain, Scandinavia, Holland, Switzerland, Australia, Canada and New Zealand."[6]

Although the American labor movement is similar to others in many respects, it differs from those of the other stable democracies in ideology, class solidarity, tactics, organizational structure, and patterns of leadership behavior. American unions are more conservative; they are more narrowly self-interested; their tactics are more militant; they are more decentralized in their collective bargaining; and they have many more full-time salaried officials, who are on the whole much more highly paid and who exhibit a somewhat greater penchant to engage in corrupt practices. American unions have also organized a smaller proportion of the labor force than have unions in these other nations.[7]

In stressing variations between American unionism and that of other countries, particularly those of northwestern Europe and Australasia, I do not mean to imply that any of these differences are of such magnitude as to make American unionism a qualitatively different phenomenon from the others. Clearly, the labor movements in all industrialized democracies have great similarities and perform similar functions. Although American

---

[4] Seymour Martin Lipset, *Political Man: The Social Bases of Politics* (Garden City, N. Y.: Doubleday, 1960), pp. 48–49.

[5] Hugh Clegg, *A New Approach to Industrial Democracy* (Oxford: Blackwell, 1960), p. 21.

[6] *Loc. cit.* My list in *Political Man* includes Belgium and Luxemburg as well.

[7] These points have been elaborated and documented in my "Le syndicalisme américain et les valeurs de la société américaine," *Sociologie du Travail*, 2 (1961), pp. 161–181.

unions are less class conscious politically than those of Europe, they are certainly involved in politics.[8] American labor leaders earn more relative to the rank and file than do European labor leaders, but the perquisites of the latter are also quite considerable in the form of high status, power, interesting work, travel, and the like. With the possible exception of leadership corruption and involvement in private business, almost every practice which may be mentioned as characteristic of American unionism is to be found in the northwestern European or Australasian movements. Clearly, as Clegg indicates, the labor movements of this industrialized, democratic "culture area" resemble each other greatly when contrasted with the types of movements found in southern and Latin Europe and in the underdeveloped states. But it is obvious also that considerable differences do exist between the labor movement of the United States and those of other countries in its "culture area."

Social Structure: the Source of American Unionism

In order to explain, in part, why American unionism differs from the unionism of the other predominantly Protestant, industrial democracies of northwestern Europe and Australasia, it is necessary to describe in more detail the way in which the trade union, as an American institution, has responded to and reflected the pressures generated by the interplay between America's basic values and the facts of social stratification in an industrial society. The stress on equality and achievement in American society has meant that Americans are much more likely to be concerned with the achievement of approved *ends*—particularly pecuniary success—than with the use of appropriate *means*—the behavior considered appropriate to a given position or status. In a country which stresses success above all, men are led to feel that the most important thing is to win the

---

[8] Their relations with the Democratic Party resemble those of many European unions with their socialist parties. However, as Cyriax and Oakeshott note: "The fact still remains that the British unions are 'in politics' in a sense in which their United States counterparts are definitely not. Their leaders still subscribe to a large body of Socialist objectives which can only be achieved through political action. . . . In America, by contrast, there is no distinct set of political beliefs superimposed on the informal working arrangements between the unions and the Democratic Party. Formally, therefore, the AFL-CIO is not affiliated to any party, and only tends to become involved in active politics when anti-union legislation is in the air." George Cyriax and Robert Oakeshott, *The Bargainers: A Survey of Modern Trade Unionism* (New York: Praeger, 1960), pp. 212–213.

game, regardless of the methods employed in doing so. American culture applies the norms of a completely competitive society to everyone. Winners take all. As Robert K. Merton has put it:

> What makes American culture relatively distinctive . . . is that it is "a society which places a high premium on economic affluence and social ascent for all its members." . . . this patterned expectation is regarded as appropriate for everyone, irrespective of his initial lot or station in life. . . .
>
> This leads naturally to the subsidiary theme that success or failure are results wholly of personal qualities, that he who fails has only himself to blame, for the corollary to the concept of the self-made man is the self-unmade man. To the extent that this cultural definition is assimilated by those who have not made their mark, failure represents a double defeat: the manifest defeat of remaining far behind in the race for success and the implicit defeat of not having the capacities and moral stamina needed for success. . . . It is in this cultural setting that, in a significant proportion of cases, the threat of defeat motivates men to the use of those tactics, beyond the law or the mores, which promise "success."
>
> The moral mandate to achieve success thus exerts pressure to succeed, by fair means if possible and by foul means if necessary.[9]

In contrast, one of the essential norms in more traditionalistic, ascriptive, or aristocratic societies is that one should behave in a manner appropriate to one's station. In the morality of aristocracy, to play the game well is more important than victory. All privileged strata seek to develop norms which justify their right to high status and which limit, if they do not eliminate, the possibility that they may be supplanted by "new men," by the upwardly mobile who succeed by "innovating"—that is, by ignoring the conventions. To emphasize correct behavior, manners, and so forth, is to reward the characteristics which those born to privilege are most likely to have. And since it is part of the logic of family life and social stratification to desire to perpetuate if not enhance the status of children and other family members, there is constant pressure in all societies to create "aristocratic" norms, or to preserve them if they have

---

[9] Robert K. Merton, *Social Theory and Social Structure* (Glencoe, Ill.: The Free Press, 1957), pp. 167–169. Merton reports considerable evidence documenting the thesis that pecuniary success is the dominant American value. I have leaned heavily on his paper, "Social Structure and Anomie," in this analysis.

been handed down from previous eras, as has been the case for most European countries.

Because of its revolutionary origins, America entered the era of a capitalist, industrial, and politically democratic society without the traditions of an aristocratic or deferential order. As a result, the norms of aristocracy, though present to a limited extent among the social elite, have not been able to make much headway. The tendency of the successful achievers to undermine equality has been checked by the recurrent victories of the forces of equality in the political order. Capitalism and industrialism have reinforced equalitarian forces in this struggle: a market economy operates best under conditions of free competition, recognizing neither family background nor social limitations.

In a society with aristocratic origins, where norms derived from a preindustrial social system still retain force and where they have often been partly accepted by the newer upper class of industrial society, there is greater emphasis on the propriety of class consciousness. Such a society, which places less emphasis on general achievement by everyone regardless of background, usually incorporates more *particular* sets of goals for each major social stratum. Thus a worker who is the son of a worker is less likely to view himself a personal failure than is a comparably situated man in a more equalitarian and achievement-oriented culture such as that of the United States. The weaker sense of personal failure felt by lower stratum individuals in such a "particularistic" social order does not mean that they feel less resentment over having inferior status, but rather that they are less likely to feel personally responsible for their "failure" or to feel the need to do something extraordinary about it. Deprived individuals are more likely to try to improve their situations *collectively* through social movements and class-conscious political parties. Or to put it in descriptive terms: in an achievement-oriented society such as the United States, the lower status person is more likely to feel impelled to drive *himself* to get ahead; in the more ascriptive European cultures, there will be greater emphasis on collective modification of the class structure.[10]

Since the emphasis is on individual success in the United States, those individuals or groups who feel themselves handicapped and who seek to resolve their consequent doubts about their personal worth are under strong pressure to "innovate," that is, to use whatever means they can find to

---

[10] Of course, these are only relative comparisons; Europeans try to get ahead, and Americans try to change the distribution of privilege. It is the difference in emphasis that I stress here.

gain recognition. This pressure to innovate may be reflected in efforts which established groups would not make—for example, the development of new and risky industries by those of recent immigrant background and low status who are barred, by limited economic resources and social discrimination, from advancing up economic ladders.[11] Similarly, urban machine politics, which required the use of "unconventional" tactics, became a road to success for various immigrant groups.

The pressure to succeed may also lead individuals and groups to serve social needs which are *outside* the law, in occupations usually described as "rackets." Organized vice—prostitution, bootlegging, and gambling— has been open to ambitious individuals from deprived social backgrounds when other fields were closed. The rackets have attracted members of minority ethnic groups who are strongly motivated by the American emphasis on achievement, but who are limited in their access to legitimate means of succeeding. Members of groups engaged in illegitimate businesses often do not conceive of themselves as engaged in crime, but rather as conforming to the achievement norms.

Criminal activities and corrupt politics may be found to some extent in all countries and may be more prevalent in impoverished regions of the world, such as Asia, southern Europe, and Latin America; but within the general culture area of the predominantly Protestant, relatively affluent, industrialized nations of northwestern Europe and the English-speaking countries of the Commonwealth, the United States is well out in the lead. As many observers have pointed out, the comparatively high crime rate in America, both in the form of lower-class rackets and white-collar and business defalcation, may be perceived as a consequence of the stress laid on success. Daniel Bell, for example, has suggested that racketeering may be seen as a natural by-product of American culture:

> Crime, in many ways, is a Coney Island mirror, caricaturing the morals and manners of a society. The jungle quality of the American business community, particularly at the turn of the century, was reflected in the mode of "business" practiced by the coarse gangster elements, most of them from new immigrant families, who were "getting ahead," just as Horatio Alger had urged. . . .
>
> The desires satisfied in extra-legal fashion were more than a hunger for the "forbidden fruits" of conventional morality. They also involved in the complex and ever shifting structure of group, class,

---

[11] The Jews, for example, played a major role in developing the motion picture industry and in introducing credit practices in retail selling.

and ethnic stratification, which is the warp and woof of America's "open" society, such "normal" goals as independence through a business of one's own, and such "moral" aspirations as the desire for social advancement and social prestige. For crime, in the language of the sociologists, has a "functional" role in the society, and the urban rackets—the illicit activity organized for continuing profit, rather than individual illegal acts— . . . [are] one of the queer ladders of social mobility in American life.[12]

Given the extent of the pressure to "innovate," it is not surprising to find evidence that the successful may win general acceptance even if there is public knowledge that they used extralegal methods to get ahead. In the mid-nineteenth century, Charles Dickens commented that in America:

The merits of a broken speculation, or a bankruptcy, or of a successful scoundrel, are not gauged by its or his observance of the golden rule, "Do as you would be done by," but are considered with reference to their smartness. . . . The following dialogue I have held a hundred times: "Is it not a very disgraceful circumstance that such a man as So-and-So should be acquiring a large property by the most infamous and odious means, and notwithstanding all the crimes of which he has been guilty, should be tolerated and abetted by your citizens? He is a public nuisance, is he not?" "Yes, Sir." "A convicted liar?" "Yes, Sir." "He has been kicked, and cuffed, and caned?" "Yes, Sir." "And he is utterly dishonourable, debased, and profligate?" "Yes, Sir." "In the name of wonder, then, what is his merit?" "Well, Sir, he is a smart man."[13]

A study of a Boston election in the 1940's in which James Curley was reelected mayor while under a charge of fraud (for which he was sub-

---

[12] Daniel Bell, *The End of Ideology* (Glencoe, Ill.: The Free Press, 1960), pp. 116–117.

[13] Charles Dickens, *American Notes, and Pictures from Italy* (New York: Oxford University Press, 1957), pp. 245–246. This quotation has been frequently cited. See Merton, *Social Theory and Social Structure*, p. 142; Gabriel Almond, *The American People and Foreign Policy* (New York: Harcourt, Brace, 1950), p. 34; and Henry Steele Commager, *America in Perspective* (New York: Mentor Books, 1947), p. 80. Dickens' comments on the willingness of Americans to accept bankrupts reiterated those of many other foreign visitors; see, for example, Gustave de Beaumont, *Marie, or Slavery in the United States* (Stanford: Stanford University Press, 1958), pp. 221–222.

sequently convicted) reported that there was a general image among his supporters, who were aware of the charges of dishonesty, that he "gets things done."[14]

Societal Values and the Union Movement

THE RELATIVE LACK OF CLASS CONSCIOUSNESS AND THE SELF-INTEREST OF INDIVIDUAL UNIONS   The lack of a class-conscious ideology in the American labor movement may be directly traced to the equalitarian, anti-class orientation of the values associated with America's national identity. Thus it may be suggested that one of the reasons unions have had trouble organizing new segments of the employed population as compared to unions in northern Europe is that they have been handicapped by their slightly illegitimate position relative to the value sytsem. "Union" connotes "class" organization.

In an interesting effort to account for the failure of socialism to take root in American society, Leon Samson has suggested that an important cause has been that Americanism is a political ideology with much the same value content as socialism.[15] It endorses the progress of the society toward the more equal distribution of privileges that socialism demands. As a result, the rank and file members of American labor unions have not had to look for an ideology that justified the changes which they desired in the society.

However, the failure of the American labor movement to identify itself as a class movement may be traced more directly to the way in which equalitarianism and achievement orientation permeated the social structure. As Schumpeter has noted, the self-interested orientation of the American labor movement is but the application, in the realm of working-class life and trade unions, of the general value scheme.[16] *Indeed, instead of reducing the individualistic orientation that Marxism associates with the early phase of capitalism, increasing industrialization in American society has reinforced the egalitarian-achievement attitudes toward stratification that early became part of the American national character. In a*

---

[14] See Jerome S. Bruner and Sheldon J. Korchin, "The Boss and the Vote: A Case Study in City Politics," *The Public Opinion Quarterly*, 10 (1946), p. 21.
[15] Leon Samson, *Towards a United Front* (New York: Farrar and Rinehart, 1933), pp. 1–90.
[16] Joseph A. Schumpeter, *Capitalism, Socialism and Democracy* (New York: Harper & Bros., 1942), pp. 331–336.

sense, industrialization has lent these attitudes continued legitimacy: industrialization and advancing technology brought about an almost unbroken increase in national wealth on both an absolute and a per capita basis, so that in the nineteenth century America became the wealthiest country in the world, a position it has never relinquished.[17] And as David Potter has well stressed, the fact of increasing abundance, no matter how unequally distributed, has served to permit the majority of the American population, including most trade-unionists, to enjoy a visible living standard roughly comparable among all groups with the exception of the extremely wealthy:

> American social distinctions, however real they may be and however difficult to break down, are not based upon or supported by great disparities in wealth, in education, in speech, in dress, etc., as they are in the old world. If the American class structure is in reality very unlike the classless society which we imagine, it is equally unlike the formalized class societies of former times. . . . the factor of abundance has . . . constantly operated to equalize the overt differences between the various classes. . . .[18]

Within this context the very success of trade unions in improving the relative position of their members *vis à vis* other groups in the population has simply contributed to the maintenance of their members' belief in the American value system.

THE MILITANT TACTICS OF UNIONS   Just as ideological conservatism and pursuit of narrow self-interests may be derived from the value system,

---

[17] Between 1869 and 1953 per capita annual income (standardized to 1929 prices) rose from $215 to $1,043. George J. Stigler, *Trends in Employment in the Service Industries* (Princeton, N. J.: Princeton University Press, 1956), p. 25. The gross national product increased five times from 1890 to 1950 as a result of a two-fold increase in population and a three-fold rise in labor productivity. Frederick C. Mills, *Productivity and Economic Progress* (New York: National Bureau of Economic Research, Inc., 1952), p. 2. This increase in the gross national product has, in turn, meant that the average income per consumption unit increased. In 1929, it was $4,190 per year, standardized to 1960 prices; in 1954, it was $6,730. Simon Kuznets, "Income Distribution and Changes in Consumption," in Hoke S. Simpson, ed., *The Changing American Population* (A Report of the Arden House Conference, jointly sponsored by the Graduate School of Business, Columbia University, and the Institute of Life Insurance, 1962), p. 30.

[18] David Potter, *People of Plenty* (Chicago: University of Chicago Press, 1954), p. 102.

so may the use of violent and militant tactics.[19] Here the labor movement, like American business, reflects the social system's relatively greater emphasis on ends as contrasted with means. One tries to win economic and social objectives by whatever means are at hand. The fact that American workers are sufficiently dissatisfied with their economic conditions to tolerate relatively frequent, long, and bitter strikes may also be explained by reference to the social structure and its values. In summing up the conclusions of late nineteenth-century foreign visitors to America, Robert Smuts points out that they saw it in this light:

> The frequency and the bitterness of industrial conflict was the most basic fault the foreigners found in American industrial life. . . .
> Most of the European visitors explained industrial conflict as a result rather than a contradiction of the material and social democracy which typified the life of the American worker. The abundance of his life, they pointed out, added to the strength of his ambition for more. His self-reliance made him sensitive to his rights. Industrial conflict in America was a man-to-man fight, with no quarter asked or given, unmitigated by the tradition of subordination on the one hand, or of benevolence and responsibility on the other.[20]

It may also be argued that we should expect more *individual* discontent with income and position among workers in America than within the more rigidly and visibly stratified European countries. The more rigid the stratification of a nation, the more candid the emphasis on the existence of differences among classes, the greater the extent to which lower status individuals will be likely to contrast their lot—*as a class*—with that of the more privileged classes. On the other hand, in a more loosely structured class system, people will be more prone to compare themselves *individually* with other workers who are relatively close to them in income and status. Thus if, in the latter system, groups or in-

---

[19] For data on the greater propensity of North American and Australian unions to strike, see Arthur M. Ross and Paul T. Hartman, *Changing Patterns of Industrial Conflict* (New York: John Wiley, 1960), pp. 141–145, 161–162. See also B. C. Roberts, *Unions in America: A British View* (Princeton, N.J.: Industrial Relations Section, Princeton University, 1959), p. 95.

[20] Smuts, *European Impressions of the American Worker*, pp. 26–27. On greater violence and bitterness, see also Roberts, *Unions in America*, p. 95; Louis Adamic, *Dynamite: The Story of Class Violence in America* (New York: Viking Press, 1934); and Henry Pelling, *America and the British Left from Bright to Bevan* (New York: New York University Press, 1956), p. 79.

dividuals improve their status, there will be resentment on the part of those left behind.

In other words, an open-class system leads workers to resent inequalities in income and status between themselves and others more frequently than does an ascriptively stratified system, where the only inequalities that count are class inequalities. America's equalitarian value system, by less clearly defining the range of groups with which workers may legitimately compare themselves, can make for greater individual discontent among workers than is the case in Europe.[21] European social structure, by regarding labor, in the words of Winston Churchill, as "an estate of the realm," makes clear to workers why they are lowly and calls upon them to act collectively; American social structure, by eschewing estates, creating vague and even illegitimate class boundaries, and stressing equality, blames individuals for being lowly and calls upon them to alleviate their resentment by improving their status in as self-interested and narrowly defined terms as possible. John L. Lewis, founder of the Congress of Industrial Organizations, president of the United Mine Workers for nearly forty years, and perhaps the most militant labor leader in the United States since the 1920's was a Republican most of his life and a strong advocate of conservative, *laissez-faire* economics (although he was willing to use state power to bolster his union and the coal industry).

There is some evidence in support of the contention that this self-interested bargaining policy does make sense for *any particular group*. Recent research dealing with the influence of trade unions on wages suggests that the existence of organized labor does not change the national distribution of income between workers and owners through collective bargaining, but it may improve the wage situation of one group of workers relative to others.[22] (As will be noted later, it has been argued, how-

[21] See Seymour Martin Lipset and Martin Trow, "Reference Group Theory and Trade-Union Wage Policy," in Mirra Komarovsky, editor, *Common Frontiers of the Social Sciences* (Glencoe, Ill.: The Free Press, 1957), pp. 391–411.

[22] See John Dunlop, *Wage Determination under Trade Unions* (New York: Macmillan, 1944), and *The Theory of Wage Determination* (New York: Macmillan, 1957); Cyriax and Oakeshott, *The Bargainers*, p. 170; and Melvin W. Reder, "Job Scarcity and the Nature of Union Power," *Industrial and Labor Relations Review*, 13, (1960), pp. 349–362. In a detailed summary of research on the subject, Clark Kerr concludes that there is no evidence that collective bargaining has increased labor's share of the national income in the United States, and further that there is "no significant relationship between the degree of unionization and labor's share, industry group by

ever, that aggressive unionism increases national wealth—and thereby workers' incomes—in absolute terms by creating constant pressure on employers to mechanize and increase productivity so as to readjust any imbalances created by increases in labor costs.) Hence the narrow self-interested policies traditionally pursued by many American unions would seem to be warranted if the objective of unionism is to secure as much as possible for the members of the given union. This is most likely to be its objective if the union movement reflects the values of achievement and individualism.

Conversely, however, there seems to be evidence that government can redistribute income among the classes through welfare, tax, and spending policies.[23] Thus, if the labor movement seeks to improve the situation of an entire class, a goal inherent in the economic conflicts which emerged in the previously aristocratic societies, a policy of concentrating on political action rather than trade union militancy is warranted.

LARGE WAGE DIFFERENTIALS   The approval of the pursuit of self-interest within the American labor movement may also help to account for the fact that wage differentials between skilled and unskilled workers are larger in America than in the other nations. A study of such differentials in six countries indicates that in France, Germany, Italy, the Netherlands, and Norway, "skill differentials are rather narrow, compared, say, with United States averages."[24] And: "Differences in wages between unskilled and skilled jobs in Swedish industry are generally much less than in America. For example, the head machine operator in an American paper mill will earn at least 50 per cent more than the lowest paid worker in the mill. In Sweden the difference is less than 20 per cent."[25]

There are many factors related to variations in wage differentials, but it

---

industry group." See his "Trade-Unionism and Distributive Shares," *The American Economic Review, Papers and Proceedings*, 44 (1954), p. 289. An opposite conclusion is reached by Robert Ozanne, "Impact of Unions on Wage Levels and Income Distribution," *Quarterly Journal of Economics*, 73 (1959), pp. 177–196.

[23] Kerr, "Trade Unionism and Distributive Shares," *op. cit.*, pp. 279–292.

[24] Adolf Sturmthal, ed., *Contemporary Collective Bargaining in Seven Countries* (Ithaca, N.Y.: Institute of International Industrial and Labor Relations, 1957), p. 335.

[25] Charles A. Myers, *Industrial Relations in Sweden* (Cambridge, Mass.: Technology Press, 1951), p. 42.

seems possible that variations in basic values may play a role. Sturmthal points this out:

> Undoubtedly also the notions of what are proper differentials . . . vary a good deal on both sides of the Atlantic. The absence of feudal concepts of the place in society to which a worker may properly aspire may have played a part in allowing the larger wage differentials to arise in the United States, just as the heritage of the feudal concepts may have helped maintain the highly compressed wage structure in Europe.[26]

The very insistence on the "formal" equality of all people in the United States places a higher value on income and conspicuous consumption than in societies in which status and occupation are closely linked. Although comparative studies of occupational status indicate that occupations tend to rank at roughly the same level in all industrial societies,[27] occupation seems to be less important than sheer income as a determinant of status in the United States, as compared with some European nations. Two surveys made at about the same time in the United States and Germany suggest this interpretation (see Table III). Although the differences in results may reflect the variations in the questions that were asked, it seems likely that both surveys touched to some extent on the same basic issue: the relative weight given to occupational prestige as compared with the size of income. In both countries those who had higher status (*i.e.*, those who were either better educated or who occupied a white-collar position) were more likely than those of lower status to favor white-collar status, even if it meant lower income than that obtained by a skilled worker. But the important result was that the majority of the American respondents, even among the college graduates, preferred the higher paid, lower status job; on the other hand,

---

[26] Sturmthal, *Contemporary Collective Bargaining in Seven Countries*, p. 343.
[27] See Alex Inkeles and Peter Rossi, "National Comparisons of Occupational Prestige," *American Journal of Sociology*, 61 (1956), p. 339. These authors compared the results of surveys completed in Japan, Great Britain, the United States, Germany, Australia, and a sample of Russian "defectors." They concluded that the rankings were roughly similar in these countries. Later studies in Brazil, the Philippines, Denmark, and the Netherlands showed similar results. For discussion and references, see S. M. Lipset and R. Bendix, *Social Mobility in Industrial Society* (Berkeley: University of California Press, 1959), pp. 14, 111.

Table III

Preference Percentages for White-Collar Status and Low Income or for Manual Position and High Income in Germany and the United States

UNITED STATES—1951

"Which of these two jobs would you personally prefer a son of yours to take, assuming he is equally qualified: a skilled worker's job at $100 a week, or a white-collar desk job at $75 a week?"

Answer	Total Sample	Years of Education			
		0–8	9–12	13–15	16
White collar	28	22	31	34	42
Skilled laborer	69	72	67	65	52
Don't know	3	6	2	1	6
Total	100.0	100.0	100.0	100.0	100.0
Number interviewed	(658)	(287)	(257)	(62)	(52)

Source: Computed from Gallup data in the files of the Roper Public Opinion Research Center at Williams College.

GERMANY—1952

"Who do you think receives more prestige from the population in general: a bookkeeper who earns 300 marks a month, or a foundry worker who brings home 450 marks a month?"

Answer	Total Sample	Manual Worker Respondents Only
The bookkeeper	58	56
The foundry worker	24	28
Don't know	18	16
Total	100.0	100.0

Source: Erich Peter Neumann and Elizabeth Noelle, Antworten, Politik im Kraftfeld der öffentlichen Meinung (*Allensbach am Bodensee: Verlag für Demoskopie, 1954), p. 107.*

the majority of the German respondents ranked the lower paid, white-collar job higher.

A report on a similar study in another European country, this time a Communist one, Poland, suggests that in that country, as in Germany, white-collar status is given more weight than income. This study, which was apparently more like the American than the German in its approach, indicates that "passage of the better paid skilled manual workers to the position of the slightly lower paid white-collar workers . . . in the majority of cases is looked on as a promotion . . . [although] from the point of view of the new criteria of prestige, this should not be considered a promotion."[28]

Assuming, therefore, that higher occupational status is more of an incentive in countries with relatively formalized status systems than in countries stressing equalitarian behavioral norms, there should be less need in the first group of societies to magnify economic incentives in order to motivate people to prepare for positions requiring long periods of training.[29] As Sturmthal has put it, "incentives that are necessary in one country to produce a certain supply of highly skilled labor may be excessive in another country or *vice versa*. This may be the result of different non-economic compensations offered to the higher skills—status and prestige—or simply of different 'styles of life' in which lesser financial rewards are sufficient to bring about the desired result."[30]

Differences in behavior of organized labor from country to country seem to reflect in some measure variations in the differentials that are considered morally appropriate. Thus, in the United States, for individuals or groups of individuals to seek to better themselves at the expense of others tends to be encouraged by the dominant achievement orientation. In the past few years, several industrial unions formed by the CIO have had difficulty with skilled workers among their membership who have insisted that the wage differentials be widened. In New York, the most highly skilled groups employed on the city's transportation system tried to break away from the Transport Workers' Union to form separate craft unions. A strike called for this purpose failed, but this relatively old industrial union made important concessions to its skilled workers. In the United Automobile Workers the skilled crafts have been allowed to form separate councils within the union and have forced the union to press their demand for greater differentials. In some old craft unions which accepted unskilled and semi-skilled workers, the

---

[28] S. Ossowski, "Social Mobility Brought About by Social Revolutions," *Fourth Working Conference on Social Stratification and Social Mobility* (International Sociological Association, December, 1957, p. 3.
[29] "The function of skill differentials is primarily to provide incentives to embark upon careers requiring longer and arduous training." Sturmthal, *Contemporary Collective Bargaining in Seven Countries*, p. 340.
[30] *Ibid.*, p. 341.

latter were often given second-class membership, *i.e.*, no voting rights, to prevent them from inhibiting the bargaining strategy of the skilled group.[31]

In much of Europe, on the other hand, the norms implicit in socialist and working-class ideology have made such behavior difficult. The Swedish labor movement for many years made a reduction of differentials one of its aims.[32] Clark Kerr notes that in Germany one of the forces which explains the greater emphasis on wage equality has been "Socialist theories of standardizing pay. . . ."[33] In Italy after World War II, "for political reasons and under the pressure of left-wing parties, the general trend was in favor of raising as much as possible the wages paid to common laborers. . . ."[34] The Norwegian labor movement followed for many years the policy of "wages solidarity," *i.e.*, the reduction of differentials.[35]

In recent years, under pressure from their skilled members and on the advice of various economists who are disturbed by the possible effects on efficiency of narrow differentials for large variations in skills, many of the European labor movements have formally dropped their insistence on narrowing the gap, and some even advocate widening it. As far as the labor economists can judge, the skill differentials, which began dropping in most countries in the late 1930's and continued falling until around 1952, have been rising slightly since then. For socialists, however, to avowedly seek to benefit a more well-to-do group at the expense of the poorer one would seem to violate essential values.[36] And the greater

---

[31] The practice is now illegal. For a general discussion of some of these problems, see David Cole, "Union Self-Discipline and the Freedom of Individual Workers," in Michael Harrington and Paul Jacobs, eds., *Labor in a Free Society* (Berkeley: University of California Press, 1959), pp. 88–101.

[32] Myers, *Industrial Relations in Sweden*, p. 43.

[33] Clark Kerr, "Collective Bargaining in Postwar Germany," in Adolf Sturmthal, ed., *Contemporary Collective Bargaining in Seven Countries*, p. 208.

[34] Luisa R. Sanseverino, "Collective Bargaining in Italy," in Sturmthal, ed,. *op. cit.*, p. 224.

[35] Sturmthal, in Sturmthal, ed., *op. cit.*, p. 339.

[36] There has, of course, been tension between the skilled and unskilled sections of the labor movement over such issues in most countries. The point here, as in the other comparisons, is always a relative rather than an absolute one. Denmark, for example, represents an extreme case of such internecine warfare. The Laborers Union, the union of the unskilled, which contains almost 40 per cent of all organized workers in the country, has had bitter battles with the craft unions over wage systems. However, as Galenson notes, "Ac-

centralization of the union movement in most of these European countries requires that such a wage policy be an explicit national one, rather than one simply reflecting adjustments to immediate pressures.

The general behavior of American unions in perpetuating wide differentials is congruent with the assumption that Americans remain more narrowly self-interested and that the more powerful groups of workers are able to maintain or occasionally even improve a relatively privileged position at the expense of the less powerful, usually less organized, and less skilled workers.[37]

Societal Values and Union Leadership

Any effort to account for the ways in which American unionism differs from unionism in northern Europe and Australasia necessarily must deal with the behavior of the leaders. As recent congressional investigations and journalistic exposés have made manifest, union officials in this country receive higher salaries, are more wont to engage in practices which violate conventional morality, and show a lesser regard for the mechanisms of democratic procedure than leaders in the other nations discussed here.

UNION LEADERS' JOB ORIENTATION, SALARIES, AND ENTRENCHED POSITIONS   The concept of "business unionism," the dominant ideology of the American labor movement which perceives unions as fighting for more money rather than for any program of social reconstruction, has important consequences in encouraging union leaders to view themselves as bound by the same standards as profit-oriented businessmen.

---

ceptance of socialism by Danish workers by no means eliminated or even dampened internecine strife when important economic interests were involved, but it did contribute to prevention of the breaches of labor solidarity sometimes witnessed in American rival union warfare." And in the 1930's, the Danish Federation of Labor adopted "the so-called 'solidaristic' wage policy, whereby lower paid workers were to receive extra wage concessions. . . ." Walter Galenson, *The Danish System of Labor Relations* (Cambridge, Mass.: Harvard University Press, 1952), pp. 50–57, 68, 186.

[37] Skill and organized collective bargaining power do not necessarily go together. Among the less skilled groups which have powerful unions are the coal miners, the truck drivers, and the West Coast longshoremen. It may also be suggested that one further reason for widespread skill differentials in the United States has been the constant addition of immigrants, most recently Negroes and Puerto Ricans, to the lowest occupational strata. Such sources of migration may involve downward pressure on the wages of the unskilled.

Usually the leaders of social movements are expected to have a "calling," to feel moved by a moral ethic toward serving certain major social values. In the early days of many American unions, when they were weak, often illegitimate, and could yield few rewards in the form of status, power, or income, their leaders did adhere to some such larger ideology, often a variant of socialism. This ideology prescribed certain standards of ethical behavior and a certain style of life. But as American union leaders shifted from social or socialist unionism to business unionism, they also changed their values and standards of comparisons. To a considerable extent, those unions which have retained important aspects of socialist values, such as the United Automobile Workers or the International Ladies Garment Workers Union, are precisely the unions whose leaders, even with great power, still insist upon relatively low officer salaries and show great concern over problems of corruption and civil liberties.[38] To the extent that union office has changed from a "calling" to a "career" as unions have aged and ideology has declined, to that extent have leaders lost their inhibitions about comparing themselves with businessmen or widening the discrepancy between their salaries and those of their members.[39]

---

[38] The two unions which have established external boards to review appeals from members who feel that they have been deprived of their rights by union officers are the United Automobile Workers and the Upholsterers International Union. Both organizations are still led by men who show various signs of having retained parts of their early socialist beliefs.

[39] For a more elaborate discussion of these concepts, see Lipset, *Political Man*, pp. 383–389. In the United States, "the gap between the members' wages and the salaries of the presidents of the larger unions has increased relatively during the 1940's and 1950's. The heads of the dozen largest unions have salaries ranging from $18,000 to $60,000 a year, plus ample expense accounts and frequently other perquisites." Richard Lester, *As Unions Mature* (Princeton, N.J.: Princeton University Press, 1958), p. 27. For data on union leaders' salaries in three different periods, see C. Wright Mills, *New Men of Power* (New York: Harcourt, Brace, 1948), p. 305; Philip Taft, *Structure and Government of Labor Unions* (Cambridge, Mass.: Harvard University Press, 1954), pp. 104–110; and Harry Cohany and Irving P. Philips, *Union Constitution Provisions: Election and Tenure of International Union Officers, 1958* (Washington: U.S. Bureau of Labor Statistics, 1958), pp. 21–24. A recent study which yields much information on the salaries of European labor leaders is Walter Galenson, *Trade Union Democracy in Western Europe* (Berkeley: University of California Press, 1961). British salaries are reported in H. A. Clegg, A. J. Killick, and Rex Adams, *Trade Union Officers* (Cambridge, Mass.: Harvard University Press, 1961), pp. 55–60.

The emphasis on pecuniary success, combined with the absence of the kind of class consciousness characteristic of more aristocratic societies, has thus served to motivate workers to use the labor movement itself as an avenue to financial and status gain. The high incomes which many union leaders receive represent their adaptation to the norm of "getting ahead." As long as a union leader has the reputation for "delivering the goods" to his members, they seem willing to allow him a high salary and sometimes the right to engage in private business, or even to be corrupt.[40]

The greater perquisites attached to high union office in America, a seeming consequence of pressure inherent in the achievement-equalitarianism syndrome, may also account for the fact that American union leaders have formally institutionalized dictatorial mechanisms which prevent the possibility of their being defeated for re-election. Although trade-union leaders in all countries have achieved a great deal by moving up from the machine or bench to the union office, this shift has nowhere meant as much in terms of money and consequent style of life as in the United States. Most high status positions carry with them some security of tenure, but political positions in democratic societies are insecure by definition. Politicians in most countries may move from electoral defeat to highly paid positions in private industry or the professions, but union leaders customarily cannot do so. This means, as I have noted elsewhere, that they are under considerable pressure to find means to protect their source of status. Thus the greater the gap between the rewards of union leadership and of those jobs from which the leader came and to which he might return on defeat, the greater the pressure to eliminate democratic rights. Within the American labor movement itself those unions in which the gap between leaders and rank and file is narrow in income or in status

---

[40] Some indication of the extent of corruption may be found in a speech by George Meany, president of the AFL-CIO, in which, discussing the revelations of the Senate Committee, he commented: "We thought we knew a few things about trade union corruption, but we didn't know the half of it, one tenth of it, or the hundredth of it." Reported in the New York *Times,* November 2, 1957, and cited in Sylvester Petro, *Power Unlimited* (New York: Ronald Press, 1959), p. 146; and in Sidney Lens, *The Crisis of American Labor* (New York: Sagamore Press, 1959), p. 105. On corruption in American unions, see also John Hutchinson, "Corruption in American Unions," *Political Quarterly,* 28 (1957), pp. 214–235; Harold Seidman, *Labor Czars—A History of Labor Racketeering* (New York: Liveright, 1938); B. C. Roberts, *Unions in America,* pp. 59–73; Petro, *op. cit.* (above), especially pp. 144–181; and Lens, *op. cit.* (above), pp. 70–132.

seem to be much more democratic than those in which the gap is great. Among the unions which fall in this former category are Actors' Equity, the American Newspaper Guild, and the International Typographical Union.[41] Thus the very forces which press for higher rewards of various types for American labor leaders also support and encourage greater restrictions on democratic politics in the unions.

It may also be argued that in societies in which deferential values are strong, union leaders may maintain an oligarchic structure with less strain than is possible in America. And as I stated in an earlier essay:

> Given the assumption that leaders in both [continents] would seek to make their tenure secure, we would expect that American labor leaders would be under greater pressure to formalize dictatorial mechanisms so as to prevent the possibility of their being overthrown. Or, to put it another way, since the values inherent in American society operate to make American union officers more vulnerable than, say, their German counterparts, they would be obliged to act more vigorously and decisively and dictatorially to stabilize their status.[42]

Some evidence that relatively elite societies are more willing to give tenure to union leaders may be found in Great Britain and Sweden, where the principal officers of many national unions are formally chosen for life.[43] Although similar commitments are much less common elsewhere, actual opposition to the re-election of national leaders is almost non-existent among most European unions. Lower level leaders and convention delegates may and often do oppose top leadership policies, but such opposition—and even successful efforts to change policies by convention vote—are rarely linked to an effort to replace the high-ranking officers.

The logic of the argument presented here is similar to that made by many foreign analysts of American stratification, who have suggested

---

[41] See Seymour Martin Lipset, Martin Trow, and James S. Coleman, *Union Democracy* (Glencoe, Ill.: The Free Press, 1956).

[42] Seymour Martin Lipset, "The Political Process in Trade Unions," in Morroe Berger, Theodore Abel, and Charles Page, eds., *Freedom and Control in Modern Society* (Princeton, N.J.: Van Nostrand, 1954), pp. 116–117. These two pages present my first efforts to suggest a relationship between societal values and variation in union structures.

[43] In Great Britain, 86 of 127 general secretaries of unions have permanent status. These unions cover 74 per cent of the total membership of the T.U.C. See V. L. Allen, *Power in Trade Unions* (New York: Longmans, Green, 1954), p. 215. On Sweden, see Galenson, *The Danish System of Labor Relations*, p. 74.

that precisely because of the antagonism to aristocratic values in the United States, upper-class Americans—as contrasted with upper-class Europeans—are more likely to be concerned with the social origins and social backgrounds of those with whom they associate at play, in clubs, in school, and so forth. Insecurity stemming from an equalitarian democracy's denial of permanent status, calls forth defensive reactions on the part of those who would preserve their positions.

THE LARGE NUMBER AND PROPORTION OF PAID UNION OFFICIALS

Perhaps even more important in affecting the varying quality of the internal political life of American and European unions is the difference in the sheer number and proportion of full-time officers. A recent ILO mission of European labor authorities studying American unions was impressed by "the number of paid posts at all levels of union organization," as contrasted with the much lower number in Europe.[44] The most recent available data for various countries are reported in Table IV. These indicate one officer for every 300 union members in the United States, while three of the northern European movements, those of Britain, Norway, and Sweden, have one officer for every 1,700 to 2,200 members. (Australia, which has one officer for every 900 members, will be discussed together with Canada in a later section.)

In Britain, Norway, Sweden, Belgium, and many other European countries, lay union officers and committees, *i.e.*, men working full time at their regular occupations while voluntarily performing union duties, carry out many of the tasks which are performed by full-time union executives and staff men in the United States. National officers clearly cannot have the same degree of control over lay subordinates which they have over paid officers whose tenure in, or advancement up, the union hierarchy usually depends on being in the good graces of the top leaders.[45]

---

[44] Report of a Mission from the International Labour Office, *The Trade Union Situation in the United States* (Geneva: 1960), p. 133. The Swedish economist and sociologist Gunnar Myrdal was startled by the differences between the size of American and European trade union bureaucracies. See his *An American Dilemma* (New York: Harper & Bros., 1944), p. 713.

[45] "There are strong, dominating personalities at the head of many Scandinavian unions, but power tends to be vested in national committees, most of which include lay members. . . . By all accounts, these rank-and-file men have strong local backing, and are quite capable of standing up to the permanent officers. . . . This pattern of the lay majority on executive boards is quite common in Scandinavia, and is regarded as an important contributor to union democracy." Galenson, *Trade Union Democracy in Western Europe*, pp. 74–75.

Table IV

Numbers and Proportions of Full-Time Union Officers in Various Countries

Country	Total union membership	Total number full-time officers	Approximate ratio of officers to members
United States	18,000,000	60,000	1:300
Australia	2,400,000	2,500–2,750	1:900
Great Britain	8,000,000	4,000	1:2,000
Sweden	1,500,000	900	1:1,700
Norway	500,000	240	1:2,200
Denmark	775,000	1,000	1:775

Sources: The American data are from Richard Lester, As Unions Mature *(Princeton, N.J.: Princeton University Press, 1958), p. 116. The British data are based on an estimate by Hugh Clegg which is an extension of the materials presented in H. A. Clegg, A. J. Killick, and Rex Adams,* Trade Union Officers *(Oxford: Blackwell, 1961), pp. 39, 94. These data, based on a detailed survey of most British unions, report 3,000 full-time officers, 2,600 national officers and 400 branch secretaries, for unions having a total membership of 5,800,000 in 1959. Earlier British estimates are reported in George Cyriax and Robert Oakeshott,* The Bargainers: A Survey of Modern Trade Unionism *(New York: New York University Press, 1960), p. 133, and in B. C. Roberts,* Trade-Union Government and Administration in Great Britain *(Cambridge, Mass.: Harvard University Press, 1956), p. 288. The Australian estimates were furnished by Dr. Tom Truman of the University of Queensland and were obtained from queries sent to union officials. The Norwegian data were gathered by Dr. Stein Rokkan of the Christen Michelsens Institute of Bergen and were supplied by the Norwegian L. O. (labor federation). The 240 Norwegians include 150 elected officers and 90 appointed ones. The Swedish materials were collected by Dr. Ingemar Lindblad of the Swedish Royal Commission on Sound Broadcasting and were secured from officials of the Swedish L. O. Danish data were obtained from officers of Danish unions by Dr. Henning Friis of the Danish National Institute of Social Research. German data which suggest a pattern similar to the British one were collected by Professor Otto Stammer of the Free University of Berlin. They are not presented here since it was not possible to obtain reports from most German unions.*

To some degree, those who serve as unpaid officers must be men with a sense of mission, who view the movement as something more than an "insurance policy" for personal success, and who expect their paid officers to adhere to the values of a social movement. Such lay leaders will clearly remain relatively close in social position and values to the rank and file. In large measure, the perpetuation of serious political debate within union movements such as the British, the Norwegian, or the Belgian reflects the fact that many lay leaders are drawn from the ranks of the more idealistic and politically motivated of the membership and are not on a union career ladder.

In the United States, the large number of paid officials at all levels often means that union conventions are to a considerable extent meetings of the full-time local, district, and national leaders. Such meetings are much less likely to create trouble for the national officers than are meetings composed largely of men who are deeply involved in union matters, but who continue to work at their trade. The British Amalgamated Engineering Union, one of the largest in the country, has a lay national committee of fifty-two members which is authorized to give the full-time executive council "instructions for the ensuing year"; and B. C. Roberts comments that this "is precisely what it does, and it enforces its constitutional authority on a not always readily compliant executive council . . . [which] is not infrequently prevented from pursuing a wise policy by the powerful national committee." In most British unions, "lay status, that is, holding of no full-time office in the union, and non-membership on the executive council is generally necessary" to be a delegate to a national convention.[46]

Extensive lay involvement in union affairs does not, of course, prevent the paid officials from effectively controlling policy on most matters most of the time. An analysis of the voting on resolutions at nine British conventions during 1950–1952 indicated that the leaders were defeated on only 31 occasions out of 428 conference votes.[47] But in countries in which most of the secondary leadership are men who work at their trade, national executives are subject to more pressure to conform to conventional norms of morality and due process than when the lower echelons are paid union officers.[48] And even though British top union

---

[46] B. C. Roberts, *Trade Union Government and Administration in Great Britain* (Cambridge, Mass.: Harvard University Press, 1956), p. 165.

[47] *Ibid.*, p. 195. This figure may be more significant than it appears, since many, if not most, conference resolutions are noncontroversial.

[48] Hugh Clegg, "The Rights of British Trade-Union Members," in Michael Harrington and Paul Jacobs, eds., *Labor in a Free Society* (Berkeley: University of California Press, 1959), pp. 133–134. Another interesting consequence of a high proportion of paid officials has been suggested by John Dunlop, in discussing the causes of jurisdictional disputes in the building trades unions in the United States. "The large number of paid union officials at the local level with direct supervision over members at job sites is a feature . . . of workers' organizations in the United States system. 'Professionals' are available to appear at job sites to draw fine lines of jurisdiction. National and local union rivalries are expressed at the work place because the machinery and manpower

officers, for example, usually remain in office as long as do the entrenched heads of American organizations, the practice of lay participation on all levels permits a greater part in decision-making by the rank-and-file activists, who become unpaid officers, committeemen, and delegates to conventions. Thus Hugh Clegg points to the fact that a major policy of the British unions, the decision made in 1948 to cooperate with the Labor Government's wage restraint policy, was reversed in 1950 "through the gradual process of branch votes and conference decisions in the individual unions. This took place without the wholesale replacement of trade-union executives and officers by opposition leaders. . . ."[49]

The fact that union activists, in the form of lay officers and committee-men, have much more influence over the policy of national unions in Britain than in America does not necessarily mean that the British unions more accurately reflect the sentiment of their general membership. The activists are much more likely to be radical than either the rank-and-file membership as a whole or the national leadership. This was clearly shown in the case of the 1960 debate over unilateral disarmament. A national opinion survey conducted in September 1960, shortly before the Labor Party conference, reported that only 16 per cent of trade-union members favored the proposal that Britain unilaterally give up its nuclear weapons, the very policy which was backed by a majority of the delegates representing the trade unions; 83 per cent of rank-and-file union members expressed the opinion that Britain should retain such weapons until other powers agreed to disarm.[50]

Although it is relatively easy to suggest some of the effects of the variation in the proportion of full-time officers on trade-union government and behavior, it is much more difficult to explain the source of the variation. Some have suggested that it reflects differences in the income

---

to express them on the job is available. In other countries . . . few full-time professionals are available to police the rules. . . . Left to themselves on the job site, the workers would engage in fewer and less severe disputes." John T. Dunlop, *Industrial Relations Systems* (New York: Holt, 1958), pp. 252–253.

[49] Clegg, "The Rights of British Trade-Union Members," *op. cit.*, p. 138.

[50] The survey, which was conducted for the London *Daily Herald*, is reported in detail in *Report on a Survey of Opinions Concerning Nuclear Disarmament* (London: Odham's Press, 1960). A survey conducted about the same time by the British Gallup Poll bearing on the same issues, although wording its question differently, also reported relatively little support (24 per cent) among Labor voters for unilateral disarmament. (Gallup did not separate out trade-union members in his report.) The Gallup survey is reported in the *Gallup Political Index*, Report No. 9, September, 1960.

of labor organizations in Europe and America. While this factor undoubtedly plays a role (though Swedish unions are quite well-to-do),
the fact remains that American unions began the practice of employing
full-time officers and staff members when many of the unions were weak
and impoverished. In discussing the American labor movement, the
Swedish sociologist and economist Gunnar Myrdal points out that the
foreign observer "is struck by the importance played by salaried
'organizers' and the relative unimportance of, or often the lack of, a
spontaneous drive from the workers themselves." He suggests that this
phenomenon reflects the general "passivity of the masses in America
[which] is, of course, a product of the nation's history." Specifically,
immigration produced cultural fragmentation and prevented strong interest-group identification, while a very high rate of social mobility
drained the working class of its potential leaders.[51]

Although the factors which Myrdal cites may account in part for the
relatively low level of "class consciousness" among American workers,
they do not explain the apparent willingness from a very early period in
trade-union history to pay leaders full-time salaries. As a further factor
contributing to this policy, it may be suggested that inherent in the ideology of an equalitarian society like ours, as contrasted with those of countries like Britain and Sweden in which aristocratic values remain significant, has been the principle that a man should be paid for his work. The
conception that public or social service is performed best when a leader
is not paid, or is paid an honorarium, is basically an aristocratic value
linked to the concept of *noblesse oblige*. In Britain, for example, recent
parliamentary discussions concerning the salaries of Members of Parliament have explicitly assumed that M. P.'s should not be paid well, because
it would be bad if men were attracted to a parliamentary career in order
to better themselves economically. The inhibitions against employing a
large number of officials permeate most voluntary associations in the European nations and reflect the historic assumption that such activities
should be the "charities" of the privileged classes. The absence of a model
of *noblesse oblige* in an equalitarian society fostered the American belief
that such voluntary associations, whether they be the "March of Dimes,"
social work agencies, or trade unions, should be staffed by men who are
paid to do the job. In a sense, therefore, it may be argued that the very
emphasis on equalitarianism in America has given rise to the large salaried
bureaucracies which permeate voluntary organizations.

---

[51] Myrdal, *The American Dilemma*, pp. 713–714.

In presenting this hypothesis, I do not mean to suggest that historic differences in ultimate values themselves account for the perpetuation and extension of the varying patterns down to the present. Rather, the different values in Europe and America helped to initiate differing early models of behavior, which became institutionalized within varying social structures. The European practice fostered—and in turn has been sustained by—the ideologies, mainly socialist, which the various labor movements adopted. Conversely, in the United States the establishment of the union career ladder made union leaders receptive to incorporating the society's achievement norms into the ideology and practice of the movement, and these norms supported further extension of the practice of maintaining a large and well-paid bureaucracy and leadership core.

The American Political System and the Union Movement

The difference between the American labor movement and those in other modern industrial countries cannot be attributed solely to the direct effect of American values on its ideology. The greater authority and power centered in the hands of American national union presidents, as compared with European leaders, [52] may also be viewed as an outgrowth of the role of the executive and of federalism in American politics.[53]

As a result of its history and size, the United States has adopted two distinct political institutions, the presidential system and the federal system. Our principal elections at the national, state, and local levels are for one man—the president, governor, or mayor. Government is largely viewed as the government of the man who holds the key executive office. His cabinet is responsible to him, not to his party nor to parliamentary colleagues. Hence there is an emphasis on personality and a relative de-

---

[52] The English labor authority B. C. Roberts has commented, "Once elected, the power of an American union president generally far exceeds that of any officer of British or Scandinavian unions." *Unions in America*, p. 36; see also Cyriax and Oakeshott, *The Bargainers*, p. 79; Walter Galenson, ed., *Comparative Labor Movements* (New York: Prentice-Hall, 1952), p. 121; and Leo Bromwich, *Union Constitutions* (New York: Fund for the Republic, 1959), p. 38.

[53] American collective bargaining "is perhaps the most decentralized in the world." Ross and Hartman, *Changing Patterns of Industrial Conflict*, p. 166. See also the ILO Mission Report, *The Trade Union Situation . . .* , pp. 24–25; Neil Chamberlain, "Collective Bargaining in the United States," in Adolf Sturmthal, ed., *Contemporary Collective Bargaining in Seven Countries*, p. 259; Roberts, *Unions in America*, p. 78; Lester, *As Unions Mature*, pp. 23–26.

emphasis of party or principles. These factors, which have become normative elements in the political sphere, undoubtedly affect the way in which other institutions, such as unions, operate.

The federal system, with its relatively strong local government institutions, has also affected the logic and organization of trade unions, since many of them are involved in various kinds of relations with the centers of political power. If political power for certain major purposes rests on the level of the municipality, this means that unions too must be able to deal with local officials. But probably at least as important as this structural parallelism is the fact that federalism and local self-government have facilitated the maintenance of strong norms of local and regional solidarity and consciousness of difference from other parts of the nation. Business power, also, is comparatively decentralized in the United States. The norms support the institutionalization of competition; this is reflected in the early passage of anti-trust laws and other legislation against unfair restraint of trade. Unions have to deal not only with local political power but with local business power as well. And business groups in various parts of the country often follow different strategies.[54]

The decentralization of authority may be related to other aspects of union behavior discussed earlier. There are fewer organizational restrictions on union militancy when authority is decentralized. National agreements require centralization of union authority and inhibit locally called strikes. Hence American union militancy may be partly a reflection of the prevalence of local agreements, which, as we have seen, may be regarded as an indirect consequence of the overreaching value system.

The militancy of American unions, which has been derived from attributes and consequences of these basic values, may in turn be one of the major factors contributing to the pattern of innovation which characterizes the economy. The editors of the London *Economist* have suggested that the historic propensity of American unions to demand "more" forces employers to find ways to resolve their dilemma by improving produc-

---

[54] The ILO Mission points out in the conclusion of its report (p. 146): "Much has been said in this report about the different conditions for trade union activity which are found in different parts of the country. . . . The general public attitude towards trade unions may vary from one state, city or locality to another. Relations with the employers vary in the same way. The relations between the unions and a company may not be the same in all the company's plants in different areas. Unions which are accepted in certain industries in some parts of the country may be opposed in the same industries in other parts."

tivity.[55] "Thus, there is generated a constant force pushing the employer into installing more labor-saving equipment, into reducing costs in other directions."[56] European unions with their involvement in making national contracts and with their regard for the over-all needs of the polity and economy—concerns which seem in some measure to stem from their political commitments—are less inclined to make "irresponsible" demands or to insist on policies which will adversely affect a sizable part of an industry. Decentralized collective bargaining is in part an *outgrowth* of a dynamic economy in which different portions are advancing at varying rates, and in part a *cause* of that very dynamism.

Decentralization of power also facilitates corruption. Corruption in American unions and other institutions is more prevalent on the local than on the national level. Where lower level officials such as union business agents or municipal inspectors deal directly with businessmen, the possibilities of undetected corruption are much greater than they are in relations among the heads of major organizations.

Political decentralization and strong local governments, as Tocqueville noted well over a century ago, strongly reinforce the norms of individualism. Americans are encouraged to press for their objectives through individual or organized group action, not to accept their lot or to hope for remedy from an established upper class or a strong central government. Over time, of course, changes in technology and the nature of social problems have led to increasing centralization of power within government, business, and labor. But it still remains true that, on a comparative scale, American institutions remain decentralized and local units retain considerable autonomy. Hence one has here another example of interrelated supports and consequences of the dominant value system.

Within the labor movement, the emphasis on strong local organizations has, in turn, facilitated the creation of the large numbers of full-time union positions referred to earlier. Thus in its decentralization, as in its

---

[55] Will Herberg, "When Social Scientists View Labor," *Commentary*, 11 (1951), p. 593.

[56] Roberts, *Unions in America*, p. 102. Sumner Slichter pointed to this phenomenon even earlier: "[T]he tendency for collective bargaining to accelerate technological discovery is undoubtedly one of its most useful effects. . . ." *The Challenge of Industrial Relations* (Ithaca, N. Y.: Cornell University Press, 1947), pp. 90–91. American union pressure to raise wages has been a major force "goading management into technical improvement and increased capital investment." Sidney Sufrin, *Union Wages and Labor's Earnings* (Syracuse, N. Y.: Syracuse University Press, 1950), p. 86; see also p. 51.

conservative politics and militant strike tactics, the American union may be viewed as an outgrowth of the American social and American value system.

Other Equalitarian Societies: Canada and Australia

In contrasting the labor movements in the various nations in the industrialized democracies' "culture area," I have largely ignored those of Canada and Australia. Both nations, like the United States, are outgrowths of the settlement of a relatively vacant frontier. There is general agreement that these two nations, along with the United States, are among the most equalitarian in their basic values.

However, as will be detailed in Chapter 7, while Canada, Australia, and the United States have value systems that are relatively similar as compared to other Western industrial nations, they differ significantly among themselves. Australia has been perceived as an even more equalitarian society than the United States. According to various interpreters of Canadian culture, Canada is somewhat less egalitarian, less achievement oriented, and less individualistic than the United States. Australia, on the other hand, seems to be even more anti-elitist in its basic values than the United States, but the values of a universalized individualism seem weaker, particularly among workers.

Given their strong similarities in basic values when *contrasted* with Old World societies, the three large, predominantly English-speaking overseas democracies also fulfill the expectations of having similarly structured labor movements. For example, these three extremely wealthy nations "have led the world in working days lost through [labor] disputes."[57] Over four decades ago, James Bryce explained the militancy of Australian labor as derivative from Australia's equalitarian emphasis, using much the same logic as has been used by such sociologists as Robert Merton to explain the propensity of Americans to engage in innovating or illegitimate actions in order to succeed:

> Neither social equality nor the standard of comfort much above that of England, which the workers enjoy, has softened the clash of economic interests . . . it is hardly a paradox to say that the more the condition of the wage-earners rises, the more does their dissatisfaction also rise. . . . Where other distinctions are absent, and

[57] Clegg, *A New Approach to Industrial Democracy*, p. 26; see also Ross and Hartman, *Changing Patterns of Industrial Conflict*, pp. 161–162.

a few years can lift a man from nothing to affluence, differences in wealth are emphasized and resented, deemed the more unjust because they often seem the result of chance, or at least of causes due to no special merit in their possessor.[58]

Most continental and British unions favor works councils or joint consultation in industry, while Australian, American, and Canadian unions are either opposed to, or uninterested in, such institutions. "What cannot be handled by a trade union and written into a collective agreement, had, in their eyes, better be left alone."[59] As in the United States, "collective bargaining . . . is not really very centralized."[60] The union movements of all three nations also tend to be legalistic and highly dependent on "labor lawyers," a category which hardly exists in Great Britain.[61] As compared with European unions, the Canadian and Australian unions, though linked to labor or socialist parties, show less of a sense of responsibility for the needs of the polity.[62] There is also some evidence that Australian and, to a lesser extent, Canadian union leaders have resembled American ones in their efforts to subvert the processes of organizational democracy in so far as these affect opposition efforts to defeat incumbent administrations. The three national union movements, which not only are influenced by

---

[58] James Bryce, *Modern Democracies* (London, Macmillan, 1921), Vol. II, p. 273. And as in the United States, Bryce reports that the Australians are too easy-going in dealing with the successful who achieve their position by corrupt means: "[M]any of their statesmen have through long and chequered careers retained the loyalty of the masses . . . their indulgent temper is apt to forget misdeeds which ought to have permanently discredited an offender. . . . Tergiversation, and still more severely pecuniary corruption, are censured at the time, yet such sins are soon covered by the charitable sentiment that 'bygones are bygones.' " *Ibid.*, pp. 276–277.

[59] Clegg, *A New Approach to Industrial Democracy*, p. 26.

[60] Ross and Hartman, *Changing Patterns of Industrial Conflict*, pp. 146, 166.

[61] A comparison of the legal profession in England and the U. S. reports: "[T]he English lawyer plays a far less important role in collective bargaining between employers and labour and in industrial relations generally. In the States this is an important and lucrative branch of legal practice; in England lawyers have been almost totally excluded from the field." L. C. B. Gower and Leolin Price, "The Profession and Practice of the Law in England and America," *Modern Law Review*, 20 (1957), p. 327. For a discussion of the role of law and lawyers in affecting union patterns in the United States, see S. M. Lipset, "The Law and Trade Union Democracy," *Virginia Law Review*, 47 (1961), pp. 1–50.

[62] See D. W. Rawson, "Politics and Responsibility in Australian Trade Unions," *Australian Journal of Politics and History*, 4 (1958), pp. 224–243.

similar national values but operate within continental, federal political systems, resemble each other too in having relatively decentralized national unions as compared to those of northern Europe. They also have extremely weak central federations. Canadian policy in these matters has been akin to the American, while the Australians have been even more decentralized. The main unit of an Australian union is the state organization, not the national body; a permanent national federation of Australian unions, the Australian Council of Trade Unions, was not established until 1927.[63] The central state federation of one state, Western Australia, remained outside of the ACTU until 1949, and the largest single union in the country, the Australian Workers Union with 200,000 members, has never affiliated.

In many other aspects of their behavior, Australia and Canada tend to behave in ways which put them intermediate between the United States and Britain or the countries of northern Europe. Thus the best available estimates of the total number of paid full-time officers, presented in Table IV above, indicate that Australia has approximately one official for every 900 members, Britain, one for 2,000, and the United States, one for 300. No reliable estimate exists for Canada, but the guess of some Canadian union leaders is that it would be somewhat closer to the United States than to the Australian figure.

With respect to officers' salaries and other perquisites, the picture is similar, although it is difficult to formulate a conclusive judgment with regard to Canadian unions, most of which are affiliates of American ones and have their salary schedules determined in some part by the pattern set by the international organization. In Australia the bulk of union officials receive relatively low salaries compared to those in North America, but their incomes are higher than those of British or northern European officials. Union officers in Australia estimate that the average salaries for the secretaries of state unions, usually the highest full-time posts, are between 1,200 and 1,600 pounds, while the average worker's annual income is about 750 pounds. Where information is public, as it is for unions which have secured awards on officers' salaries from the Arbitration Court, secretaries' salaries are known to be 2,000 pounds a year. The Australian Workers Union, which is a general union of laborers and which has close to 10 per cent of the total national union membership, seems to operate on American standards. Its general secretary receives 4,500 pounds

---

[63] See Lloyd M. Ross, "Trade Unionism" in *Australian Encyclopedia* (East Lansing: Michigan State University Press, 1958) Vol. 9, p. 9.

a year plus a 600 pound tax-free allowance for expenses. In addition to this regular income, the union gives him a traveling allowance of five pounds a day, the use of an automobile together with its operating costs, long-service leave worth 6,000 pounds on retirement, an insurance policy subsidized by union funds, and a loan of 6,000 pounds at 1 per cent interest to purchase a home.[64]

There seems to be much less corruption among union officials in Australia and Canada, as compared with the United States.[65] However, English visitors to Australia are struck with the extent to which they "will put up with boss-rule and corruption in trade-unions."[66] On the whole, labor groups in both Canada and Australia would appear to be less law-abiding than similar organizations in northern Europe and Britain. Australian unions "can reduce the law, or parts of the law, to impotence. Practically every strike of any size in Australia is illegal, yet the Australian record of man-days lost per head since the war is challenged only by the United States."[67] In Canada, as compared with the United States, "there has generally been less violent conflict between workers and employers. Professional strikebreakers, labor spies, 'goon squads,' 'vigilante' groups, armed militia, and other spectacular features of industrial warfare in the United States in previous decades have been absent from the Canadian scene—again with several notable exceptions.[68]

Many differences among these three nations are analyzed in detail later, and they will not be pursued further here. It does seem appropriate, however, to call attention to the fact that individually Canada, Australia, and the United States may each be contrasted with most, if not all, of the industrial democracies of northwestern Europe in terms of differences in value orientation, and that in most respects the differences between the behavior of their individual labor movements and those of Europe fit the assumptions made here about the consequences of varying national value systems and social structures on trade-union behavior.[69]

---

[64] I am indebted to Dr. Tom Truman of the University of Queensland for gathering these data. The materials on the Australian Workers Union are taken from *Voice*, the organ of the Council for Membership Control.

[65] Lester, *As Unions Mature*, p. 62.

[66] Jeanne Mackenzie, *Australian Paradox* (London: Macgibbon and Kee, 1962), p. 164.

[67] Clegg, *A New Approach to Industrial Democracy*, p. 22.

[68] Jamieson, *Industrial Relations in Canada*, p. 7.

[69] Other reasons accounting for the number of strikes in the three countries are presented in Ross and Hartman, *Changing Patterns of Industrial Conflict*, pp. 141–151, 161–170.

Conclusion

The basic values—equality and achievement—that America acquired from its Revolutionary and Puritan origins have continued to shape American institutions. From early in their histories to the present day, many of the unique features in American institutions may be attributed to them.

Thus the American labor movement has been less class conscious and more militant than those in European countries where there is less emphasis on individual achievement and equality. Since the American emphasis has been upon individual responsibility for success or failure, the American worker has not seen himself as a member of a class. He has felt his lower status as a personal affront, while he has felt that his attempts to better himself, collectively as well as individually, were legitimate. As a result there have been pressures, unchecked by traditional deference relations between classes, to support aggressive union action.

While the principle of equality has thus extended pressures to succeed to all members of the society, regardless of class, the stress on achievement has created inequalities. The difference between the income and status of union leaders and the union rank and file is but one example of the way in which the stress on both equality and achievement may bring about institutional features that appear contradictory to one another.

The ability of American trade unionists calmly to accept such a paradox may be partially explained by the fact that labor unions, like other American associations, tend to play a specific rather than diffuse role in the lives of their members. From time to time union leaders have espoused radical class conscious ideologies, but the members generally have not followed them. Rather they have viewed the union as a means of specifically improving their wages and working conditions, rather than as a means of raising them from their generally "lowly status." These ideologies did not convince them that they were part of an underprivileged class, because they believed that, as individuals, they had as good a chance as anyone else.

The paradox of ideological conservatism and militant tactics parallels, to some extent, the paradox that American society is, at the same time, one of the most religious (moral) and one of the most secular (materialistic) societies in the world. Both paradoxes are made possible by the specificity of the role that these two institutions play in American society. Thus, both the church and the trade union are allowed to express generalizations that people do not necessarily accept because they judge religious and trade union institutions in terms of their specific roles rather than their ideologies. But whereas, in the area of religion, this has simply meant that Americans limit the degree to which religious principles govern their daily lives, it has deeply affected the structure of the labor movement.

Democracy has divorced religion from political power, and made the organization of its Protestant sects democratic. It is antagonistic to the self-righteous concept of "the elect" in Calvinism. As such, democracy has made religious institutions an inappropriate place to satisfy the individual's ambition to succeed. On the other hand, trade unions deal with money and power, both of which provide very tangible evidence of where one stands in relation to others. In a sense, trade unions represent an organized attempt to achieve individual equality and as such they are permeated by the peculiarly American characteristic, the pressure to succeed.

Much of the behavior which we deplore in the American labor movement is the expression of the tension inherent in valuing both equality and achievement. The American trade union, like the American church, behaves in ways which often displease those whose institutional model is of European origin. True believers in one area desire militant class consciousness and honest unionism, just as, in the other, they desire devout, theologically serious religion with a high level of participation in observances. America gives them some traits which they like, combined with some which they dislike. But such contradictions are seemingly inherent in complex social structures. To illustrate the way in which the differing value systems of all societies, resulting from variations in history, produce comparable structural paradoxes, the next section of this book turns to a more detailed examination of comparative social systems.

DEMOCRACY IN COMPARATIVE PERSPECTIVE

PART **III**

Values and
Democratic
Stability

6 ★★★

Parts I and II of this study examined how the United States produced a particular set of "structured predispositions," which is one way of defining values, for handling strains generated by social change. These predispositions have affected the status system, the "American character," the pattern of American religion, and the development of class interests among the workers. The effort has been to demonstrate that American status concerns, "other-directedness," religious participation, church organization, labor union structure, and the like, differed from those of other nations because of our distinctive value system. Within self-imposed limitations, this has represented an effort to present an integrated view of American society. Only in the treatment of trade-union behavior did the analysis move toward an attempt also to explain behavior in other countries.

In this concluding section of the book, I turn from a concentration on the United States to comparative analysis of a given institutional structure—the organization of democratic polities.[1] In a sense, the dis-

---

[1] I have dealt with such problems in preceding publications. Thus *Political Man: The Social Bases of Politics* (Garden City, N.Y.: Doubleday, 1960) is addressed to an analysis of the relationship between stages or degrees of economic development and political systems, and to the effect of varying types of legitimacy on the intensity of conflict within political systems. *Union Democracy*, with Martin Trow and James Coleman (Glencoe, Ill.: The Free Press, 1956) and *Agrarian Socialism* (Berkeley: University of California Press,

cussion here represents a further effort to illustrate the worth of the preceding analyses of American society by a systematic presentation of the way American institutions differ from those of other nations with varying value systems. It represents an effort to extend the type of value analysis employed in preceding chapters to locate some of the sources of variation among a number of national polities, including the American. However, it should be obvious that institutions and reactions cannot be derived soley or even primarily from the basic value systems; and, as one illustration of the way in which specific legal enactments may influence the course of nations, I turn in the final chapter of this section to a discussion of the processes through which the varying structure of the polity may itself affect the form and stability of the political system.

Since I have attempted elsewhere to elaborate a sociologically meaningful definition of a democratic system, I do not want to repeat these discussions here.[2] Essentially, I have urged the view that *realistically* the distinctive and most valuable element of democracy in complex societies is the formation of a political elite in the competitive struggle for the votes of a mainly passive electorate. This definition is premised on the common assumption that democracy means a system in which those outside of the formal authority structure are able significantly to influence the basic direction of policy. If the citizenry as a whole are to have access to decisions, there must be a meaningful competitive struggle within the political elite which leads factions within this elite to look for generalized as well as specific support. But the political elite can be leaders *and representatives* only if there are mechanisms within the culture which foster the kinds of personal motivations that lead men to perceive and strongly support their interests within a political system which has relatively well-defined rules. Mechanisms that undermine the democratic rules or which inhibit institutionalized conflict are destructive of democracy, in that they restrict the general population's access to, or power over, key societal decisions. Hence it is necessary to look for factors which, on the one hand, sustain the separation of the political system from the excesses inherent in the populist assumptions of democracy—

1950) dealt with the ways in which variation in the number and type of secondary organizations mediate between the population and the government and thus affect the conditions for democracy or dictatorship.

[2] See *Political Man*, pp. 21–41 and 45–48; and my Introduction to a new paperback edition of Robert Michels, *Political Parties* (New York: Collier Books, 1962), pp. 15–39, especially pp. 33–38.

the belief that the majority will is always sovereign—*and*, on the other, encourage participation in organizations that conflict with one another and with state agencies concerning the direction of public policy on all major issues.

Earlier I argued that the effects of American values on the American labor movement could best be specified by comparing that movement with those in countries at relatively similar levels of development. The same argument applies to any attempt systematically to examine the way in which a nation's values affect its polity.

Value Patterns and a Democratic Polity

To compare national value systems, we must be able to classify them and distinguish among them. Talcott Parsons has provided a useful tool for this purpose in his concept of "pattern variables." These were originally developed by Parsons as an extension of the classic distinction by Ferdinand Tönnies between "community" and "society"—between those systems which emphasized *Gemeinschaft* (primary, small, traditional, integrated) values, and those which stressed *Gesellschaft* (impersonal, secondary, large, socially differentiated) values.[3] The pattern variables to be used in the following analysis are achievement–ascription, universalism–particularism, and specificity–diffuseness. According to the achievement–ascription distinction, a society's value system may emphasize individual ability or performance or it may emphasize ascribed or inherited qualities (such as race or high birth) in judging individuals and placing them in various roles. According to the universalism-particularism distinction, it may emphasize that all people shall be treated according to the same standard (*e.g.*, equality before the law), or that individuals shall be treated differently according to their personal qualities or their particular membership in a class or group. Specificity–diffuseness refers to the difference between treating individuals in terms of the specific positions

---

[3] Ferdinand Tönnies, *Community and Society, Gemeinschaft und Gesellschaft* (East Lansing: Michigan State University Press, 1957). A somewhat more complex specification of the component elements of these two concepts may be found in Charles P. Loomis, *Social Systems: Essays on Their Persistence and Change* (Princeton, N.J.: Van Nostrand, 1961), especially pp. 57–63. The pattern variables may also be seen as derived from Max Weber's types of social action, especially the traditional and the instrumentally rational. See Max Weber, *The Theory of Social and Economic Organization* (New York: Oxford University Press, 1947), pp. 115–118.

which they happen to occupy, rather than diffusely as individual members of the collectivity.[4]

The pattern variables provide us with a much more sensitive way of classifying values than the older polar concepts of sociology, such as the folk–urban, mechanical–organic, primary–secondary, or *Gemeinschaft–Gesellschaft*, etc. For instance, they make it possible for us to establish differences in value structures between two nations that are at the same end of the *Gemeinschaft–Gesellschaft* continuum, or are at similar levels of economic development or social complexity. They are also useful for describing differences within a society. Thus the family is inherently ascriptive and particularistic while the market is universalistic and achievement oriented—the weaker the kinship ties in a given society, the greater the national emphasis on achievement is likely to be.

The manner in which any set of values is introduced will obviously affect the way the values are incorporated into a nation's institutions. In France, for instance, where the values of universalism, achievement, and specificity were introduced primarily through a political revolution, we would expect to find them most prominent in the political institutions; in Germany, where they have been introduced primarily through industrialization, we would expect to find them most prominent in its economic institutions. The American example suggests that for democratic values to become legitimate in a post-revolutionary polity the norms of universalism, achievement, and specificity must be introduced into its economic institutions as well. This fosters rapid economic development, and encourages the underprivileged to believe that they as individuals may personally improve their status.[5]

---

[4] Parsons has two other pattern variables which I ignore here, largely for reasons of parsimony: affectivity–affective neutrality, and the instrumental-consummatory distinction. A third set—self-orientation–collectivity-orientation —is discussed briefly toward the end of Chapter 7. For a detailed presentation of the pattern variables, see Talcott Parsons, *The Social System* (Glencoe, Ill.: The Free Press, 1951), pp. 58–67. Parsons' most recent elaboration of the relationship of pattern variable analysis to other elements in his conceptual framework is "Pattern Variables Revisited," *American Sociological Review*, 25 (1960), pp. 467–483; see also his article, "The Point of View of the Author," in Max Black, ed., *The Social Theories of Talcott Parsons* (Englewood Cliffs, N.J.: Prentice-Hall, 1961), pp. 319–320, 329–336.

[5] Karl W. Deutsch, S. A. Burrell, R. A. Kann, M. Lee, Jr., M. Lichterman, R. E. Lindgren, F. L. Loewenheim, R. W. Van Wagenen, *Political Community and the North Atlantic Area* (Princeton, N.J.: Princeton University Press, 1957).

I shall add the equalitarian–elitist distinction to the pattern variables just outlined. According to this, a society's values may stress that all persons must be given respect simply because they are human beings, or it may stress the general superiority of those who hold positions of power and privilege. In an equalitarian society, the differences between low status and high status people are not stressed in social relationships and do not convey to the high status person a general claim to social deference. In contrast, in an elitist society, those who hold high positions in any structure, whether it be in business, in intellectual activities, or in government, are thought to deserve, and are actually given, general respect and deference.[6] All ascriptively oriented societies are necessarily also elitist in this use of the term. On the other hand, achievement orientation and egalitarianism are not necessarily highly correlated, since a stress on achievement is not incompatible with giving generalized deference to all who have achieved their elite positions. To a considerable degree societies which are in the process of changing from an emphasis on ascription to one on achievement seem disposed, as we shall see later, to retain their elitist orientations and institutions when contrasted with societies in which ascriptive values have never had a preeminent role.

In actual fact, *no society is ever fully explicable by these analytic concepts, nor does the theory even contemplate the possible existence of such a society.*[7] Every society incorporates some aspect of each polarity.

---

[6] Although all four polarity distinctions are important to the analysis of the political system, ascription–achievement and universalism–particularism seem more important than the other two. As Parsons has suggested, these are the variables which have the most reference to the total social system, rather than to subparts or to the motivation of individuals. "They are concerned . . . with the type of value-norms which enter into the structure of the social system." Combinations of these pairs are also most useful to help account for "structural differentiation and variability of social systems." See Parsons, *The Social System*, p. 106. The other two pairs, specificity–diffuseness and equalitarianism–elitism, are to a considerable degree dependent on the particular combinations of the first two.

[7] As Parsons has put it: "In a very broad way the differentiations between types of social systems do correspond to this order of cultural value pattern differentiation, but *only* in a very broad way. Actual social structures are not value-pattern types, but *resultants* of the integration of value-patterns with the other components of the system." *Ibid.*, p. 112. (Emphases in the original.) Gabriel Almond has criticized the utility of pattern-variable analysis for the study of comparative politics on the grounds that it results in exaggerations of the differences among political systems, particularly between Western and non-Western and primitive ones. He argues that "all political systems—the

We may, however, differentiate among social structures by the extent to which they emphasize one or another of these polarities.[8] It should be added that classifications of the relative emphases among nations with respect to certain value polarities do not imply that such values are either prescriptive or descriptive of actual behavior. Rather, they are intended to provide base lines for comparative analysis.

I have chosen to discuss the United States, Great Britain, Canada, Australia, France, and Germany to illustrate the relationship between values and the stability of democratic political systems.[9] These nations are all relatively industrialized, all have capitalist or mixed economies, and the religious traditions of all can be traced back to the same Hebraic-Christian source. They all have democratic political systems. Yet they

---

developed Western ones as well as the less-developed non-Western ones—are transitional systems in which cultural change is taking place." Thus they both include elements of each polarity of the pattern variables in many of their institutions. See Gabriel Almond, "Introduction: A Functional Approach to Comparative Politics," in Gabriel Almond and James S. Coleman, eds., *The Politics of Developing Areas* (Princeton, N.J.: Princeton University Press, 1960), pp. 20–25. This criticism is useful if it is considered as a warning against reifying these concepts, or tending to exaggerate the integrated character of societies, whether large or small. However, there is no reason why use of the pattern variables for analytic purposes need fall into these errors, and Parsons himself repeatedly stresses that systems and structures are never wholly one.

A detailed criticism of Parsons' analysis of politics, which, however, does not touch on the concepts dealt with here may be found in Andrew Hacker, "Sociology and Ideology," in Max Black, ed., *The Social Theories of Talcott Parsons* (Englewood Cliffs, N.J.: Prentice-Hall, 1961) pp. 289–310.

[8] It is important to note also that the pattern variables can be and have been used to distinguish among and within different orders of social systems or structures. Thus we may characterize total epochs (feudalism compared to capitalism), whole nations (the United States compared to Britain), subsystems within nations that logically may operate with different combinations of the variables (the state, or industry), subsystems within nations that logically must follow a specific set of pattern variables (the family), and subsystems within which there is conflict between different pattern variables (*e.g.*, the French business system, to be discussed later).

[9] There have been other efforts at using the pattern variables for political analysis. For the most part, however, they do so in the context of specifying differences between Western and agrarian societies and hence posit ideal types of integrated *Gemeinschaft* and *Gesellschaft* cultures. A paper which does attempt to use the variables to analyze contemporary differences is William Evan, "Social Structure, Trade Unionism, and Consumer Cooperation," *Industrial and Labor Relations Review*, 10 (1957), pp. 440–447.

differ in one important respect: the United States, Britain, Canada, and Australia have stable polities, while France and Germany have (or have had) unstable ones. The prime empirical focus in this chapter is on the four most populous countries; the two overseas dominions of the British Crown are contrasted with the United States and Britain in the next chapter.

The United States and Great Britain

Though the United States and Great Britain are both urbanized, industrialized, and stable politically, they are integrated around different values and class relations. Tocqueville's *Democracy in America* and Bagehot's *The English Constitution* accurately specified these different organizing principles. According to Tocqueville, American democratic society was equalitarian and competitive (achievement oriented); according to Bagehot, Britain was deferential (elitist) and ascriptive. As both Tocqueville and Bagehot indicated, a society in which the historic ties of traditional legitimacy had been forcibly broken could sustain a stable democratic polity only if it emphasized equality and if it contained strong, independent, and competitive institutions. Conversely, if the privileged classes persisted and continued to expect ascriptive (aristocratic) and elitist rights, a society could have a stable democratic system only if the lower classes accepted the status system. These differences will be explored in more detail subsequently. Suffice it to say now that a stable democracy can result from different combinations of pattern variables.

The United States, more than any other modern non-Communist industrial nation, emphasizes achievement, equalitarianism, universalism, and specificity.[10] These four tend to be mutually supportive. This does not mean that other stable combinations are not possible or that the "American" combination does not exhibit tensions. From the perspective of the polity, however, this combination of variables does encourage

---

[10] For a discussion of the American value system, see Robin Williams, *American Society* (New York: Alfred A. Knopf, 1951), pp. 372–442; see also Talcott Parsons and Winston White, "The Link Between Character and Society," in S. M. Lipset and Leo Lowenthal, eds., *Culture and Social Character* (New York: The Free Press, 1961), pp. 98–103; on values and the political system see William Mitchell, *The American Polity* (New York: The Free Press, 1963). I devote less space here to elaborating on American values than on those of the other nations, since I have already dealt with them in detail in the earlier chapters of this book.

stable democracy. The upper classes can accept improvements in the status and power of the lower strata *without feeling morally offended.* Since all men and groups are expected to try to improve their position *vis à vis* others, success by a previously deprived group is not resented as deeply as in countries whose values stress the moral worth of ascription.[11] Similarly, the emphasis on equalitarianism, universalism, and specificity means that men can expect—and within limits do receive— fair treatment according to the merits of the case or their ability. Lower-class individuals and groups which desire to change their social position *need not be revolutionary;* consequently their political goals and methods are relatively moderate. There is little class consciousness on their part, since this consciousness is in part an adaptation to the behavior of the upper class in those societies characterized by ascription, elitism, particularism, and diffuseness. The latter values imply that men will be treated by others and will treat each other diffusely in terms of class status. American values support interaction with an individual in terms of his role as worker in one situation, as suburban dweller in another, as a member of the American Legion in a third, and so forth.

The above comments are, of course, an oversimplification. In fact, American society does display ascriptive, elitist, particularistic, and diffuse culture traits. These are not completely dysfunctional, as will be shown. They do create frictions (see the analyses of McCarthyism as a reaction to "status-panic"),[12] but in general, with the exception of race and ethnic relations, these have not affected the basic stability of the polity.

The American South, which has stressed ascriptive-elitist-particularistic-diffuse values in race relations and to some extent in its total social system, has constituted a major source of instability in the American polity. It was retained in the nation only by force, and down to the present it does not have a stable, democratic polity. To the extent that its citizens have felt the pull of the dominant value system, the South

---

[11] Like all comparative generalizations, this is a relative rather than an absolute statement. It is obvious that in the United States, as in other countries, those with higher status dislike any challenge to their privileged positions, and resist and resent new claimants. The common resistance to the claims for status equality of upwardly mobile ethnic groups such as the Jews, the Irish, and the Italians illustrates this. Status resentments against rising groups have been a frequent source of social tension all through American history.

[12] Daniel Bell, ed., *The Radical Right* (Garden City, N.Y.: Doubleday, 1963).

has always found it difficult to build an integrated regional social order on its own terms.[13]

Britain has come to accept the values of achievement in its economic and educational system, and to some extent in its political system, but retains a substantial degree of elitism (the assumption that those who hold high position be given generalized deference) and ascription (that those born to high place should retain it).[14] Tocqueville described the British class system as an "open aristocracy," which can be entered by

[13] See the essays in Charles Sellers, ed., *The Southerner as American* (Chapel Hill: University of North Carolina Press, 1960), for interesting insights on the difficulties faced by Southern whites both before and after the Civil War in resolving the conflicts generated within the society and within the individuals by the sharply varying dictates of alternative value systems.

[14] The general concept of elitism explicitly affects the training given to prospective members of the British upper class. Thus a description of the English public schools (private in the American sense) reports that "learning and the getting-fit are represented as part of the 'training for leadership' which many public-schoolmasters see as their social role. . . . It infects the whole set-up with a certain smugness and a certain frightening *elite* concept. The word 'breeding' is often on their lips. . . . Many of these boys go around looking for people to lead: they actually say at the University interviews that they feel they have been trained to lead . . ." John Vaizey, "The Public Schools," in Hugh Thomas, ed., *The Establishment* (New York: Clarkson Potter, 1959), pp. 28–29.

"What does the middle-class Briton mean when he says that Eton or some obscure public school in the Midlands will develop his son's character? . . . I would say that he includes in character such traits as willingness to take responsibility, loyalty to the class concept of the nation's interests, readiness to lead, which implies, of course, a belief that he is fit to lead and that people are willing to be led. . . ." Drew Middleton, *The British* (London: Pan Books, 1958), pp. 230–231.

The role of the public schools as a means of training an elitist upper class which took into itself the best of the *arrivistes* was an explicit objective of the reforms of the public school system initiated by Thomas Arnold in the 1830's. He strongly admired aristocracy, saw respect for it at the heart of England's security and freedom, and wanted to make certain that it would not be corrupted. As he saw it, public school boys were "destined to become the new masters, the epitome of all the new tendencies, annexed and made subservient to the old aristocratic order of things. 'You should feel,' he said in addressing the boys of the Sixth Form, 'like officers in the Army or Navy.' Officers! This comparison has been applied ever since to the public school men of England." G. J. Renier, *The English: Are They Human?* (New York: Roy Publishers, 1952), p. 249 and pp. 229–270; see also Asa Briggs, *Victorian People* (Chicago: University of Chicago Press, 1954), pp. 150–177; and Denis Brogan, *The English People* (New York: Alfred A. Knopf, 1943), pp. 18–56.

achievement but which confers on new entrants many of the diffuse perquisites of rank enjoyed by those whose membership stems from their social background.[15] Thus Britain differs from the United States in having, in terms of pattern variables, a strong emphasis on ascriptive, elitist, particularistic, and diffuse values.

In the nineteenth century the British business classes challenged the traditional pre-industrial value integration.[16] But the British upper class

---

[15] Writing in Thomas Arnold's day in 1833, Tocqueville pointed out that what distinguished the English aristocracy "from all others is the ease with which it has opened its ranks. . . . [W]ith great riches, anybody could hope to enter into the ranks of the aristocracy. . . . The reason why the French nobles were the butt of all hatreds, was not chiefly that only nobles had the right to everything, but because nobody could become a noble. . . . The English aristocracy in feelings and prejudices resembles all the aristocracies of the world, but it is not in the least founded on birth, that inaccessible thing, but on wealth that everyone can acquire, and this one difference makes it stand, while the others succumb. . . .

"[O]ne can clearly see in England where the aristocracy begins, but it is impossible to say where it ends. It could be compared to the Rhine whose source is to be found on the peak of a high mountain, but which divides into a thousand little streams and, in a manner of speaking, disappears before it reaches the sea. The difference between England and France in this manner turns on the examination of a single word in each language. 'Gentleman' and 'gentilhomme' evidently have the same derivation but 'gentleman' in England is applied to every well-educated man whatever his birth, while in France *gentilhomme* applies only to a noble by birth. . . . This grammatical observation is more illuminating than many long arguments. . . .

"[I]f you speak to a member of the middle classes; you will find he hates some aristocrats but not the aristocracy. . . .

"The whole of English society is still clearly based on an aristocratic footing, and has contracted habits that only a violent revolution or the slow and continual action of new laws can destroy. . . ." Alexis de Tocqueville, *Journeys to England and Ireland* (New Haven, Conn.: Yale University Press, 1958), pp. 59–60, 67, 70–71.

Similarly, the great French student of English history, Elie Halévy, described the English upper class as "an aristocracy in which no rank was a closed caste, an aristocracy in which the inferior regarded the superior not with envy but respect. It was not impossible to climb into a superior class and those who respected those above them were respected in turn by those below. . . ." *History of the English People in the Nineteenth Century* (London: Ernest Benn Ltd., 1961), Vol. IV, p. 345. See also Vol. I, pp. 221–222.

For a recent discussion stressing the same point, see Anthony Sampson, *Anatomy of Britain* (New York: Harper & Bros., 1962), especially pp. 3–30.

[16] For a detailed analysis of the way in which the values regulating class relations gradually changed with the rise of industry, see Reinhard Bendix, *Work and Authority in Industry* (New York: John Wiley, 1956), pp. 100–116.

(in contrast to most Continental aristocracies) did not strongly resist the claims of the new business classes, and later those of the workers, to take part in politics. For reasons to be discussed later, when pressure for political participation developed within these classes in Britain, it was members of already enfranchised classes who took the leadership in reform movements. If communication between the different strata in Britain had been blocked by jealously guarded privileges—as it had been in France—conflicts over the suffrage might have become more divisive. As Robert Michels once pointed out, the presence of upper-class leaders in a working-class party serves to reduce conservatives' hostility toward it. To the extent that the social system permits a "left" party to recruit leaders from the existing elite, it is easier for this party to become an accepted part of the polity. It is worth noting that, unlike the British Labour Party, the German socialists have recruited few, if any, leaders from the old upper classes.

Thus the *economy* and *polity* in Britain have been characterized by achievement, elitism, universalism, and diffuseness. The *social class* system, however, retains many elements of ascription, elitism, particularism, and diffuseness. The traditional upper classes and their institutions—the public schools, the ancient universities, and the titled aristocracy—remain at the summit of the social structure.[17] At the same time, achievers in job and school are not barred from securing diffuse elite status, and the lower classes feel that the political institutions operate for their benefit. Like the liberal bourgeoisie before them, the British workers have never seriously developed the objective of eliminating the old privileged classes, either socially or economically.[18] Having been allowed into the political

---

[17] See C. A. R. Crosland, *The Future of Socialism* (London: Jonathan Cape, 1956), pp. 232–237; Raymond Williams, *The Long Revolution* (New York: Columbia University Press, 1961), pp. 318–321; Sampson, *Anatomy of Britain*, pp. 160–217.

[18] Writing in the early 1860's, before Bagehot laid down his thesis that the stability of the British polity rested on the strength of deferential ties, Taine predicted that these social relations would maintain the class structure even under conditions of universal suffrage: "[B]eneath the institutions and charters, the bill of rights and the official almanacs, there are the ideas, the habits and customs and character of the people and the classes; there are the respective positions of the classes, their reciprocal feelings—in short a complex of deep and branching invisible roots beneath the visible trunk and foliage. . . . We admire the stability of British government; but this stability is the final product, the fine flower at the extremity of an infinite number of living fibres firmly planted in the soil of the entire country. . . .

"For the grip of tradition, sentiment and instinct is tenacious. There is no stronger attachment than—attachment. . . . Even at the time of the rotten

club almost as soon as British labor developed organizations of its own, working-class leaders have supported the rules of the parliamentary game. Unlike many early continental socialist parties, they were willing, while a small minority party, to cooperate with one of the older parties. And currently they remain the only socialist party whose policies "sustain" the legitimacy of aristocracy; their leaders, like other members of the Establishment, willingly accept aristocratic titles and other honors from the Crown.[19]

---

boroughs Parliament was representative of the people's will, as it is today although the number of people having a vote is rather small. And it will still be so in ten years' time, if the Reform Bill extends the suffrage. In my view changes in the law relating to the suffrage do no more than perfect the system in detail, without affecting fundamentals. The important thing remains the same, public assent. And, enfranchised or not, the labourer and the 'shopkeeper' agrees in wanting a man of the upper classes at the helm." On the other hand, Taine felt that "attachment" to leaders or representatives was absent in his native France; democracy could not work well there because France was characterized by "egalitarian envy," while at the same time it lacked the educated mass base which made possible "an intelligent democracy" in the United States. Hippolyte Taine, *Notes on England* (Fair Lawn, N.J.: Essential Books, 1958), pp. 162, 164–165.

[19] Clement Atlee, speaking as leader of the Labour Party in the House of Commons on July 9, 1952, opposed sweeping economies in royal expenditures on the following grounds: "It is a great mistake to make government too dull. That, I think, was the fault of the German Republic after the first World War. They were very drab and dull." Cited in Edward Shils and Michael Young, "The Meaning of the Coronation," in S. M. Lipset and Neil Smelser, eds., *Sociology: The Progress of a Decade* (Englewood Cliffs, N.J.: Prentice-Hall, 1961), p. 221.

"In 1957, three people in five throughout the country were still keeping souvenirs from the 1953 Coronation; and three in ten claimed to have a picture of a royal person in their house." Tom Harrison, *Britain Revisited* (London: Victor Gollancz, 1961), p. 232.

George Orwell suggested that elitist sentiments are strong among British workers as well. "Even in socialist literature it is common to find contemptuous references to slum-dwellers. . . . There is also, probably, more disposition to accept class distinctions as permanent, and even to accept the upper classes as natural leaders, than survives in most countries. . . . The word 'Sir' is much used in England, and the man of obviously upper-class appearance can usually get more than his fair share of deference from commissionaires, ticket-collectors, policemen, and the like. It is this aspect of English life that seems most shocking to visitors from America and the Dominions." *The English People* (London: Collins, 1947), p. 29.

The British journalist Jenny Nasmyth has pointed out that "most Labour M.P.s who can afford it, and many who cannot, send their children to the

The deference shown to the system by the leaders and the rank and file of the labor movement is not simply a reaction to the strength of the status system. The British upper class has long shown a high level of sophistication in handling the admission of new strata to the "club." Thus in 1923, as Labour was about to form its first government, the *Sunday Times* printed a manifesto by Richard Haldane (Viscount of Cloan) urging that the two old parties give Labour a fair chance at government:

> We have to recognize that a great change is in progress. Labour has attained to commanding power and to a new status. There is no need for alarm. All may go well if as a nation we keep in mind the necessity of the satisfaction of two new demands—that for recognition of the title to equality, and for more knowledge and its systematic application to industry and to the rest of life. . . . The result of the General Election may prove a blessing to us if it has awakened us to our neglect of something momentous which has been slowly emerging for years past. . . . Three quarters of a century since, the old Whigs, wise in their limited way, refused to meet the Chartist movement merely with a blank refusal. Thereby they earned our gratitude. For while most of the nations of Europe were plunged into revolution as a result of turning deaf ears to their violent progressives, we were saved, and remained in comparative quiet. . . . We had spoken with the enemy in the gate, and he had turned out to be of the same flesh and blood as ourselves. . . .[20]

Edward Shils, in *The Torment of Secrecy*, seeks to account for the great emphasis on publicity concerning political matters in the United States, *e.g.*, congressional investigations, as contrasted with the stress on privacy and secrecy in Britain. His explanation hinges on the fact that Britain is still a deferential society as compared with the United States:

> The United States has been committed to the principle of publicity since its origin. The atmosphere of distrust of aristocracy and of pretensions to aristocracy in which the American Republic spent its

---

traditional [public] schools of the governing classes. They do this, perhaps, not primarily because they are snobs, but because, having themselves assumed the obligations of governing, they have an easy conscience (so easy that they seem blind to the inconsistencies between their political principles and their private lives) about partaking in the privileges of the governing classes." "Dons and Gadflies," *The Twentieth Century*, 162 (1957), p. 386.

[20] Quoted in Kingsley Martin, *The Crown and the Establishment* (London: Hutchinson, 1962), p. 88.

formative years has persisted in many forms. Repugnance for governmental secretiveness was an offspring of the distrust of aristocracy.

In the United States, the political elite could never claim the immunities and privileges of the rulers of an aristocratic society. . . .

American culture is a populistic culture. As such, it seeks publicity as a good in itself. Extremely suspicious of anything which smacks of "holding back," it appreciates publicity, not merely as a curb on the arrogance of rulers but as a condition in which the members of society are brought into a maximum of contact with each other.

. . . Great Britain is a modern, large-scale society with a politicized population, a tradition of institutionalized pluralism, a system of representative institutions and great freedom of enquiry, discussion, and reporting. . . . British political life is strikingly quiet and confined. Modern publicity is hemmed about by a generally well-respected privacy. . . .

Although democratic and pluralistic, British society is not populist. Great Britain is a hierarchical country. Even when it is distrusted, the Government, instead of being looked down upon, as it often is in the United States, is, as such, the object of deference because the Government is still diffused with the symbolism of a monarchical and aristocratic society. The British Government, of course, is no longer aristocratic . . . [But it] enjoys· the deference which is aroused in the breast of Englishmen by the symbols of hierarchy which find their highest expression in the Monarchy. . . .

The acceptance of hierarchy in British society permits the Government to retain its secrets, with little challenge or resentment. . . . The deferential attitude of the working and middle classes is matched by the uncommunicativeness of the upper-middle classes and of those who govern. . . . The traditional sense of the privacy of executive deliberations characteristic of the ruling classes of Great Britain has imposed itself on the rest of the society and has established a barrier beyond which publicity may not justifiably penetrate.[21]

---

[21] Edward A. Shils, *The Torment of Secrecy* (Glencoe, Ill.: The Free Press, 1956), pp. 37–51. This book deserves recognition as at least a minor classic of sociological analysis of a social problem; and yet curiously is not well known. There are few other books I know of which are as illuminating concerning the interrelationships of American society and polity. The earlier article by Shils and Michael Young on the monarchy is also well worth reading in the context of problems raised in this chapter. "The Meaning of the Coronation," *op. cit.,* pp. 220–233. See also H. H. Hyman, "England and America: Climates of Tolerance and Intolerance," in Daniel Bell, ed., *The Radical Right,* pp. 227–258.

Other articles and books which present interesting case materials on

The protection from populist criticism which an elitist system gives to all who possess the diffuse status of "leaders" extends not only to the political and intellectual elites but to school teachers and the school system as well. A study of the comparative position of teachers in England and America points this out well:

> Conservative, Labour, and Liberal parties alike have consistently held to the view that the content of education and methods of instruction are not matters for popular debate and decision, but should be left in the hands of teachers themselves and of other professional educators. This being so, individuals or groups seeking to "use" the schools for their own purposes are confronted, not by the hastily constructed defenses of the teacher or of a single school or school board, as in America, but by the massive disregard of experienced politicians and administrators. This willing delegation of educational issues to educators is possible because the latter form a coherent and predictable element in the authority structure that moulds society. . . .
>
> The relation between the school and the family also differs in the two countries. In America, for the most part, the parents hand over their child to the school system, but maintain a continuous scrutiny over progress. In England, "interference" by the parents in the school is resisted both by teachers and by educational administrators. Parents' associations and parent-teacher associations are becoming increasingly common, but they limit their activities to social functions and to meetings at which school policy is explained but not debated.[22]

significant differences between various aspects of British and American society are: Stephen Richardson, "Organizational Contrasts on British and American Ships," *Administration Science Quarterly*, 1 (1956), pp. 189–207; L. C. B. Gower and Leolin Price, "The Profession and Practice of Law in England and America," *Modern Law Review*, 20 (1957), pp. 317–346; Roy Lewis and Rosemary Stewart, *The Managers: A New Examination of the English, German, and American Executive* (New York: Mentor Books, 1961); P. S. Florence, *The Logic of British and American Industry* (Chapel Hill: The University of North Carolina Press, 1953); E. Lipson, *Reflections on Britain and the United States—Mainly Economic* (London: The Pall Mall Press, 1959), see especially Chapter 1, "The American and British Way of Life"; C. A. R. Crosland, *The Future of Socialism*, pp. 238–257 and *passim*; and George Baron and Asher Tropp, "Teachers in England and America," in A. H. Halsey, Jean Floud, and C. A. Anderson, eds., *Education, Economy, and Society* (New York: The Free Press, 1961), pp. 545–557.

[22] Baron and Tropp, "Teachers in England and America," *op. cit.*, p. 548.

Ralph Turner also shows how variations in the basic values of the two societies impinge on their educational systems. American education reflects the norms of *contest mobility*, "a system in which elite status is the prize in an open contest and is taken by the aspirants' own efforts. . . . Since the 'prize' of successful upward mobility is not in the hands of the established elite to give out, the latter are not in a position to determine who shall attain it and who shall not." Conversely, British education reflects the norms of *sponsored mobility*, in which "elite recruits are chosen by the established elite or their agents, and elite status is *given* on the basis of some criterion of supposed merit and cannot be *taken* by any amount of effort or strategy. Upward mobility is like entry into a private club, where each candidate must be 'sponsored' by one or more of the members."

The American system, with its emphasis on the common school and opportunities for further education at every level, encourages all to advance themselves through their own efforts. "Every individual is encouraged to think of himself as competing for an elite position, so that in preparation he cultivates loyalty to the system and conventional attitudes."[23] Conversely, the British system has always selected the minority who will go ahead in the educational system at a relatively early age. Those not selected, the large bulk of the population, are taught to "regard themselves as relatively incompetent to manage society. . . . The earlier that selection of the elite recruits can be made, the sooner the masses can be taught to accept their inferiority and to make 'realistic' rather than phantasy plans."[24] Those selected for the elite, on the other

---

[23] Ralph Turner, "Modes of Social Ascent through Education: Sponsored and Contest Mobility," in Halsey, Floud, and Anderson, *Education, Economy, and Society*, pp. 122, 125. (Emphasis in original.) For a discussion of the elitist assumptions and consequences of the English school system by a Labour Party leader who is much impressed by the egalitarian aspects of the American educational system, see Crosland, *The Future of Socialism*, pp. 258–277 and *passim*; see also Sampson, *Anatomy of Britain*, pp. 174–194.

[24] Turner, "Modes of Social Ascent . . . ," *op. cit.*, p. 126. One of the key differences between England and the United States that has been noted as most clearly reflecting the contrast between an egalitarian society with a "common school" and an elitist society with a highly class segregated system of education is accent variations. As C. A. R. Crosland has put it: "[P]art of the reason why these differences [between classes in England] make so strong an impact is that they are associated with, and exaggerated by, the most supremely unmistakeable of all symbols of social standing—differences of accent and vocabulary. In no other country is it possible in the same way to assess a person's social standing the moment he opens his mouth. . . ." *The Future of Socialism*, pp. 177–178.

hand, are removed from competition and admitted to a school, either public or grammar, in which there is great emphasis on absorbing the elite's aesthetic culture, manners, and sense of paternalism toward the non-elite. Unlike the situation in America, where in the absence of a sense of a special elite culture the masses retain their right and ability to determine taste, English society operates on the assumption that only the elite may determine what is high or low quality.[25]

And in a recent report on English life, the founder of Mass Observation (an organization which has studied mass behavior through systematic observation techniques since 1937), writing about working-class life, comments that in spite of all the other major changes that have occurred since they began their observations: "No voice changes can be detected between 1937 and 1960. Radio, television and other outside impacts oriented to a more standard English appear to have had little or no effect. A tiny minority have consciously altered their voices. But elocution and speech training are still not important here. An English master at one of the big local schools . . . gave his considered opinion that if anything the standard of speaking of what he called 'King's English' had gone *down*." Harrison, *Britain Revisited*, p. 32. (Emphasis in original.)

[25] For an analysis of the way in which the variations in the status of elites, diffuse or specific, affect the position of intellectuals in England and America, see my *Political Man*, pp. 326–328. A. G. Nicholas has argued that although intellectuals do not have high status *within* the elite in England, the intellectual there receives more overt respect from the population as a whole than does his compeer in America because the former "has been in some degree sheltered by his very position in what Bagehot called a 'deferential' society. Not *very* deferential to him, perhaps; less deferential than to the landowner, the administrator, the soldier, the clergyman, or the lawyer, over. all of whom the protective gabardine of the appellation 'gentleman' has fallen more inclusively, with fewer ends sticking out. Nevertheless the [English] intellectual has shared in it too. . . ." "Intellectuals and Politics in the U.S.A.," *Occidente*, 10 (1954), p. 47; see also Gertrude Himmelfarb, "American Democracy and European Critics," *The Twentieth Century*, 151 (1952), pp. 320–327.

A clear indication of the differences in the values of those in charge of English elite education and those of comparably placed Americans may be seen in the criticism of the views of the former president of the highest status American university, Harvard, by the Master of the Manchester Grammar School: "When Professor Conant demands 'a common core of general education which will unite in one cultural pattern the future carpenter, factory workers, bishop, lawyer, doctor, sales-manager, professor and garage mechanic,' he is simply asking for the impossible. The demand for such a common culture rests either on an altogether over-optimistic belief in the educability of the majority that is certainly not justified by experience or on a willingness to surrender the highest standards of taste and judgment to the incessant demands of mediocrity." Cited from E. James, *Education for*

In his discussion of the sources of stability of English democracy, Harry Eckstein observes that authority patterns vary among the classes—authoritarian relations increase as one moves down the social ladder. Within the British elite, he suggests, social relations

> tend to be quite surprisingly democratic, or at least consultative and comradely; here . . . we might note the ubiquity of committees at every conceivable level in the higher civil service, the unusual use of staff committees in the military services, and the easy relations among officers of all ranks in military regiments, especially in elitist regiments like the Guards . . . , while behavior among pupils [in upper-class public schools] is modeled to a remarkable extent on the political system.
>
> [Conversely, where hierarchical relations are involved, as] between members of the Administrative Class [of the Civil Service] and their underlings, officers and their men, managers and their help, relations are highly non-consultative and certainly not comradely. . . .[26]

The United States and Great Britain differ, of course, not only in these patterns, but in the extent to which the same value orientations dominate the key status, economic, and political subsystems of the society. Presumably, Eckstein would relate the stability of American populist democracy to the fact that there are egalitarian social relations within all levels. American society has more homogeneity of values than the British. On the other hand, the particular distribution of different value orientations in Britain would also seem to be congruent with the stability of an industrialized democracy, since it legitimates open participation by all groups in the economy and polity, while the diffuse elitism rewards all with a claim to high position.

France and Germany

The values of France and Germany—our politically unstable cases—resemble those of the United States and Britain in many respects. France, through her Great Revolution of 1789, sought to adopt the same syndrome of values which the United States developed: achievement,

---

Leadership, in Michael Young, *The Rise of the Meritocracy* (New York: Random House, 1959), p. 40.

[26] Harry Eckstein, *A Theory of Stable Democracy* (Princeton, N.J.: Monograph No. 10. Center for International Studies, Princeton University, 1961), pp. 15–16.

equalitarianism, universalism, specificity. The Declaration of the Rights of Man, like the Declaration of Independence, proclaims doctrines subsumed by these concepts. Germany has resembled Britain in that the pressures stemming from economic change and the rise of new social groupings in the nineteenth century did not result in a political revolution which proclaimed a new value ethos. Rather, Germany seemingly sought to modify existing institutions and to create diverse value patterns in different hierarchical subsystems in ways very similar to those which developed in Britain. The French failure stems from the fact that, in contrast to America, the forces of the Revolution were not strong enough to sustain value consensus among the key social groupings; in Germany the new combinations of values, though powerful, were basically incompatible with the requirements for a stable *non-authoritarian* political system.

French society is difficult to classify in terms of basic values. Its internal political tensions flow in large measure from the fact that major social groupings adhere to largely incompatible values. The French sociologist François Bourricaud has pointed this out:

> It is . . . difficult to seize upon and isolate the unconscious or semi-conscious motivations [basic values] which give French institutions their tone and their specific color. They are more apparent in some groups than in others. Certain themes of French culture are more clearly discernible, more sharply outlined, among the bourgeois than among the workers. All research of this nature begins by determining what social groups are culturally dominant. America, for example, has developed a culture of the middle classes. But in France a group can be culturally dominant in one area and not at all present in another. . . . For example, the tradition of the noble life continues without doubt to be very influential in French society even though the nobility as a social group does not amount to much. . . . In brief, cultural themes are very far from being unified even within the society, both by reason of the diversity of the groups which make up this society and the diversity of activities by which this culture is expressed.[27]

These internal cleavages result from the fact that the French Revolution succeeded in eliminating neither the old set of ascriptive-particularis-

---

[27] François Bourricaud, "France," in Arnold M. Rose, ed., *The Institutions of Advanced Societies*, (Minneapolis: University of Minnesota Press, 1958), pp. 500–501.

tic values nor some of their key institutional supports, particularly the Church. A large part of the French bourgeoisie, whose status and economic objectives sustained the Revolution, never completely rejected the traditional value system.[28] And, as François Goguel points out, this traditional value system was directly hostile to democracy:

> A pessimistic idea of human nature—an idea of Catholic origin, and directly opposed to the optimism of J. J. Rousseau—is at the basis of this conviction; man, being naturally evil, must have teachers, or guides, to direct him toward good. These guides are the traditional institutions, the social authorities. The first is the authority of monarchy, temporally the highest, and then the First Families, predestined by birth and wealth to a leading role. Finally, above all, there is the Catholic Church, charged with shaping conscience and soul and conditioning them toward the social order and eternal salvation. These theocratic ideas, expounded by Bonald at the time of the Restoration, survived much longer than one would have thought possible. . . .[29]

France has maintained particularistic values in commerce and industry more than any other industrial nation. The economic policies of many French small businessmen emphasize the maintenance of the family fortune and status. They refuse to take economic risks or to enter into serious competition with one another.[30] The politics of the petty bourgeoisie has stressed the stability of existing business, even though

---

[28] Tocqueville has argued that fear of social revolution led the bourgeoisie to return to Catholicism. As he put it: "The Revolution of 1792, when striking the upper classes, had cured them of their irreligiousness; it had taught them, if not the truth, at least the social usefulness of belief. . . . The Revolution of 1848 had just done on a small scale for our tradesmen what that of 1792 had done for the nobility. . . . The clergy had facilitated this conversion by [giving] . . . to long established interests, the guarantees of its traditions, its customs and its hierarchy." *The Recollections of Alexis de Tocqueville* (London: The Harvill Press, 1948), p. 120.

[29] François Goguel, "The Idea of Democracy and the Political Institutions," in Saul K. Padover, *French Institutions, Values and Politics* (Stanford, Calif.: Stanford University Press, 1954), pp. 12–13.

[30] See the articles by John E. Sawyer, "Strains in the Social Structure of Modern France," and by David S. Landes, "French Business and the Businessman: A Social and Cultural Analysis," in Edward M. Earle, ed., *Modern France* (Princeton, N.J.: Princeton University Press, 1951), pp. 293–312; 334–353. See also Roy Lewis and Rosemary Stewart, *The Managers*, pp. 182–187. For a discussion of similar attitudes and consequences in Italy, see Maurice F. Neufeld, *Italy: School for Awakening Countries* (Ithaca: N.Y. State School of Industrial and Labor Relations, 1961), pp. 36 and *passim*.

this has limited the economy's potential for expansion.[31] French employers, particularly in small plants, have expected particularistic loyalties from their employees.[32] All through its history, French industry has attempted to deny representation rights to trade unions, and when forced to grant them has undermined these concessions as soon as possible. To permit the unions rights of representation—and thereby to acknowledge universalistic norms—has been seen as morally offensive. The behavior of the French businessman is, of course, more complicated than this brief analysis suggests, since a capitalist system inevitably dictates a considerable degree of universalism.[33] As François Bourricaud has pointed out: "Between the 'bourgeois' money criterion and more aristocratic criteria—antiquity of family and connection—the bourgeois hesitates. This ambiguity explains in part, perhaps, why his relations with the workers have been so difficult."[34]

---

[31] Raymond Aron, who differs from most analysts of the French scene in arguing that there has been a rapid rate of growth in the total French economy in most of this century, agrees, however, that "the usual idea that France is still the nation of small business is, then, not false. . . . It is quite likely that in many sectors there are still large numbers of firms which are too small and more or less unproductive. Sometimes these marginal enterprises are protected rather than opposed by the larger ones, which thus ensure extra profits by maintaining prices at levels desired by the former.

"This relative slowness in concentration is attended by the survival of precapitalistic legal entities. . . .

"The French seem to attach importance to independence and at times to prefer it to higher income. Resistance [to incorporation into larger units] . . . expresses a characteristic of the national psychology just as it is a result of a policy adopted by governments under pressure from the electorate or grouped interests." *France: Steadfast and Changing* (Cambridge, Mass.: Harvard University Press, 1960), pp. 60–62.

[32] In discussing the French businessman, Roy Lewis and Rosemary Stewart have pointed out these tendencies in detail: "The businessman is paternalistic and autocratic, treating his employees as '*mes enfants*,' as much a part of his '*maison*' as his own children and domestics. In an age of rapid technological change, this has led not only to discontent among the children, but also to a failure to modernize. . . .

"Their labor relations are also prejudiced, and even French big business lacks 'industrial-relations sense.' In France, the dogged anti-labor attitude of the businessman has ended not only with businesses paying for social welfare out of their own pockets directly, but also with an irreconcilably bitter anticapitalist feeling among the workers, who vote Communist often for that reason and no other." *The Managers*, pp. 186–187.

[33] See Aron, *France: Steadfast and Changing*, pp. 45–77.

[34] Bourricaud, "France," *op. cit.*, p. 478.

The French working class, on the other hand, has supported in ideology, if not always in action, the revolutionary values of achievement, equalitarianism, universalism. However, it has been faced with a situation in which individual and collective mobility are morally disapproved of by the more privileged orders—although, of course, as in other industrial societies, considerable individual mobility does occur.[35] French workers' efforts to improve their lot through collective action are bitterly resisted by the bourgeoisie, and the emphasis on local particularism inhibits the unions' efforts to form strong nation-wide organizations.[36] There is perhaps no more impressive evidence of the deep moral hostility of many French employers towards unions than the systematic effort to demolish all union rights during the period of the "phony" war, from September 1939 to May 1940. Seemingly both employers and their political representatives in the government put "teaching the workers and unions a lesson" ahead of national unity and, in the last analysis, national survival.[37]

The effort to sustain traditionalist norms within a growing economy has inhibited the creation of a democratic parliamentary system based on achievement and universalism. Every French republic has sought to institutionalize these values, and has given the lower classes equal rights of access to government. In most other countries such rights and norms have led to the tempering of aggressive ideologies in the lower classes; in France it has led to an intensification of these ideologies.

Thus the most disruptive element in French culture has been the cleavage between pre-industrial values, supported by the upper classes and the church, which have continued to affect the economic sector, and the legitimacy of the Revolution, which has formally dominated the political structure. The ascriptive, elitist, and particularistic aspects of French values facilitated the emergence of politics along class lines, while the emphasis on equalitarianism, universalism, and achievement has led the less privileged strata to sharply resent their position. Tocqueville pointed to this problem in an exaggerated form when he suggested: "To conceive

---

[35] There is some evidence and opinion to sustain the belief that successfully mobile French are more likely to hide this fact than would be true for comparable individuals in other countries. See S. M. Lipset and R. Bendix, *Social Mobility in Industrial Society* (Berkeley: University of California Press, 1959), pp. 19, 82–83.

[36] Val Lorwin, *The French Labor Movement* (Cambridge, Mass.: Harvard University Press, 1954), pp. 36–37.

[37] See Herbert Luethy, *The State of France* (London: Secker and Warburg, 1955), p. 87; Val Lorwin, *The French Labor Movement*, pp. 87–88; Henry W. Ehrmann, *French Labor, From Popular Front to Liberation* (New York: Oxford University Press, 1947), pp. 169–232.

of men remaining forever unequal upon a single point, yet equal on all others, is impossible; they must come in the end to be equal upon all."[38]

The retention of pre-industrial values within French capitalism did not mean, of course, that all of French industry adhered to them. Within large-scale industry as within government, the corollaries of bureaucratization and rationalization emerged: stable definition of rights and duties, systematic universalistic ordering of authority relationships, publicity of decisions, the appearance of personnel experts or specialists in labor relations as a consequence of the division of labor. And though one generally expects workers to be more radical in large-scale industry than in small, in those sections of France where industry was large and bureaucratic—in general the North—the business classes demonstrated a greater willingness to accept trade unions as a legitimate and permanent part of the industrial system; there, syndicalism and Communism were weakest. Before 1914, the Socialists were strongest in the areas of the country with large industry, while the anarcho-syndicalists had their greatest strength in those parts of the nation where the particularistic values of small business were dominant. These differences were paralleled between the two great wars by the variations in support of the Socialists and Communists. The Communists, in general, took over the centers of syndicalist strength, though since World War II they have become the party of the French industrial workers almost everywhere.

The picture of a relatively stagnant France with "stalemate" politics, a reluctance to take advantage of economic opportunities, and a low birthrate, which was accurate enough before World War II, has changed drastically since then. The European economic miracle—great and rapid economic growth and a sharp increase in the consumption of mass-produced items—has affected France as much as any country. The net reproduction birth rate, which stood below 100 (the rate at which a population reproduces itself) all during the inter-war years, has hovered around 125 since 1946.[39] A number of observers of the French scene have argued that "the combination of 'new men and new attitudes' inherited from the war period has made French society much less different from the societies of other industrial nations."

---

[38] Alexis de Tocqueville, *Democracy in America* (New York: Vintage Books, 1956), Vol. I, p. 55. (Equality in this sense does not mean equality of condition, but rather universalistic treatment in all sectors.)

[39] Charles P. Kindleberger, "The Postwar Resurgence of the French Economy," in Stanley Hoffman, Charles P. Kindleberger, Laurence Wylie, Jesse R. Pitts, Jean-Baptiste Duroselle, and François Goguel, *In Search of France* (Cambridge, Mass.: Harvard University Press, 1963), p. 133.

In the civil service, in business, in professional organizations, even in the military forces, new groups of "technocrats" appear—men who specialize in the management of a highly industrialized and bureaucratic society, men who earn high incomes without necessarily owning much capital. . . .

Within the business world, a kind of managerial revolution has led to a new conception of profits, in which management and ownership are less tightly fused and in which the firm's power counts more than the owner's fortune.[40]

The emergence of a "modern" France would seem to be negated by the continued strength of the Communists as a party and union movement (CGT) among the industrial workers, and the highly unstable political system. It may be argued, however, that the current instabilities of the political system now reflect the tensions of rapid change superimposed on a polity whose political leadership has a traditional bent toward uncompromising rhetoric. The Communists have retained most of the working-class electoral following which they secured in the late 1930's and the 1940's. They have not gained new votes, and they have lost a large proportion of their party and trade-union membership. But if the majority of French workers still vote Communist, various opinion surveys suggest a relatively low level of class alienation among the workers. On the "right," the principal version of anti-democratic extremism—the Poujadist movement—secured almost all of its backing from the declining middle-class strata, often in regions that were being economically impoverished. That is, those who found their relative or absolute economic and social position worsening as a result of changes in French society were attracted to a politics that was "against the system." The tensions over the Algerian War similarly involved efforts to resist inherent "modernizing" tendencies. In a real sense, the Gaullist fifth republic is engaged in an effort to bring France's polity and values into line with the changing reality of its class and economic structures. But political and organizational loyalties do not disappear quickly, and consequently the political system, in which conflicts over these values are acted out, seems much more resistant to change than are other institutions.

The way in which historic tensions are maintained may be seen most clearly by examining the sources of the perpetuation of value differences between those white-collar workers who are employed in the bureaucracy

---

[40] Stanley Hoffman, "Paradoxes of the French Political Community," in Hoffman, *et al.*, *In Search of France*, p. 61.

of industry and those employed by government. In France, it has not been possible to speak of the "white-collar worker" as such; rather, there are the sharply differing backgrounds of the *employé* (private employee) and the *fonctionnaire* (civil servant). As the French sociologist Michel Crozier has described the situation in his country:

> We meet two opposite types of participation and integration in society; one type which can be described as paternalistic and which is present among traditional white-collar workers (bank employees, insurance employees, and those employed in industry), and an egalitarian type, present in the world of the lower civil servants. . . . The same basic psychological situation has produced two role types, and with these two roles, two different concepts of society, two sets of religious attitudes, two approaches to politics. These differences have tended to decline since the second World War, but there are still two different worlds which are determined in one case by channels of social mobility through the lay and anti-clerical sector of the society, and in the other through paternalistic and even confessional methods of entrance.[41]

These two non-manual strata are recruited from different sectors of French society. Private industry tends to secure its employees from the graduates of the Catholic schools, often on the basis of personal recommendations, and "many private firms examine carefully the family origins . . . of prospective employees." The Civil Service is recruited almost exclusively from state schools whose faculties are overwhelmingly on the political left. Its recruitment procedures and operation emphasize rigorous selection criteria and formal academic achievement. These differences in the recruitment and membership deeply affect French trade-union political life, since the Catholic trade-union federation (CFTC) and the liberal Catholic party (the MRP) have their principal base of support in the white-collar workers employed in private industry, while the socialist-influenced union federation, *Force Ouvrier* (FO), and the socialist party (SFIO), have their strongest supporters among the lower echelons of civil service workers.

> The political consequences of these differences are known; the inability of the parties of the Center, of the Third Force, to overcome their differences and to form any permanent unity. These differences

---

[41] Michel Crozier, "Classes san conscience ou préfiguration de las société sans classes," *European Journal of Sociology*, 1 (1960), pp. 244–245.

support, and are in turn nourished by, the opposition of the socialist
FO and the Catholic CFTC unions, a conflict based in the last analysis on the essential incompatibility between the religious mentality
of the old Federation of White-Collar workers, the base of the
CFTC, and the lay mentality of the federations of Civil Servants in
the FO.[42]

Thus France remains unstable politically. It may currently be in the
final process of cultural "modernization," but historic institutional commitments still prevent the emergence of a fully modern domestic politics,
one in which the basic internal issues revolve around an interest struggle
for the division of national income within a welfare state. Rather, issues
concerning the legitimacy of various institutions, the role of the religious
and secular school, and the structure of authority still divide the nation.
Historically, the resistance of the French ascriptive and particularistic
"right" to accepting changes in power relations within industry, to legitimating (i.e., morally accepting) unions, was in large measure responsible for the fact that the French workers, though possessors of the suffrage
before workers elsewhere in Europe, remain alienated from the polity.[43]
Conversely, to the extent that the workers have supported extremist tendencies, anarcho-syndicalism and Communism, the conservative strata have
been enabled to feel morally sustained in their refusal to share power. To
break through this vicious cycle of extremism and counter-extremism is
not an easy task, even though the cleavages in basic values may be ending.

The difficulties of the German polity stem from sources which are, in
one sense, the obverse of the French. Where France has encouraged political participation by the lower classes but denied them rights in industry,
the German system has given the working class rights and protection
within industry while limiting their access to the polity. Until 1918 at
least, the German aristocratic classes successfully maintained ascriptive
and particularistic values in the non-economic areas of life, while encouraging achievement and universalism, but not equalitarianism, in the
economic order. That is, the old upper classes permitted, and sometimes
even encouraged, the working class to improve its economic position

---

[42] *Loc cit.*

[43] It should also be noted that this alienation cannot be explained primarily
by low wages. "In comparison with European wages, they are not low.
Higher than in Italy or Holland, certainly not as high as in Sweden or
Switzerland, a little lower than in Great Britain, they have been somewhat
better in buying power than in Germany and are still at least equal in that
respect." Raymond Aron, *France: Steadfast and Changing*, p. 49.

through social legislation and trade unions. They were not willing, however, to accede to achievement criteria in the status and political orders. Individuals were still judged and rejected according to their social origins. This meant that, as is usual in an ascriptively oriented status system, political movements emerged based on distinct status or class lines which were buttressed by the class organizations in industry. However, these political groupings could never gain a secure foothold in the political system.

Concretely, the Prussian aristocracy and the Wilhelmine monarchy, while sympathetic to the objectives of the unions in industry, first attempted to suppress the Socialists as a party between 1878 and 1891, and then refused to accept a democratic electoral system in Prussia, the chief state of the Reich, up to the overthrow of the monarchy in 1918. This refusal to allow the workers' political representatives a share in political power forced the Socialist movement to maintain a revolutionary ideological posture which was at complete variance with its social position and aspirations. The workers' movement did not want to destroy the state, but rather to be admitted to it. In southern Germany, where ascriptive status lines were much less rigid than in Prussia, and where the conservative classes admitted the workers' political movements into the body politic, the Socialist parties quickly developed a moderate, reformist, and pragmatic ideology. In these states, the revisionist doctrines of Eduard Bernstein had their earliest and strongest advocates; in some, the Social-Democrats supported cooperation with non-socialist parties, thereby reducing the emphasis on class warfare.[44] In Weimar Germany, the Social Democratic Party developed into a moderate organization, and, until the outbreak of the Great Depression and the rise of Nazism, absorbed most of the old socialist and Communist electoral strength.

Many conservative groups, particularly those which had been involved in the status system of the old empire—for example, the landed aristocracy, the teachers, the professional officers, and much of the civil service —never accepted the Weimar Republic and its universalistic norms.[45] The

---

[44] Peter Gay, *The Dilemma of Democratic Socialism: Eduard Bernstein's Challenge to Marx* (New York: Columbia University Press, 1952), pp. 254–255 and *passim*. See also Arthur Rosenberg, *The Birth of the German Republic* (New York: Oxford University Press, 1931), pp. 48 ff.

[45] "From 1920 onwards the history of the Weimar Republic was only a rearguard action against the revitalized social forces on which the German state structure had been built under Bismarck: Army, *Junkers*, big industrialists, and the higher strata of the Civil Service." J. P. Mayer, *Max Weber and German Politics* (London: Faber and Faber, 1956), p. 64.

middle classes wavered between embracing a political system which incorporated the universalistic values that they had long supported and reacting against the challenge to the privileges and the deferential norms they retained as part of the socially privileged. The support which both the old and new middle classes gave to Nazism in the early 1930's has been linked by many observers to the strong German emphasis on ascription and elitism. Faced with a dire economic threat to their status, the middle classes turned to the Nazis, who promised a national socialism which would restore prosperity and preserve the values of the *Ständestaat* (strong respect for hierarchical rankings).

In discussing the pattern variables, I have assumed that the industrial economic order requires a greater application of universalistic, specific, and achievement criteria than do the political and social orders. Employers must deal with workers in terms of these values, and workers, in turn, are constrained to secure a stable, universalistic definition of their rights in industry. The demand for universalistic treatment in the factory is a prime demand of workers in modern society. The demand for universalistic treatment in the political sphere occurs often as part of the struggle in the economic order. On the other hand, the middle and upper classes tend to be more oriented toward maintaining their privileged position in terms of status rather than in economic terms—that is, toward enforcing the norms inherent in elitism. Hence, a working class which has made gains in the economic order will be relatively satisfied, while a middle and upper class which feels threatened in its position of status will react aggressively. It may be contended that in Weimar Germany the majority of the workers were relatively moderate politically because they had secured access to the economic and political orders, while traditional conservative groupings and the middle classes were disposed to accept militant politics in a crisis because their value orientations of elitism and ascription led them to perceive such gains on the part of the workers as a threat to their over-all status position and to their sense of "the way things ought to be."

Harry Eckstein argues that the instability of the Weimar Republic was a result of the strains between the authoritarian norms which characterized all non-governmental institutions and the democratic patterns of the political system:

> The German governmental pattern was . . . one-sidely democratic, at any rate if we confine analysis to the level of parliamentary representation and decision-making. . . . On the other hand, social life,

including life in parties and political interest groups, was highly authoritarian. . . . Not only were society and polity to some degree incongruent; they existed in unprecedented contradiction with one another. . . .

This unalleviated democracy (pure proportional representation, strong detailed bill of rights) was superimposed upon a society pervaded by authoritarian relationships and obsessed with authoritarianism. . . . German family life, German schools, and German business firms were all exceedingly authoritarian. German families were dominated, more often than not, by tyrannical husbands and fathers, German schools by tyrannical teachers, German firms by tyrannical bosses.[46]

Eckstein does not contend that the Germans as individuals always preferred authoritarian politics. Rather, he points to the fact that from the first universal suffrage elections in Imperial Germany down to 1928, liberal, center, and socialist parties secured between 80 and 90 per cent of the vote, and that anti-democratic pre-Nazi parties were always in a small minority. He seems to suggest that a more authoritarian kind of "democratic" regime, such as that of Imperial Germany, would have provided a "proper base" for a stable regime. It might be argued, in line with the reasoning behind both my own and Eckstein's analyses, that Germany could have best evolved into a stable constitutional democracy through the gradual growth of a system which retained elitist and monarchical forms and strong executive power in the hands of a powerful Chancellor. The symbolic retention of legitimate power in the hands of a Kaiser conceivably might have preserved the allegiance of the middle and upper classes to a democratic political system.

Arguments such as these are impossible to prove, but it may be suggested that the political history of Sweden illustrates "what might have been" in Germany. In many ways, pre-World War I Swedish social structure resembled that of Germany. The Swedish privileged classes strongly resisted universal suffrage, and adult suffrage was adopted only in 1909 for the lower house and in 1921 for the upper one.[47] Swedish social life contained many of the same authoritarian patterns that characterized Germany's, and Sweden instinctively looked to Germany for intellectual and cultural leadership. But Sweden was both small and geographically isolated from European wars; it escaped the tensions resulting from the

[46] Eckstein, *A Theory of Stable Democracy*, pp. 17–18.
[47] Dankwart Rustow, *The Politics of Compromise* (Princeton, N.J.: Princeton University Press, 1955), pp. 65–85; Douglas Verney, *Parliamentary Reform in Sweden* (New York: Oxford University Press, 1957), pp. 159–173, 202–214.

overthrow of a monarchy after military defeat. Its radical Socialist party became moderate and its extreme conservatives and upper class came to accept the right of the workers to participate in, and ultimately to dominate, the polity. But even today, the values of the Swedish status system contain strong elements of ascription, elitism, particularism, and diffuseness.

Much of the elitist quality of Swedish life has gradually declined under the impact of thirty years of Socialist government. Successful political rule by this party, many of whose leaders began life as workers, has undoubtedly weakened the value orientations which sustained elitism. Yet Swedish politics remain highly particularistic. For example, Swedish telephone books still list individuals alphabetically *within* occupational groups. So to look up a Swede in the phone book, you must know his occupation. He is still a doctor, printer, or carpenter before he is a person.

To a considerable extent the egalitarian changes reflect conscious policies of the governing Socialists. Thus the Swedish educational system has been changing, from one similar to that of Britain and other parts of Europe with their class-stratified divisions of secondary schools—modern, technical, and grammar—to "single-type comprehensive schools, into which all the existing schools are to be incorporated. . . . The eventual aim is a 9 year school, with differentiation beginning in a very mild form in the 6th year, and only taking shape in 3 different 9th classes [at age 16] (preparation for higher education; general finishing class with mainly theoretical bent; and preparatory vocational training with some theoretical courses)."[48]

C. A. R. Crosland, who sees class values in his own England as little changed in spite of the great structural reforms introduced by the Labour government of 1945–1951, twenty years of full employment, and the welfare state, has pointed to at least one of the major conditions required for a political impact on class values in a democracy:

> Political power can also have an influence on class attitudes, but in a democracy only, I think, *if one party remains in office for a long time. . . .*
>
> Thus in Britain, before the war, when Conservative Governments seemed the natural thing, collective feelings of superiority and in-

---

[48] Perry Anderson, "Sweden," *New Left Review*, No. 7, (1961) pp. 6–7. For other objective factors which have served to reduce hierarchical differentiation and class tension in Sweden, see the second part of Anderson's article, *New Left Review*, No. 9 (1961), pp. 34–35.

feriority were intensified by the belief that political power was an additional, semi-permanent attribute of a class which already appeared to possess all the other attributes of a ruling class. Conversely in Sweden, the fact that a Socialist Government now seems the natural order of things has a profound effect in weakening collective class feelings, since at least the attribute of political power is differently located from the other attributes of the "upper class."

It creates, in other words, a definite "scatter," and prevents a concentration of "top-class attributes". . . . Thus political power counterbalances the influence of other class determinants, and hence diminishes the likelihood of strong, coagulated class feelings. But this will occur only if the period of one-party rule is sufficiently prolonged to cause a definite adjustment in psychological attitudes.[49]

Evidence secured in a Swedish survey study confirms the thesis that long tenure in office by a workers' party may modify the traditional assumptions concerning the inter-relationship of different indicators of high position. Those interviewed were asked, "Which class do you think is the most influential in our society today?" The responses indicate that Swedes who perceive their status as "working class" are most likely to believe that their class is the most influential one than self-defined "middle-class" individuals believe is the case with the middle class. And to explain this phenomenon of consensus across class lines concerning the greater power of the working class, Torgny Segerstedt comments: "Perhaps I ought to remind you that we have had a Labour government in office in Sweden for more than 20 years."[50]

To return to Germany briefly, major changes in its value system, which weaken ascriptive values, appear to have been developing since the end of the last war. Two of the major bulwarks of ascriptive and particularistic values in the society no longer exist or have been weakened: the army and the Prussian aristocracy. The major regions of Germany previously dominated by these values (most of old Prussia) are now in Russia, Poland, or Communist East Germany. What is now West Germany is largely composed of areas which even before World War I were willing to admit the working class into the political club. In addition, the upheav-

---

[49] Crosland, *The Future of Socialism*, pp. 181–182. (Emphasis mine.)
[50] Torgny Segerstedt, "An Investigation of Class-Consciousness among Office Employees and Workers in Swedish Factories," *Transactions of the Second World Congress of Sociology* (London: International Sociological Association, 1954), Vol. II, pp. 300–301, 305.

als of Nazism and World War II have upset the old German class structure and have reduced the significance of ascriptive elements.[51]

Yet ascriptive, elitist values are far from dead in West Germany. To some extent, the society still emphasizes social origins as a determinant of status, and men are still reacted to in terms of status position—professors, engineers, industrialists, and others are members of an elite. While workers are part of the body politic and not outside it, they have not secured an end to a diffuse emphasis on class. The continued significance of elitist values has been pointed up in a recent study of the German entrepreneurial class. Heinz Hartmann suggests that this stratum has laid claim to diffuse respect: "[M]anagement does not claim elite status with respect to a specific task, area, or group but rather in relation to the total society."[52] In effect, the German *Unternehmer* (entrepreneurs) have laid explicit claim to the deference and authority once received by now decimated classes:

> Management's drive toward ascendancy quite frequently is justified by reference to the death or incapacitation of previous elite groups. When Winschuh, for instance, addressed a conference of Young *Unternehmer* in 1950, he pointed out that "due to the destruction of old elites, the importance of the *Unternehmer* for the formation of a new elite group has increased." He reminded his audience of the "mass annihilation and expatriation of the Elbian feudatory" and called the attention of his listeners to "the decimation of numerous families of officers and civil service officials." . . . All of this led up to the finding that "society needs more authority in leadership, more determination and speed in administration" than it enjoys at the time and that the *Unternehmer* were willing and able to provide all of this.[53]

---

[51] There are relatively few men of aristocratic or Junker origin in the various elites of contemporary Germany as contrasted with Weimar or Imperial times. "In the German Federal Republic, the . . . barriers of class have become greatly simplified, compared to the past. . . . In terms of social origins, all elites are now predominantly middle-class, with the exception only of the SPD [Social Democrats] and trade union leaders. The aristocracy has largely disappeared. . . . For the average of . . . twelve elites, 70 per cent are of middle-class background, while only 8 per cent bear aristocratic names and 10 per cent indicate some working-class background. . . ." Karl W. Deutsch and Lewis J. Edinger, *Germany Rejoins the Powers* (Stanford, Calif.: Stanford University Press, 1959), p. 125; see also p. 139.

[52] Heinz Hartmann, *Authority and Organization in German Management* (Princeton, N.J.: Princeton University Press, 1959), p. 11.

[53] *Ibid.*, p. 242.

The West German system is probably moving toward the British or the Swedish model. There is also much more authoritarianism—or perhaps, more accurately, executive power—in Bonn than there was in Weimar. Chancellor Adenauer has played a role much more comparable to that of Bismarck in the Imperial system than to any of the Weimar chancellors, and elections have been fought to a considerable degree as contests for the Chancellorship.[54] Whether Germany will actually maintain itself as a stable democracy, only time will tell. Particularly crucial will be the resolution of the challenge to the values of the privileged classes when the working-class-based Social Democrats actually move toward national office.[55]

Social Change and Political Stability

One problem faced by all developing societies is that the legitimacy of the existing distribution of resources and privileges, and of the political decision-making process itself, comes under severe tension. A new economic class usually achieves high position by the use of methods which have been traditionally defined as inappropriate or illegitimate. The social system, in turn, may adjust by incorporating the new class into the ascriptive elites, or by insulating the old ascriptive elites from the new ones (for example, by reserving for the old elite certain privileged positions, often in government, the military, religion, and education). The first course maintains the unity of high status strata, and augments the tendency of the lowly to accept the existing structure of authority as legitimate. The "insulative" course precipitates a reactionary–radical polarization, quickly rationalized in uncompromisable, absolute value terms.

The "incorporative" response and its effects are illustrated best in

---

[54] See Eckstein, *A Theory of Stable Democracy*, p. 37.

[55] Contemporary West Germany, of course, continues to differ from Britain and Sweden, which retain deferential elements in their status system, by not being a monarchy. This, as I have tried to demonstrate in *Political Man* (pp. 78–79), is not an unimportant difference. To create legitimacy is much more difficult than to transfer the symbolic legitimacy of the older political system to a new one, as is done in monarchical democracies. I will discuss some of the sharp differences between the Bonn Republic and its predecessors in Chapter 9. It should be stressed, however, that a variety of public opinion polls and studies of elite opinion indicate that attachment to democratic values is extremely fragile in Germany. For detailed summaries and discussion of such data, see Deutsch and Edinger, *Germany Rejoins the Powers*.

British parliamentary history.[56] As we have already seen, the articulate leadership of the bourgeoisie, and later of labor, were given access to political decision making, and were then incorporated into the ranks of the Whig party and the Liberal and Labour parties respectively. Not only did the old ascriptive elites admit those of achieved position into the formal institutional structure, but they acculturated the newcomers to many ascriptive orientations.[57] Hence the House of Lords has been able to

---

[56] The English sociologist A. H. Halsey has well described the "incorporative" process in the class structure of Great Britain: "Perhaps the most outstanding characteristic of the English class structure historically has been the remarkable absorptive capacity, the judicious and un-Marxist Fabianism of the upper classes. The culture of the gentry and of higher officialdom never quite lost control of the rising provincial centers. If the successful northern businessmen were themselves excluded from entry into 'the establishment,' their sons could cross the social barrier by southward movement through the public schools and Oxford, by movement of religious adherence from Chapel to Church, and by occupational movement from trade to profession or from a northern works to a London central office." "British Universities and Intellectual Life," in A. H. Halsey, Jean Floud and C. A. Anderson, eds, *Education, Economy, and Society*, pp. 506–507.

Philip Toynbee has suggested that the reason that the British " *bourgeois* . . . never emerged as the ruling class was that each individual who had risen high enough was immediately transformed into a member of the upper class. Or at least he was put into a position from which he could transform his son. The age-long operation was performed with a fantastic degree of instinctive skill, which was exhibited quite as much by each successive generation of qualifying New Men as by the ever-changing never-changing class to which they had successfully aspired. What mattered to both was to preserve the ethos, not the personnel. If, at any point, the middle class had simply *become* the ruling class, then a genuine social revolution would have been achieved and a whole new set of values and behavior patterns would have supplanted the old ones." Philip Toynbee, "The Governing Class," *The Twentieth Century*, 162 (1957), p. 298.

[57] Bagehot well recognized the importance of these processes for the polity: "In all countries new wealth is ready to worship old wealth, if old wealth will only let it, and I need not say that in England new wealth is eager in its worship. . . . Rank probably in no country whatever has so much 'market' value as it has in England just now. Of course there have been many countries in which certain old families, whether rich or poor, were worshipped by whole populations with a more intense and poetic homage; but I doubt if there has ever been any in which all old families and all titled families received more ready observance from those who were their equals, perhaps their superiors, in wealth, their equals in culture, and their inferiors only in descent and rank. The possessors of the 'material' distinctions of life . . . rush to worship those who possess the *im*material distinctions. Nothing can be

withstand the influx of bourgeoisie and labor into the political process, and one is presented with the interesting phenomenon of the Labour peer.

France provides an example of the "insulative" response and its effects. The *ancien régime* provided virtually no institutional access for the rising bourgeoisie to political decision making, much less incorporation into the ranks of the decision makers. A potent, hostile counter-elite was thus formed which, in collusion with disaffected elements of the nobility, provided the leadership for the Revolution of 1789. This carnage did not, however, mark the end of the insulative response. Rather, the antagonistic role into which the aristocracy was cast produced a new and durable counter-elite of the right. Moreover, the bourgeoisie themselves adopted an insulative attitude toward aspiring labor elites. The rising bourgeoisie did not absorb the *noblesse oblige* ethic of the traditional aristocracies. They were thus prone not to feel responsible for the welfare of the lower orders just at a time when those classes were undergoing severe material deprivation and social dislocation; no particularistic protection was provided, but particularistic loyalty was demanded. The lower classes, in turn, were increasingly alienated from the system. In this manner, France arrived at the difficult position of having counter-elites of both the left and the right, each with a considerable following in the electorate, and with neither according legitimacy to the political process as such.

The German experience also failed to develop an "integrated" response; it shared features of both the British and French experiences. A strong business class arose, but it was unable to reach the pinnacle of a society in which the monarchy and nobility resisted accepting it as a partner in government or as an equal in status. As Roy Lewis and Rosemary Stewart described the situation:

> The growth of capitalism in Germany was affected, to a far greater extent than in Britain or France, by a rigid structure of class and status. . . .
>
> Capitalism, technology and business came to Germany in various ways. But the structure of a society based on status—and still divided between Catholic and Protestant states—was so strong that it had to shape itself largely to the form of the society. . . .
>
> Bismarck made the mold into which German business was poured in the last half of the nineteenth century. He broke the out-of-date

more politically useful than such homage, if it be skillfully used; no folly can be idler than to repel and reject it." *The English Constitution* (New York: Oxford University Press, 1952), pp. 277–278. (Emphasis in original.)

medievalism of the *Junker* (land-owning) squires, but maintained the autocracy of their king (and later emperor). . . . However, top businessmen did not find themselves, as in England, at the apex of society. Status remained decisive, and the army retained its caste privileges. The successful businessman might in time be allowed to put "von" in front of his name, but he could not aspire to become a full part of the nobility; and the purchase of a great estate did not (as, again, it did in England) provide his children with a springboard into the ruling circles.[58]

The German upper class, as represented by Bismarck and the Kaiser, sought to make the workers as a class loyal to the polity by "protecting" them against the bourgeoisie through a variety of social welfare legislation. The aristocracy, in fact, saw the workers as potential allies against the power and status claims of the "vulgar" business classes, and perceived their own actions on behalf of the workers as reflecting the morality of *noblesse oblige*, of the responsibility toward their inferiors of those born to rule. In a real sense, Bismarck and Disraeli reflected similar reactions by the political spokesmen of comparable strata. The Germans differed from the British, however, in that they refused to "incorporate" the leaders of the new classes, in particular the workers, into the political process.

To give an adequate account of the differing ways in which nations with ascriptive traditions met the tensions of entering a commercial and industrial era requires reference to many unique factors.[59] Much of the

---

[58] Lewis and Stewart, *The Managers*, pp. 166–168.

[59] Schumpeter explicitly addressed himself to this problem, but curiously put the responsibility for the differences between British and German political systems on the behavior of one man, Bismarck: "But, why was it that the English methods and tactics did not prevail in Germany? . . . The fatal mistake was really Bismarck's. It consisted in the attempt, explicable only on the hypothesis that he completely misconceived the nature of the problem, at suppressing socialist activities by coercion. . . ." *Capitalism, Socialism, and Democracy* (New York: Harper & Bros., 1950), pp. 341, 343.

Writing in 1917, Max Weber saw the failure of Bismarck to share political power with the various opposition parties as a prime cause of the latter's inability to function as a responsible and loyal opposition: "Bismarck left behind as a political heritage a nation without any political education. . . . Above all he left behind a nation without any political will, accustomed to allow the great statesman at its head to look after its policy for it. Moreover . . . he left a nation accustomed to submit, under the label of constitutional monarchy, to anything which was decided for it . . ." Cited in Mayer, *Max Weber and German Politics*, p. 78; see also Edward Shils, "The

difference between northern and southern Europe is related to the success or failure of the Protestant Reformation. Britain's position as an island was important because, among other things, it eased the problem of national unification and national defense, and reduced the role of the military as a major factor affecting the special course of its economic and political development. Also the historic timing with which different nations entered the industrial age or were unified politically cannot be ignored. However, on the level of the specific variables with which this book is concerned, one factor would seem to stand out, and that is the cluster of variables which produced "open" or "closed" aristocracies. In seeking to account for the differences in the political adaptation of Britain and France to the tensions occasioned by modernization, Tocqueville found the key precisely in the variations between the British and continental upper classes. As he put it:

> I have always been surprised that a circumstance that renders England so different from all other modern nations and which alone explains the peculiarities of her laws, history, and traditions has not received more attention.
>
> . . . England was the only country in which the caste system had been totally abolished, not merely modified. Nobility and commoners joined forces in business enterprises, entered the same professions, and—what is still more significant—intermarried. The daughter of the greatest lord in the land could marry a "new" man without the least compunction. . . .
>
> The reason why the English middle class, far from being actively hostile to the aristocracy, inclined to fraternize with it, was not so much that the aristocracy kept open house as that its barriers were ill defined; not so much that entrance into it was easy as that you never knew when you had got there. The result was that everyone who hovered on its outskirts nursed the agreeable illusion that he belonged to it and joined forces with it in the hope of acquiring prestige or some practical advantage under its aegis.[60]

Intellectuals in the Political Development of New States" (mimeographed, 1962), p. 45.

Addressing himself to the same problem in terms of why Britain succeeded in avoiding major class tension, a French historian also credits the insight of individuals. G. E. Lavau urges that England avoided a revolutionary working class because of "the practical intelligence—at the right moment—of some Conservative [Disraeli, Randolph Churchill, Joseph Chamberlain] and Liberal [Asquith, Lloyd George] leaders." *Partis politiques et réalités sociales* (Paris: Armand Colin, 1953), p. 95.

[60] Alexis de Tocqueville, *The Old Regime and the French Revolution* (New York: Anchor Books, 1955), pp. 82, 88–89.

The British aristocracy obviously was not inherently more sophisticated than the French or German, but its *structural position* made it more adaptive to a changing class structure. This situation has been well summarized by Robert Ulich in a discussion of Britain as she entered the modern age:

> Despite terrific social contrasts between the upper and middle classes on the one hand and the poor on the other, there was no exclusive ruling caste as in France up to 1789 and again in the latter periods of reaction, and as in Germany up to the twentieth century. Greater mobility . . . was secured by the English custom of succession, or primogeniture, according to which the title of the parent is transmitted only to the eldest son of a noble family, while the other children become commoners. In contrast, in France and Germany every descendant of a nobleman, whether male or female, inherits the title. Until the modern democratic revolutions the mere name made the bearer a privileged person. Intermarriage with commoners meant degradation; even scholarship could only be a hobby. Only through some middleman could the nobleman go into business. . . . [T]his aloofness from modern occupations involved a kind of glorified poverty. There remained nothing but to fight desperately for the monopoly of officers' positions in the army and the higher offices of the civil and diplomatic service. . . .[61]

Unencumbered by a title and seeking ways to regain a firm claim to high status, the "younger sons" of British aristocracy entered the new occupations and married with the new families much more rapidly than their continental brothers. And since many of the "new men" and their families often had family connections with the aristocracy, the problem of "integrating" the new and old elites was nowhere near as difficult as in countries where the aristocracy sought to differentiate itself as much as possible from the corrupting contact with the "vulgar" moneymakers.

---

[61] Robert Ulich, *Education of Nations* (Cambridge, Mass.: Harvard University Press, 1961), p. 95. "The great distinction between the English aristocracy and any other has always been that, whereas abroad every member of a noble family is noble, in England none are noble except the head of the family. . . . The descendants of younger sons, who on the Continent would all be counts or barons, in England have no titles and sit even below knights. Furthermore, the younger sons and daughters of the very richest lords receive, by English custom, but little money from their families, barely enough to live on. The sons are given the same education as their eldest brother and then turned out." Nancy Mitford, "The English Aristocracy," in Nancy Mitford, ed., *Noblesse Oblige* (Harmondsworth: Penguin Books, 1959), pp. 36–37.

Nor was it [in England], in contrast to Germany, considered a sort of high treason—at least after the middle of the nineteenth century —if a member of the privileged group joined the masses in their struggle for better conditions. Leftists have come from all groups of English society including graduates from Eton; they have provided an organic exchange of ideas, however controversial; and they have supplied labor with men whose background and experience gave them that sense of social security, grace, and freedom that political leaders in other countries, having come from the working class, so often lacked.[62]

Up to this point the discussion has focused on the way in which ascriptive values have been handled in establishing who should have the right to rule in a political democracy. There is, however, an alternative basis of gaining support for a new system: effectiveness, or demonstrated and successful achievements. But as a sole foundation for legitimacy, it is tenuous. Any government can become involved in crises; major groupings will oppose specific policies, sometimes to the point of alienation. Consequently any government which persists must have ascriptive grounds for support—*i.e.*, a sense of traditional legitimacy. Where a polity does not have such legitimacy to begin with, as in the case of new states or post-revolutionary governments, it is inherently unstable. If the basic value pattern of the society includes a strong emphasis on ascription, new governments will find it difficult to rule by any means except force. Only where the value pattern stresses achievement will the political system, like other institutions and positions, be evaluated by achievement criteria. Thus the success of the American Republic in establishing a post-revolutionary democratic legitimacy may be related to the strength of achievement values in the society.

These analyses suggest that the persistence of ascriptive and particularistic norms is compatible with democracy only in societies which have retained ascriptive legitimacy for their polity, that is, in monarchies.[63] Where such a traditional support is missing, the only way to create a legitimate regime is through long-term effectiveness, that is achievement.

---

[62] Ulich, *Education of Nations*, p. 96.

[63] For detailed analyses of these problems in the new states, see Edward Shils, "Political Development in the New States," *Comparative Studies in Society and History*, 2 (1960), pp. 265–292, 379–411; S. N. Eisenstadt, "Soziale Entwicklung und Politische Stabilität in Nichtwestlichen Gesellschaften," *Koelner Zeitschrift für Soziologie und Sozialpsychologie*, 12 (1960), pp. 189–203, and *Essays on Sociological Aspects of Political and Economic Development* (The Hague: Mouton and Co., 1961).

This is a difficult method at best. To succeed, it requires rapid change in fundamental values. A look at new societies which have attempted to achieve political legitimacy while retaining strong ascriptive elements indicates how problematic this is. (Such nations include most of Latin America, Spain, Germany, Italy, France, Turkey, and many others.)

A genuine problem for achievement or effectiveness as a basis for legitimacy arises in the contemporary "new states," almost all of which, like the Latin American republics in the early nineteenth century, lack traditional legitimacy. The problem of ascriptive and particularistic values apart, the need for effectiveness poses a real dilemma, because in contemporary times "effectiveness" is apt to consist of a demand for the equitable distribution of a rapidly increasing social product. But in the developing areas there are formidable obstacles to such effectiveness: the economy is primitive and unbalanced, the bulk of the population is impoverished, capital is lacking, political experience and skills are rare, and much of the available store of political and entrepreneurial experience is distributed among individuals associated with the former colonial masters. And as Weber and others have pointed out, rapid economic growth may often engender violent class and political conflict, rather than faith in the social system.[64] To the extent, therefore, that democratic rulers who lack legitimacy are responsible for a rapid increase in the pace of economic transformation, to that extent they may also serve to undermine the capacity of the system to receive generalized support. By fostering rapid transformation, the new political system provokes dislocations in such basic social relationships as the extended kinship system, the emphasis on mutual aid within pre-industrial communities, and traditional orientations to work and time.

In applying these considerations to the prospects for political and economic development in the "new" and/or "underdeveloped" states, it is important to recognize that the now economically developed, stable democracies were able to develop either in societies which for the most part possessed traditional legitimacy, or in an achievement oriented society like the United States which also had widespread and relatively equitable distribution of land ownership for much of its early history. In addition, these societies did not have to counter a (partly artificially— that is, politically—stimulated) rising "level of expectation" which was beyond the capacity of the economy or polity. As it is clearly difficult to generate support in the new states on grounds of either ascription or

---

[64] H. H. Gerth and C. W. Mills, eds., *From Max Weber: Essays in Sociology* (New York: Oxford University Press, 1946), pp. 193–194.

achievement, the chances for stable democracy in any Western sense are slim. Communism and other forms of totalitarian rule apart, the general alternatives available are either particularistic appeals to the existing ascriptive solidarities—family, village, tribe, religion, linguistic unit, or caste—an approach which is obviously dysfunctional from the standpoint of developing a consensus in new territorial political systems, or charismatic domination by party or leader, as pursued in such countries as Mexico, Ghana, or Tunisia.

Value Differences,
Absolute or Relative:
The English-Speaking
Democracies

7 ★★★

As has been remarked, to compare nations or societies which are highly similar in basic values may be even more fruitful analytically than to contrast those which are very different. As a final illustration of this mode of inquiry, I will briefly expand the analysis of the stable democracies to include Australia and Canada, nations which like the United States are former colonies of Great Britain, which settled a relatively open continental frontier, and are today continent-spanning federal states. There is general agreement that, on a world-wide comparative scale, these two large, predominantly English-speaking states resemble the United States in stressing equalitarianism, achievement, universalism, and specificity.[1] But if Canada and Australia share these basic values with the United

---

[1] An illustration of the relativity of such comparative statements may be found in an interesting book on England by an Indian, Nirad C. Chaudhuri, *A Passage to England* (London: Readers Union, 1960). Many of his comments on England are similar to those made about the United States by visiting Europeans. For Chaudhuri, England is the model of an achievement-oriented and universalistic society. Elie Halévy was well aware of the problem which this posed for a foreign student of England: "[W]hatever the differences between English and continental life, we must beware of exaggerating their importance. To be sure, the Frenchman feels himself in a

States, they differ with it also, and it is these differences which sharply illustrate the way in which even relatively slight variations in value patterns help account for important differences among the stable and highly developed democracies.

The very tentative rankings which may be given to the positions of the four major, predominantly English-speaking democracies on the four pattern-variable dimensions are presented in Table V below. It is obviously extremely difficult to be precise about such variations, and these should be considered as at best an informed guess.

Table V

Tentative Estimates of Relative Rankings of the Four English-Speaking Democracies According to Strength of Certain Pattern Variables (Rankings according to First Term in Polarity)

	United States	Australia	Canada	Great Britain
Elitism–Equalitarianism	3	4	2	1
Ascription–Achievement	4	2.5	2.5	1
Particularism–Universalism	4	2	3	1
Diffuseness–Specificity	4	2.5	2.5	1

According to my estimates, Australia differs from the United States in being slightly more equalitarian, but less achievement oriented, universalistic, and specific. It also seems less universalistic and more equalitarian than Canada, but it is difficult to estimate the differences on the other two polarities. Canada differs somewhat from the United States on all four dimensions of equalitarianism, achievement, universalism, and specificity, while Britain in turn is less oriented toward these values than Canada.

To demonstrate that such differences really exist would involve a

foreign land when he crosses from Calais to Dover, but how insignificant the difference would seem to an Asiatic traveller from Calcutta or Pekin. Between Latin Catholicism and Anglo-Saxon Protestantism the gulf seems wide, but what is the distance which divides European Christianity as a whole from Brahminism?" *History of the English People in the Nineteenth Century.* (London: Ernest Benn Ltd., 1961), Vol. I, p. xiii. David Landes reports that his as yet unfinished study of writings about England by eighteenth-century French travelers indicates that they viewed English customs and values in much the same light as visiting Englishmen have regarded the United States.

considerable research program. However, I have drawn on a considerable number of writings which have argued and given some evidence that these differences are as they are presented here and, for the time being, we must depend on such impressionistic evidence to support the discussion to follow. In this chapter, I will first seek to account for the differences by indicating variations in the social development of these countries which presumably created and sustained structures carrying these values, and then "derive" differences in their political systems which seem related to value patterns.

The Canadian pattern, as has been noted earlier, seems to reflect the fact that Canada always has been more conservative than the United States, that its early political history from 1776 on involved the defeat of radical reform, and that consequently some of the traditionalist "Tory" values which declined in the United States continued in Canada. The Canadian historian Frank Underhill has described the situation in the following terms:

> The mental climate of English Canada in its early formative years was determined by men who were fleeing from the practical application of the doctrines that all men are born equal and are endowed by their creator with certain unalienable rights amongst which are life, liberty and the pursuit of happiness. . . . In Canada we have no revolutionary tradition; and our historians, political scientists, and philosophers have assiduously tried to educate us to be proud of this fact. . . .[2]

It is true, of course, that Canadian frontier conditions were just as destructive of traditional social relations as were those on the American frontier. "Distinctions of social class found little recognition in the pioneer communities where the demands of neighborhood association pressed so heavily upon the inhabitants."[3] Pressures toward egalitarianism

---

[2] Frank H. Underhill, *In Search of Canadian Liberalism* (Toronto: The Macmillan Co. of Canada, 1960), p. 12. He goes on to point out that, while Jacksonian Democracy triumphed in the United States in the 1830's and "swept away most of the old aristocratic survivals and made a strong attack on the new plutocratic forces," its equivalent in Canada, the movements of Papineau in Quebec and Mackenzie in Ontario, were defeated and discredited. Hence in Canada, unlike the United States, the "social pyramid . . . was *not* upset." pp. 12–33.

[3] S. D. Clark, *The Canadian Community* (Toronto: University of Toronto Press, 1962), p. 65.

and individualism resulted; but there were counter forces which prevented individualism of the American type from becoming the accepted way of life on the Canadian frontier.

Canada had to be constantly on its guard against the expansionist tendencies of the United States. It could not leave its frontier communities unprotected, or autonomous. Law and order in the form of the centrally controlled North West Mounted Police moved into frontier settlements along with the settlers. This contributed to the establishment of a greater tradition of respect for the *institutions* of law and order on the Canadian as compared to the American frontier. At the same time, frontier egalitarianism and individualism were played down in Canada because they were linked to American values and might conceivably undermine national integrity:

> Efforts to strengthen the political ties of Empire or of nation led to deliberate attempts, through land grants and political preferments, to create and strengthen an aristocracy in the colonies . . . and later in a less obvious fashion, in the Canadian nation. The democratic movement it was felt was liable to draw Canadian people closer to their neighbors to the south; and a privileged upper class was a bulwark of loyalty and conservatism.[4]

One consequence of the value system which emerged is that Canadians have always been less intolerant of economic inequality and social stratification.[5] Horatio Algèr has never been a Canadian hero. As the Canadian sociologist Kaspar Naegele put it in his excellent discussion of his society:

> [T]here is *less* emphasis in Canada on equality than there is in the United States. . . . In Canada there seems to be a greater acceptance of *limitation*, of hierarchical patterns. There seems to be less optimism, less faith in the future, less willingness to risk capital or

---

[4] *Ibid.*, p. 194.

[5] A sociological study made in the mid-1930's in English-speaking Montreal based on a small sample of "seventy people, who were thought to be representative," reports that the "notion of a social elite, of a culture based upon the traditions and ideals of aristocratic Britain, reappears over and over again in the interviews." These attitudes, the authors note, are probably not characteristic of Canadian opinion much west of Montreal. S. D. Clark, assisted by C. A. Dawson and E. C. Hughes, "Opinions and Attitudes in English-Speaking Quebec," in H. F. Angus, ed., *Canada and Her Great Neighbor* (Toronto: Ryerson Press, 1938), pp. 383–389.

reputation. In contrast to America, Canada is a country of greater caution, reserve, and restraint.[6]

But if there is agreement that Canada lies somewhere between America and Britain as concerns equalitarianism (although it is closer to America),[7] this is not the case with Australia. The scanty available evidence or, more properly speaking, impressions would suggest that equalitarianism is stronger in Australia than in Canada or the United States, but that universalism is weaker in Australia than in the United States, particularly among the workers. The particularistic and equalitarian value of "mate-ship," the "uncritical acceptance of reciprocal obligations to provide companionship and material or ego support as required," is viewed by many Australians as contradictory to the value of "success-ship," (achieve-ment) although many feel that the latter value is "gradually gaining ascendency . . ."[8] A number of commentators have recently called

---

[6] Kaspar Naegele, "Canadian Society: Some Reflections," in Bernard Blishen, *et al.*, eds., *Canadian Society* (Toronto: Macmillan, 1961), p. 27. (Emphases in original.) This article is the best effort to sum up the general value system of Canada. Naegele argues strongly for the thesis that Canada on many matters lies "in the middle between America and England," and that it both accepts and rejects various aspects of the English and American models.

[7] Some of the flavor of the social differences between Canada and the United States which reflect the greater strength of traditionalist and conservative val-ues in the former country have been well summed up by an Australian histo-rian who spent some time in Canada studying its values and attitudes: "I con-sider it not unfair to suggest, however, that if some Canadians think some Americans brash and loud, most Americans think Canadians generally are not only quiet and standoffish on occasion but also—let's be frank about it, rather dull and often very drab. Even an overseas visitor to North America may detect the contrast with the friendly, talkative habits of the curious American which he finds among reserved Canadians in trains, in cafes, and even in some private homes. American women, moreover, find a sharp contrast in the apparent readiness of their Canadian sisters to leave public life in many forms to their husbands and to their brothers." Fred Alexander, *Canadians and Foreign Policy* (Toronto: University of Toronto Press, 1960), p. 121.

[8] Ronald Taft and Kenneth F. Walker, "Australia," in Arnold M. Rose, ed., *The Institutions of Advanced Societies* (Minneapolis: University of Minnesota Press, 1958), pp. 144–145. These two Australian social psychologists sum up Australian values as being militantly equalitarian, "set in the background of politico-economic class consciousness. . . . These equalitarian attitudes have taken the form of militant attempts to eliminate the material and prestige liabilities of the working class. . . . Thus a high value is placed on activities aimed at protecting and promoting the standing of the 'underdog' by abusing privileged or would-be privileged persons. Although, as we have seen, middle-

attention to what they describe as the "Americanization" of Australia, by which they mean "the growth of competitiveness and the success ethic."[9] It may be, therefore, that Tocqueville's proposition that equalitarianism demands an emphasis on competition, that the absence of status barriers presses men toward achievement, may turn out to be valid for Australia. Certainly, the growth of facilities for higher education in Australia, discussed below, suggests that Australians may be losing their disdain for "success-ship." But whatever the facts are concerning the relative emphasis on achievement in contemporary Australia, there still seems to be general agreement that it stands out in its commitment to egalitarian social relations. For example, a visiting Englishwoman observes:

> The Australian concern, at least with the semblance of equality, is deep rooted and probably accounts, for instance, for the fact that it is the only western country which long resisted the noxious habit of tipping. . . . [I]n 1884 Francis Adams—whose book *The Australians* was movingly perceptive—was emphasizing the same quality. "This is a true republic," he said, "the truest, I take it, in the world. In England the average man feels he is an inferior; in America he feels he is superior; in Australia he feels he is an equal. Here the people is neither servile nor insolent, but only shows respect for itself by its respect for others."[10]

And she also points to the continued difference in attitudes toward work and achievement in Australia and the United States:

> In America there is a drive to work which exists quite apart from the incentive of material comforts. Perhaps it is a legacy from the Puritan heritage but, whatever the reason may be, the American has a compulsive attitude to work itself. The powerful big business executive in America does not relax even when he has reached the top of his profession. . . .

---

class Australians avoid identifying themselves as workers, they nonetheless typically share this militant equalitarianism against authority or prestige figures . . . Thus the middle class, by and large, supports the welfare state, maintains the right of workers to strike and to look after their own interests, and eschews the servility associated with certain necessary occupational roles. Australians are poor at providing personal service and are reluctant to demand it."
[9] Jeanne Mackenzie, *Australian Paradox* (London: Macgibbon and Kee, 1962), p. 8.
[10] *Ibid.*, p. 102.

An Australian is not concerned with work for its own sake. He will fight on a union basis for shorter hours and more pay, but he isn't interested in increasing his output in order to meet bigger demands. He would prefer to reduce his needs in order that they may be fulfilled.[11]

Frederick Eggleston argues that "in Australia, there is little respect for wealth as such. . . . It is harder for an industrial magnate to enter politics than for a camel to pass through the eye of a needle. . . . The wealthy classes have never provided leaders or shown the community any guidance in political matters.[12]

A report by an Australian professor of education on the school system of his country complains that the equalitarian values and behavior pattern built into the school systems prevent the emergence of any concern for leadership. Compare the comments on the British educational system cited earlier with these statements about the Sydney school system:

> The almost century-old tradition of equalitarianism militates against class leadership of any kind. . . . Nowhere, thus, in his education does he [the young Sydney citizen] receive inspiration and encouragement to strive for a position of leadership in the community. . . .
> The general effect in secondary education here appears to have been a blurring of distinctions between different secondary schools [public and private]. . . . The tendency of the system appears to be towards the elimination of distinctions between schools and thus the elimination of characteristics, in so far as schools can provide them, distinctive of an upper class which has special knowledge, attitude, or skills built into it by the schools.[13]

Leslie Lipson accounts for the differences between Australia (and New Zealand) and the mother country by the fact that nations which were settled "in large part by representatives of the laboring and lower middle

---

[11] *Ibid.*, pp. 107–108.

[12] Frederick W. Eggleston, "The Australian Nation," in George Caiger, ed., *The Australian Way of Life* (London: Heinemann, 1953), p. 11; see also A. P. Rowe, *If the Gown Fits* (Melbourne: Melbourne University Press, 1960), pp. 59–67; and J. D. B. Miller, *Australian Government and Politics* (London: Duckworth, 1954), pp. 22–24.

[13] W. F. Connell, "Education and Social Mobility in Australia, *Transactions of the Third World Congress of Sociology* (London: International Sociological Association, 1954), Vol. V, pp. 75–76.

classes could be expected to react instinctively against any whiff of the mother country's social stratification."[14] Australia was originally founded as a penal colony. As late as the 1850's, before its Gold Rush, the *majority* of the population were convicts, ex-convicts, or the children of convicts. Many of the later "free immigrants" were people who had been involved in Chartist and similar movements in Britain.[15] It is also important to note that "Australia is one of the very few countries whose whole development has taken place since the beginnings of the Industrial Revolution," and consequently it developed its national ethos and class structure in a period in which traditional and aristocratic values were under sharp attack.[16] Unlike Canada, Australia did not emerge out of a vanquished democratic revolution, and has no history of defeated nineteenth-century reformist movements.[17] If anything, the reverse is true: the "left" played the major role in defining political and social institutions in the periods in which national identity was established.

The difference between the Australian focus on equality and the American emphasis on individual achievement is also connected with the fact that the Australian frontier experience was quite different from that in both Canada and the United States. While its influence on Australian values was not restrained and restricted as in Canada, it was conducive to an equalitarianism from which the individualism produced on the American frontier was absent.[18] In America, each individual attempted

---

[14] Leslie Lipson, *The Politics of Equality* (Chicago: University of Chicago Press, 1948), pp. 487–488.

[15] Russel Ward, *The Australian Legend* (New York: Oxford University Press, 1959), pp. 14–16, 157–158.

[16] *Ibid.*, p. 18.

[17] Canadian unification in 1867 is associated with the Conservative Party, while the federating of Australia around the turn of the century was pressed by the Labour Party, which existed in most states. It is noteworthy that the "conservative" party in Australia has constantly changed its name to avoid association with traditional and privileged elements. "Not by accident but by design the term conservative early in the twentieth century disappeared from the nomenclature of parties in Australia and New Zealand. It could not obviously win enough varied backing among the surviving elements of conservative opinion. . . . In Canada a conservative outlook in many respects found great favor." Alexander Brady, *Democracy in the Dominions* (Toronto: University of Toronto Press, 1958), p. 528.

[18] Carter Goodrich has suggested that "the United States owes its individualism largely to its small man's frontier; I think it not fanciful to suggest that Australia owes much of its collectivism [particularism] to the fact that its frontier was hospitable to large men instead." See "The Australian and American La-

to find his own plot of land. The Australian pioneer, on the other hand, faced a foreboding climate. Many of the frontier enterprises involved large-scale cattle and sheep grazing, both of which required considerable capital if the enterprise was to be worthwhile:

> Big men came to control the Australian frontier development while in America the westward drive consisted of ordinary individuals, men "on the make," where there was sufficient room for manoeuvre to support a pro-capitalist outlook. . . . But, in Australia, it left the man still a wage earner. . . . Thus, Australia did not develop a large middle class of small property owners. Rather was there a nomad tribe of pastoral workers, who retained their working class attitudes.[19]

In a certain sense, the differences in outlook between Canada and Australia may be seen as reflections of the need of each country to dissociate itself from that major power which has had the most direct cultural and economic influence on it. Canadians—as Frank Underhill, the eminent elder statesman of Canadian historians, put it recently in a public lecture—are the world's oldest and continuing "anti-Americans." The Canadian sense of nationality has always felt itself threatened by the United States, physically in earlier days, and culturally and economically in more recent years. Not only have Canadians found it necessary to protect themselves against American expansion, they have also found it necessary to define why they are not and should not become Americans, and they have done so by disparaging various elements in American life, mainly those which seemingly are an outgrowth of mass democracy and an excessive emphasis on equalitarianism.[20] For example, the president

---

bour Movements," The Economic Record, 4 (1928), pp. 206–207. In Australia, unlike the United States and Canada, frontier farms were immensely large, and employed large numbers of workers. This pattern to a considerable degree reflected the difficulties of desert farming and ranching: "The typical Australian frontiersman in the last century was a wage-worker who did not, usually, expect to become anything else." Ward, *The Australian Legend* p. 226. Large groups of land laborers developed a sense of group consciousness, and very early formed a major trade union, now the largest in the country, the Australian Workers Union. See also Fred Alexander, *Moving Frontiers* (Melbourne: Melbourne University Press, 1947).

[19] Mackenzie, *Australian Paradox*, p. 106.

[20] Frank H. Underhill, "The Image of Canada," address given at the University of New Brunswick Founders' Day, March 8, 1962. In an earlier book Underhill pointed to "the effect of British influences in slowing down all movements throughout the nineteenth century in the direction of the democratiza-

of the University of Toronto, Claude T. Bissell, has attempted to explain why the image of America has generally had a negative impact on Canadian writers in this way:

> [T]he Canadian political heritage and development created an atmosphere that was inimical to much of American literature. There was no revolutionary tradition in Canada, no glorification of force as a means of winning freedom and release. Moreover, the Canadian nation had been fashioned in a spirit of cautious defensiveness as a means of preserving what might at any moment be snatched away. All of this led to an innate suspicion of violence, and a tendency to equate the exuberant and the expansive with the empty and the vulgar. Here, I think, we have the source of the assumption on the part of Canadians of a quiet moral superiority to their more splendid and affluent neighbors.[21]

The "assumption of a quiet moral superiority" as a means of distinguishing Canada from the United States may be seen in the first literary attempts to comment upon the Canadian scene. John Pengwerne Matthews points out that Thomas Chandler Haliburton, an eighteenth-century Canadian writer, created a "figure of the irrepressible Yankee [peddler], Sam Slick," as a "goad he could apply to the inert elements of Nova Scotia life": "Sam Slick represented all those traits of bumptiousness which Haliburton so detested, and while his self confidence and ingenuity are characteristics that Nova Scotians would do well to copy, he is the caricature of a national prototype that Haliburton did not admire."[22] Haliburton was using Sam Slick as a moral lesson to make Nova Scotians better Canadians, but this was largely ignored, because in their distaste for the American emphasis upon equality and achievement, Canadian writers could not see the difference between "the synthesis that Haliburton had created and the unadulterated American slick humor south of the border. As a result, Canadian writers and critics drew back in well-bred horror from the distasteful crudities of the frontier, and looked,

---

tion of politics and society. Inevitably, . . . the urge towards greater democracy was likely to appear in Canada as an American influence; and since the survival of Canada as a separate entity depended on her not being submerged under an American flood, such influences were fought as dangerous to our Canadian ethos." Underhill, *In Search of Canadian Liberalism*, p. 15.

[21] Claude T. Bissell, "The Image of America in Canada," Address delivered at the Canadian Studies Seminar, University of Rochester, March 16, 1962.

[22] John Pengwerne Matthews, *Tradition in Exile* (Toronto: University of Toronto Press, 1962), p. 38.

more resolutely than ever, eastward across the Atlantic to the source of all good things."[23]

Insofar as elements that distinguished it from Britain, such as a frontier experience and virgin land, were also shared by the United States, Canadians turned away from them as a source of defining themselves. As a result, whereas the frontier experience in both Australia and the United States, though quite different, brought equalitarian values into the nation's image of itself, it did not do so in Canada.

Canadian intellectuals attempted to overcome their sense of colonial inferiority by trying to be as good as the British in their own medium rather than trying to find a medium that suited the attributes of their native land. Thus, whereas Canadian critics praised the poet Charles Sangster because "he may be regarded as the Canadian Wordsworth," Australian critics praised Charles Harpur for those poems in which he "was *not* the Australian Wordsworth."[24] Such attitudes kept Canadian intellectuals from supporting the populist doctrines espoused by many intellectuals in both Australia and the United States.

Australian nationalism, in contrast, inspired efforts to dissociate Australia from Britain, first politically, and later in terms of social values.[25] Britain was perceived antagonistically as the stronghold of rigid inequality. Australian writers romanticized the virtues of the gold rush experience or the nomadic life of the sheep-shearers. R. M. Crawford has pointed out that the self-image forged for the nation by Australian writers drawing on this local heritage was always more radical than actual social conditions, precisely because of these writers' efforts to differentiate Australia from Britain.[26] Thus where Canada retained a more elitist attitude in reaction to American equalitarianism, Australia emulated various American equalitarian patterns in reaction to British elitism.[27]

---

[23] *Ibid.*, p. 40.

[24] *Ibid.*, pp. 58–59.

[25] James Bryce was struck by these attitudes before World War I. Thus he reports, "I was amazed to find in 1912 how many Australians believed Britain to be a declining and almost decadent country." *Modern Democracies* (London: Macmillan, 1921), Vol. I, p. 268.

[26] R. M. Crawford, "The Australian National Character: Myth and Reality," *Cahiers d'histoire mondiale*, 2 (1955), p. 715.

[27] See Robin Gollan, *Radical and Working Class Politics: A Study of Eastern Australia* (Melbourne: Melbourne University Press, 1960), especially pp. 113–115. In drawing up their constitution, the Australians consciously modeled it "upon the American rather than the Canadian model." See Brady, *Democracy in the Dominions*, p. 153.

American literature, particularly that growing out of a vaguely populist intellectual tradition, has found resonance among Australian writers but has been largely ignored by Canadian writers:

> [I]n the field of literature, one could argue that Canadian writers have been less responsive than the Australian to American influences. As between English and American influences, they have preferred the English. . . . Canadian writers found it more difficult than the Australian to absorb the exuberant realism that went with the expansion of American democracy. Whitman excited only feeblest discipleship in Canada but he was a political bible and a literary inspiration to Bernard O'Dowd, perhaps the best of pre-modern Australian poets. American Utopian and protest literature found eager readers in Australia, comparatively few in Canada.[28]

Some quantitative indicators for the value differences among the four major English-speaking nations, particularly as they pertain to achievement, may be deduced from variations in the numbers securing higher education. Perhaps the most striking evidence of the difference between American and British values is the variation in such opportunities. In the United States, the strong and successful efforts to extend the opportunities to attend colleges and universities have, to some considerable degree, reflected both pressures by those in lower status positions to secure the means to succeed, and recognition on the part of the privileged that American values of equality and achievement require giving the means to take part in the "race for success" to all those who are qualified.

Thus if we relate the number enrolled in institutions of higher learning to the size of the age cohort 20 to 24, we find that almost seven times as large a group was attending such schools in 1956–1957 in the United States as in England and Wales.[29] Some proof that these differences reflect variation in values, and not simply differences in wealth or oc-

---

[28] Claude T. Bissell, "A Common Ancestry: Literature in Australia and Canada," *University of Toronto Quarterly,* 25 (1955–56), pp. 133–134.

[29] The number attending institutions of higher learning (post-high school) has been related to the four year age category 20–24, since in most countries the bulk of such students are in this age group. The best category for such analysis would probably be 18–21, but the more or less standardized census categories are 15–19, and 20–24. Since these two groups are about the same size, using the category 20–24 probably gives as good an estimate as is needed of the national variations in the proportion of the relevant age cohort attending schools of higher education.

Table VI

Students Enrolled in Institutions of Higher Learning as Per Cent
of Age Group 20–24, by Country, about 1956

COUNTRY

United States	27.2
Australia	12.05*
Canada	8.0
England and Wales	3.7*
Scotland	5.1*
Philippines	14.5
Jamaica	.7
Puerto Rico	11.9
Western Europe	4.5
Denmark	6.6
France	5.8
Germany (West)	4.1
U.S.S.R.	11.1

*Source: The educational data for the first eight countries and the U.S.S.R. are
calculated from materials in UNESCO, Basic Facts and Figures, 1958 (Paris:
1959), and the Demographic Yearbook 1960, (New York: Statistical Office of the
United Nations, 1960). The data for the Western European countries other than
Britain are taken from J. F. Dewhurst, et al., Europe's Needs and Resources (New
York: Twentieth Century Fund, 1961), p. 315.*

* The proportion of Britons and Australians attending institutions of higher
education is somewhat higher than the figures given in the table proper,
which include those in universities and teachers' colleges only. Both countries have a system of technical colleges, most of which are designed for
vocational training in technical subjects for students who have not completed high schools. However, some of these "colleges" do give university
level education in engineering and scientific subjects. No precise estimate
of the size of this group has been located, but one report indicates that as of
1957, approximately 20,000 students were taking work comparable to that
in universities in British technical colleges. See E. J. King, *Other Schools and
Ours* (London: Methuen and Co., 1958), p. 98. If this group is added to the
English total, then it would indicate about 4 per cent of the age cohort in
higher education. Since there are over 200,000 students in Australian technical
colleges, the "true" Australian figure may also be somewhat higher than the
one presented in the table. On the other hand, it should be noted also that
a higher proportion of students in English universities are foreigners (over
10 per cent) than is true in most other countries. The Russian figure is
probably a low estimate since it is based on educational enrollment for 1956,
but on a population cohort taken from 1959 census data.

Since definitions of higher education and methods of training for different
professions vary so much from country to country, it is necessary to stress

cupational structures, may be deduced from the fact that the one major former American colony, the Philippines, has a much larger proportion enrolled in colleges and universities than any country in Europe or the British Commonwealth, a phenomenon which seemingly reflects the successful effort of Americans to export their belief that "everyone" should be given a chance at college education. A comparison of the variation in enrollment in such institutions in the two major Caribbean nations long under the hegemony of Britain and the United States, Jamaica and Puerto Rico, is also instructive. Thus Jamaica, like many other former British colonies in Africa and Asia, has a higher education system which seems premised on the belief that only a tiny elite should receive such training; while the system in Puerto Rico, like the one in the Philippines, clearly reflects the continued impact of American assumptions concerning widespread educational opportunity. Canada, though it appears to many American tourists to be so similar to the United States, has apparently not accepted its commitments to spreading educational advantages as much; it has less than one-third the United States' proportion in colleges and universities, twice that of the English but—amazingly—less than the Filipinos or Puerto Ricans.[30] Australia is closer to the United States in this respect, particularly since the percentage reported for it is probably not based on as complete an estimate of those in higher education as the North American data. The assumptions made by various observers of the Australian scene that achievement values are gaining there would seem to be congruent with the evidence that a much larger proportion of Australians than Canadians are enrolled in institutions of higher learning.[31]

---

the fact that statistics such as these, though derived from official national bodies and censuses, are subject to considerable error, particularly when used comparatively.

[30] The assumption is often made that Quebec, which is a more traditionalist and Catholic area, shows lower proportions on statistics such as these. This assumption is not valid in the case of university education. In the academic year 1959–1960, the proportion of the population aged 18–21 attending universities was higher in Quebec than in Canada as a whole, or than in the neighboring predominantly English-speaking province of Ontario. See Dominion Bureau of Statistics, *Fall Enrollment of Universities and Colleges,* 1959 (Ottawa: Queen's Printer, 1960), p. 9.

[31] Some indication that these differences operate within the United Kingdom itself may be seen in the fact that the Scots, whose society is both more equalitarian and achievement oriented than the English, though much poorer economically, have many more students enrolled in universities than the English, holding population size constant.

American and Australian egalitarianism is perhaps most clearly reflected politically in the relative strength of "populist" movements through which popular passions wreak their aggression against the structure of the polity. Most recently Australia and the United States both sustained large-scale, popularly based efforts to drive suspected Communists out of key positions in unions and politics.[32] J. B. Priestley has in fact argued that "Australia's attitude to men of independent thought was the same as that of America when McCarthy was at his peak."[33] Conversely in Canada, as in Britain, such problems have been handled in a much more discreet fashion, reflecting in some part the ability of a more unified and powerful political elite to control the system. The Canadian sociologist S. D. Clark has explained these differences as due to variations in patterns of political integration:

> [In the nineteenth century] Canada maintained her separate political existence . . . only by resisting any movement on the part of her population which had the effects of weakening the controls of central political authority [and thus encouraging the possibility of American take-over]. The claims to the interior of the continent were staked not by advancing frontiersmen, acting on their own, but by advancing armies and police forces, large corporate economic enterprises and ecclesiastical organizations supported by the state. The Canadian political temper, as a result, has run sharply counter to the American. Those creeds of American political life—individual rights, local autonomy, and limitation of executive power— . . . have found less strong support within the Canadian political system.

---

[32] There have been a number of cases in recent Australian history of restrictions on academic freedom and outside political interference in the life of universities. Perhaps the most scandalous involved the refusal of the University of New South Wales to appoint an important scholar to its faculty because of objections by government security officers. He had apparently belonged to the Communist Party in the 1940's. See "Security in the Quad," *Nation* (Australia), December 3, 1960, p. 7; see also W. M. Bell, "Secure No More," *Nation* (Australia), October 8, 1960, pp. 6–8.

[33] Cited in Mackenzie, *Australian Paradox*, p. 155. Mrs. Mackenzie agrees that the pressures toward intolerance and conformity in Australia are great, but she feels that Australia has not been as bad as the United States during the height of the McCarthy era. Rather, she seems to agree with a statement that she quotes from the *Sydney Morning Herald*, which commented in February, 1955, that, "While there is nothing that can properly be called McCarthyism in Australia, there is a discouragement of free and unpopular or politically unconventional thinking."

... [the] conditions of rule in Canada required the maintenance of a highly centralized political community.

... Critics outside [the United States] might well pause to consider not the intolerance which finds expression in McCarthyism but the tolerance which makes it possible for McCarthyism to develop. In Canada it would be hard to conceive of a state of political freedom great enough to permit the kind of attacks upon responsible leaders of the government which have been carried out in the United States. More careful examination of the American community ... would probably reveal that, in spite of the witch hunts in that country, the people of the United States enjoy in fact a much greater degree of freedom than do the people of Canada.[34]

Forty years earlier, James Bryce also called attention to these aspects of Canadian life:

Demagogism is supposed to be a malady incident to democracies. Canada has suffered from it less than any other modern free country except Switzerland. . . . The spirit of licence, a contempt of authority, a negligence in enforcing the laws, have been so often dwelt upon as characteristic of democracies that their absence from Canada is a thing of which she may well be proud. To what shall we ascribe the strength of the Executive, the efficiency of the police, the strict application of criminal justice, the habit of obedience to the law? . . . The habit was formed under governments that were in those days monarchical in fact as well as in name and it has persisted.[35]

The greater similarity between Australia and the United States, as contrasted with Canada (and to a much greater degree with Britain), in the extent to which populist explosions and threats to systematic due process occur, is reflected to some degree in their attitudes toward law and order. Again a reading of largely impressionistic literature suggests that the first two seemingly more equalitarian nations are more willing to tolerate lawlessness. The reason for this may be that the absence of traditional mechanisms of social control in these societies has weakened the pressure to

---

[34] S. D. Clark, "The Frontier and Democratic Theory," *Transactions of the Royal Society of Canada*, 48 (1954), Series III, Section Two, pp. 71–72; see also S. D. Clark, *Movements of Political Protest in Canada* (Toronto: University of Toronto Press, 1959), pp. 3–10.

[35] Bryce, *Modern Democracies*, Vol. I, pp. 559–560.

conform without coercion. As the Australian historian Russel Ward has well put it, the deferential "respect for the squire" which underlies the acceptance of authority and informal social controls in Britain is "based on traditional obligations which were, or had been, to some extent mutual." This was not easily transferred to new equalitarian societies which emphasized the universalistic cash nexus as a source of social relations.[36] The complaints found in the United States that corrupt means of achieving success are socially accepted have also been expressed by Australians.[37] "They will put up with boss-rule and corruption in trade unions; they are not greatly concerned about gerrymandering at elections."[38] Neither union corruption, as we have seen, nor gerrymandering are so prevalent in Britain or Canada.

One indicator of the relative strength of the informal normative mechanisms of social control as compared with the restrictive emphases of legal sanctions seems to be the extent to which given nations need lawyers. Among the English-speaking democracies, the United States and Britain stand at polar extremes. As of 1955, the United States had 241,514 lawyers "of whom approximately 190,000 were engaged in private practice. This means there was one lawyer in private practice per 868 of population. . . . [T]he total English legal profession seems to number about 25,000, and those in private practice can hardly be more than 20,000, or one lawyer per 2,222 population."[39] The comparable ratio for Australia, considering all men reported as employed in private practice in the legal profession as practicing lawyers, is one for every 1,210 persons, while in Canada the figure is about one for every 1,630.[40]

The emphasis on populist values derivative from equalitarianism in the United States as contrasted with the very different value emphases in Britain is reflected in the differential status and role of judge and jury in the two countries. The American system has stressed the notion of the judge as a neutral "umpire," in a contest which is decided by a jury drawn from

---

[36] Ward, *The Australian Legend*, p. 27.

[37] Bryce, *Modern Democracies*, Vol. II, pp. 276–277; MacKenzie, *Australian Paradox*, pp. 154, 220–222.

[38] Mackenzie, *Australian Paradox*, p. 154.

[39] L. C. B. Gower and Leolin Price, "The Profession and Practice of Law in England and America," *Modern Law Review*, 20 (1957), p. 317.

[40] The Canadian estimate of about 11,000 practicing lawyers (and notaries) in Quebec is from a study of the Taxation Division of the Department of National Revenue reported in a letter from the Information Officer of the Canadian Embassy in Washington; the Australian data were supplied by the Australian Reference Library in New York City.

the population, while the British have placed more stress on the positive role of the judge and less on the role of the jury. In a detailed study of changes in the British conception of the jury, Joseph Hamburger points out the relationship between these differences and the larger social systems:

> The main difference between England and America that led to the different status of the jury system in the estimate of public opinion arises from the differences in social and political backgrounds. America, a new country in which people had a greater freedom to form their opinions without the restraints of tradition or the influences of an established class system, allowed wider range for populistic fantasies. There were, particularly in the frontier communities, few ancient traditions or vested interests of an established society to keep people from modelling their institutions on the popular democratic beliefs that seemed to emerge almost naturally in such an atmosphere. It is not surprising, therefore, that the jury was seen, not in its English historical context, but as a microcosm of the popular will, a positive instrument of democracy. Accompanying such an image, there were hostilities to any ideas or practices that spoiled the pure, democratic character of this picture; thus, the impatience with judges who asserted more authority than an umpire needed or who insisted on the authority of a law that was not only complex but also foreign. The jury appeared to be an ideal instrument for allowing the sovereign people to form and interpret the laws that regulated their conduct.[41]

The contempt for law in Australia is expressed by the behavior of their trade unions, which "can reduce the law, or parts of the law to impotence. Practically every strike of any size in Australia is illegal, yet the Australian record of man-days lost per head since the war is challenged only by the United States."[42] Lack of respect for the police and for law enforcement in general, an attitude linked not only to equalitarian attitudes toward authority but also perhaps to the country's penal-colony origins, is evident in the many press reports and editorials which report incidents and complaints that bystanders "refuse to help, in fact

---

[41] See his chapter, "Trial by Jury and Liberty of the Press," in Harry Kalven, ed., *The Public Image of the Jury System* (Boston: Little, Brown, forthcoming); see also Hamburger's chapter, "Decline of the Jury Trial in England," in the same volume.

[42] Hugh Clegg, *A New Approach to Industrial Democracy* (London: Basil Blackwell, 1960), p. 22.

their inclination [is] to hinder a policeman in trouble."[43] A study of Australian national character states unequivocally that "dislike and distrust of policemen . . . has sunk deeply into the national consciousness.[44]

This judgment may be contrasted with the emphasis placed, in a report of a detailed questionnaire-based study of English national character, on the great respect for the police in that country. Geoffrey Gorer describes "the enthusiastic appreciation of the police, disclosed by this study" and comments that he does "not think the English police have ever been felt to be the enemy of sizeable non-criminal sections of the population. . . ."[45] Similarly in Canada, the respect given the national police force, the Royal Canadian Mounted Police, far exceeds that ever given the police in the United States, and crime statistics for English Canada indicate a much lower rate of law violation than occurs south of the border.

But if the differences among the English-speaking nations discussed so far reflect their variations on a scale of elitism–equalitarianism, the strength and policies of their labor movements would seem to be linked to alternative attitudes toward particularism. As was noted earlier, most commentators agree that Australia differs from the United States and also, to a somewhat lesser degree, from Canada in the extent to which its social structure is tied to strong particularistic sentiments, especially the emphasis on "mateship." And the same strong emphasis on "mateship" has been suggested as a major cause of the fact that Australia shows a much lower wage differential for skill as compared with the United States. However, it should be noted that this egalitarian wage tendency is not limited only to manual workers: "The differential between the low-

---

[43] Ward, *op. cit.*, p. 6. Jeanne Mackenzie has commented: "While I was in Australia a young man, Kevin John Simmonds, escaped from gaol; 38 days later he was captured and brought into court. The newspaper report read: 'More than 500 people lined Central Lane today to cheer the shoeless Simmonds as he appeared in the courtyard. Simmonds, still unshaven, limped across the courtyard and waved to the crowd.' It would seem that he was a national hero but then the report went on to list the charges against him. They were: 'The murder of Emu Plains training centre warder Cecil Mills on 11 October; escape from custody; one robbery while armed; seven breaking and entering and stealing charges; six charges of car stealing; one charge of stealing from a dwelling.' " *Op. cit.*, p. 154.

[44] *Ibid.*, p. 149.

[45] Geoffrey Gorer, *Exploring English Character*, "A Study of the Morals and Behavior of the English People" (New York: Criterion Books, 1955), p. 295.

est and highest incomes is low in Australia. Within any commercial or industrial organization the salary of the second-highest level executives is usually not more than three times that of the lowest paid adult male employee (before income tax, which levels the incomes considerably more)."[46] Thus the lower wage differentials in Australia must also be linked to its emphasis upon equalitarianism. However, Australian equalitarianism has a somewhat different emphasis than it does in the United States:

> [The Australian] is indifferent to the fact that some can be educated privately and some simply acquire a state education, that some go to a university and others have neither the money nor inclination to do so. But he is concerned that those who are educationally privileged should not thereby stand on the shoulders of others and be blessed by a social cachet because of it.[47]

The Australians' instinctive desire to "cut down the tall poppies" perhaps results from the fact that equalitarianism grew out of a tradition that stressed common lower-class origins, as expressed in mateship, whereas equalitarianism in the United States was reenforced by an emphasis upon all individuals having equal potentiality. The Australian pattern thus emerges in a culture where equalitarianism is combined with somewhat less emphasis upon achievement and somewhat greater emphasis on particularism than it is in the United States.

Canada is seemingly less particularistic than Australia and Britain, but more so than the United States. Quantitative evidence of the greater emphasis on particularism in Australian and British politics as contrasted with the two North American democracies may be found in a detailed comparative analysis of the factors associated with electoral support for different parties in these four countries. Although there is a clear correlation between class and voting in each country (the poorer a group or the lower its status, the more likely it is to be "leftist" in its voting behavior), the relationship is "consistently higher in Australia and Great Britain than in Canada and the United States."[48]

---

[46] Kenneth F. Walker, *Industrial Relations in Australia* (Cambridge, Mass.: Harvard University Press, 1956), pp. 329–330.

[47] MacKenzie, *Australian Paradox*, p. 129.

[48] Robert Alford, *Social Class and Voting in Four Anglo-American Democracies* (Berkeley: Survey Research Center, University of California, dittoed, 1961), p. 89.

Similarities in basic values derived from comparable institutionalized historical experiences in Australia and the United States have made each more like the other than either is to Canada or Britain.[49] These comparable value patterns over-ride the influences flowing from the fact that Australia is in closer cultural contact with Britain than with the United States, or from the fact that Canada is in relatively intimate contact with the United States and has much less direct stimulation from Britain.[50]

Values and the Democratic Process

While the stability of a democracy demands that the values of universalism and achievement be dominant in both the economic and political spheres, it does not require them to be dominant in the status hierarchies. That is, the status hierarchy may lean toward elitism, as it does in Britain, or toward equalitarianism, as in the United States, yet both of these nations are stable democracies.

However, these differences do have their effects on the ways in which the political system functions, particularly in the viability of the "rules of the game," and in such matters as the tolerance of opposition and nonconformity and in the respect shown for the due process of the law.

Although popular agreement about the importance of such rules would seem an important requisite for their effectiveness, the empirical data do not clearly sustain this expectation. The less educated and the lower strata in most countries do not accept the need for tolerance of what they consider to be "error" or "wickedness," that is, opposition to what is "clearly right." Conversely, the "rules of the game" are most respected where they are most significant, that is, among the various politically relevant

---

[49] It has been suggested by some that these similarities and differences in values showed up in vivid form in reactions to the demands that military life has made on civilian conscripts in the four countries. The British and, to a lesser degree, the Canadians accepted the need to conform to the rigid hierarchical structure of the military; while Australians and Americans showed deep resentment at having to exhibit deference to superiors. I have been told by nationals of different countries that in London bars during both world wars Americans and Australians tended to associate with each other, while Canadians were more likely than the Australians to prefer British companions to Americans. I am indebted to Professor Frank Underhill for first calling my attention to such behavior patterns.

[50] As the Australian writer J. D. Pringle has put it: "Australia is less English than it appears and more American than it looks." Cited in Mackenzie, *Australian Paradox*, p. 28.

and involved elites.[51] Perhaps the highest degree of tolerance for political deviance is found, therefore, in democratic systems which are most strongly characterized by the values of elitism and diffuseness. Diffuse elitism of the variety which exists in most of the democratic monarchies of Europe tends to place a buffer between the elites and the population. The generalized deference which the latter give to the former means that even if the bulk of the electorate do not understand or support the "rules," they accept the leadership of those who do. It is deferential respect for the elite rather than tolerant popular opinion which underlies the vaunted freedom of dissent in countries like Britain and Sweden. The ability of countries to operate with an unwritten constitution which places no formal restrictions on parliamentary violations of civil liberties is in some considerable measure made possible by the emphasis on diffuseness and elitism in the system.[52] In these societies, the elites, whether those of the

---

[51] See S. M. Lipset, *Political Man: The Social Bases of Politics* (Garden City, N. Y.: Doubleday, 1960), pp. 101–105, 109–114, for a summary of studies bearing on this problem. The reverse proposition will be true in countries in which democratic "rules of the game" have not been institutionalized. Where privileged classes are fighting to retain their traditional oligarchic rights and powers, they will strongly resist the claims for participation in the polity of groups based on the lower strata.

[52] In an extremely interesting paper comparing life and social organization on ships in the American and British merchant marines, Stephen Richardson indicates that variations in basic national values deeply affect authority relationships within identical economic institutions: "Comparison of British and American crews suggests that the British realize and accept the authority of competent persons and are not as fearful of the misuse of authority as Americans. This acceptance of authority is closely related to acceptance of social stratification and the symbols of these differences. Status symbols function as cues for self-regulation, in conformity with the status and role requirements of the ship. British seamen are conditioned before coming to sea to accept authority, and consequently the change in attitudes required when a man becomes a seaman is slight. . . .

"Among American crews a far greater fear and suspicion of authority appears to exist. Social stratification is not widely accepted and is often denied. Many symbols of social stratification have been removed, and, because they are suspect, the remaining symbols do little to enhance self-regulation of the man in conformity with the status and role demands of the ship's social organization." Since the norms of the social structure undermine authority on American ships, there is a necessity for a "far greater formalization of the social system than [on] the British," and American ships have many more explicit rules and regulations. Richardson, "Organizational Contrasts on British and American Ships," *Administration Science Quarterly*, 1 (1956), pp. 206–207.

intellect, of business, of politics, or of mass organizations, are both protected and controlled by their membership in the "club."

The seemingly lesser respect for civil liberties and minority rights in
the more equalitarian democracies such as the United States and Australia may be viewed as a consequence of a social system in which elite
status is more specific, so that contending elites do not receive diffuse
respect and feel less acutely the need to conform to an appropriate set of
rules when in conflict with one another. They do not see themselves as part
of the same club, as members of "an establishment." Hence disagreement
about *the rules,* as well as over policies, are thrown to the broader public
for settlement. And this entails appealing in some degree to a mass electorate to adjudicate on rules whose utility, in some measure, they cannot
be expected to understand; appreciation of the necessity for such rules
often involves a long-term socialization to the nature of the political and
juridical process, secured primarily through education and/or participation. Thus, though civil liberties will be stronger in elitist democracies
than in equalitarian ones, the latter may be regarded as more "democratic"
in the sense that the electorate has more access to or power over the elite.

Another of Parsons' pattern variables not discussed earlier suggests
specific sources of political strain in contemporary American society. His
distinction between self-orientation and collectivity-orientation stresses
the extent to which values emphasize that a collectivity has a claim on
the individual units within it to conform to the defined interests of the
larger group, as contrasted to a stress on actions predominantly reflecting
the perceived needs of the units. An emphasis on particularism tends to
be linked to collectivity-orientation. Moreover, the *noblesse oblige*
morality inherent in aristocracy is an aspect of collectivity-orientation.
Traditionally, Britain and Australia appear to have stressed collectivity
obligations more than have Canada and the United States. Consequently,
the rise of socialist and welfare-state concepts have placed less of a strain
on British and Australian values than on American. Canada, with its
greater stress on elitism and particularism than the United States, would
be somewhat more collectivity-oriented than this country. Although
modern industrial society, including the United States, appears to be
moving generally toward a greater acceptance of collectivity-orientations,
the American values' emphasis on self-orientation results in a stronger resistance to accepting the new community welfare concepts than occurs
elsewhere. In discussing the rise of right-wing extremism in American
society, Parsons has argued that they are the most self-oriented segments
of the American population which currently find the greatest need for

political scapegoats and which strongly resist political changes which are accepted by the upper classes in such countries as Britain and Sweden.[53] Thus, the values of elitism and ascription may protect an operating democracy from the excesses of populism and may facilitate the acceptance by the privileged strata of the welfare planning state, whereas emphases on self-orientation and anti-elitism may be conducive to right-wing populism.

Elitism in the status hierarchy has major dysfunctions which should be noted here.[54] A system of differential status rankings requires that a large proportion of the population accept a negative conception of their own worth as compared with others in more privileged positions. To be socially defined as being low according to a system of values which one respects, must mean that, to some unspecified degree, such low status is experienced as "punishment" in a psychological sense. This felt sense of deprivation or punishment is often manifested in "self-hatred," a phenomenon which, when perceived as characteristic of inferior ascriptive racial or ethnic status, has often been deplored. The features of such self-hatred are: rejection of behavior patterns associated with one's own group as uncouth, negative judgments concerning the value of occupational roles characteristic of one's own group, and the desire to leave one's own group and "pass" into a dominant group. It is universally recognized that such feelings on the part of a Negro or a Jew are indicators of psychic punishment; yet the same reactions among the lower class are often not perceived in the same way.

To a considerable degree, the social mechanisms which operate to legitimate an existing distribution of status inequalities succeed in repressing such discontent, sometimes by structuring perceptions so that even low status individuals may view themselves as higher and therefore "better" than some others, or by creating bonds of vicarious identification with those in higher positions. The latter mechanism is particularly prevalent in systems which emphasize ascriptive and elitist values. However, it is doubtful that such mechanisms alone are a sufficient solution for the problem of social rejection and psychological self-punishment inherent in low status.

There are different adaptive mechanism which have emerged to rec-

---

[53] See Talcott Parsons, "Social Strains in America," in Daniel Bell, ed., *The Radical Right* (Garden City, N.Y.: Doubleday, 1963), pp. 183–184.

[54] For a good discussion of the dysfunctions inherent in an elitist society see C. A. R. Crosland, *The Future of Socialism* (London: Jonathan Cape, 1956), pp. 227–237.

oncile low status individuals to their position and thus contribute to the stability and legitimacy of the larger system. The three most common appear to be:

1. Religion—Belief in a religion with a transvaluational theology, one which emphasizes the possibility or even the probability that the poor on earth will enjoy higher status in heaven or in a reincarnation, operates to adjust them to their station, and motivates those in low positions to carry out their role requirements.[55]

2. Social Mobility—The belief that achievement is possible and that virtue will be rewarded by success for one's self or one's children provides stabilizing functions comparable to those suggested for religion.

3. Political Action—Participation in or support for political movements which aim to raise the position of depressed groups, and which in their ideology contain transvaluational elements—the assumption that the lower strata are morally better than the upper classes—also helps to adjust the deprived groups to their situation.

Since the three mechanisms may be regarded as functional alternatives to one another, that is, as satisfying similar needs, it may be posited that where one or more is weakly present, the other(s) will be strongly in evidence. Specifically, for example, where belief in religion or social mobility is weak, the lower strata should be especially receptive to radical transvaluational political or economic appeals.[56] Social systems undergoing major institutional changes, which weaken faith in traditional religion and which do not replace this lost faith by the value system of an open, achievement-oriented society, have experienced major extremist political movements. It has been argued by some that one of the factors sustaining the bases for Communist and anarchist movements in countries like Spain, France, and Italy has been the perpetuation in society of

---

[55] Religious movements may also, of course, constitute a major element in secular political protest. This is the case today among American Negroes. Lower-class churches and their ministers may directly or indirectly help form class-based political movements. And, of course, sectarian groupings have often expressed the hostility of the depressed strata to the privileged order and their religion. But such forms of institutionalized protest, like radical political movements, themselves serve as means of defining lower status in forms which are palatable to those occupying lower status positions.

[56] The thesis that revolutionary socialism and transvaluational religion have served similar functions for oppressed groups was elaborated by Friedrich Engels, "On the Early History of Christianity," in K. Marx and F. Engels, *On Religion* (Moscow: Foreign Language Publishing House, 1957), pp. 312–320.

strong ascriptive and elitist value elements together with a "dechristianized" lower stratum.[57]

A strong societal emphasis on achievement and equalitarianism (which in part may be perceived as a secular transvaluational ideology) combined with strong religious belief, particularly among the lower strata, should maximize the legitimacy of the existing distribution of privilege and thus minimize the conditions for extremist protest. This is, of course, the situation in the United States. The strong emphasis in American culture on the need to "get ahead," to be successful, seems to be accompanied by powerful transvaluational religions among those who have the least access to the approved means of success.

---

[57] In France, for example, ecological studies which contrast degree of religious practice with Communist strength show that the Communists are most successful in regions in which the "anti-clerical" wave had previously suppressed much of the traditional fidelity to Catholicism. See G. LeBras, "Géographie électorale et géographie religieuse," in *Etudes de sociologie electorale*, Cahiers de la fondation nationale des sciences politiques, n. 1 (Paris: Armand Colin, 1949); and François Goguel, *Géographie des élections Françaises de 1870 à 1951*, Cahiers de la fondation nationale des sciences politiques, n. 27 (Paris: Armand Colin, 1951), pp. 134–135.

Values, Social Character, and the Democratic Polity

8

★★

The relationship between the value patterns and the political process of a society may be considered on another level than has been discussed so far—that of the effect of these patterns on the social character of the citizen. As pointed out in Chapter 3, European travelers to America have remarked over the course of American history that, compared to parents in their own countries, American parents were much more permissive with their children. This they perceived as related to the general emphasis on equalitarianism. Anthropologists and psychologists, in their recent work on "national character," would agree that there is a relationship between such differences in child-rearing practices and the modal personalities of the members of various societies. The character of the citizens may in turn affect the functioning of the society's political system.

There is ample evidence that the differences in early socialization and training reported in the nineteenth century between American and European countries have persisted to this day. American children are much more likely than their European counterparts to feel free to "talk back" to their parents or their teachers, to have their wishes respected, to be paid attention, and to perform duties in the family which would in other countries be restricted to adults. The retention of more ascriptive values in European societies may account for such differences in child-rearing practices.[1] British middle-class respondents are somewhat more likely than

---

[1] See Max Horkheimer, ed., *Studien über Autorität und Familie* (Paris: Alcan, 1936).

their American counterparts to stress obedience as something to be culti-
vated in the child.[2] And the feature that stands out most prominently in
French socialization practices is the separation between the world of
adults and the child's world.[3] It may also be suggested that, in many ways,
Swedish and German family systems and socialization patterns are highly
similar, because both cultures only a short time ago placed a high emphasis
on ascriptive authority.

A very provocative study comparing American and German socialization practices suggests the ways that differences in values between the
two nations affect their socialization practices and the ways these in turn
may affect children's behavior. The authors report that, in general, German parents are much more likely to assume "parenting" behavior than
American parents, both in the form of "direct punishment and control"
and in the form of "affection and companionship."[4] As a counter to their
lesser control over their children, and in congruence with the other major
themes in American culture, American parents, particularly American
mothers, are more likely than German parents to put pressure on their
children to achieve.

These differences in the relationship between parents and children are
in turn reflected in differences in the way parents reward and punish their
children. American parents are more likely than German parents to show
their disapproval of a child's actions by rejecting him or depriving him of
his privileges; German parents are somewhat more likely than American
parents to use "principled discipline" and "physical punishment." The
American type of discipline combined with the greater pressure on the
American child to achieve seems to stimulate him to assume responsibility
for himself at an earlier age than a comparable German child. The researchers conclude that "German children are exposed to appreciably
more affection and control than their American age-mates. This, in turn,
implies a prolongation of dependency, postponement of participation in
semi-autonomous peer-group activity, and delay in the development of
motives for self-directed achievement."[5]

We have seen how Americans' orientation toward individuality and

---

[2] Maurice L. Farber, "English and American Values in the Socialization
Process," *Journal of Psychology*, 36 (1953), p. 245.

[3] Rhoda Metraux and Margaret Mead, *Themes in French Culture* (Stanford,
Calif.: Stanford University Press, 1954), pp. 27–34.

[4] Edward C. Devereux, Jr., Urie Bronfenbrenner, and George Suci, "Patterns
of Parent Behavior in the United States of America and the Federal Republic of Germany: A Cross-national Comparison," *International Social
Science Journal*, 14 (1962), p. 496.

[5] *Ibid.*, p. 505.

achievement, and their tendency to choose reference groups outside the family, have affected their reaction to stratification. Their characteristically universalistic, self-interested approach has influenced the character of the institutions, such as trade unions, that are associated with it. A psychiatric study comparing American and German reactions to military life suggests that Americans approach the military hierarchy also in terms of a need for individual achievement which has been fostered by American socialization practices. It concludes:

> The abuse of the privileges accorded status by the officers, the widespread black-market and looting activities of all lower ranks, the rejection of authoritarian and disciplinary demands that tend to overwhelm and subordinate the self, the reluctance to expose ego to damage until machine power has done all it can, and the relatively speedy withdrawal from the group when under stress, are all very positive indications . . . [that] the central orientation of the American character is self interest. It is the dynamic force that binds all the traits together, that gives the type its Gestalt.[6]

Thus the value system of a society influences the character of its institutions and these shape the character of its citizens as they grow up. The character of a society's members in turn reacts upon the character of its institutions. Several versions of such an argument have been proposed specifically with regard to the political system.[7] Alex Inkeles reports generally that:

> There is substantial and rather compelling evidence of a regular and intimate connection between personality and the mode of political participation by individuals and groups within any one political system. In many different institutional settings and in many parts of the world, those who adhere to the more extreme political positions have distinctive personality traits separating them from those taking more moderate positions in the same setting.[8]

---

[6] G. Dearborn Spindler, "American Character as Revealed by the Military," *Psychiatry*, 11 (1948), p. 279.

[7] The effort of Harry Eckstein to relate the stability of democratic systems to the type of authority relations in different societies is closely related to the attempts to link political systems to modal personal character in given cultures. *A Theory of Stable Democracy* (Princeton, N.J.: Princeton University Center of International Studies, 1961).

[8] Alex Inkeles, "National Character and Modern Political Systems," in Francis Hsu, ed., *Psychological Anthropology* (Homewood, Ill.: Dorset Press, 1961), p. 193.

Unfortunately, systematic comparative studies relating personality characteristics to political behavior are scarce. But since the main purpose of this book is to suggest the utility of relating value orientations to structural correlates of behavior, I will briefly indicate possible links with character analysis as well.

The Authoritarian versus the Democratic Personality

One of the personality distinctions on which there is a fair amount of data is that developed by Horkheimer and his associates in Germany in the 1930's and elaborated by Adorno and his associates in the United States in the 1950's. This is the distinction between the authoritarian and the democratic personality.[9] On the basis of these writings and others in this field, Inkeles has summarized this distinction as follows:

> The . . . [democratic person] should be accepting of others rather than alienated and harshly rejecting; open to new experiences, to ideas and impulses rather than excessively timid, fearful, or extremely conventional with regard to new ideas and ways of acting; able to be responsible with constituted authority even though always watchful, rather than blindly submissive to or hostilely rejecting of all authority; tolerant of differences and of ambiguity, rather than rigid and inflexible; able to recognize, control and channel his emotions, rather than immaturely projecting hostility and other impulses on to others.[10]

Inkeles cites, among other studies, one by D. V. McGranahan which secured attitude responses from comparable groups of German and American boys.[11] The Germans were much more likely to favor obedience to authority, to admire people with power, and to have less faith in the common man. Another comparative study of college students in a number of countries reported that the Japanese were high among various nationals in their sense of obligation to the group, and in feeling that children should learn the need for service to society. Conversely, Ameri-

---

[9] See Horkheimer, ed., *Studien über Authorität und Familie;* and T. W. Adorno, Else Frenkel-Brunswick, Daniel J. Levinson, and R. Nevitt Sanford, *The Authoritarian Personality* (New York: Harper & Bros., 1950).

[10] Inkeles, "National Character and Modern Political Systems," *op. cit.,* p. 198.

[11] Donald V. McGranahan, "A Comparison of Social Attitudes among American and German Youth," *Journal of Abnormal and Social Psychology,* 41 (1946), pp. 245–257.

cans and New Zealanders emphasized "rights rather than duties," and stressed individuality and privacy.[12]

A comparison of German and English boys' answers to a projective test also suggests differences between the two national characters along the lines outlined by Inkeles' definition of the democratic as opposed to the authoritarian person. The German boys were most likely to dislike *cowards*, whereas English boys were most likely to dislike *bullies*, ruffians, and girls. The German boys were in almost complete agreement in seeing corporal punishment as the only sequence to an offense, whereas English boys showed greater flexibility, sometimes trying "to fit the punishment to the crime." In general, there was a marked tendency toward conventionalism and rigidity in the German boys' answers, whereas the English boys seemed to "allow more free play to their imaginations."[13]

A comparison between German and American popular plays also suggests that "the needs, assumptions and values" expressed in the drama of the two nations differ along these same dimensions. Thus the greatest percentage of German plays analyzed are concerned with idealism and power whereas the greatest percentage of American plays are concerned with love and morality. As the authors point out:

> . . . the German plays are strikingly more preoccupied with social and political problems than are the American plays. Their level of action is primarily ideological. . . . The problems portrayed in the American plays, on the other hand, are overwhelmingly personal. . . . The German ideological emphasis is obviously tied up closely with the emphasis on the idealism theme.[14]

As a result, the American hero is seen as struggling against immoral or anti-social tendencies in himself, whereas the German hero rises above the masses in pursuit of an ideal goal. American plays are often climaxed by a marshaling of evidence that causes the hero to change his attitude;

---

[12] James M. Gillespie and Gordon W. Allport, *Youth's Outlook on the Future: A Cross-National Study* (Garden City, N.Y.: Doubleday, 1955), p. 29.

[13] A. Kaldegg, "Responses of German and English Secondary School Boys to a Projective Test," *British Journal of Psychology*, 39 (1948), p. 51. (Emphasis in original.)

[14] Donald V. McGranahan and Ivor Wayne, "A Comparative Study of National Characteristics," in James Grier Miller, ed., *Experiments in Social Process* (New York: McGraw-Hill, 1950), p. 112.

German plays are often resolved through an exercise of power, since the characters are usually portrayed as inflexible and uncompromising.

But if these and other studies are suggestive of a relationship between the social requirements of political systems and the model, if not the dominant, cluster of personal traits of its citizens, the evidence to justify this conclusion is far from in.

If we assume with Inkeles that what he calls the democratic personality facilitates the stabilization of democratic institutions and reduces the potential appeal which extremist tendencies may have, then it is necessary to posit the aspects of the social structure which are conducive to the predominance of such traits. Psychological analysis confirms that in large measure such traits are derivative from childhood experiences, particularly parent–child relationships.[15] In its extreme form we have the conclusion of Ralph Linton that "nations with authoritarian family structure inevitably seem to develop authoritarian governments, no matter what their official government forms may be."[16] Such conclusions are clearly unwarranted by any substantial body of data. They do point, however, to the need to relate the types of family structures and child-rearing experiences found under different systems of stratification and value orientations to the ability of people to adapt to the operation of a democratic polity, with its inherent need for the toleration of differences.

It would be in line with the general approach being discussed here to argue that American children have more "democratic" characters—in the sense that they have a greater independence of mind and tolerance for ambiguity—than do the children in Europe, since there is less stress on home discipline in the United States.[17] Some of the direct evidence available would seem to support this contention. For instance, Maurice Farber's study comparing British and American attitudes toward socialization

---

[15] A questionnaire study based on a Swedish sample reports that "significant positive correlations were also found between authoritarianism of upbringing and authoritarianism of both political and child-rearing attitudes." R. H. Willis, "Political and Child-Rearing Attitudes in Sweden," *Journal of Abnormal and Social Psychology*, 53 (1956), p. 77.

[16] Ralph Linton, "The Concept of National Character," in Alfred H. Stanton and Stewart E. Perry, eds., *Personality and Political Crisis* (Glencoe, Ill.: The Free Press, 1951), p. 146.

[17] Ralph Linton argues: "It seems highly improbable that any totalitarian type of organization could be made to operate in the United States for any length of time. The average American is reared with little respect for his parents' authority and finds this attitude reinforced by a general indifference or hostility toward government." *Loc. cit.*

(cited earlier), shows that in bringing up children the British try to "suppress those impulses which are socially disturbing," whereas the American pattern aims at developing the skills required to succeed.[18] It could be argued that this difference reflects national personality differences as demonstrated in the variations in the mosaics that British and American children construct when subjected to psychological tests. British children are much more likely than American children to construct "abstract, symmetrical, balanced, conventional patterns," whereas even when American children construct this type of pattern "it is much more apt to show a color or piece variant which breaks its symmetrical perfection."[19] And British youth, in turn, are seemingly less rigid than German youth. These variations among the psychological responses of American, British, and German young people would appear to agree with the hypothesis that national personality traits and political systems are closely related. Such a conclusion would be unwarranted, however. British values, for example, emphasize more rigid family authority relations than do American—but, as we have seen, the greater British acceptance of elitism also fosters a viable parliamentary democracy!

Could we say, however, that there is some minimum level of so-called democratic traits that are requisite in "national character" for a nation successfully to develop a democratic polity? The French case suggests that even this relating of the degree to which "democratic" traits are prevalent to a polity's democratic potential is too simple. French youth fall somewhere between British and American personality responses along a continuum between individual free expression and traditional ways of thinking. While insisting that the child copy pre-existing models in order to train his mind, the French school also encourages individual thinking and the development of *l'esprit critique*.[20] The object is not so much to suppress impulses as to train them. And although discipline is strict in the French family, the father takes more of a supervising than a strictly authoritarian role.[21] "Democratic" traits do show up in tests of French national character; but France has not been able to develop a viable democracy. Thus, simply ranking polities according to the degree to which "democratic" traits are prevalent does not tell us much about the necessary conditions for successful democratic institutions.

---

[18] Farber, "English and American Values . . . ," *op. cit.*, pp. 245–246.

[19] U. Steward and L. Leland, "American versus English Mosaics," *Journal of Projective Techniques*, 16 (1952), pp. 246–248.

[20] Metraux and Mead, *Themes in French Culture*, pp. 32–35.

[21] *Ibid.*, pp. 16–18.

Since similar family and educational structures are to be found in both stable and unstable democracies, the question clearly arises whether a democratic system requires "democratic personalities." If we recognize, as the previous chapters have argued, that stable democracy is possible under varying value systems and kinds of hierarchical relationships, it is probable that the kind of personality most congruent with any given political structure varies, not with the political structure itself, but rather with *the value system* of that political structure. The modal personality response which encourages democratic stability in a society emphasizing the values of achievement and equality may be very different from the one best related to a social system organized around ascriptive and elitist norms.[22] For instance, an emphasis on respect for authority and the need for discipline can conceivably be linked to the absence of organized expressions of populist intolerance, as in Sweden or Switzerland. But similar emphases on home discipline in the German context are frequently cited as being causally related to the supposed propensity for political authoritarianism of many Germans.

Research in this as yet underdeveloped area of political inquiry will be considerably strengthened if it continues with the recognition that highly different social structures and value systems are congruent with stable democracy or authoritarianism, and that varying ways of organizing social systems around different value patterns may each be related to different modal personality characteristics.

The Inner-directed versus the Other-directed Personality

There has also been considerable discussion in the last decade on the way in which value patterns affect the propensity of citizens of various societies to exhibit "inner" or "other" directed behavioral or personality traits. These distinctions of David Riesman, discussed in Chapter 3, refer to the sources of individual goals. As we have seen, Riesman suggests that the inner-directed individual has his goals implanted in him from strict disciplinary parents, has internalized these goals, and works toward them relatively protected from the "buffetings of his external environment." In contrast, the other-directed person has been led by different socialization processes to find his source of direction from his contemporaries; as

---

[22] Eckstein, *A Theory of Stable Democracy*, suggests, in effect, that societies with more authoritarian social relations require a more "authoritarian" form of democracy than those with more equalitarian patterns of behavior.

their "signals" shift, so do his goals.[23] (For purposes of this discussion, the issue of whether or not the reactions subsumed under these headings are deeply rooted in personality is irrelevant.)

Earlier I attempted to demonstrate that there is a causal relationship between an emphasis on achievement and equalitarianism *and* other-directedness, together with the converse proposition, that inner-directed behavior is more prevalent in ascriptive and elitist oriented societies. Specifically, I argued that the achievement-equalitarian pattern results in a stratification system which denies stable status, and that the consequent acute status anxiety presses people to behave in an other-directed manner. Conversely, ascription and elitism reduce the need to propitiate others in order to establish or perpetuate a claim to high esteem.

These behavioral or personality constructs may be linked to a specification of the functional requisites for democracy, since democracy obviously entails a great deal of bargaining and compromise, behavior which seems more in line with other-directedness than with inner-directedness. Hence, the effect of a stress on achievement and equalitarianism, together with the growth of bureaucracy and urbanism—factors which Reisman suggests increase other-directedness—would seem to strengthen the conditions for democracy. However, this conclusion seems less obvious when we consider the implications of a purely other-directed populace attempting to function in a consensual-decision process. Such a populace would be engaged in an endless search for approval and for direction, a situation conducive to high anxiety and great anomic potentialities on the level of the total population, and to weak leadership on the elite level. It is this supposed emphasis in American society on other-directedness that leads Riesman to suggest that power in America is fragmented and is characterized by interaction among various "veto-groups." He argues that the American elites are so concerned with the need for approval that they are inhibited from acting in ways that will be opposed by a significant segment of the polity. Democracy requires conflict as well as consensus, and other-directed man is incapable of participating in sustained real conflict, in taking positions that will make him unpopular.

Ralf Dahrendorf, in a perceptive essay on this very problem of the

[23] See *The Lonely Crowd* (New Haven, Conn.: Yale University Press, 1950). An excellent experimental study which indicates that these concepts actually correspond to deep-rooted personality traits is reported by Elaine Graham Sofer, "Inner-Direction, Other-Direction, and Autonomy: A Study of College Students," in S. M. Lipset and Leo Lowenthal, eds., *Culture and Social Character* (New York: The Free Press, 1961), pp. 316–348.

viability of democracy in a country of other-directed citizens, puts the matter even more strongly.[24] He points out that in modern democracies a considerable amount of political power is lodged in the governmental bureaucracy. This bureaucracy, which maintains itself through the vicissitudes of changing political parties and leaderships, structurally requires someone to provide it with policies which it can then administer. If, as is likely in an other-directed society, such a leader, or group of leaders, cannot be found in the prevailing political parties, they will be found elsewhere, possibly in totalitarian parties.

The inner-directed man, if he is sufficiently aware of his own long-run interests, and if he has internalized the rules of the game, would seem better able to fulfill the role requirements for democratic citizens and leaders. Inner-direction, however, also posits some problems for democracy. Decision-making within a group or society predominantly composed of such types is apt to be a painfully slow process. Perhaps even more significant, the purely inner-directed type, if he existed, would have difficulty in adjusting his values to encompass the span between the situation in which he internalized them and that in which he is called upon to apply them.

Indeed, one could argue that the French electorate find the pragmatic compromises necessary to maintain a populist democracy difficult precisely because they are more inner-directed than Americans. The socialization of the French child, in comparison to that of the American child, seems conducive to greater inner direction. As a French child analyst has put it: "The French child must constantly 'prepare his future'; he must not have fun because he must learn how to live."[25] French parents mediate the child's contact with the world outside the family and discourage those contacts with his peers that the child seeks out on his own.[26] This practice is justified by the argument that before setting out on his own a child must be taught "good habits (*les bonnes habitudes*) and given education (*education, formation*) and training (*instruction*) in the specific

---

[24] Ralf Dahrendorf, "Democracy without Liberty: An Essay on the Politics of Other-directed Man," in S. M. Lipset and Leo Lowenthal, eds., *Culture and Social Character* (New York: The Free Press, 1961), pp. 175–206.

[25] Francoise Dolto, "French and American Children as Seen by a French Child Analyst," in Margaret Mead and Martha Wolfenstein, eds., *Childhood in Contemporary Cultures* (Chicago: University of Chicago Press, 1956), pp. 408–423.

[26] Martha Wolfenstein, "French Parents Take Their Children to the Park," in M. Mead and M. Wolfenstein, eds., *Childhood in Contemporary Cultures* (Chicago: University of Chicago Press, 1956), pp. 300–305.

skills on which the achievement of individuality and adulthood depend. Thereafter they are able to make reasonable choices, to elaborate in their own way upon what they already are; they are formed."[27]

However, the difference between the fostering of inner direction in French and American socialization practices can be only a matter of degree. As in the case of the pattern variables, the personality or behavioral constructs of inner- and other-directed men cannot and do not involve any assumption that men or groups are entirely one or the other. Clearly, noone who reacted wholly in the way assumed by one or the other type could function. The matter at issue at any time is the extent to which the socialization process or structural conditions press men to behave more like one polar type than the other. Requisite to the functioning of a political democracy are citizens (and especially political leaders) who are sufficiently inner-directed to sustain a desired policy direction, and to have internalized a strong valuation of certain rules of the game. However, they should be sufficiently other-directed to be willing to re-examine their premises when faced with the disapproval of others, to perceive needed adjustments and compromises, and to make these without experiencing traumatic psychological disturbances.[28]

To prescribe the type of social structure which would produce the optimum ratio between "inner" and "other" directedness is clearly impossible. The very notion of optimum ratio is itself merely an analytic construct: every social and political system will be somewhat different. If we assume, however, the need to "protect" individuals from constant concern with what others think of them, then a certain degree of ascription–particularism–diffuseness–elitism is necessary. This conclusion relates back to the previous discussion of the conditions which would inhibit the destructive tendencies of populist contempt for due process. To

---

[27] Metraux and Mead, *Themes in French Culture*, p. 27.

[28] In a perceptive essay which attempts to find implications of personality typologies for political and social science, Robert Lane suggests that "other-direction" is functional in a pluralist society such as the contemporary United States, while "inner-direction" best fits the political needs of a non-pluralistic democracy, that is, one in which the citizenry is relatively "atomized" and not linked to the polity by identification with various secondary, mediating institutions. In the latter situation, supposedly characteristic of the early days of the American Republic, strong ·moral attitudes dictated political participation and concern; pluralism, however, has too many sources of conflict among the various organizations and interest groups to operate well if those involved in such groups all feel they must win—or else. See "Political Character and Political Analysis," *Psychiatry*, 16 (1953), pp. 387–398.

avoid the excesses which may be perceived as inherent in populism and in other-direction, mechanisms are necessary which will limit the dependence of the politically relevant elites upon the day-to-day fluctuations in mass opinion. And in addition to such mechanisms the normative processes required seem derivative from the same value patterns.

But while efforts to relate national character to the characteristics of the polity—such as those discussed here—should be encouraged, it must be noted that any attempt closely to link personality and child-rearing patterns to the political or other macroscopic structures of so complex and differentiated a unit as a nation, must fail. Talcott Parsons has well stressed the point that "no social system is really well integrated or fully integrated. There is no neat one-to-one correspondence between social structure and personality; the social system has to be seen as a functioning system . . . dynamically changing and dynamically interacting with its individual members, not only in an early child-training period but throughout their lives."[29]

---

[29] Talcott Parsons, "Personality and Social Structure," in Alfred H. Stanton and Stewart E. Perry, eds., *Personality and Political Crisis* (Glencoe, Ill.: The Free Press, 1951), p. 65.

Party Systems and the Representation of Social Groups

9

★★

Thus far in this book, I have largely stressed the influence of national value systems on specific institutions. This form of "sociological determinism" is properly subject to the criticism that it ignores ways in which men may change their society and its values by changing its structure. We know that men may modify their conditions of existence by changing the laws which govern them, a process which may be the first step on the road to changing values. So I would like to bring to a close this analysis of the relation of values to the stability of American and other polities by pointing out ways in which the governmental institutions of the polity itself may affect stability. The conclusion of this discussion returns to some of the issues raised in the first section of the book, the factors which affect the polity formed in new nations.

We have had major extremist social movements in this country, of which the Know Nothing Party and the Ku Klux Klan are perhaps the most extreme, but among which must be included Abolitionism, Populism, Prohibitionism, and the like. Although some of these movements have become organized into political parties, they have never been able to sustain themselves, and their programs have been dependent upon endorsement by one of the major political parties for influence in the national power arena. To a considerable degree one must recognize that the failure of these and other movements, such as the Socialist, to create viable third parties which would change the political system is as much a consequence of the legal structure of the polity as it is of elements in the value system or of the distribution of wealth.

In order to generalize about the significance of a nation's constitutional system in stabilizing its polity, we need concepts which permit us to distinguish the role played by the legal structure from the effect of various social forces within the polity. A step in this direction has been taken by Talcott Parsons.[1] He has argued that the polity can be seen as providing generalized leadership for the larger social system in setting and attaining collective goals, and that this is acknowledged by interested social groups who supply generalized support in the expectation of "a good life," as they understand it. Within this polity, a variety of social groups form and advocate the particular policies that eventually result in the specific decisions of public officers, which then become binding on all citizens. The competitive struggle within the elite, sometimes for generalized but usually for specific support, gives those outside the authority structure *access* to political power.

This process works through the representation system.[2] It is given shape by those institutional practices which have been developed in democratic societies—notably party systems and interest organizations—to facilitate interchange between authority and the spontaneous groupings of society. This internal differentiation produces its own power structure and its own problems of integration, which within limits may also affect the stability of the polity.

Within the representative system, some of the aspirations of the subgroups in the society are transformed into demands; these demands are then killed, compromised, or magnified into issues that are fed into the authority system as party policies or as the detailed recommendations of interest groups. Inchoate loyalties are turned into organized support. Thus the system provides grist for the political mill and also some of the power that drives it, depending upon how far the polity derives its effectiveness and legitimacy from organized support.

---

[1] Talcott Parsons, "Voting and the Equilibrium of the American Political System," in Eugene Burdick and Arthur Brodbeck, eds., *American Voting Behavior* (Glencoe, Ill.: The Free Press, 1959), pp. 80–120; see also William Mitchell, *The American Polity* (New York: The Free Press, 1963).

[2] For a comprehensive summary of definitions, see John A. Fairlie, "The Nature of Political Representation," *The American Political Science Review*, 34 (1940), pp. 236–248, 456–466; for articles dealing with various aspects of the system, see Harry Eckstein and David E. Apter, eds., *Comparative Politics* (New York: The Free Press, 1963), pp. 97–132.

On the other hand, the representative system also receives information and public policy commitments from the authority structure wherein decisions are reached and implemented. These in turn shape the demands within the system, and legitimate the leadership and domination. This "input" from the side of authority may be general (political leadership at various levels, party discipline) or specific (electoral laws, regulation of the lobby), suppressing some demands, raising others into issues, and enforcing compromise. Into the social base the political system puts the political education of citizens and the political consciousness of groups. Whether or not these have consequences that are functional for the polity as a whole depends largely upon the form and working of the representative structure.

Viewed in this way, representation is neither simply a means of political adjustment to social pressures nor an instrument of manipulation. It may contribute to the maintenance or dissolution of primary ties, to the perception of common or diverse interests, to the socialization or alienation of elites, to the effectiveness or feebleness of the polity in attaining societal goals, and to the political unity or incoherence of society as a whole. This chapter will consider some aspects of the behavior of social groups in politics, taking into account the political alternatives which face the electorates of different countries, with special reference to the ways in which various party systems organize and affect their social bases. It is not primarily concerned with the *differentials* between power wielded by various social groups, nor will economic variables be given much prominence. Its aim is to show how certain combinations of relationships between parties and social bases contribute to the possibility of stable and efficient government.

Parties are by far the most important part of the representative structure in complex democratic societies. Such societies show some variation in the salience of particular solidary groupings as the source of demands and support; but generally, under contemporary industrial conditions, the stratification system has been the prime source of sustained internal cleavage—classes have been the most important bases of political diversity.[3]

The character and number of the political parties in a country are

---

[3] They, of course, are far from being the only important such bases. Others, such as religious, ethnic, or linguistic groups, regions, and rural–urban groupings, have formed the basis for separate parties or differential backings for particular parties. For a detailed discussion of the way in which different groups have varied in support for parties in different democratic countries, see S. M. Lipset, *Political Man: The Social Bases of Politics* (Garden City, N.Y.: Doubleday, 1960), pp. 228–282.

perhaps the chief determinants of the extent to which the government acts through a stable system of interchanges between the key solidary groups and the political elite. Discussions of the causes and consequences of diverse party systems often turn upon the question of whether it is social structure or electoral arrangements that mainly determine the different types. Some argue that the character and number of parties flow almost directly from the social cleavages in a country; others have claimed that the electoral system in use—proportional representation or the single-member district plurality method—has been the main source of stability or instability in democracies. On the whole, this is a sham dispute. There is no reason to believe either that social cleavage creates political cleavage, or that political cleavage will give rise to social controversies. As Maurice Duverger has said: "The party system and the electoral system are two realities that are indissolubly linked, and even difficult sometimes to separate by analysis."[4]

Social Structure and the Character of the Party System

The representative system may be said to have a singular influence on the stability of the polity only when the economic and social conditions for stable democracy that I have described in the previous chapters (and in my *Political Man*) have been taken into account. Yet, paradoxically, these conditions affect the workings of the democracy precisely through their influence on the representative system. The ability of a democratic political system to win or retain the support of different solidary group-ings depends largely on whether all the major parties already accept democratic principles. If some parties reject the system, it may break down even if democracy is favored by a substantial majority.

---

[4] Maurice Duverger, *Political Parties* (London: Methuen, 1954), p. 204. Duverger's book, however, is the best recent effort to demonstrate the causal effect of electoral systems. A sophisticated critique of Duverger and the general emphasis on electoral systems may be found in G. E. Lavau, *Partis politiques et réalités sociales* (Paris: Armand Colin, 1953); see also Aaron Wildavsky, "A Methodological Critique of Duverger's *Political Parties*," in Eckstein and Apter, *Comparative Politics*, pp. 368–375. There is a comprehensive statement of all the arguments for and against proportional representation in Alfred De Grazia, *Public and Republic* (New York: Alfred A. Knopf, 1951). A good general discussion of the theory of electoral systems is D. Hogan, *Election and Representation* (Cork: Cork University Press, 1945). Differing analyses and points of view are reprinted in Eckstein and Apter, eds., *Comparative Politics*, pp. 247–324.

The evidence seems quite clear that stable democracies are largely to be found in more well-to-do nations, where greater wealth is associated with patterns which reduce internal tension—for example, more equal distribution of income and of education, less emphasis on barriers between classes, and the existence of a relatively large middle class. In addition, the stability of democratic systems depends upon the extent to which they have retained or developed legitimacy, a "believed-in title to rule," for the political elite. Such legitimacy, as we have seen, has been most secure where the society could admit the lower strata to full citizenship and to the rights of participation in the economic and political systems, and could at the same time allow the traditionally privileged strata to keep their high status while yielding their power.

But if legitimacy and economic development define the boundaries within which political conflict occurs, there nevertheless remains great variation in the nature of party systems. Why do they take so many different forms? I have suggested that to some extent this depends upon the ways in which varying combinations of value orientations have permeated the attitudes toward stratification in a nation. The basic (and obvious) fact is that the more clear-cut the status demarcation lines in a country, the more likely there exist explicitly strata-oriented parties. The failure of Canada and the United States to develop a major working-class party, and the relative stability of their democratic systems, may be partially explained by the difficulty of developing a working-class political consciousness where no rigid status groups already existed to create a perception of common interests. On the European continent, workers were placed in a common class by the value system of the society, and they absorbed a political "consciousness of kind" from the social structure. Marxists did not have to teach European workers that they formed a class; the ascriptive values of the society did it for them.

In the English-speaking parts of the Commonwealth, Labour parties have been class oriented and class based, yet much less imbued with class feeling than those of continental Europe, as is shown by their early willingness to cooperate with bourgeois parties, and their consistent opposition to Marxist and revolutionary ideology. The absence of a base for intense class conflict is also affirmed by the bent toward a two-party system which has characterized their politics, since inherent in a two-party system is the need for cooperation among diverse strata. In Australia and New Zealand, this pattern may be explained, as it can in Canada and the United States, by the absence of feudal tradition. In Britain, the weakness of working-class extremism is often attributed to the country having borne the early tensions of industrialization before the rise of modern socialism, and, after the working-class movement had appeared, to its prosperity. On the other hand, as I have argued in Chapter 6, the uniquely "open" and "responsible" character of the British aristocracy enabled it to retain power and influence late into the capitalist period, thus helping to soften the antagonism of the working classes to the state and to society.[5]

The great emphasis on status differentiation in Germany may also have been responsible for the large number of middle- and upper-class parties, each representing a distinct status group on a national or regional basis and each possessing its own ideology, which existed in pre-Nazi Germany.[6] Similarly, it has been suggested that the relative failure of the German Socialists to gain rural backing, and their weakness among the poorer urban working class, reflected the hostility of the better paid and more skilled workers, who dominated the movement, toward other depressed segments of the population such as the so-called *Lumpenproletariat*—a hostility which has not existed in other countries.[7] The split within the working class between Socialists and Communists in Weimar Germany was also partly due to this status consciousness of the skilled workers in the Social-Democratic Party, who left the more depressed sector to be recruited by the Communists. Robert Michels has pointed out how their sense of superiority was reflected in party literature, which attacked the Communists by arguing that their supporters were largely the shiftless *Lumpenproletariat*.[8]

The failure of the multi-party system based on distinct and rigid status groups to revive in the Federal Republic is due to a number of causes.[9] Fundamentally, it reflects the weakening of the old status structure during

---

[5] Joseph Schumpeter, *Capitalism, Socialism and Democracy* (New York: Harper & Bros., 1947), pp. 134–139.

[6] Sigmund Neumann, *Die deutschen Parteien: Wesen und Wandel nach dem Kriege* (Berlin: Junder und Dunnhaupt, 1932); Theodor Geiger, *Die soziale Schichtung des deutschen Volkes* (Stuttgart: Ferdinand Enke, 1932), p. 79.

[7] See Robert Michels, "Die deutschen Sozialdemokratie, I: Parteimitgliedschaft und soziale Zusammensetzung," *Archiv für Sozialwissenschaft und Sozialpolitik*, 26 (1906), pp. 512–513; Robert Lowie, *Toward Understanding Germany* (Chicago: University of Chicago Press, 1954), p. 138. For detailed evidence that the contemporary German Social-Democratic Party remains weak among the less skilled, a pattern which remains almost unique among left parties, see Lipset, *Political Man*, pp. 240–241.

[8] Robert Michels, *Sozialismus und Fascismus I* (Karlsruhe: G. Braun, 1925), pp. 78–79.

[9] It is interesting to note that in 1918 Max Weber believed that there were four parties "structurally inherent within German Society: a conservative, a democratic [liberal], a socialist, and a Catholic party." J. P. Mayer, *Max Weber and German Politics* (London: Faber and Faber, 1956), p. 101.

the Nazi and wartime upheavals and the final blow delivered by the end of Prussian domination. Partition removed from view the glaring inequalities of the east and destroyed the stronghold from which the Junkers had dominated the army and defied the Weimar Republic; simultaneously, the greater homogeneity of western Germany now became a national homogeneity, reinforced by the economic growth which strengthened the achievement values of a profoundly bourgeois culture.[10] This homogeneity seems to be expressed in a genuine, if rather skeptical, consensus, rejecting both the Nazi past and the Communist alternative, and more easily accepted by a generation maturing in an era of expansion when the old ruling groups play little part either as authority or model. Its political manifestation is an interest-group structure much like that of Britain, thoroughly interlaced with the party system, and bringing with it an increasing political professionalism. The former bearers of ideology—the intellectuals, the jurists, and the bureaucrats—have largely abdicated their special role under the *Rechtsstaat*, and a pragmatic approach has replaced the old emphasis upon the objective rationality of the expert. The Social-Democratic Party has more and more disowned its Marxist heritage, and the interdenominational Christianity of the Christian Democratic Union is more a catch-all than an ideology. The accompanying bureaucratization of the two major parties had led to a pattern of occasional, mediated participation by the ordinary citizen in politics, which is generally regarded as a major source of both stability and flexibility in modern democratic electorates.

These general causes were supplemented by the circumstances attending the birth of the present parties. The power to make certain major decisions was retained by the occupying forces until the early 1950's, which restricted the scope of political contention. The parties called into existence by the Allies in 1946 to fill the political vacuum became, as Dolf Sternberger has put it, like "stakes rammed into a swamp," and were able to give shape to most of the emerging tendencies. This position was consolidated by the subsequent modifications of proportional representation, by the legal restrictions upon extremist parties, and by the statesmanship of Adenauer. In particular, the stability of the parties has been aided by their ascendancy over the bureaucracy. The acceptance by civil servants of the constitution and the parties as legitimate is largely a product of the social changes mentioned above and the political stability resulting from them; it is symbolized, and also advanced, by the practice of staffing top

---

[10] See Karl W. Deutsch and Lewis J. Edinger, *Germany Rejoins the Powers* (Stanford, Calif.: Stanford University Press, 1959), pp. 35–47.

civil service positions below the ministerial level with political appointees.[11]

The discussion so far has sketched some of the conditions under which support will be available for *different kinds* of political leadership. But the number and nature of political parties, the claims they stake out, and the policies they advocate, do not result automatically from underlying social cleavages. Political systems possess a certain (varying) autonomy within the larger social system, and it is appropriate to ask how the restraints imposed by the political order itself affect the capacity of parties to provide generalized leadership in different countries.

Social Structure and Electoral Systems

Concern with formal constitutional provisions has generally been outside the province of political sociology. Sociologists tend to see party cleavages as reflections of an underlying structure, and hence, wittingly or not, frown on efforts to present the enacted rules of the game as key *causal* elements of a social structure. The sociologist's image of a social system, all of whose parts are interdependent, is at odds with the view of many political scientists, who believe that such seemingly minor differences in systems as variations in the way in which officials are elected can lead to stability or instability. An examination of comparative politics suggests that the political scientists are right, in that electoral laws determine the nature of the party system as much as any other structural variable.

The available evidence gathered together by political scientists such as E. E. Schattschneider, F. A. Hermens, Maurice Duverger, and many others indicates that proportional representation encourages the appearance or continuance of more relatively large parties than does the plurality system, in which the candidate receiving the most votes in an electoral unit is elected. Wherever we find a two-party system working (wherever the usual situation is the alternating control of government by one of two parties, with an over-all majority of representatives) we find also an electoral system which debars from representation in government those parties which cannot win a plurality of votes in a geographical election district. On the other hand, every country which uses proportional representation has four or more parties represented in the legislature and, except in Norway, Sweden, and Ireland in recent decades, absolute parliamentary majorities of one party have been extremely rare.

---

[11] See Otto Kirchheimer, "The Political Scene in West Germany," *World Politics*, 9 (1957), pp. 433–445, and the sources cited there.

If enough cases existed for analysis, the following rank-order correlation might be found between electoral systems and the number of political parties: presidential system with single-member districts and one plurality election—two parties; parliamentary system with single-member districts and one plurality election—tendency to two parties; parliamentary system with single-member districts and alternative ballot or run-off (second) election—tendency to many parties; proportional representation—many parties.

The thesis that the plurality system tends to produce or maintain a two-party system needs some qualification. Groups centered in distinct regions or political units may gain representation, and may sometimes influence policy, within such systems, even where cabinet government is conducted by means of a parliamentary majority. In Great Britain, Parnell's Irish party was able to hold its own in the House of Commons during the latter part of the nineteenth century through solid regional support. The initial growth of socialist parties in European countries with single-member districts depended on their winning in solidly working-class constituencies, just as various ethnic parties have achieved regional support in India, and from time to time agrarian "third parties" have won considerable backing in the more rural provinces of Canada.

But the requirement of ecological isolation limits the type of third party which can succeed in a two-party system with single-member districts. It must possess a strong appeal to a homogeneous part of the population whose residential areas correspond to electoral units. The problem which this poses is illustrated by the British Liberal Party, which, according to some public opinion studies, would secure as much as 25 per cent of the national vote in a parliamentary election under proportional representation, where every vote counted. The existing single-member districts reduce the Liberals to impotence, since their appeal is not to groups which dominate electoral districts but to a large middle-class sector which is usually in a minority in every constituency. This not only keeps the Liberals out of Parliament but deprives them of most of their votes, since many prospective Liberals prefer to vote for the lesser of two electable evils. To take another case, all efforts to form third parties in the United States have proved futile because the effective constituency in national elections is really the entire country, and in state elections the entire state is the effective constituency. The emphasis on presidential or gubernatorial elections has prevented American third parties from building up local constituency strength as labor, agrarian, religious, or ethnic parties have done in some other single-member constituency systems.[12] As evidence for this view, third parties have gained their greatest strength in municipal or occasionally state elections, and have almost invariably lost strength in subsequent presidential elections. The American Socialist Party attained its greatest electoral success in municipal elections and actually captured the government of a number of cities. Its high point as an electoral force was in the municipal elections of 1917, in which it attained an average vote of 20 per cent in a number of major cities.[13] In general, American third parties have been much more successful in Congressional elections conducted in non-presidential election years than in those in which a president was also being elected.

Recognition of the inability to create a new national party has led many American leftists, who would have preferred a new radical party, to operate as factions within one of the old parties, and at different times since 1920 socialist or near-socialist groups have either controlled or greatly influenced one of the two major parties in a large number of states.

The motives underlying the electorate's refusal to sustain third parties, in systems where the candidate with the most votes is elected and where third parties are effectively barred from representation, have been analyzed in detail in the numerous studies of electoral systems, and I will not discuss them here. Essentially, polarization between two parties is maintained by those factors which lead people to see a third party vote as a "wasted vote."[14]

Party Systems and the Bases of Social Cleavage

The interrelated effects of electoral systems and social cleavages may be seen in a comparison of the party systems in different parts of the British Commonwealth, in the United States, and in France.

There is general recognition that stable two-party government works

---

[12] The argument and best evidence for this thesis may be found in E. E. Schattschneider, *Party Government* (New York: Rinehart and Co., 1942), especially pp. 65–98.

[13] James Weinstein, "Anti-war Sentiment and the Socialist Party, 1917–1918," *Political Science Quarterly*, 74 (1959), pp. 223–239; Paul H. Douglas, "The Socialist Vote in the 1917 Municipal Elections," *National Municipal Review*, 7 (1918), pp. 131–139.

[14] See Duverger, *Political Parties*, pp. 224–228, 246–250; and E. E. Schattschneider, *Party Government*, pp. 80–84.

"best in Great Britain. Members of Parliament are elected in single-member constituencies in which one factor—class position—is the basic source of political difference.[15] Differences based on regions, religious or ethnic allegiances, urban–rural conflicts, or past historical feuds are unimportant or affect groups too small to organize on their own behalf. But if two-party government presents its best and simplest face in Britain, multi-party government has created the most difficult and complicated conditions in France. Until the Gaullist presidential system began to press the French parties together, France had at least six important political groupings, in addition to some minor ones. For many decades it has been divided between clericals and anti-clericals, supporters and opponents of a planned economy, and supporters and opponents of parliamentary government, with a few rural–urban and regional cleavages as well. Table VII shows the ways these differences have been reflected in French party life during the period from 1955 to 1963.[16]

Before De Gaulle created a presidency directly elected by the people, France appeared to be a country whose social fragmentation dictated the need for a multi-party system, whatever electoral laws were in force. The fact remains, however, that the various parliamentary electoral systems in use throughout most of the history of the Third, Fourth, and Fifth republics encouraged the creation or perpetuation of small parties. The experiences of Britain and France, standing near the extremes of stable and unstable government, might suggest that the nature of group differences is the key to the number of parties in a system; yet even for these nations this conclusion may be questioned. Since the development of adult suffrage, Britain has never had a *pure* two-party system. In the late nineteenth century there was a strong Irish third party; before World War I, four parties were represented in the Commons: the Liberals, the

---

[15] "British politics are almost wholly innocent of those issues which cross the social lines in other lands, for example, race, nationality, religion, town and country interests, regional interest, or the conflict between authoritarian and parliamentary methods." See John Bonham, *The Middle Class Vote* (London: Faber and Faber, 1954), pp. 194–195; and Leslie Lipson, "The Two-Party System in British Politics," *American Political Science Review*, 47 (1953), pp. 337–358.

[16] The table, of course, oversimplifies present divisions. Almost no political group in France is actually for a "free economy." The Gaullist government has continued and even extended the comprehensive system of planning begun under the Fourth Republic. This system, however, is a voluntary one; private industry need not conform, though the state has extensive powers through its ownership of banks, insurance companies, and many industries. Communist and Gaullist "anti-parliamentary" positions are quite different. The first favors a dictator; the second, an "American-type" president.

Table VII

Overlapping of Cleavages in France*

CLERICAL			
PLANNED ECONOMY		**FREE ECONOMY**	
Parliamentary	*Anti-Parliamentary*	*Parliamentary*	*Anti-Parliamentary*
M.R.P.		Independents	U.N.R.
(Catholics)	(left Gaullists)	(conservatives)	(Gaullists)

ANTI-CLERICAL			
PLANNED ECONOMY		**FREE ECONOMY**	
Parliamentary	*Anti-Parliamentary*	*Parliamentary*	*Anti-Parliamentary*
Socialists	Communists	Radicals	Poujadists†

* *Adapted from a somewhat similar diagram in Duverger,* Political Parties
(London: Methuen, 1954), p. 232.
† *Now practically dead.*

Conservatives, the Irish, and Labour; between 1918 and 1931 three major parties were represented; and since then the Liberal Party has remained a serious electoral force even though the plurality system minimizes its strength in Parliament.[17]

[17] For a detailed report on the issues and facts involved, see D. E. Butler, *The Electoral System in Britain 1918–1951* (New York: Oxford University Press, 1953). Though many argue from historical evidence that the British two-party system derives from particular national characteristics, since two parties or tendencies preceded the introduction of the present single-member constituency in the mid-nineteenth century, this argument also may be questioned. G. E. Lavau, *Partis politiques et réalités sociales,* has pointed out that the House of Commons had unstable majorities, with members shifting their support from government to opposition throughout much of the nineteenth century. Duverger contends that in France itself the contemporary complex political substructure was built "upon the fundamental conflict which dominated the nineteenth century, that between conservatives and liberals. . . . The principal actors were a landowning aristocracy, bound to monarchical principles . . . and, opposed to this aristocracy, an industrial, commercial and intellectual bourgeoisie, attracted to the principles of political liberty. . . . The first phase in the moulding of the prevailing spirit in modern Europe ended wth the appearance and development of the socialist parties. . . . Between 1900 and 1914, the bipartisan tendency which had dominated the preceding century was replaced everywhere by a swing towards tripartisanship; the 'conservative-liberal' duo now changed to a 'conservative-liberal-socialist' trio." Maurice Duverger, "Public Opinion and Political Parties in France," *American Political Science Review,* 46 (1952), p. 1070. See also Club Jean Moulin, *L'État et le citoyen* (Paris: Éditions du Seuil, 1961), pp. 249–253, 325–343.

French political history offers striking examples of the ways in which formal political institutions may decisively affect political cleavage, and therefore the stability of the democratic system. Despite deep-rooted social tensions and lack of consensus on fundamental political, religious, and economic issues, the Third Republic's electoral system diverted considerable support from the anti-democratic extremists. Its double ballot effectively stopped the French Communist Party from becoming a major force during this period. For after an auspicious start in 1921, supported by a majority of the former Socialist Party and controlling its principal newspaper, *L'Humanité*, it lost ground seemingly because it was unable to elect members to the Chamber. As a revolutionary party opposed to constitutional government, it could not combine with other parties for the decisive second ballot, so that many of its potential voters obviously returned to the Socialist fold. Thus in 1928, the Communists secured 11 per cent of the vote in the first ballot, but only 14 out of 600 seats. In the following election of 1932, held in the depths of the depression, the Communist first-ballot vote dropped to 8 per cent, and it elected less than 2 per cent of the representatives. Almost half the Communist first-ballot supporters backed candidates of other parties on the second ballot, though the Communists did not withdraw any candidates. Even Communist party discipline and the worst depression in history could not induce many voters to "waste" their ballots. Similarly, Maurice Duverger notes "the complete impossibility" for fascist and right-wing extremist movements "to obtain any representation in parliament," although there were many strong fascist groups during the 1930's.[18]

The Communists became a major force in French politics only after they pretended to give up their opposition to parliamentary government, and formed the Popular Front coalition with the Radicals and Socialists in 1936. This enabled them to increase their first-ballot percentage to 15.6, and their representation in the Chamber from 11 to 72.[19]

But if the Third Republic demonstrated how electoral rules may punish and inhibit parties which oppose the system, the Fourth Republic showed how different rules may facilitate the ruin of democracy by nourishing

---

[18] *Political Parties*, pp. 319–320; see also F. A. Hermens, *Europe between Democracy and Anarchy* (Notre Dame, Ind.: University of Notre Dame Press, 1951), pp. 41–44, and Club Jean Moulin, *L'État et le citoyen*, pp. 349–350.

[19] For a detailed account of the events leading up to this election as well as an analysis of the vote, see Georges Dupeux, *Le Front populaire et les élections de 1936* (Paris: Armand Colin, 1959).

such parties.[20] Throughout its history, the Fourth Republic employed different versions of proportional representation. Its last Parliament, elected in 1956, was hampered by the presence of 150 Communists and 50 Poujadists. The latter, who secured about 10 per cent of the vote, could probably have elected no candidates under the double ballot with single-member constituencies. The Fifth Republic, having returned to that system, elected only ten Communists and one Poujadist to its first Chamber and 40 Communists to its second. The Communist gains between 1958 and 1962 were largely a result of an informal electoral alliance with the Socialists. And for the first time in French history, the combination of a strong presidential system and the absence of proportional representation has given one tendency, the Gaullists, a parliamentary majority.

The United States and Canada offer a still more complex picture of the way in which party systems can be affected by the interrelationship between social cleavages and methods of election. For though two-party politics have predominated at the national level in both countries, it is clear that their solidarity structure is in some ways more like that of France than that of Britain. Both are divided along class, ethnic, religious, and regional lines, and while the chief issues for groups like the southern whites or the French Canadians tend to separate them from the rest of the nation, internally they remain sharply divided over non-ethnic questions.

It seems likely that if the United States had ever adopted proportional representation or even the second ballot run-off, it would have developed several main parties, such as the following: 1) a labor party, based on urban workers and perhaps on ethnic minorities outside the South; 2) a northern conservative party, based on the urban middle class and the higher-status ethnic and religious groups; 3) a southern conservative party,

---

[20] "It is especially important, in order to understand what the fundamental political problems of France actually are, to investigate why the state for too many years has seemed so completely powerless to hold the antagonisms and the divisions between the parties within reasonable bounds and to make the divergent forces act in concert for the general welfare. This raises the question of political institutions, the most important problem facing France. *The present difficulties in this sphere stem from the fact that the political institutions that were adopted in 1946 in no way satisfy the requirements of the economic, social, and political situation. . . .*" François Goguel, *France under the Fourth Republic* (Ithaca, N.Y.: Cornell University Press, 1952), p. 146. (Emphasis mine.)

comparable in support to the *ante-bellum* southern Whigs and Constitutional Unionists, i.e., the urban middle classes, and the more well-to-do rural whites; 4) a southern populist party, based on the lower white strata comparable to those who backed the Jacksonian Democrats in the 1830's and 1840's, Breckenridge and the secessionist Democrats in the election of 1860, and various "populist" parties and agrarian factions of the Democrats in the late nineteenth century; and 5) a farmer's party, based on rural elements outside the South. There would probably also have been a number of smaller parties from time to time.

Such differentiation has been prevented, not only by the disadvantages which the American presidential system lays on small parties, as discussed above, but also by the peculiar device of the party primary. This arrangement, by which different factions within the party may compete in state-conducted, intra-party contests to determine party candidates and officials, permits the interests and values of different groups, which elsewhere would give rise to separate parties, to be expressed within the major parties. First, the various groups have been forced by the electoral system to identify with one or the other of the two major blocs on whatever basis of division matters most to them;[21] then their differences are fought out within each party in the primaries, although they may often still lead to cross-party alliances in Congress afterward.

Few observers have been willing to recognize how comparable are the social bases for multiple parties in France and the United States, and how far the difference between them in political stability has been due to varying constitutional structures. The French two-ballot system may be regarded as a functional equivalent to the American primary elections. In both cases, different tendencies may compete in various ways up to the decisive final election. Thus, in most elections of the Third Republic, "at the first ballot few candidates could obtain an absolute majority, so that at this stage there was no fear of splitting the vote and no deterrent to 'splinter parties'; but at the second this fear became as effective as in Britain.

---

[21] The one other country which I know of that has a system akin to the American primaries is Uruguay, the most stable democracy in Latin America. In Uruguay, the various factions within the two major parties may each nominate a presidential candidate. On election day, the voters choose the man they prefer. When votes are counted, the party which has a majority, counting the votes of *all* its presidential candidates, wins the election, and the candidate of that party who received more votes than any other one of the party is elected president. In other words, Uruguay combines the primary and the final election on the same ballot.

Most constituencies then had a straight fight between a candidate of the Right and one of the Left.[22]

Under the Third Republic, the electoral alliances which gave decisive majorities to the Left or Right would always break down in parliament, hence the constant reshuffling of cabinets. The common assumption that these coalitions were so fragile because they tried to harmonize incompatible views and interests—such as those of the Radicals, as the party of small business, with those of the Socialists, as the workers' party—overlooks the fact that these differences have been no sharper than some *within* the American parties. The divergencies on domestic issues between conservative southern Democrats and left-liberal northern Democrats, or on foreign affairs between Republicans from the provincial Midwest and Republicans from the metropolitan centers of the East, with their close ties to international big business, are fully as great. The American party factions have been held together largely by the presidential system. Thus, the changing congressional majorities on questions which cut across party lines are comparable to the shifts in the Chamber as new issues were taken up. Since in America this cannot change the party in control of the executive, however, there has been continuity of executive action and also a substantial amount of party loyalty in important congressional votes, as David Truman has demonstrated.[23] And the "American" elements introduced into the French constitution by General De Gaulle seem to be having comparable effects on the party system there.

Canada is perhaps an even more interesting case of interaction of the various elements which have been discussed. Its social structure and bases for political division are complex and comparable to the American and French. It retains, however, the British electoral and parliamentary system, which requires disciplined parliamentary action and does not permit the American practices of cross-party alignments in the House, of ideo-

---

[22] Philip Williams, *Politics in Post-War France* (New York: Longmans, Green and Co., 1954), p. 310. (Emphasis mine.) This book contains an excellent discussion of the nature and effects of the French electoral systems. For a detailed description of the way in which the double ballot worked in the first elections of the Fifth Republic in 1958, see Philip Williams and Martin Harrison, "France 1958," in D. E. Butler, ed., *Elections Abroad* (New York: St. Martins, 1960), pp. 13–90.

[23] David Truman, *The Congressional Party: A Case Study* (New York: John Wiley, 1959); see also Duncan MacRae, Jr., *Dimensions of Congressional Voting* (Berkeley: University of California Press, 1958); and V. O. Key, Jr., *Politics, Parties and Pressure Groups* (New York: Thos. Y. Crowell, 1958), p. 729.

logical divergencies between local party machines, or the resolution by public primary elections of differences within the parties. Whenever a Canadian region, class, ethnic group, or province comes into serious conflict with its party of traditional allegiance, it must either change over to the other party, with which it may be in even greater disagreement on other issues, or form a new "third" party. The result of combining this social diversity with a rigid constitutional structure has been the regular rise and fall of relatively powerful "third" parties. Every single Canadian province, except Prince Edward Island and New Brunswick, has been governed for some time since World War I by a "third" party. At least three such parties, the Progressives in the 1920's and, since 1933, Social Credit (monetary reformers supported by farmers and small businessmen) and the socialist Cooperative Commonwealth Federation (CCF), renamed in 1961 the New Democratic Party, have had significant strength in a number of provinces. Nationalist parties, often at odds with one another, have arisen in Quebec; one of them, the *Union Nationale*, governed the province almost unbrokenly from 1936 to 1957. Most recently, in 1962, Social Credit, which was almost non-existent in Quebec in the 1958 election, won twenty-six constituencies in the national election in that province, and it retained most of this strength in the 1963 election. The rise and fall of these parties, mainly at the provincial level, are not the result of any general discontent in Canada, but largely of the interaction between constitutional arrangements and social and economic divisions.[24]

Although the Canadian two-party system has repeatedly broken down, it has been able, especially on the national level, to reabsorb most of the rebellious elements, since the single-member plurality method of election necessarily represses minorities. At the provincial level, however, it has been much easier for them to survive by becoming one of the two major *local* parties. Unlike the situation in the United States, in which state and presidential elections are often on the same ballot, in Canada this never occurs. Hence, voters are not pressed to bring their national and provincial party preferences into line.

South Africa, which also combines British constitutional procedure with

[24] See S. M. Lipset, "Democracy in Alberta," *Canadian Forum*, 34 (1954), pp. 175–177 and 196–198. For British Columbia, where Social Credit rose from no seats to the provincial government in one election, see H. F. Angus, "The British Columbia Election, 1952," *Canadian Journal of Economics and Political Science*, 18 (1952), pp. 518–525; and Margaret Ormsby, *British Columbia: A History* (Vancouver: Macmillan, 1958), pp. 477–489.

complex internal bases of cleavage, has exhibited the same rapid rise and fall of minor parties as Canada. Within the limits of the dominant ethnic divisions, other sources of conflict still exist. Thus for long periods the Afrikaners were divided into two parties; today they are united in the National Party, but the English are split. In addition to the old but sharply declining Labour party, a number of parties, mainly English, have come into being in the last decade as splinters from the United Party. All these minor parties have met, in an aggravated form, the same difficulties as the Canadian.[25]

In New Zealand, the two non-socialist parties merged after Labour had risen to a position in which it seemed able to win a three-cornered fight. Social Credit has shown on at least two occasions that it could get the support of about 10 per cent of the New Zealand electorate, but, being unable to win seats, it has failed to sustain any permanent strength.[26] In Australia, the two major non-socialist parties—the Country and Liberal parties—have not merged, but generally follow a policy of exchanging seats and refraining from competition.[27] Similar electoral alliances took place in some of the Scandinavian countries before the introduction of proportional representation.

Conversely, in one former dominion of the British Crown, Eire, which

---

[25] See Gwendolen M. Carter, *The Politics of Inequality, South Africa Since 1948* (New York: Frederick A. Praeger, 1958); for a further report see R. R. Farquharson, "South Africa 1958", in D. E. Butler, ed., *Elections Abroad* (New York: St. Martins, 1960), pp. 229–275.

[26] Peter Campbell, "Politicians, Public Servants, and the People in New Zealand, I," *Political Studies*, 3 (1955), pp. 196–197.

[27] Although the Country and Liberal parties usually do not run against each other and act, in effect, electorally as the rural and urban wing of the non-socialist party, the continued existence of two such parties is facilitated by the fact that Australia has adopted the preferential ballot system with the single-member constituency. Under this system voters list the order of preference for all candidates on the ballot. Thus when there are Liberal and Country candidates in the same constituency, a Liberal voter will mark the Country candidate as his number two choice, and Country party supporters will do the same for the Liberals. This system has also encouraged occasional splits from the Labour Party, since minority party candidates can pick up first votes without these votes being permanently lost to the major party backed by such protest voters. The Democratic Labor Party, a right-wing split from Labour, has urged its followers to vote Liberal as their second preference as a means of pressing the Labour Party to accept their terms. See J. D. B. Miller, *Australian Government and Politics* (London: Duckworth, 1954), pp. 85–86.

has a relatively simple basis for political cleavage, the perpetuation of proportional representation ever since the birth of the Irish Republic in 1922 has meant the continued existence of at least five parties. Only one party, Fianna Fáil, has been able to govern without a coalition under these conditions. The second largest party, Fine Gael, which is somewhat more conservative, can hope to form a government only with the help of minor and often more leftist parties, such as Labour and the Republicans.[28]

Had Eire adopted the British election system, it would now no doubt have a stable two-party system and cabinets as responsible as the United Kingdom. This failure, like some other Irish difficulties, must be attributed to the English, because when yielding power in southern Ireland, they insisted on a system of proportional representation to ensure representation of Protestant and other more pro-Commonwealth minorities. Fianna Fáil, as the dominant party, has tried hard to change the electoral system, but as in other countries the smaller parties oppose such changes for fear that the single-member plurality district system would weaken their electoral position. The result is that the need for "inter-party" governments has led to periodic breakdowns in the traditional pattern of responsible cabinet government.[29]

Similarly, in Israel, another state once governed by Great Britain, independence was followed by the continuance of the system of proportional representation previously used in elections to the council of the Jewish Agency, the dominant pre-independence organ of the Zionist community. Hence, in this immigrant society formed by men from many states and cultures, over thirty different parties have taken part in the elections. There have been at least five different socialist parties, excluding the Communists, represented in the Knesset, and some half dozen religious parties. Basically, however, the Israeli political structure consists of three groups: the socialist parties, the largest of which, the Mapai, has about 40 per cent of the vote, while the others have between 10 and 15 per cent; the non-socialist secular parties, which range from liberal to conservative (in the American sense of the terms), and which poll about 30 to 35 per cent of the vote; and the religious parties, which poll from 10 to 15 per cent and are divided fairly equally between pro- and anti-socialist groups. A single-member district plurality system would probably create a two-party system, socialist versus conservative, with each party bidding for the

[28] See Enid Lakeman and James D. Lambert, *Voting in Democracies* (London: Faber and Faber, 1955), pp. 223–230.

[29] Basil Chubb, "Cabinet Government in Ireland," *Political Studies,* 3 (1955), p. 272.

support of the religious. This solution is favored by Mapai, the largest party in the country; but, as in Ireland, it is opposed by the others, since none of them feels certain of survival without proportional representation. An Israeli social research institute, in a study of the effects of electoral systems on national life, has strongly urged a change in the Israeli system.

> In sum: while the present system of proportional representation aggravates existing social evils in the Israeli society, i.e., absolute rule of central party machines, deepening social divisions and the perpetuation of factional fanaticism, the system of constituency election is designed to counteract and finally to eliminate them, by weakening party power at the centre, placing emphasis on common, integrative, cohesive elements in our society and encouraging the growth of tolerance, fellow-feeling and social compromise. . . .
> The condition for constructive democratic life in the country becomes largely a function of the development of social forces which can combat and counteract these negative features [toward intense destructive conflict]. And the web of social institutions is the most potent powerful instrument at our disposal to accomplish this end.[30]

Maurice Duverger has described the conscious and successful effort made in Belgium to prevent a two-party system reasserting itself when the Socialists rose to second place, displacing the anti-clerical Liberal opposition, after the adoption of universal manhood suffrage in 1893. By the next election in 1898, the Liberals had declined to parliamentary insignificance with only thirteen seats. Rather than see the Liberals disappear, which would have meant, eventually, a Socialist government, the Catholics, who were then in power, introduced proportional representation and thus preserved the Liberals as a major third party.[31] The anti-clerical vote has almost always been above 50 per cent, but the Socialists have never reached 40 per cent, while the Liberals have constantly secured between 10 and 15 per cent.[32]

The strain between the institutionalization of specific social cleavages

[30] Beth Hillel (Society for Social Research in Israel), *Electoral Reform in Israel* (Tel Aviv: Beth Hillel Publications, 1953), pp. 24, 26.

[31] Duverger, *Political Parties*, pp. 246–247.

[32] Felix E. Oppenheim, "Belgium: Party Cleavage and Compromise," in Sigmund Neumann, ed., *Modern Political Parties* (Chicago: University of Chicago Press, 1958), p. 167.

in a multi-party structure and a plurality electoral system is aggravated by the distorted representation which usually results. The major party whose support is most evenly distributed throughout the country tends to be over-represented, and sometimes the largest single party does not win the most seats. In Canada between 1935 and 1957 the Liberal party dominated Parliament with overbearing majorities, though it had a majority of the electorate on only one occasion.[33] Similarly, in India the Congress Party has over 75 per cent of the seats in the House with less than 50 per cent of the vote, while the Communist Party ruled the Indian state of Kerala for one term with a legislative majority based on 35 per cent of the electorate.[34] In 1945, the British Labour Party took over with an overwhelming majority of 146 seats in the House of Commons, and nationalized a number of industries, despite the fact that over half of the electorate had voted for non-socialist candidates. Conversely, the three British Conservative governments since 1951 have governed with parliamentary majorities although the country had given a majority of its votes to Labour and the Liberals.[35]

Essentially, the evidence suggests that whatever potential cleavages exist in the social structure, there is a fundamental incompatibility between a multi-party system and a plurality method of election; where the two co-exist, the instability is ultimately resolved by a change to one of the following situations: 1) a change in the electoral system to proportional representation, which preserves declining parties and facilitates the growth of new ones; 2) an arrangement by which different parties continue to exist, but support each other in more or less permanent alliances; 3) mergers between parties which re-create a two-party situation, as has occurred a number of times with American third parties; or 4) the elimination over time of the weaker parties and a return to a two-party system, as has occurred in various countries of the Commonwealth and in the United States.

---

[33] Gwendolen M. Carter, "The Commonwealth Overseas: Variations on a British Theme," *ibid.*, p. 104.

[34] Avery Leiserson, *Parties and Politics* (New York: Alfred A. Knopf, 1958), p. 286.

[35] Detailed discussion of the relation between votes and seats in the British system can be found in R. B. McCallum, *The British General Election of 1945* (New York: Oxford University Press, 1947), pp. 277–292; for a table giving votes and seats in British elections since 1900, see Samuel Beer, "Great Britain: From Governing Elite to Organized Mass Parties," in Sigmund Neumann, ed., *Modern Political Parties* (Chicago: University of Chicago Press, 1958), p. 57.

Consequences of the Different Systems

A number of consequences for the nature of representation and the stability of democracy have been attributed to the two-party and the multi-party systems.

In a two-party system, both parties aim at securing a majority. Hence, they must seek support among groups which may be preponderantly loyal to their opponents and must avoid accentuating too heavily the interests of their customary supporters. Elections become occasions for seeking the broadest possible base of support by convincing divergent groups of their common interests. The system thus encourages compromise and the incorporation into party values of those general elements of consensus upon which the polity rests. For similar reasons the system encourages emphasis by both parties upon material interests (concessions and patronage) as against a stress upon ideal interests, thus reducing ideological conflict.[36] The "out" party can always realistically aspire to gain office within a few years, and this has the effect of stifling exaggerated commitments on its part to ideal or ideological goals which may gain votes but embarrass office holders, and it also reinforces the adherence of the opposition to the "rules of the game." The weakness of ideology that is inherent in two-party systems has the further consequences of reducing intense concern with particular issues dividing the parties, and sharpening the focus on party leaders. The plebiscitary nature of electoral struggles in two-party systems is largely an effect of the system itself.

In a multi-party system, where parties do not hope to gain a majority, they usually seek to win the greatest possible electoral support from a limited base. They therefore stress the interests of that base and the cleavages which set it apart from other groups in society. The party's function as a representative of a group is separated from the function of integrating the group in the body politic, which requires a stress on similarities with others and commitments to them.[37] The multi-party system with proportional representation in fact substitutes the interest group (or group of common believers) for the territorial unit as the

---

[36] See Carl Friedrich, *Constitutional Government and Democracy* (Boston: Ginn and Co., 1950), pp. 416–417; Parsons, "Voting and the Equilibrium of the American Political System," *op. cit.*

[37] See F. A. Hermens, *The Representative Republic* (Notre Dame, Ind.: University of Notre Dame Press, 1958), p. 201.

basis of representation.[38] The small size of many parties and the absence of a need in most multi-party systems for compromise at the electoral level enhances the ideological content of the conflict. This divisiveness encouraged by a multi-party system is perpetuated by the tendency of most parties to attack most virulently those with whom they have most in common and with whom they thus compete for a similar vote; this magnifies the differences between them.

The two-party system helps to maintain the commitment of the entire electorate to the system itself, rather than to the regime, and encourages the elector to devote his efforts to the quite clear-cut task of replacing the incumbents with their traditional opponents. The necessity for coalition government in most multi-party systems—where the lesser parties wield so disproportionate an influence that election results may scarcely affect the composition of the government—deprives the elector of the feeling that he is able to turn out leaders who have forfeited his confidence, and weakens his commitment to the system as a whole.

There are, however, conditions under which a two-party system is *less* conducive to the preservation of democratic order than is a multi-party system. The two-party system works best where it is based on an elaborate, cross-cutting solidarity structure, in which men and groups are pulled in different directions only by their diverse roles and interests. Wherever the solidarity structure is polarized by class, race, or religion, and the political lines follow those of social cleavage, a two-party system may intensify internal conflict rather than help to integrate the society. For example, the first Austrian republic (1919–1934) was largely a two-party system, but one which was divided along the interrelated lines of religion, class, and region. The parties represented two almost completely separate cultural units, and the civil war which followed was a nearly inevitable consequence of the system.[39] Similarly, in Italy today the lines

---

[38] "Electoral procedures based on territorial . . . [as distinct from 'representation through interest-groups'] is [*sic*] precisely the technique for the organic integration of the whole. As a matter of principle the individual delegate represents the entire area. The ensuing separation into parties according to *political* tendencies implies then only differences of belief concerning the means by which the welfare of the nation is to be achieved." Georg Simmel, *The Web of Group Affiliations* (Glencoe, Ill.: The Free Press, 1955), p. 194.

[39] For a detailed description of the system and an analysis of the events leading to the downfall of the first Austrian republic, see Charles Gulick, *Austria: From Hapsburg to Hitler* (Berkeley, Calif.: University of California Press, 1948). A recent study of elections in the first and second republics demonstrates that the second one is genuinely different from the first in that the

of division between the Christian Democrats and the Communist opposition are such as to reduce consensus rather than increase it. In South Africa, a division into two parties largely based on two ethnic groups, the Afrikaner Nationalists and English United Party, is destructive of national unity and democratic norms.[40]

In general, where the class struggle is superimposed upon a conflict between religion and irreligion, or between different ethnic groups— wherever opposing groups see elections as a fight between good and evil, so that conversion from one political faith to another is almost impossible—a two-party system is more destructive of political stability than is one which center parties can mediate between extreme opponents. Consequently, though it may be validly argued that a two-party system makes for a more stable and effective democratic polity than a multi-party one, this is true only if both actors in the system accord a certain degree of legitimacy to each other; each party must be willing to view the other as an acceptable alternative government.

Considerations such as these have led many to suggest that a system of proportional representation, though making for more parties, may help to unify a nation of low consensus by forcing all parties to look for votes in every major group and region in the country. A committee of the United States Senate urged this view as early as 1869, arguing that the Civil War might have been avoided if the electoral system had permitted minorities in the North and South who agreed with dominant opinion in the other regions to elect representatives. The committee argued that the absence of minority representation "in the states of the South when rebellion was plotted, and when open steps were taken to break the Union, was unfortunate, for it would have held the Union men of these

---

two major parties, though based on the same groups as before 1934, have much more support today within "opposition strata" than their predecessors did. Thus the conservative People's party is much stronger today among workers, residents of Vienna, Protestants, and irreligious people, than was the pre-1934 Christian Social party. Conversely, the Socialists, though weaker in Vienna, are much stronger in the outlying provinces than earlier, and they have considerably increased their vote among peasants. Paralleling the growth of the two parties within segments once overwhelmingly opposed to them has been a sharp decline in ideological cleavage. The conservative party is no longer a Christian or Catholic party, and the Socialists have dropped their adherence to Marxist doctrine. See Walter B. Simon, "Politische Ethik und Politische Struktur," *Kölner Zeitschrift für Soziologie und Sozialpsychologie*, 11 (1959), pp. 445–459.

[40] Carter, *op. cit.*

states together and have given them a voice. . . . Dispersed, unorganized, unrepresented, without due voice and power, they could interpose no effectual resistance to secession and to civil war."[41] John Humphreys suggested that the same system of proportional representation, which is sometimes thought to have prevented stable two-party government in Belgium, has actually reduced the conflict between the Flemish and Walloon groups. Since all parties seek votes in both ethnic groups, the South African pattern of parties representing distinct ethnic and language groups is avoided.[42]

The Swedish political scientist Herbert Tingsten has suggested, from the experience of his own country, that a multi-party system rooted in proportional representation lowers the vitality of political life by eliminating the slightly spurious dramatics which two-party elections can call forth even among rather homogeneous and satisfied electorates.[43] This is not incompatible with the supposed tendency of the multi-party system to increase the purely numerical participation of the electorate. Thus, when Switzerland changed in 1919 from a plurality system of elections to proportional representation within cantons, not only did the number of significant parties increase, but the average percentage of the eligible electorate who voted jumped from 50 per cent to nearly 80 per cent. The Swiss changeover was extremely revealing, as there were a number of variations among the cantons which permitted some controlled comparisons. For example, in those cantons which had previously been "safe seats" for one party under the plurality system, only 30 to 40 per cent of the eligible electorate had voted before proportional representation. The vote in these previously "safe" cantons doubled after the change in the system. However, in comparable safe cantons which elected only one member to the national parliament, so that proportional representation could not alter the result, participation did not increase and remained at about 40 per cent. A somewhat similar situation occurred with comparable

---

[41] Cited in John H. Humphreys, *Proportional Representation, A Study in Methods of Election* (London: Methuen, 1911), p. 58.

[42] *Ibid.*, p. 57. A similar point is made by Maurice Duverger in *L'influence des systèmes électoraux sur la vie politique* (Paris: Armand Colin, 1950), pp. 39–40; see also Lakeman and Lambert, *Voting in Democracies*, pp. 63–64. The latter contend also that "an instance of the unifying effect of proportional representation is Czechoslovakia after the first world war, where representation of their respective minorities prevented what might have been a sharp cleavage between Bohemia and Slovakia." *Loc cit.*

[43] Herbert Tingsten, "Stability and Vitality in Swedish Democracy," *The Political Quarterly*, 26 (1955), pp. 140–151.

results in Norway in 1921.[44] A situation in which every vote "counts" seems to increase both the concern of the voter with the need to participate and the concern of the parties with the reactions of all voters.

The differences between the two types of party system must be tested also for their capacity to provide generalized leadership in return for generalized support, to serve as the interchange mechanism between the solidary groups of society and the wielders of political power. The experiences of Western industrial society suggest that, in general, a two-party system is much the better adapted to these needs.

The ability of the two-party system to provide for generalized leadership is closely linked to the fact that one party always represents the government and actually rules the country, so that the party in power *temporarily* becomes identical with the State. Both parties are organized to be able to take full responsibility, at home and abroad, for the conduct of the nation's affairs; the opposition is always conscious of its role as the government of tomorrow, and in order to be able to *govern* it must look beyond electoral victory to its chance of inspiring at least some confidence among the supporters of the other party. Insofar as the party itself overtly represents interests, these are represented *within* the party and disciplined by the necessity of being able to govern in the national interest; the same applies to the party's relationship with pressure groups. A party, in these circumstances, is above all a way of organizing citizens to take part in *public* affairs. It is clearly damaging to a party, especially to the party in power, if it appears in a light where its opponents can accuse it of obvious favoritism to a group of party supporters. Further, since the legitimacy of a party rests ultimately upon its actual or potential effectiveness as a *national* government, there is strong pressure on both parties in a two-party system to reduce or eliminate ideology as a basis for political decision. The access of a given party to the full power of the state is quite straightforward so long as almost everyone is convinced that it will use that power to solve problems from a national standpoint.

In contrast to the two-party system, where each party tries to appear as a plausible representative of the whole society, multi-party systems have been mainly based upon the premise that a party should consciously represent the private interests of a section of the population. Only the State, and no one party, can claim to represent the interests of the whole. Thus individuals are citizens, and enjoy public roles, in relation only to the State, not to the party; and patriotism tends to be found only in

---

[44] Herbert Tingsten, *Political Behaviour* (London: P. S. King, 1937), pp. 219–220, 224–225.

action which "transcends" party, rather than as a value which can infuse party action as such. As a result, bourgeois and peasant parties have tended to reflect rather than sublimate the *incivisme* of their constituents. Minority working-class parties have often regarded constitutionalism—the basis of any notion of public interest—as a matter of socially irrelevant technicalities, and parties of the right have been tempted to aspire to a position "above parties."

But while almost all minority parties in a multi-party system could ideologically reject responsibility for the political community at large, many have in fact found themselves wielding State power in coalition governments. The consequent divorce between party symbols and party actions for all who participate in coalitions, and the bargaining necessary to fill public offices and obtain parliamentary support, may lead to cynicism or to attitudes resembling that unmediated attachment to abstractions which, as Philip Selznick argues, is a source of irresponsibility, extremism, and manipulability in mass society.[45] These extreme manifestations have, of course, appeared in some multi-party systems only under conditions of stress. It seems likely, however, that multi-party systems accentuate the development of such dangerous traits, while two-party systems are better able to resist political and civic irresponsibility on the part of different solidary groups and their representatives.

While the two-party system has these great advantages, under certain conditions a multi-party system may produce a relatively permanent coalition cabinet which adequately reflects the main groupings of society and can effectively interchange leadership and support. In such systems all parties become, in a sense, "State parties." This development seems to have occurred in Switzerland and, to a lesser degree, in Austria, Uruguay, Benelux, and the Scandinavian countries. There is some reason to anticipate that the Swiss "solution" to the problem of multi-party government—the inclusion of all democratic parties in the cabinet, so that issues are fought out there as well as in the parliament—may spread to other countries as well.

Conclusion

Political sociologists tend to regard formal political devices as peripheral items, having little effect upon the main features of societies. One purpose of this chapter has been to distinguish between the more "natural"

---

[45] Philip Selznick, *The Organizational Weapon* (New York: McGraw-Hill, 1952), pp. 276–291.

elements in the social structure, derivative from the value system discussed in the earlier parts of this book, which influence the political process and the enacted rules which help determine the nature of parties and of representation. As we have seen in the American example, constitutions and electoral systems are the outcome of particular decisions which may permanently affect the type of social system which a country develops. It is especially important to emphasize this at a time when men in various new nations are trying to set up democratic procedures and to foster an open society. For sociologists to treat formal political structures as epiphenomena is not only wrong from a theoretical point of view, but may also reinforce the appeal of a vulgar Marxism which would have democracy wait solely upon economic development.

On the other side, it is fairly obvious that a simple change in electoral laws cannot guarantee the transformation of a multi-party system into a two-party one. In unstable multi-party countries, the alternative to numerous, rather rigid parties has been the *rassemblement* (rally) type of organization, which, while possessing a loose structure, has also just those authoritarian traits which its purpose demands. Movements of this type arise because parliamentary democracy has failed to produce effective leadership, and since their purpose is to establish a new source of authority in their leader's charisma, they are often opposed to democracy itself.

This brings us back to a consideration of the problem of authority in relation to party systems. Democratic stability, as I noted in the Introduction, requires that the *source* of authority be out of reach of any of the contending parties, which should aspire to become the *agents* of authority, not its creators. In all stable democracies we do in fact find an institutionalized separation of the *source* from the *agencies* of authority. In the stable parliamentary monarchies of Northern Europe and the Commonwealth, the monarchy remains the latent source of authority, effectively divorced from its exercise.[46] In the United States and Switzerland, since their systems acquired a traditional legitimacy

---

[46] See Lipset, *Political Man*, pp. 77–96. As Walter Bagehot put it almost a century ago: "The functions of royalty are for the most part *latent*. It seems to order, but it never seems to struggle. . . . The nation is divided into parties, but the crown is of no party. Its apparent separation from business is that which removes it both from enmities and from desecration, which preserves its mystery, which enables it to combine the affection of conflicting parties —to a visible symbol of unity." *The English Constitution* (New York: Oxford University Press, 1958), p. 40. Bagehot's use of the distinction between manifest and latent activities and functions is, I think, one of the first uses of these concepts in social science.

through prolonged effectiveness, it was the constitution that became the supreme symbol of authority. And in contrast to France and many other countries, the American and Swiss constitutions are beyond the direct reach of the elected representatives and are not easily amended. It is unthinkable that they can be abolished or fundamentally revised.

Two-party democracy, therefore, in addition to an electoral system which tends to polarize the electorate, requires that: 1) the groups composing the two potentially dominant parties not be committed to incompatible ideologies; and 2) the source and agents of authority be institutionally and legitimately separated, so that neither major party can aspire to become the source of authority.

It would therefore appear that those countries with multi-party systems, in which the possibility of change to a two-party system exists, are in fact those which already have fairly efficient ways of exchanging leadership and support. In none of the chronically unstable democracies are the source and agencies of authority sufficiently separate to insure against a sudden authoritarian turn.

But although too great a faith in the manipulation of electoral laws cannot be justified, some conclusions for action may be drawn: to create democracy it may be necessary to use the legal system to exclude those who would destroy it. Thus the French double ballot, in which the democratic parties could unite for the second ballot against an opponent of the system, limited both the participation and the strength of the Communists and Fascists in the 1930's.[47] Such a system in Weimar Germany would obviously have kept the Nazis out of the Reichstag in the 1920's and reduced the parliamentary strength of the Communists to insignificance. It would have guaranteed a large democratic majority in the election of 1930, and even in 1932.[48]

The question is most urgent in the new states of Africa and Asia. There, the source and agencies of authority are not separated. In none of these countries do the underlying structural conditions exist for a stable democratic party system, either two-party or multi-party.[49] Lack

[47] Michel Debré, the first prime minister of the Fifth Republic, argued in 1947 that the Fourth Republic would *inevitably* collapse because it used proportional representation. See his *La mort de l'état républicain* (Paris: Gallimard, 1947).

[48] Dankwart Rustow, "Some Observations on Proportional Representation," *The Journal of Politics*, 12 (1950), pp. 107–127.

[49] For a general theoretical discussion of how to deal with these problems comparatively, see Francis X. Sutton, "Representation and the Nature of Political Systems," *Contemporary Studies in Society and History*, 2 (1959),

of experience and leadership, illiteracy, poverty, traditional cultures and status structures, dependence upon primary products which often provide insufficient resources for expensive government—all militate against parliamentary rule. These strains are frequently intensified by the lack of any sense of historical unity, and by the conjunction of all the tensions of rapid industrialization with the opportunities for demagogic license afforded by universal suffrage. A further major factor is the differential impact of Communism, Russian or Chinese, upon these emerging polities. Whether it appears as an imperialistic threat, as a tempting solution to urgent and overwhelming problems, or as a source of irresponsible exploitation of discontent, it adds to the already formidable obstacles to peaceful democratic growth. Under these conditions, the form of one-party "democratic" government which is emerging in many of these countries may hold some hope for the future. Such parties tend to be loosely structured, more like a *rassemblement* than a party of ideology or interest. They combine a number of interests and strata, either through the charisma of the leader or through the original need for unity in the struggle for independence. Charisma, as has been noted, is necessary if the system is to survive in its early stages, and the absence of opposition may prove beneficial if it preserves the often frail mystique upon which authority depends. Such opposition as does exist must remain factional, even where it has a nominal right of appeal to the electorate. Other parties may be permitted, as in Ghana, Tunisia, and Mexico (the model in this pattern for other underdeveloped societies), but they cannot be allowed a chance of electoral victory. Any failure in effectiveness—and there are bound to be many—may become grounds for challenging the entire system if an opposition can hope to gain mass support and power.

Ever since the rise of Sun Yat-sen in China, many leaders of such states have spoken of their particular type of government as a "guided" or a "tutelary" democracy. Unlike Communists or other totalitarians, these leaders have as their point of reference, and their image of the good society, not a one-party state or a society without internal conflict, but rather the existing stable Western democracies. They regard the existence of opposition, free elections, and public criticism as ideals to be attained. Turkey, for example, has already developed from a one-party into a two-party state, and Mexico seems to be moving gradually in the same

---

pp. 1–10. For a detailed description of the party systems and elections in various African states, see W. J. M. Mackenzie and K. E. Robinson, eds., *Five Elections in Africa* (New York: Oxford University Press, 1960).

direction.[50] The dominant parties in both states have tolerated much internal diversity, and acknowledged their opponents' rights to discussion and organization—while at the same time denying them a chance of electoral victory.

Democracy cannot be created by fiat. It grew through many centuries in the West, during which time the concept of representation changed greatly, and the norms regulating the access of different groups to governmental power were slowly modified in the course of great social and political upheavals. As Max Weber pointed out, democracy must be regarded as a process rather than as an attribute which a system does or does not possess. In his view, *democratization* involves two traits: 1) "prevention of the development of a closed status group of officials in the interest of a universal accessibility of office, and 2) minimization of the authority of officialdom in the interest of expanding the sphere of influence of 'public opinion' as far as practicable."[51]

In Western societies the absolute power and charismatic authority of the monarch were gradually eroded, mainly through pressure from groups who were consciously loyal to the monarchy. The title of His Majesty's Loyal Opposition echoes this development. Similarly, in some of the dominant charismatic parties of the underdeveloped states, the growth of politically significant solidary groups and of restrictions on the authority of officials has been taking place *within* the ruling party, much as in an earlier age it took place under the shadow of the monarchy. In Mexico, to take the most developed case of this phenomenon, these groups have been brought into the *Partido*, often as formally affiliated groupings—for example, trade unions and professional associations. As was true in the monarchies of the eighteenth and nineteenth centuries, which were in transition from absolutism to constitutionalism, considerable factionalism exists in many of these parties, which gives the different groups within them access to power. "Insofar as factions develop freely inside a single party this becomes simply a framework which limits political rivalries without destroying them; prohibited outside the single

---

[50] See Duverger, *Political Parties*, pp. 275–280; Robert E. Scott, *Mexican Government in Transition* (Urbana: University of Illinois Press, 1959), especially pp. 145–243; and Kemal H. Karpat, *Turkey's Politics: The Transition to a Multi-Party System* (Princeton, N.J.: Princeton University Press, 1959).
[51] H. H. Gerth and C. W. Mills, eds., *From Max Weber: Essays in Sociology* (New York: Oxford University Press, 1946), p. 226. These concepts are elaborated in an unpublished seminar paper by Patricia Richmond, "Democracy and Party: The Problem of Political Stability in the Mexican 'One-Party' System," which has influenced my thinking on these issues.

party, pluralism is reborn within the party, and there it can play the same part."[52] An analysis of the political changes in Mexico over the past three decades concludes:

> Intra-party pluralism has produced the following stabilizing consequences in present-day industrial Mexico . . . : an increase in the organizational strength of significant secondary groupings; an increase in the legitimacy of the system and of the incumbents; an increase in the representation of all the significant segments in society with a corresponding decrease in the arbitrary power of the president as well as an increase in his resourcefulness; and an increase in the legitimacy and tolerance of opposition groups.[53]

To justify the manipulation of political systems so as to limit the rights of opposition in underdeveloped states, or to deny the rights of anti-democratic forces to equal representation, may seem itself to be a basic denial of democracy. But as the Founding Fathers of the American Republic well recognized, the problem of democracy is not simply to maximize popular influence on government policy; it also involves finding the best way to protect the stability of the political system. They sought to safeguard the infant republic by framing a constitution which would favorably "prejudice the outcome of democracy," and which would reduce "the likelihood that the majority would decide certain political issues in bad ways."[54]

Wherever democracy has not been institutionalized, whether in the old states of Europe or the new states of Asia and Africa, it is important to recognize that particular political forms will not emerge automatically in response to developments in other parts of the social system.[55] Whether these states develop a stable interchange of leadership and support in a democratic framework also depends in part on the rules they adopt for their polities. The study of the social effects of diverse constitutional arrangements should remain a major concern for the student of politics and comparative institutions.

---

[52] Duverger, *Political Parties*, p. 278.

[53] Patricia Richmond, "Democracy and Party," p. 29.

[54] Martin Diamond, "Democracy and The Federalist: A Reconsideration of the Framers' Intent," *American Political Science Review*, 53 (1959), pp. 56–57.

[55] For a detailed analysis of the factors which influence political forms in these societies, see Edward Shils, *Political Development in the New States* (The Hague: Mouton, 1962); see also S. N. Eisenstadt, "Sociological Aspects of Political Development in New States," in his *Essays on Sociological Aspects of Political and Economic Development* (The Hague: Mouton, 1961), pp. 9–53.

Epilogue: Some Personal Views on Equality, Inequality, and Comparative Social Science

10 ★★★

This book has had two major purposes, a substantive one and a methodological one. The second purpose is discussed later in this chapter. Substantively, it has sought to present a perspective on American society, first, by looking at it historically and, second, by showing how it differs from other modern Western States. Essentially, I have argued that the American Creed, with its emphasis on equality and opportunity, is still a dynamic part of the culture. The concern for equality still determines how Americans interact with each other. The "other-directedness" of Americans, the flattery, the use of first names among people who hardly know each other or are in a superior–subordinate relation, the elaborate efforts to avoid hurting the feelings of others, all reflect the fact that deeply rooted in our values is the mandate that all men should respect one another.

The accounts of visitors from abroad continue to support the contention that the two emphases, on equality (respect for others) and achievement (competition), are clearly linked together in the United States. Recently, some Canadian academic friends who spent a year in California told me how impressed they were with the effect of one year in an American junior high school on the outlook of their eleven-year-old daughter. The girl, who did extremely well in school, had looked down on her less able schoolmates back home in Vancouver. In California, according to my friends, she developed much more respect for her classmates, regardless of intellectual achievement. Her parents felt this new respect taught her by the American school did not lead to a reduction in her intellectual interests or her concern for knowledge. Rather, both strands were present in the American school—the need to do well, and the need to respect others with lesser ability.

Similar impressions were reported by a South African writer, Dan Jacobson, now a resident of Britain, who lived for a year in an American surburban community.[1] He was particularly struck with the extent to which the elementary school system tried to foster a concern for the feelings of others. Thus, he reports that his seven-year-old daughter came home one day with the request that she bring twenty-three valentines to school for St. Valentine's Day. Her teacher wanted each child in the class to receive the same number of cards. She was concerned that no child should feel deprived or that he was not liked.

The comments of two European Marxists, one a pro-Soviet fellow traveler and the other a Polish sociologist and member of the Communist party, are also relevant here. The first, an Englishwoman whom I saw in Britain shortly after her return from six months in the United States, reported that a visit to America always brings home to her the class-differentiated character of British society. In America a well-educated member of the upper middle class will discuss politics or other such topics with a cab driver, a hairdresser, and others at that occupational level; but in Britain, a person from the upper middle class still finds it difficult to interact informally with people that far below him in the social scale. When viewed in comparison with America, Britain—even in the 1960's —remains a rigidly stratified society.

The Polish Communist's comments were perhaps even more note-worthy. He knows English extremely well and had written about some aspects of American society before his first visit here. I saw him in Warsaw after he had spent a year in America, and he remarked that much to his surprise he had felt much more at home, more at ease in social relations, in the South than in other parts of the United States. This reaction naturally puzzled him, since he was bitterly hostile to the pattern of race relations in southern life and thought he disliked everything the South stood for. On thinking the matter through, he realized

---

[1] Dan Jacobson, *No Further West: California Visited* (New York: Macmillan, 1961).

that the reason for his apparently contradictory feelings was that interpersonal relations in the South—race relations apart—were more like
those of Europe, including Communist Poland, than those of the northern
states. The fact that the South is a caste society not only defines Negro–
white relations but also affects the pattern of life within white society
as well. Thus this Polish sociologist reported that there is much less
informality between superiors and inferiors among southern whites than
among northern ones. Southern white children show more respect to
adults than do those in the North, there is more formality in relations
between the sexes in the South than in the North, and persons in higher
status occupations are shown more deference in the South than in the
North. The American South, in other words, places more emphasis on
elitism, on ascription, on particularism, and on diffuseness, than does the
North, and this makes the South more like Europe than are other parts
of the United States.

In much of Europe, for example, diffuse elitism requires that subordinates address superiors with the impersonal form of "you" (*Sie* in
German and *vous* in French), while one of higher status will address one
of lower, such as an employee or a servant, with the more personal
form, which is also the form used in speaking to children (*Du* in German
and *tu* in French). In the American South, a similar pattern is followed.
Although English has only one form of "you," whites address Negroes by
their first names, that is, familiarly, as if speaking to a child, while a
Negro must always call a white man "Mister." And a study of Soviet
literature indicates that this indicator of the existence of diffuse superior
status continues in Communist Russia. Alexander Gerschenkron finds "in
Kruzilikha and elsewhere in Soviet fiction that the manager, in addressing
subordinates, uses the time-consecrated feudal *ty* (thou), while the
subordinates use the respectful *vy* (you)."[2] Given the continuation of
pre-revolutionary forms of interpersonal relationships after many decades
of Communism in Russia it is not surprising that even a committed
Polish Communist should find that the more ascriptive and elitist South
is more like his homeland, in terms of social relations, than is the more
equalitarian area of the United States.

Because equality and achievement have been linked throughout
America's development as a nation, the concept of equality has had a
special character. As David Potter has stressed, "the American ideal and
practice of equality . . . has implied for the individual . . . opportunity

---

[2] Alexander Gerschenkron, "Economic Life in Soviet Literature," in Alex
Inkeles and Kent Geiger, eds., *Soviet Society* (Boston: Houghton Mifflin,
1961), p. 401.

to make his own place in society and . . . emancipation from a system of status."[3] It must be emphasized that the American concept of equality, which focuses on opportunity and the quality of social relations, does not demand equality of income. This fact, as Potter has well pointed out, has been one of the sources of confusion concerning the very use of the term "equality" to describe aspects of the American reality.

> [T]he connotations [of the term "equality"] to an American are quite unlike what they might be to a European. A European advocating equality might very well mean that all men should occupy positions that are roughly the same level in wealth, power, or enviability. But the American, with his emphasis upon equality of opportunity, has never conceived of it in this sense. He has traditionally expected to find a gamut ranging from rags to riches, from tramps to millionaires. . . . Thus equality did not mean uniform position on a common level, but it did mean universal opportunity to move through a scale which traversed many levels. . . . The emphasis upon unrestricted latitude as the essence of equality in turn involved a heavy emphasis upon liberty as an essential means for keeping the scale open and hence making equality a reality as well as a theoretical condition. . . . As for social distinctions, certainly they exist; but whatever their power may be, social rank can seldom assert an open claim to deference in this country, and it usually makes at least a pretense of conformity to equalitarian ways.[4]

The focus on the ideology of equal opportunity for each individual has made Americans relatively insensitive to gross inequalities of income and wealth in their country. If the stress on equality serves to moderate relations among those who are unequal in class position, it may be argued that this very emphasis, which leads Americans to speak of their country as a "classless society," may serve to inhibit efforts to reduce inequality in the economic system through political and other means.

Inequality in America

The United States, like all other nations, has an enormous concentration of personal wealth in the hands of relatively few individuals. The most recent detailed investigation of the subject, which is based on estate tax records, estimates that the group of persons who ". . . have had $60,000

---

[3] David M. Potter, *People of Plenty* (Chicago: University of Chicago Press, 1954), p. 91.
[4] *Ibid.*, pp. 91–92, 96.

Table VIII

Distribution of Total Family Personal Income Among Consumer
Units Grouped by Size of Income Per Unit, Selected Years, 1929–
1959, After Deduction of Federal Income Tax Liability

Income Groups as Fifths of the Population	1929	1941	1951	1954	1959
	Per Cent				
Lowest and next lowest fifth	12.6	14.2	17.3	16.9	16.3
Third	13.9	15.9	17.2	17.1	16.8
Fourth	19.5	23.1	22.8	22.8	23.1
Top fifth	54.0	46.9	42.7	43.2	43.8
Top 5 per cent	29.5	21.5	18.4	18.3	17.8
Average after-tax income per unit (1960 prices)	$4,160	$4,360	$5,070	$5,340	$6,040

Source: Simon Kuznets, "Income Distribution and Changes in Consumption," in
  H. S. Simpson, ed., The Changing American Population (New York: Institute
  for Life Insurance, 1962), p. 30.

or more of gross estate in 1953 comprised 1.04 per cent of the total population, and 1.6 per cent of the adult population. This group of top wealth-
holders held over a quarter of the total personal wealth. . . ."[5] This finding
is substantiated by the 1953 Survey of Consumer Finances, which dealt
with net worth; it reported that those with $60,000 or more constituted
3 per cent of all spending units, and that they held 30 per cent of total
assets.[6] Efforts to estimate changes in the pattern of inequality in personal
wealth indicate that between 1922 and 1929 the top one per cent of the
population, in terms of wealth, increased their share from 33.9 to 38.8
per cent. However, this share dropped considerably during the 1930's
and 1940's; it fell to 33.8 per cent in 1939 and 22.8 per cent in 1949.
Between 1949 and 1953, the last year reported in this analysis, the top
one per cent gained somewhat, owning 27.4 per cent of all personal assets,
but was still considerably below 1929.[7]

Simon Kuznets finds that the proportion of the wealth going to the
bottom section of the population has increased since 1929, while the
upper groups' portion (the top fifth and top 5 per cent) dropped con-

---

[5] Robert J. Lampman, *The Share of Top Wealth-Holders in National Wealth
1922–1956* (Princeton, N.J.: Princeton University Press, 1962), p. 191.
[6] *Ibid.*, p. 195.
[7] *Ibid.*, p. 209.

siderably during the 1930's and 1940's. Table VIII shows the distribution of income from selected years after 1929. Most recently, a comparison of data from the various censuses, including that of 1960, suggests similar conclusions. Herman Miller of the Census Bureau concludes that, since the end of the war, income distribution "has not changed significantly."[8]

The data reported by Lampman, Kuznets, and Miller suggest that the tendency to reduce the relative disproportion in income between the higher and lower groups which characterized the 1930's and 1940's has ended, and may even be moving slightly in the reverse direction. Given the widespread opportunities to increase family income available to the growing middle-class and white-collar strata, there has been a general reluctance to press for an extension of an egalitarian-oriented progressive taxation policy, such as that fostered during the Roosevelt depression and wartime era. In fact, changes in tax legislation have served to reduce the severity of taxes. "Most noteworthy among the latter changes was the introduction of the marital deduction on the estate tax, and the extension to residents of all states of community property rights for both federal income and gift tax purposes in 1948."[9] This change in national mood with regard to tax policy probably reflects one of the fluctuations in relative emphasis on the values of equalitarianism and achievement discussed in Chapter 3. In a period of high levels of employment and economic opportunity, the concern for achievement, for incentives, becomes greater than that for equality.

It is far from certain, however, that the egalitarian trend with respect to income is disappearing. The largest "occupational" group among the lowest fifth in income is made up of those without regular employment, the large majority of whom are retired. And this tendency for the retired to form an increasingly larger segment of the low-income group may serve to conceal a continued move toward equality of income among those in the labor force. As Kuznets puts it:

> This trend towards the domination of the lowest group of consumer units by retired family heads reflects the spread of social insurance and the "splitting up" of consumer units, the separation of generations [parents and children living apart after the latter go to work]. . . . Splitting up would, all other conditions being equal, widen the inequality in the distribution of income among consumer units—as

---

[8] Herman Miller, "Is the Income Gap Closed? 'No!' " *The New York Times Magazine,* (November 11, 1962), p. 50.

[9] Lampman, *The Share of Top Wealth-Holders* . . . , p. 239.

measured; for it would create an increasingly large group of units at
the lower end of the distribution, whose needs are relatively modest,
and whose drive toward or capacity for substantial earnings is
limited.

If reaching retirement age means passing the optimum earning
phase of one's life and declining into a position below the average
not unlike that held in the early stages of life, i.e., before the
acquisition of experience and maturity, the separation of aged heads
from the younger consumer units only lengthens the lower tail of
the income distribution and makes for greater measured inequality
than would be the case if retired folks continued to live with their
children in one consuming unit. Inequality would also be intensified
if splitting up of the very young into separate consumer units increased, since their income also would be much below the average.
. . . The point to be stressed is that in so far as splitting up began in
the 1930's and continued thereafter, inequality in the distribution of
income among consumer units declined until 1947 and was constant
thereafter *despite* the underlying trend in the structure of consuming units. In other words, even in the 1950's there may have been
forces making for narrower income inequality, but their effects may
have been offset by the greater fractionalization of consuming units
at both ends of the age distribution of heads, i.e., the very old and
the very young, and at one end of the income distribution, i.e., the
low one.[10]

But whatever the inequality in personal wealth and income in the
United States, it remains true that in spite of the activities of the 1945–
1951 Labour government, Britain is not only less egalitarian in its value
system but also evidences greater disparities in distribution of wealth.
"In 1946–47 the top 1.5 per cent of adults owned 53 per cent of the
total wealth in England and Wales, while in 1953 the top 1.5 per cent

---

[10] Simon Kuznets, "Income Distribution and Changes in Consumption," in
H. S. Simpson, ed., *The Changing American Population* (New York: Institute
of Life Insurance, 1962), pp. 36–37. The magnitude of the effect of retirement on any discussion of income distribution can be realized when it is
noted that, while the longevity of the population has been constantly rising,
so that those over sixty-five constitute an increasing portion of the population,
from 1890 to 1960 the proportion of men in this age group who are still in
the labor force declined from more than two-thirds to less than a third.
"Between 1950 and 1960 the percentage declined steeply, from 41.4 to 30.5."
Philip M. Hauser, "More from the Census of 1960," *Scientific American*,
207 (October 1962), p. 35.

of adults in the United States owned only 27 per cent of the wealth."[11] A comparison based on sample survey data of the net worth of spending units in both countries in 1953 supports these conclusions. In Britain, in that year, the top one-tenth of the population held 75.7 per cent of the total net worth, as contrasted with 56 per cent for the comparable group in the United States.[12] And a recent study of wealth distribution in Great Britain concludes that "the ownership of wealth, which is far more highly concentrated in the United Kingdom than in the United States, has probably become still more unequal and, in terms of family ownership, possibly strikingly more unequal, in recent years."[13]

While any discussion of equality cannot ignore the distribution of wealth and income, it is important to recognize that the higher standard of living of the majority in America, as compared with other countries, may contribute to sustaining the characteristically American assumption that no man may claim the right to generalized deference from another, that no elite has the right to dominance outside of its area of very special competence. The concern for equality may in some part be satisfied by the fact that the United States is at the point where the majority of the population can enjoy a high level of consumption. (The situation of the minority of very poor will be discussed below.) In a real sense, in spite of considerable inequality of wealth and income, the consumption indicators of status become more equally distributed with a high national wealth level. Thus in terms of 1960 prices, the average income per American family rose from $4,160 in 1929 to $5,070 in 1951 and to $6,040 in 1959.[14] "Between 1909 and 1929, consumer expenditure per head rose almost 45 per cent, and from 1929 to 1958–60 another 52 per cent."[15] Such increases, particularly when combined with a reduction in relative wealth and in inequality of income, means a substantial shift in the direction of equalizing consumption. And it is notable that the distribution of personal savings as well became much more equitable between the 1920's and the 1950's. A comparison of the distribution of consumer durables and property in the United States and Britain indicates that net worth "is much more widely distributed in America than in Britain.

[11] Lampman, *The Share of Top Wealth-Holders* . . . , p. 211.
[12] *Ibid.*, p. 215.
[13] Richard M. Titmuss, *Income Distribution and Social Change* (London: Allen and Unwin, 1962), p. 198.
[14] Kuznets, "Income Distribution and Changes in Consumption," *op. cit.*, p. 30.
[15] *Ibid.*, p. 46.

There are comparatively few Americans who own nothing [15 per cent]: there are many Britons who own nothing [34 per cent]. . . ."[16]

> [T]he over-all difference between the British and American patterns of property ownership is largely attributable to differences between the lower-paid occupations in the two countries. Property is more widely held in America than in Britain, not because the higher-paid occupations have more property in America, but because more manual workers, more clerical and sales workers, and more retired and unoccupied persons have property in America. . . .
>
> These figures suggest that in respect of property ownership there is more difference between the social classes in Britain than in the United States. . . . British spending units headed by managers and technical employees have net worth which is more than twice the all-British average, while American spending units in this group have net worth only slightly above the all-American average. At the other extreme, British manual worker spending units—especially skilled manual workers—are relatively badly off. The gap between them and the managers is very great, while in America it is only moderate.[17]

While the American distribution of *wealth* seems less steep than in Britain, and seemingly less than some other European nations for which data exist, the variations in *income* in the United States are among the highest in the world. As was noted earlier in the discussion of trade-union policy, the stress placed on achievement in America seemingly fosters a concern with, and an acceptance of, relatively large differences in pay among those of varying skills, responsibility, and power. It is interesting to note, therefore, that the other great nation which places high stress on the value of achievement, the Soviet Union, seems comparable to the United States in inequality of income. This is true, both with respect to differences in reward for varying levels of worker skills, and in variations between incomes of factory managers and workers. The economist David Granick has recently concluded:

> Managers comprise part of the high-income group of Soviet society, just as they do in the United States. . . . In terms of income in-equality the relation between worker and manager in Russia and

---

[16] Harold Lydall and John B. Lansing, "A Comparison of the Distribution of Personal Income and Wealth in the United States and Great Britain," *The American Economic Review*, 49 (1959), p. 59.

[17] *Ibid.*, pp. 61–62, 64.

in the United States does not differ too greatly. Pre-tax, the American manager would be a bit ahead; but then his income tax is higher.[18]

Comparisons such as these, of course, ignore the social implications of the fact that a majority of the American population earn enough to purchase some form of the "good" things of the society, a fact which is certainly not true of the Soviet Union or of most other nations. But if the greater absolute level of income makes possible a more comparable style of life among the classes, this pattern of seeming equality in social relations is perhaps facilitated even more by what is probably the most equitably distributed item in America from a comparative point of view—education. The pressures to equalize educational facilities reflect the emphasis on both equality and achievement, and these pressures are still operating.

Between 1910 and 1960, according to United States Census data, the proportion of sixteen- and seventeen-year-olds attending school increased from 43.1 to 80.9 per cent. And the enrollment of those of post-high school age, eighteen and nineteen years old, as full time students jumped from 18.7 to 42.2 per cent.[19] The sharp increase in the educational attainments of the American people may be seen in a comparison of the educational achievements of a 1959 national sample of heads of families (Table IX). Only 15 per cent of the youngest group did not go on to high school, as compared with 53 per cent of the oldest one, while 30 per cent of those under thirty-four have attended college as contrasted with 17 per cent among those over fifty-four years old. These figures underestimate the increase in education among those eighteen to thirty-four years old, since the sample cited is one based on heads of families, and consequently the unmarried college students who are still supported by their parents are not included in the returns.

Today, over two-thirds of all Americans in the relevant age groups graduate from high school, and over one-third enters colleges or universities. These proportions are even higher in the wealthier urbanized

---

[18] David Granick, "Soviet-American Management Comparisons," U.S. Congress, Joint Economic Committee, Subcommittee on Economic Statistics, 86th Congress, *Comparisons of the United States and Soviet Economics*, Part I (Washington, D.C.: U.S. Government Printing Office, 1959), p. 144. See also Herbert McClosky and John E. Turner, *The Soviet Dictatorship* (New York: McGraw-Hill, 1960), pp. 384–385.

[19] Hauser, "More from the Census of 1960," *op. cit.*, p. 33.

Table IX

Education and Age, 1959

Education	55 and older (Born Before 1905)	35 to 54 (Born 1905–1925)	18 to 34 (Born 1925–1942)
		Per Cent	
None	4	1	0
Grades 1 through 8	49	26	15
Grades 9 through 11	17	23	23
Grade 12	8	18	21
Grade 12 plus non-academic courses	5	11	11
Some college or more	17	21	30

Source: James N. Morgan, Martin H. David, Wilbur J. Cohen and Harvey E. Brazer, Income and Welfare in the United States (*New York: McGraw-Hill, 1962*), *p. 332.*

northern and western states. In California, well over 40 per cent of all college age youth enter an institution of higher learning. But even such figures as these do not satisfy the American passion to equalize opportunity. A Presidential Commission on Higher Education set as a desirable and attainable objective that two-thirds of the college age population should attend such institutions. And the various public agencies are planning to enlarge facilities to reach that figure in the latter decades of this century.

Since a college education is a necessary prerequisite for a place on the bureaucratic ladder in business and government, it becomes essential to Americans to tax themselves to provide such educational opportunities. Evidence that Americans are more than willing to pay these costs may be seen in the 1959 survey study cited in Table IX. When asked whether taxes should pay *more* of the cost of higher education than they are now doing, 52 per cent of the sample of 3,000 family heads said that they should, while only 18 per cent favored decreasing the tax burden; 30 per cent would continue the present policies. Those family heads with dependent children were, not unexpectedly more in favor of increasing taxes for college than those without them. However, even among the latter group, 48 per cent favored higher taxes, as compared with 21 per cent who supported a reduction. And even when the respondents were differentiated according to income, the highest income group, those earning $10,000 or more, showed many more favoring a tax increase

(41 per cent) than a cut (22 per cent). Strong Democratic partisans were more likely than were committed Republicans to favor increasing taxes for higher education (56 per cent to 40 per cent), but it is perhaps more significant that many more Republicans favored raising taxes than advocated a decrease.[20]

The continued strength of liberal social and economic political forces in the wealthiest nation of the world also attests to the continued significance of the basic value system in the power arena. Some political experts had seen Democratic and liberal strength primarily as an after-effect of the Great Depression, and predicted that post-depression generations reared in affluent America would vote Republican and conservative.[21] Such analysts saw in the election of Eisenhower in 1952 the beginning of a long-term Republican era. But in fact, even during the Eisenhower years, the Republicans could not elect a majority in either house of Congress (1952 apart), and they lost strength on the local level. *In my judgment, it was the prolonged post-Civil War Republican reign that was the major deviant case in the general American political pattern of liberal domination.* It was brought about by the increment of Negro and northern white votes which the Civil War gave to the Republicans as the party which freed the slaves and saved the Union. Once the Republicans lost their hold on groups won by these issues, the nation returned to the electoral patterns set in the eras of Jefferson and Jackson, which ensure a normal majority for the party of equality. Today, as before the Civil War, it is an electoral handicap to be identified with the party of the elite.[22] Republican candidates today, like Whig and Federalist candidates a century or more ago, seek to run as personalities rather than as Republicans. In many states, it is difficult to find the Republican label on the campaign literature of

---

[20] James N. Morgan, Martin H. David, Wilbur J. Cohen and Harvey E. Brazer, *Income and Welfare in the United States* (New York: McGraw-Hill, 1962), pp. 416–418.

[21] Samuel Lubell, *The Future of American Politics* (Garden City, N.Y.: Doubleday Anchor, 1956).

[22] "In America, of course, status, as fixed differential social position, has long been in disrepute. Ever since the Revolutionary War, it has borne the hateful implications of privilege and subservience. . . . Thus status incurred obloquy, and even the party of conservatism—that is, the Republican party—rejected it. Probably nothing has contributed more to the weakness of the conservative position in the United States than the fact that this principle, which the great conservative leaders like Edmund Burke and Benjamin Disraeli have recognized as the foundation stone of conservatism, has been so sharply rejected by American conservatives. . . ." Potter, *People of Plenty*, pp. 104–105.

that party's nominees. Democrats, on the other hand, recognize that the party label, the label of the party of the common man, is an asset, and they emphasize it.

Although the majority of employed Americans (primarily those in white-collar jobs) do not belong to trade unions, and although unions have been subject to continuous criticism as dictatorial, corrupt, and excessively powerful organizations, efforts to hamper their activities have been defeated by the electorate when subject to referenda in northern and western industrial states. Goodly majorities, including the residents of well-to-do suburban counties, have voted down anti-union "right-to-work" laws. When the voters are asked to cast ballots on issues that are defined as business versus unions, the latter almost invariably win. There is a strong bias in favor of them as organizations protecting poor people against wealthy business interests.

American egalitarianism is, of course, for white men only. The treatment of the Negro makes a mockery of this value now as it has in the past. During the early nineteenth century, when European leftists and liberals were pointing to the United States as a nation which demonstrated the viability of equality and democracy, America was also the land of slavery. The trauma of slavery is deeply rooted in the American psyche. The contradiction between the American value system and the way in which the Negro has been treated has, if anything, forced many Americans to think even more harshly of the Negro than they might if they lived in a more explicitly ascriptive culture. There is no justification in an egalitarian society to repress a group such as the Negroes unless they are defined as a congenitally inferior race. Therefore, Americans have been under pressure either to deny the Negro's right to participate in the society, because he is inferior, or to ignore his existence, to make him an "invisible" man. The South has always insisted on the first alternative. The North tried for many decades after the Civil War to follow the second. But once the Negro appeared on the northern urban scene with his demands for equality, there was no legitimate way to hold him down. As Gunnar Myrdal has convincingly demonstrated in his *An American Dilemma*, the American Creed is on the side of the Negro, and even men who have strong prejudices against Negroes must assent publicly to their rights. The pace is all too slow; the poison of anti-Negro prejudice is a part of American culture, and almost all white Americans have it, to a greater or lesser degree. White Americans can no more fail to absorb anti-Negro sentiments than Christians can avoid assimilating some anti-Semitic feelings. But racist sentiments are in sharp conflict with American values and create a strain in the minds of Americans, a strain which provides an important weapon for those pressing for Negro equality.

It is important to note that what makes the Negro issue so difficult of quick resolution, as compared to prejudice against various immigrant groups, is that two centuries of slavery left the American Negro without a stable family or community structure.[23] Existence under slavery also resulted in a negative reaction to work or achievement. Working hard led nowhere. Exhibiting or developing high intelligence often resulted in punishment. These negative rewards for conforming to the normal American achievement standards continued until deep into the present century for most southern Negroes. Hence, the Negro now enters white urban society at a much greater disadvantage than any white immigrant group ever did. He appears "undesirable." The white community, therefore, continues to punish him for the sins which its forefathers committed against his.

Perhaps the most important fact to recognize about the current situation of the American Negro is that *equality is not enough to assure his movement into the larger society*. The greatest progress in the direction of securing equal rights for Negroes has occurred since World War II, with integration in the armed services, the Supreme Court's decision outlawing segregation in schools and other public places, and the passage in various northern states and cities of legislation designed to prevent discrimination in employment and housing. In spite of all these gains, however, the national median income for the non-white population in 1960 was only 54 per cent of that for whites. (It should be noted, however, that there is a tremendous disparity between the South and the rest of the country. Thus, southern non-whites average 43.4 per cent of the regional median white income, while in the rest of the country the non-white median income is 70 per cent of that received by whites.[24]) On a national basis, employed Negroes in 1960 received about 60 per cent of the income of whites—a figure that was almost identical to that of 1950.[25] Unemployment, which has been around 5 per cent of the labor force since 1958, has been disproportionately concentrated among Negroes. As of mid-year 1963, more than 10 per cent of Negroes were unemployed, and

---

[23] Stanley Elkins, *Slavery* (Chicago: University of Chicago Press, 1959).
[24] Hauser, "More from the Census of 1960," *op. cit.*, p. 37.
[25] Miller, "Is the Income Gap Closed? 'No!'" *op. cit.*, pp. 50–52.

another 10 per cent had only part-time work.[26] One out of four Negroes under nineteen years of age in the labor force was unemployed.

The reasons for the Negro's seemingly slow rate of economic progress do not lie solely in discrimination in the labor market. The fact that the Negro population has a much lower level of education and skill means that automation has been eliminating the very jobs in which Negroes are concentrated. Fair employment legislation does little good if there are no decent jobs available for which the bulk of Negroes are qualifed. According to the 1960 Census, 23.4 per cent of the non-white population is functionally illiterate, "unable to read a newspaper easily."[27] The problem is a continuing one, since Negro youth do much less well than whites in school. The low emphasis on achievement resulting from their past, their weak family structure, and their segregated and inferior schools, all adversely affect their capacity to gain from education. To break this vicious cycle, it is necessary to treat the Negro *more than equally*, to spend more money rather than equal amounts for Negro education, to have smaller classes with better teachers in predominantly Negro schools, to enlarge the scope of counseling and recreation facilities available for Negro youth, and the like. The white community must be forced to recognize its moral responsibility to subsidize the training of Negroes. If the former imperialist nations such as France and Great Britain now feel the responsibility to contribute to the economic development of the successor states formed from their empires, white Americans today should be prepared to assume responsibility for the educational and economic development of the descendants of those whom earlier white Americans dragooned from Africa to serve them as slaves.

The equalitarian pressures in American society obviously do not operate independently of the minds of men, and they have meaning only insofar as they affect behavior. The abolition of slavery did not occur simply because it violated basic morality; it required a heroic struggle by the abolitionists to activate the conscience of white America. White Ameri-

---

[26] E. W. Kenworthy, "Rise in Negro Jobs Linked to Growth," *The New York Times*, June 28, 1963, p. 1; John D. Pomfret, "Literacy Act Tied to Equality," *ibid.* (Western Edition), p. 4.

[27] Hauser, "More from the Census of 1960," *op. cit.*, p. 34. In testifying before Congress on the problem of Negro unemployment in July, 1963, Secretary of Labor Willard Wirtz reported that 44 per cent of unemployed Negroes had not finished the eighth grade. He stated that "many applicants for a recent training program for janitors in the District of Columbia could not read the labels on boxes of detergent and rat poison." Pomfret, *op. cit.*

cans, like all people, prefer to be left in peace; they do not want to be told that their behavior violates their sense of right. Equalitarian values are a force in the Negro's favor, but their efficacy depends on whether men are willing to use them as political weapons. And while the Negroes themselves have been a major force pressing for their rights, appealing to the morality of the majority group, the very social and economic inequality of the Negroes reduces their political power. Like all depressed and uneducated groups, Negroes vote less and participate less in politically relevant organizations than do more advantaged groups. Even the Negro Revolt of 1963 is largely the work of college students and others from the middle-class Negro minority. Unless whites are willing to take up their cause in order to force politicians, businessmen, labor organizations, and other relevant groups to support the necessary measures, Negro inequality will remain a blot on the American claim to be democratic and will prevent foreigners from recognizing how real and significant is the national commitment to equalitarianism—as is evidenced in other spheres of American life.

While Negroes constitute the most visible example of economic and social deprivation in the United States, they are joined at the bottom of the economic ladder by a large white group. Various estimates, by economists, government agencies, and labor organizations, of those living in poverty in the United States have varied from 20 to 40 per cent of the population.[28] Negroes constitute about 25 per cent of the poverty-stricken, twice their proportion in the population, but are still outnumbered by the poor whites.

The modern American poor are significantly different from the poor in the economically less developed countries and in the past of this country. They vary from the poor elsewhere in having a much higher absolute standard of living. This fact, however, should not be a matter for self-congratulation. The lowest fifth of the population of the United States had an average income in 1958 of $1,460 per family. This is considerably higher than the income per family in many nations, but the standard of what constitutes a decent level of life obviously is much different for an American than for an Iranian village dweller or for the resident of a Chinese commune. Living in a nation in which success is expected of all,

[28] For a discussion of these estimates and their sources see Michael Harrington, *The Other America: Poverty in the United States* (New York: Macmillan, 1962), pp. 175–191. The most comprehensive set of references to the literature on this subject may be found in Morgan *et al., Income and Welfare in the United States.*

and in which the poor are aware that they live on a level much below that of the great majority, must result in a sense of frustration, of alienation from the society. It will be of a different order from that which exists among those who must worry about enough food to eat and who see some of their children die while young, but the sense of relative deprivation, of personal inadequacy, may be greater than exists among the poor in nations where they can feel that they are living a life akin to the majority of their fellow men. By the standards which the highest 60 per cent of the American population use to define the modicum of a livable existence, the poor, those with less than $3,000 to $5,000 a year income (to take a low point which must vary with size of family) are living in miserable conditions. They lack decent housing, a good diet, adequate clothing, and, most important of all, the ability to have pride in themselves.

But the greater income, or the possibly increased sense of relative deprivation, which characterizes the American poor as compared with those elsewhere, is not the most significant fact about the condition of this group in the United States of the 1960's. Rather, as John Kenneth Galbraith and Michael Harrington have emphasized, poverty is not a general condition of the lower strata as it once was in the American past and still is in most nations. Where the majority of the working-class or the rural population are poor, they constitute an actual or potential force pressing for a general improvement in their lot. Thus, in the underdeveloped countries, the dominant parties seek to foster rapid economic growth so as to reduce mass poverty. In the United States, the lower classes once provided the mass base for political movements, farm organizations, and trade unions, which advocated reform legislation designed to improve the situation of the more deprived groups. The leaders of parties and mass organizations were sensitive to the demands and plight of the depressed. Many middle-class intellectuals devoted considerable energies to publicizing their situation and to supporting measures for economic betterment.

Today, however, poverty is not general; it is located in special pockets of the society. And these pockets are both politically weak and relatively invisible. The affluent middle class and the well-paid, skilled section of the working class are almost unaware of the existence of large numbers of the very poor. The poor today are not the bulk of the urban proletariat or the majority of a predominant farm population; rather, they are concentrated among the Negroes, the aged, the uneducated, the unskilled, the migrant farm workers, small farm operators, families which have lost their male head, and that large group of persons with individual handicaps (those with low I.Q.'s or those suffering from mental illness, physical deformities, or other chronic illnesses). The handicaps of many in the latter group, of course, are as much a consequence as a cause of poverty, since the poor are disproportionately subjected to such morbidities precisely because of their poverty. In evaluating the social sources of poverty for a Senate Committee, Robert Lampman estimated that over two-thirds of the low-income group have an eighth grade education or less, one-quarter are over sixty-five years of age, one-quarter are in families in which the woman is the chief breadwinner, and one-fifth are non-white.[29] These categories overlap considerably, of course. Lampman reports that 70 per cent of the low-income group have at least one of these characteristics, a finding which suggests that low education is the principal intervening variable which determines income opportunities, since race, age, and family instability are associated with extent of education. Lampman's analysis has since been reiterated in a comprehensive study of factors related to low income completed by a group at the University of Michigan's Survey Research Center.[30] It is significant to note that beyond the variables cited above, one-half of the poor families in this survey live in the South, and that a "sizable majority of poor families live in areas beyond the suburban belts surrounding metropolitan areas, where the variety and number of jobs available are not as great as in the large cities and their environs."[31]

It is difficult to predict whether existing trends will operate to reduce the proportion of the very poor in succeeding decades. Robert Lampman, who estimates that about 20 per cent are now in the poverty-stricken class, concludes on the basis of his analysis of long-run trends that by 1977–1987 this will decline to 10 per cent.[32] He bases this conclusion on the assumption of a continuing rate of economic growth. In addition to this factor, the expansion of educational facilities should reduce the proportion of individuals who lack the skills to hold relatively well-paying

[29] Robert J. Lampman, *The Low Income Population and Economic Growth*, U.S. Congress, Joint Economic Committee, Study Paper No. 12, 86th Congress, 1st Session, December, 1959, pp. 6–9.

[30] Morgan *et al.*, *Income and Welfare in the United States*, pp. 188–217.

[31] *Ibid.*, p. 212. Poverty in this study is defined as not earning enough to maintain a necessary minimum standard of living, as defined by social agencies in determining eligibility for assistance and free medical care. According to this standard 20 per cent of all families are living in poverty, and another 20 per cent are slightly above this minimum.

[32] Lampman, *The Low Income Population and Economic Growth*, p. 24.

jobs. And it should be noted that changes in the occupational structure are constantly reducing those positions which are least rewarding economically: small farms, farm labor, and unskilled manual labor.

These optimistic projections are countered, however, by the fact that the United States' economic growth rate (2 per cent) has remained for a number of years the lowest of any developed country except Britain's; by the fact that, over the past five years, the economy has been unable to create new jobs to replace those eliminated by automation or made necessary by the expansion of the labor force as a result of population growth; and, finally, by the implications of the fact that the poverty-stricken have much larger families than do the well-to-do. Lampman indicates that one-third of the 20 per cent of the population in the low-income class are under eighteen. And we know from a variety of studies that poverty tends to sustain itself in a self-maintaining cycle; the children of the very poor as compared to others are less motivated to achieve, do less well in school, and enter the labor market with fewer of the skills which might enable them to compete for good jobs. Increasing automation also contributes—over the short run, at least—to an increase in the very poor, since older men (age forty or older), once they are displaced by the elimination of the need for their traditional skill, find it extremely difficult to relocate in a well-paying position.

The data from the University of Michigan Survey Research Center study do offer some hope that the younger, better educated children of the poor succeed in securing better jobs than their fathers. Two-thirds of those from poverty-stricken families who had completed their education at the time of the interviews in 1959 had secured more than an eighth grade education and almost half of them (45 per cent) had finished high school.[33] Among the children of unskilled workers, 44 per cent of those fifty-five or older in 1959 were in unskilled jobs, in contrast to 31 per cent among those in the thirty-five to forty-four bracket and only 21 per cent among those under thirty-five years old.[34] In other words, as a group, the younger offspring of the unskilled are now working in jobs which require more education and skill, which pay more, and which are less vulnerable to economic fluctuations than those held by their fathers.

But if structural trends with respect to education and skill are favorable to a long-term decline in the proportion among the population who

---

[33] Morgan *et al.*, *Income and Welfare in the United States*, p. 211.
[34] *Ibid.*, p. 337.

live at the level of poverty, the data for the 1950's indicate that it is impossible to rely on structural trends alone to eliminate or sharply reduce income inequality. As has been noted, the very forces which have upgraded the economy have also served to make a hard-core minority out of the poor, the clearly underprivileged. The economically well-to-do, the middle class, both self-employed and employed, and the organized workers in the skilled crafts and mass production industries constitute a majority of the population. The Democratic Party, the more left-wing party, is today largely responsive to pressures from middle-class liberal intellectuals and relatively well-paid trade unionists. And though it continues to espouse the cause of Negro equality, and to favor the extension of welfare measures and the equalization of opportunity—for example, medical care for the aged and federal aid to education—on the whole it has not fostered a drive for a massive (and therefore costly) attack on poverty. No prominent Democrat, for example, has proposed to extend old age pensions to the point where the State will provide for a pension of 65 per cent of the average of the top fifteen years of a man's earnings, as has been enacted in Sweden; or to reduce the pressures on older workers who face elimination by automation, by means of lowering the retirement age to fifty-five which has been done in a number of nations; or to extend leisure and increase the need for labor by guaranteeing a three- or four-week vacation with pay, as the Swedish government is proposing and as a number of other countries have already provided. Few Democrats in high places seriously propose to increase sharply the contribution of the government to community leisure resources, as Galbraith has advocated. Many liberal intellectuals, believing that they live in an affluent, relatively equalitarian society, have in fact deliberately turned away from a concern with economic betterment of the underprivileged (the Negroes apart). They now direct the bulk of their criticism at the quality of American culture, and their targets include mediocre taste in architecture, bad urban planning, the corrupting character of the mass media, the uninspired quality of public education (the weaknesses of high schools in preparing students for college is of much more concern to them than the lack of school resources in lower-class areas), the dilution of taste fostered by advertising and by companies seeking the largest possible market, and the supposedly new emphases on conformity and status seeking in middle-class suburbs and corporate bureaucracies. The trade unions, like all interest groups, are primarily concerned with serving the particular needs of their own members and with preserving and extending their organizational influence on industry and the polity.

Most of these causes are well worth the effort put into them, but they also serve to deflect attention from the fact that for thirty to fifty million people, America is not an affluent society, that for this group the very emphasis on equality and achievement may intensify their sense of frustration. The Negroes are not the only depressed group left in America, and it ill becomes those who see this country as legitimately dominated by an egalitarian ethos to desist from the battle to extend economic equality. If the Democratic Party ignores its historic mandate to press for egalitarian reforms, then it may well suffer another catastrophe, equivalent to that which affected it in the 1850's when it failed to meet the slavery issue. For the American class system will not stand still, nor will it automatically continue to become more equalitarian. The changes occasioned by technology and the requirements of America's world role upset existing relationships. Men must respond deliberately to the requirements of their day; the fact that our basic values are still those set down in the Declaration of Independence means that the left, now as in the past, has the strength of these beliefs working on its side. But it must work to convert such national predispositions into meaningful policies. If it does not, then the pressures toward stabilizing the privileges of the more well-to-do and the more powerful, which are characteristic of all complex human societies, may reverse the trend toward equality—and if allowed to operate unchecked, may even begin to change these very values themselves.

An example of the way in which the American value system may be negated can be seen in the passage and continued existence of restrictive immigration legislation biased in favor of Nordic Protestants. The passage of this law in 1924 eliminated the universalistic and egalitarian principle which asserted that anyone had a right to become an American, that to become one required only that one wanted to be an American, not that one be lucky in having chosen one's parents. And though it is possible to argue that the imposition of numerical restrictions on immigration was necessary with an end of an open land frontier, the fact remains that to have imposed particularistic ethnic and religious restrictions on immigration constituted a fundamental violation of traditional American values.

Fortunately, an examination of the forces which precipitated the passage of this law suggests that it did not reflect a clear-cut rejection of the American Creed. Rather, in the 1920's its enactment—together with the passage of the Prohibition Amendment to the United States Constitution which occurred a few years earlier, the enactment in many states of laws barring the teaching of evolution, and the rise of the Ku Klux Klan—represented the power of the backwash of provincial resentment against structural changes within the society which were weakening the social and political influence of the more fundamentalist small-town and rural Protestants. The 1920 census reported that for the first time in American history, a majority lived in "urban areas." And the urban areas, particularly the culturally and economically dominant metropolitan cities, were centers of opposition to evangelical Protestant influence, an opposition consisting of Catholics, Jews, and adherents of the liberal high-status Protestant denominations. To the ascetic smalltown Protestants, these cities represented drunkenness, immorality, political corruption, and cosmopolitanism. Many evangelical Protestants backed Prohibition and nativism because they saw real evidence that the increase in the size of the non-Protestant population and the growth of the metropolis were undermining their way of life, were relegating them and their communities to a minority position.

The crusade to keep America Protestant by imposing ascetic norms on the total population and by barring massive non-Protestant immigration is actually almost as old as the United States itself. From Jefferson's day to Wilson's, there was an association between conservative politics, efforts to impose ascetic Protestant morality on the lower classes—often viewed as largely immigrant in composition—and attempts to limit immigration of (or to withhold equal rights from) the foreign-born. In almost every generation, "old American" groups which saw themselves "displaced," relatively demoted in status or power by processes rooted in social change, have sought to reverse these processes through the activities of moralistic movements or political action groups. Conflict between the advocates of ascetic and nativist doctrines, usually associated with the Federalist-Whig-Republican party, and their more culturally cosmopolitan and egalitarian opponents, most often located in the non-Southern Democratic Party, has characterized much of American history.

The victories which these fundamentalist groups attained after World War I did not, however, indicate that the basic values had been adjusted in their favor. If anything, as I have suggested above, they won their legislative battle on the very eve of their loss of a numerical majority in the nation.[35] Their strength at the time was in part a result of the

---

[35] The chief national lobbyist of the Anti-Saloon League pressed for the enactment of Prohibition before 1920 because, as he openly stated at a convention of the League: "We have got to win it now because when 1920 comes and reapportionment is here, forty new wet Congressmen will come from the

coincident combination of, first, the greatest Republican electoral victory in history, resulting from the resentment of many traditional Democratic ethnic groups to the fact that Wilson had taken the country into a war they opposed, and second, the intensity of fundamentalist feeling occasioned by the fact that their real decline had become more manifest than ever.

The sources of support for such policies began to disintegrate almost as soon as they were enacted into law. The Ku Klux Klan collapsed before the 1920's ended. In 1928, Al Smith, though a Catholic and an avowed anti-Prohibitionist, secured a larger proportion of votes outside of the fundamentalist, Prohibitionist, and rural South than any previous Democratic presidential candidate in the twentieth century, with the exception of Woodrow Wilson in 1916. The Great Depression provided the death blow for prohibition; repeal was regarded as a measure that would help spur business and increase employment. The existence of mass unemployment, however, strengthened the sentiment supporting restrictions on immigration, and the nationalist fervor occasioned by war and continued postwar international tensions have reinforced them. Gradually, however, the more bigoted aspects of the restrictions are being eliminated. The United States has taken many "non-quota" European refugees from non-Nordic Protestant areas, and the administration of the quotas is being slowly liberalized. The country will probably never return to a state of unrestricted immigration; but it will probably curtail discrimination based on national origins as a means of differentiating among those who may enter.

The Ever-Present Conflict between Equality and Inequality

In evaluating the continued effect of the value system on various institutions, I am not arguing the case for sociological determinism as an alternative to economic determinism. In presenting the thesis that there was a relationship between the Protestant ethic and economic development, Max Weber did not argue in terms of any necessary condition. Rather, he advanced the generalization that certain values inherent in

---

great wet centers with their rapidly increasing population." Wayne B. Wheeler, quoted in Peter Odegard, *Pressure Politics, The Story of the Anti-Saloon League* (New York: Columbia University Press, 1928), p. 173. The majority of Democrats outside of the South voted against the Prohibition Amendment in the House of Representatives. It was passed with the support of the Republicans and Southern Democrats.

ascetic Protestantism were extremely encouraging to the capitalist accumulation of wealth. In the same way, I have been urging here that
certain elements of the American value system encourage various forms
of behavior and institutional reaction and development. But the precise
developments which occur at any given time in history are a result of a
multitude of factors. Men must act to secure the kind of social order that
they want. American values, more than those of other nations, have
encouraged men to apply equalitarian and achievement orientations to
the polity and its various institutions. But other forces have pressed
men in very different directions. The privileged strata in America, as in
other countries, have sought to maintain and enhance their advantages.
And they have been able to win victories in the struggle with the
egalitarian left. The Civil War, led in the North by the party allied
with business, ironically strengthened economic and class conservatism
greatly. The very success of the American Revolution and its leftist
political aftermath, which gave the lower strata a place in society
superior to that of lower classes in any other nation, also meant that
there was less that they would want in the future. The subsequent
moderation of American class politics is related to the fact that
egalitarianism and democracy triumphed *before* the workers were a
politically relevant force. Unlike the workers in Europe, they did not
have to fight their way into the polity; the door was already open.
Hence, they had little use for socialist revolutionary theories, for approaches which argued the class domination of the society. And the lack
of a social base for a really radical working-class party has given a seemingly conservative face to American politics and even to its ideology,
when viewed from the vantage point of Marxist doctrine.

In a world in which radicalism is equated with some form of Marxism
and socialism, a nation without such movements or ideological tendencies
seems conservative. But as Leon Samson argued, the weakness of socialism
as an American ideology reflects, in part, the similarities between the
ideological content of socialism and that of Americanism as laid down in
the Declaration of Independence.[36] Americans have always defined the
preferred relationships among men in the same terms as have most
socialists. And since their self-conception leads them to believe that such
relationships actually characterize America—or are the agreed-upon objectives toward which the nation is moving—socialism as such has never
been able to make much headway. In a real sense, the more conservative

[36] Leon Samson, *Towards a United Front* (New York: Farrar and Rinehart,
1933), pp. 1–90.

the adjustment which a nation made to facing the problems of industrialization, that is, the more it preserved aspects of traditional pre-industrial values, particularly ascription and elitism, the greater the strength of radical lower-class movements within it. The United States, which retained fewer of these values than did any industrialized European country, has consequently been able to adjust to the structural changes imposed by economic and population growth with much less intense class conflict. Since progress is part of America's national self-image, progressive movements have been able to induce change without becoming radical. And the very success of earlier progressive movements has often eased the way for the victory of latter-day ones, so that these, when they arose, could hope to triumph by following moderate techniques. As Selig Perlman has pointed out, a major reason for the political moderation of the American labor movement lies in the fact that battles, such as the struggle for adult suffrage, which organized workers had to win in other nations, were already won and finished with before trade unions appeared on the scene:

> Another cause for the lack of "class consciousness" in American labor was the free gift of the ballot which came to labor at an early date as a by-product of the Jeffersonian democratic movement. In other countries where the labor movement started while the working-men were still denied the franchise, there was in the last analysis no need for a theory of "surplus value" to convince them that they were a class apart and should therefore be "class conscious." There ran a line like a red thread between the laboring class and the other classes.[37]

Ironically, though many foreigners view the United States as the one great stronghold of conservatism, it is the right-wingers, the American practical conservatives, who feel most alienated from the polity. The radical right finds a mass base; the radical left has little support. This fact tells a great deal about contemporary American society. Conservative businessmen and right-wing ideologists speak of the "liberal Establishment"; they believe that the dominant center of power in the country is on the left. American businessmen and conservatives, like their Swedish counterparts, report that the government and the society is opposed to

---

[37] Selig Perlman, *The Theory of the Labor Movement* (New York: Augustus M. Kelley, 1949), p. 167.

them. While this feeling of inferiority leads to a gross exaggeration of the realities of liberal power, since the strengths of business outside of the electoral arena are enormous, the fact remains that the United States is a nation in which the upper social and economic classes do not regard themselves as being in power. Businessmen are harangued by their associations and journals to learn how to participate in politics, and to follow the example of the liberals, intellectuals, and trade unionists, who, in their view, dominate the polity.

The recurrent conflict between liberal and conservative forces, between groups linked to equality or achievement, will continue as long as America is free. The forces making for elitism, for inequality, will seek, often successfully, to strengthen themselves. If they achieve a major permanent breakthrough, then America will become a different nation in terms of its values. If, for example, the values of a military society, which are elitist and diffuse, increasingly dictate the norms of the entire society, then one will not be able to speak of the continuity of values. To build and maintain a free and equalitarian society is the most difficult task political man has ever set himself. There are tendencies inherent in human social organization which seek to destroy freedom and to foster inequality. Hence the effort to prevent them from dominating must be a constant one. It must be directed against poverty and its related evils at one hand, and against ascription and elitism at the other. Most efforts to erect or continue democratic polities have disintegrated. The American experiment may very well fail. On the other hand, the fact that this New Nation has succeeded in fostering economic growth and democracy under the aegis of equalitarian values holds out hope for the rest of the world. For prosperity, freedom, and equality cannot be for white men only. If they are, then they will prove to have been as illusory and impermanent as the slave-based democracies of ancient Greece.

Comparative Analysis

From a methodological vantage point, that is, the concern with the creation of social science, this book is designed to illuminate the way in which sociological value analysis may contribute to generalizations about the sources of variation among complex societies. I write "illuminate" deliberately, since it should be clear that this work has not "proved" anything about the causes of differences among social systems. What I have attempted, rather, is to use a certain conceptual framework to point out possible relationships between the pattern of dominant value orientations and the content of their internal differentiation.

Clearly, if we are to move from purely descriptive comparative analysis, or narrowly focused historical comparison, to hypotheses concerning the generalized characteristics of such differences, we must have concepts, for which reliable indicators can be found, that permit systematic comparisons of different nations. As I suggested earlier, Talcott Parsons has inaugurated the major effort in this direction. His concepts, while obviously subject to considerable further refinements, do permit the comparison of complex units in terms of a number of predominant value orientations. As yet, however, little work has been done on the problem of linking such concepts to systematic empirical indicators (for example, how to differentiate units as being higher or lower in particularism or diffuseness).

Perhaps the most important efforts to test hypotheses about comparative national development by the rigorous methodology of modern social science have been initiated by Karl Deutsch. His study, *Nationalism and Social Communication*, demonstrated ways in which social scientists could test hypotheses concerning magnitudes in the variation of significant characteristics among different segments of a nation, and concerning its prospects for surviving as an integrated society.[38] In *Political Community and the North Atlantic Area*, he and a group of historians examined twenty historical efforts to create new national communities out of what had been separate entities. As has been noted earlier, some of their hypotheses are comparable to those suggested by the specific early American experience. They, however, sought to define the conditions for a particular type of new state by extensive comparative references to events in these societies, rather than an intensive case study of one society.[39] Still a third approach to the problem of testing hypotheses concerning the conditions for social and political development has involved the use

---

[38] Karl Deutsch, *Nationalism and Social Communication* (New York: John Wiley, 1953). Stein Rokkan's efforts to systematize analysis of the sources and consequences of ways in which new strata were admitted to the suffrage in various societies is also noteworthy in this respect. See his, "The Comparative Study of Participation," in Austin Ranney, ed., *Essays on the Behavioral Study of Politics* (Urbana: University of Illinois Press, 1962), esp. pp. 66–85.

[39] Karl Deutsch, S. A. Burrell, R. A. Kann, M. Lee, Jr., M. Lichterman, R. E. Lindgren, F. L. Loewenheim, and R. W. Van Wagenen, *Political Community and the North Atlantic Area* (Princeton: Princeton University Press, 1957), and Gabriel Almond and James S. Coleman, eds., *The Politics of Developing Areas* (Princeton: Princeton University Press, 1960).

of quantitative parameter data.[40] These data, however, are for the most part originally collected without reference to a complex conceptual scheme. They do yield much knowledge about the interrelated correlates of social structure; but the data collectors and manipulators will in the future have to be guided by theory which directs them to sources of data which census takers do not normally gather and might not think of looking for.

To find indicators of elitism in a culture, it might be useful to do a content analysis of symbols in samples of fiction, both popular and elite; or one might make a comparative study of military manuals among various nations. The sources of recruitment to different schools, government units, business organizations, and so forth would be hard data bearing on the extent of particularism in a society. Data from public opinion polls in various nations is an obvious source of evidence to test and elaborate hypotheses such as have been offered in this book. For the most part there has been little such comparative research explicitly guided by general theoretical considerations of a comparative sort. Perhaps the best example of such work is that of David McClelland and his collaborators, who have attempted to test various hypotheses concerning the psychological factors related to economic development on a comparative scale. As has been noted, McClelland has made detailed content analyses of the themes of children's stories in many countries and over considerable periods of time. He has also secured field data, based on interviews and questionnaires, designed to relate variations in personality patterns to occupational orientations in a number of countries. There are few methods or types of data, whether from ancient Greece or the modern Communist world, that McClelland is not prepared to use to elaborate his approach.[41]

---

[40] For example, see Lyle Shannon, "Is Level of Development Related to Capacity for Self-Government?" *American Journal of Economics and Sociology*, 17 (1958), pp. 367–382; Russell H. Fitzgibbon, "A Statistical Evaluation of Latin American Democracy," *Western Political Quarterly*, 9 (1956), pp. 607–619; Daniel Lerner, *The Passing of Traditional Society* (Glencoe, Ill.: The Free Press, 1958), especially p. 63; S. M. Lipset, *Political Man: The Social Bases of Politics* (Garden City, N.Y.; Doubleday, 1960), chapter 2; Karl Deutsch, "Toward an Inventory of Basic Trends and Patterns in Comparative and International Politics," *American Political Science Review*, 54 (1960), pp. 34–57; and *idem*, "Social Mobilization and Political Development," *ibid.*, 55 (1961), pp. 493–514.

[41] See David C. McClelland, *The Achieving Society* (Princeton, N.J.: Van Nostrand, 1961); McClelland, J. W. Atkinson, R. A. Clark, and E. L. Lowell,

We do not really know how similar and how different are men in various cultures. This book has emphasized differences among people living in such highly similar societies as those of the major English-speaking democracies. However, it would be possible to write an interesting and important book about similarities in taste and behavior among men in comparable or even highly varied societies.[42] What is one to make of the fact that the *Reader's Digest,* the most popular magazine in the United States, edited and published for Americans, is also the most popular magazine in many other countries in Europe, Africa, Asia, and Latin America? Why do Finns, Arabs, or Latins prefer a translated version of an American magazine largely dealing with American themes to magazines written by their compatriots? The *Digest* apparently has located a common bond of taste which unifies men in different cultures. Similarly, other popular cultural activities—the movies, jazz, various sports—have all had considerable appeal to the residents of nations which vary greatly in literacy, wealth, cultural history, religious values, and so forth. A study of the social prestige of occupations in various parts of the developed and underdeveloped world indicates high similarities in the rankings of comparable occupations in these nations.[43] If one may argue that any two nations, even two as similar as the United States and Canada, can be shown to be quite different, it is also possible to demonstrate that people everywhere have much in common.

Whether one stresses similarities or differences is to some extent a matter of taste or, rather, of conceptual frameworks. One may say about many things, "as much as" or "as little as." If one assumes that stratification and the pressure to pass on one's privileges to one's offspring are inherent in human social organization, then a national rate of social mobility in which one-third move down the class ladder appears high. If, however, one judges a system against a norm which demands perfect

---

The Achievement Motive (New York: Appleton-Century-Crofts, 1953); and McClelland and G. A. Friedman, "A Cross-Cultural Achievement Motivation Appearing in Folk-Tales," in G. E. Swanson, T. M. Newcomb, and E. L. Hartley, eds., *Readings in Social Psychology* (New York: Henry Holt, 1952), pp. 243–249. For an interesting effort by an economist to apply psychological concepts to the comparative and historical analysis of problems of economic development, see Everett E. Hagen, *On the Theory of Social Change* (Homewood, Ill.: The Dorsey Press, 1962).

[42] Deutsch, *et al., Political Community and the North Atlantic Area,* do this with respect to the relatively similar nations of the North Atlantic area.

[43] Alex Inkeles and Peter Rossi, "National Comparisons of Occupational Prestige," *American Journal of Sociology,* 61 (1956), pp. 329–339.

equality of opportunity, then the fact that most of the privileged strata do not fall seems inequitable. The way that one looks at social data depends in large measure on the questions asked, the theory employed, and the classifications used. It should be obvious that in dealing with complex subjects, no matter how rigorous the methodology employed, in elaborating or presenting a thesis which involves interrelating such structural variables as national values, class, personality, and the like, most social scientists basically present an argument which they then "validate" by showing that there are more positive than negative data available. Most of our concepts, however, are necessarily very imprecise, and consequently leave a great deal of room for the analyst unwittingly to find reasons for selecting those indicators which best fit the conceptual framework he is using. And when existing data are confirmatory, we are not motivated to look further. It is only when the data are in conflict with our theory, hunches, or prejudices that most social scientists decide there must be something wrong with the data or with the concepts underlying the selection of the data, and look further. In reading the work of others, we are normally inclined to accept their findings as both valid and reliable, as long as they agree with our predispositions. Disagreement, however, results in efforts to re-analyze the evidence and to demonstrate that previous work has drastically oversimplified, or simply ignored, much data.

It is important to recognize that by looking at the same problem from different theoretical perspectives, we increase knowledge about social processes. Different conceptual frameworks lead one man to highlight certain aspects which another ignores. Often findings that appear to be contradictory merely reflect the fact that different scholars have used different concepts. Thus a definition of class which is stated exclusively in terms of income may result in the conclusion that there has been no change in the class structure. On the other hand, a view of the class structure of the same society in terms of power or status may suggest that important changes have occurred.[44]

This book, like any effort at comparative analysis, is necessarily subject to the sins of oversimplification and exaggeration. Oversimplification comes about because, in comparing such complex phenomena as national value systems and national organizational structures, one must necessarily gloss over the internal differences that exist. Exaggeration is

---

[44] A brilliant discussion of the implications of various conceptualizations of class is Stanislaw Ossowski, *Class Structure in the Social Consciousness* (London: Routledge and Kegan Paul, 1963).

present because any effort to analyze the influence of only one set of factors, even if it is as important as the national value system, tends to disregard many other variables which are obviously necessary for the proper understanding of the variations involved. For example, important economic variables, such as differences in past rates of economic growth, in current levels of productivity, and in international market situations, all of which may have an independent effect on the various national patterns discussed, have largely been ignored here, partly because I have dealt with them in other works, but more significantly because a major purpose of this book has been to demonstrate the independent explanatory power of value analysis, seen as the codification of historical experiences.[45]

But while the principal scientific contribution of comparative analysis is to permit the testing of hypotheses concerning complex social systems, it has another less ambitious function, and those who reject the first as intellectually unattainable should be able to accept the second. A look at the same institution in varying cultural contexts is basic to any effort to understand why it has the character it does. To understand the American labor movement, American religion, American education, American law, or any other institution, it is necessary to know how it differs from the comparable institution in other cultures. Only when one knows what is unique on a comparative scale can one begin to ask significant questions about causal relationships within a country. Hence, even that most particularistic of all social scientists, the historian, can learn much about American history by studying the history of somewhat comparable foreign nations at equivalent points in their development. And if this is true for the historian, then it is even more valid for the rest of us.

A meaningful scientific dialogue requires, of course, certain basic levels of agreement on the rules of the discussion. Where problems are stated in fundamentally differing terms, as between political "true believers" and empirically, behaviorally oriented social scientists, no effective communication is possible. One must agree concerning the levels of hypothesis and the nature of evidence. Where this occurs, the dialogue can result in replication and the growth of knowledge. This method has been the very meaning of scholarly verification in history. The social sciences, however, with their desire to employ the same approaches to the verification of hypotheses as the natural sciences, have been reluctant to recognize that dialogue or controversy remains a principal means of scientific verification of hypotheses in their disciplines as well.

---

[45] An excellent analysis of much the same aspects of American values and behavior that have been discussed here which places the brunt of explanation on American economic development is Potter, *People of Plenty*.

Name Index

Aaron, Daniel, 40n.
Abegglen, J. C., 125n.
Abel, Theodore, 190n.
Abrams, Mark, ix
Adamic, Louis, 180n.
Adams, Abijah, 42n.
Adams, Francis, 253
Adams, Henry, 59, 65n.
Adams, John, 19, 21, 44
Adams, John Quincy, 44, 65
Adams, Rex, 188n., 192
Adenauer, Konrad, 239
Adorno, T. W., 277
Alexander, Fred, 252n., 256n.
Alford, Robert, 267n.
Allen, V. L., 190n.
Allport, Gordon W., 278n.
Almond, Gabriel, 24n., 113n., 115n., 132n., 177n., 211n., 212n., 344n.
Anderson, C. A., 221n., 222n., 240n.
Anderson, D. R., 64n.
Anderson, Perry, 236n.
Angus, H. F., 251n., 302n.,
Apter, David E., ix, 14, 18, 36n., 37n., 287n., 289n.
Argyle, Michael, 157n.
Arnold, Matthew, 115n.
Arnold, Thomas, 215n., 216n.
Aron, Raymond, 227n., 232n.
Aronson, Sidney, 101n., 102
Aschinger, F. E., 66n.
Asquith, Herbert Henry, 243n.
Atkinson, J. W., 345n.
Atlee, Clement, 218n.
Austin, Dennis, 36n.

Backmer, Donald L. M., 24n.
Baedeker, Karl, 110
Bagehot, Walter, 76, 213, 217n., 223n., 240n., 313n.
Bailyn, Bernard, 95n.
Baird, Robert, 142–146, 160n.
Baltzell, E. Digby, 153
Bancroft, Aaron, 22
Bancroft, George, 72
Baring Brothers, 55n.
Baron, George, 221n.

Barzun, Jacques, 109n.
Bassett, John Spencer, 40n., 77n.
Bayard, James A., 119n.
Beard, Earl S., 54n.
Beaumont, Gustave de, 17n., 19n., 22n., 73n., 74n., 154–155, 177n.
Becker, Carl L., 116
Beecher, Lyman, 82
Beer, Samuel, 306n.
Bell, Daniel, ix, 105, 138, 176, 214n., 220n., 271n.
Bell, W. M., 262
Bemis, Samuel F., 66n.
Benda, Harry J., 25n., 35n., 69n.
Bendix, Reinhard, vii, ix, 6, 129n., 170n., 183n., 216n., 228n.
Benson, Lee, 82n., 83n., 85n.
Berger, Max, 110n., 119n., 142n.
Berger, Morroe, 190n.
Bernardi, Gene, ix
Berthoff, Rowland, 113, 138
Bismarck, Otto von, 233n., 242
Bissell, Claude T., 257, 259n.
Black, Max, 7n., 210n., 212n.
Blishen, Bernard, 252n.
Blumenthal, Albert, 131n.
Boardman, J., 120n.
Bodo, John R., 59n., 82
Boisen, A. T., 157 n.
Bonham, John, 296n.
Boorstin, Daniel J., 70, 106
Bourget, Paul, 113
Bourricaud, François, 225, 227
Brady, Alexander, 225n., 258n.
Brazer, Harvey E., 329n.
Breckenridge, John C., 300
Bridenbaugh, Carl, 92, 160n.
Briggs, Asa, 215n.
Brock,W. R., 41n.
Brodbeck, Arthur, 287n.
Brodersen, Arvid, 133n.
Brogan, Denis W., 60, 112, 113n., 156n., 215n.
Bromwich, Leo, 196n.
Bronfenbrenner, Urie, 275n.
Brooks, John Graham, 109, 115, 120n.
Brotz, Howard, 117n.

Brown, Stuart Gerry, 64n.
Bruckberger, R. L., 1, 152n.
Bruner, Jerome S., 178n.
Bryce, James, 108, 110, 112, 116–117, 141, 142n., 199–200, 258n., 263, 264n.
Buckingham, J. S., 120n.
Burdick, Eugene, 287n.
Burke, Edmund, 40n., 329n.
Burne-Jones, Philip, 110n.
Burr, Aaron, 33
Burrell, S. A., 9n., 26n., 91n., 210n., 344n.
Butler, D. E., 297n., 301n., 303n.
Butts, R. Freeman, 165n.

Caiger, George, 254n.
Calhoun, Arthur W., 120n., 121n.
Calhoun, Daniel H., 130n.
Callender, G. S., 48, 51n., 56n.
Campbell, Peter, 303n.
Cantril, Hadley, 150n.
Carroll, H. K., 146n., 147n.
Carter, Gwendolen M., 303n., 306n., 309n.
Chamberlain, Joseph, 243n.
Chambers, William Nisbet, x, 27n., 30n., 32n., 33, 38n., 61n.
Chapman, John Jay, 109
Charles, Joseph, 19n., 22n., 38n.
Chaudhuri, Nirad C., 248n.
Chubb, Basil, 303n.
Churchill, Randolph, 243n.
Clark, E. T., 157n.
Clark, R. A., 345n.
Clark, S. D., ix, 88, 166n., 250n., 251n., 262, 263n.
Clegg, Hugh A., 172–173, 188n., 192n., 193n., 194, 199n., 200n., 202n., 265n.
Clinton, George, 33, 42n.
Cohany, Harry, 188n.
Cohen, Wilbur J., 329n.
Cole, A. H., 55n.
Cole, David, 186n.
Coleman, James S., viii, 23n., 24, 35n., 36n., 190n., 207n., 212n., 344n.
Coleman, Lee, 106n.
Colton, Calvin, 161n., 162n.
Commager, Henry Steele, 105–106, 177n.
Conant, James B., 223n.
Connell, W. F., 254n.
Coxe, Tench, 47n.
Crawford, R. M., 258
Crèvecoeur, M. G. J. de (J. Hector St. John), 92, 94
Crosland, C. A. R., ix, 217n., 221n., 222n., 236, 271n.
Crozier, Michel, ix, 231
Cunliffe, Marcus, 18, 19n., 20, 22n., 40n., 104–105

Curley, James, 177
Curti, Merle, 69n., 72n., 86n.
Cyriax, George, 173n., 181n., 192, 196n.

Dahl, Robert, ix
Dahrendorf, Ralf, ix, 89, 90n., 282–283
Dandakar, V. M., 70n.
Dangerfield, George, 45n.
Dauer, Manning, 152n.
David, Martin H., 329n.
Davis, Jefferson, 34n.
Dawson, C. A., 251n.
Debré, Michel, 314n.
De Gaulle, Charles André, 296, 301
De Grazia, Alfred, 289n.
Deutsch, Karl W., viii, 4, 9n., 25–26, 46n., 75, 91n., 93n., 210n., 238n., 292n., 344, 345n., 346
Devereux, Edward C., Jr., 275n.
Dewey, John, 122
Dewhurst, J. F., 260
Diamond, Martin, 317n.
Dickens, Charles, 177
Disraeli, Benjamin, 242, 243n., 329n.
Dogan, Mattei, ix
Dolto, Françoise, 283n.
Donald, David, 72n.
Douglas, Paul H., 295n.
Dunlop, John T., 181n., 193n., 194n.
Dupeux, George, 298n.
Duroselle, Jean-Baptiste, 229n.
Duverger, Maurice, 289, 293, 295n., 297n., 298, 305, 310n., 316n., 317n.

Earle, Edward M., 226n.
Eckstein, Harry, x, 4n., 224, 234–235, 239n., 276n., 281n., 287n., 289n.
Edinger, Lewis J., 238n., 292n.
Edwards, Alba M., 149
Eggleston, Frederick, 254
Ehrmann, Henry W., 228n.
Eisenhower, Dwight D., 329
Eisenstadt, S. N., 245n., 317n.
Elizabeth I, 96
Elkins, Stanley, 28n., 30n., 162n., 331n.
Emerson, Ralph Waldo, 72n.
Emerson, Rupert, 37n.
Engels, Friedrich, 5–6, 7n., 272n.
Erikkson, Erik M., 101n.
Etzioni, Amitai, 74n.
Evan, William, 212n.
Everett, Edward, 22

Fairlie, John A., 287n.
Farber, Maurice L., 133n., 275n., 279
Fee, Walter, 78n.
Feuer, Lewis S., 8, 9n.
Fidler, Isaac, 122

Finney, Charles G., 83 n.
Fish, Carl R., 85 n.
Fisher, Marvin, 60 n.
Fitzgibbon, Russell H., 345 n.
Flexner, James T., 71 n., 73 n.
Florence, P. S., 221 n.
Floud, Jean, 221 n., 222 n., 240 n.
Ford, Thomas, 131 n.
Ford, W. C., 43 n.
Fox, Dixon Ryan, 73 n.
Franklin, Benjamin, 69 n.
Frenkel-Brunswick, Else, 277 n.
Friedman, G. A., 346 n.
Friedman, Milton, 128 n.
Friedrich, Carl, 307 n.
Friis, Henning, 192
Fromm, Erich, 132 n.

Gabriel, Ralph H., 106
Galbraith, John Kenneth, 334, 337
Galenson, Walter, 187 n., 188 n., 190 n., 191 n., 196 n.
Gallatin, Albert, 48
Gallup, George, 134 n.
Garrison, W. L., 34
Gay, Peter, 233 n.
Geiger, Kent, 320 n.
Geiger, Theodore, 291 n.
Gerschenkron, Alexander, 320
Gerth, H. H., 94 n., 115 n., 126 n., 142 n., 156, 246 n., 316 n.
Gilbert, Felix, 65 n.
Gillespie, James M., 278 n.
Goguel, François, 226, 229 n., 273 n., 299 n.
Goldberg, Arthur, *ix*
Gollan, Robin, 258 n.
Goodrich, Carter, 48, 52 n., 54 n., 255 n., 256 n.
Gorer, Geoffrey, 266
Gower, L. C. B., 200 n., 221 n., 264 n.
Grand Pierre, J. H., 154 n.
Granick, David, 326, 327 n.
Grassi, Giovanni, 153
Grattan, Thomas C., 153 n.
Greeley, Horace, 83 n.
Greene, Evarts B., 166 n.
Griesinger, Karl T., 143 n.
Griffin, Clifford S., 80 n., 161 n.
Grund, Francis J., 108 n., 116
Gulick, Charles, 308 n.
Gunderson, Robert G., 84 n.
Gusfield, Joseph, 81 n.

Habakkuk, H. J., 57 n.
Hacker, Andrew, 7 n., 212 n.
Hagen, Everett E., 346 n.
Haldane, Richard, 219

Halévy, Elie, 6 n., 216 n., 248 n.
Haliburton, Thomas Chandler, 257
Halsey, A. H., 221 n., 222 n., 240 n.
Hamburger, Joseph, 265
Hamilton, Alexander, 20, 27 n., 32, 37, 44, 65–66; forms "government party," 38; neutralism of, 63–64; "Report on Manufactures," 47 n.
Handlin, M. F., 49 n.
Handlin, Oscar, 49 n., 143 n., 153 n.
Harpur, Charles, 258
Harrington, Michael, 186 n., 193 n., 333 n., 334
Harris, Seymour, 170 n.
Harrison, Martin, 301 n.
Harrison, Tom, 218 n., 223 n.
Harrison, William Henry, 84
Hartley, E. L., 346 n.
Hartman, Paul T., 180 n., 199 n., 200 n., 202 n.
Hartmann, Heinz, 238
Hartz, Louis, 50 n., 52 n., 54 n., 78 n., 83 n., 85 n., 106
Hauser, Philip M., 324 n., 327 n., 331 n., 332 n.
Heath, Milton S., 53 n.
Heckscher, August, 136 n.
Herberg, Will, 141, 158, 198 n.
Hermens, F. A., 293, 298 n., 307 n.
Higham, John, 95 n.
Hill, Evan, 134 n.
Himmelfarb, Gertrude, 223 n.
Hobsbawn, Eric, 6 n.
Hodgkin, Thomas, 24, 31 n., 32 n.
Hoffman, Stanley, 229 n., 230 n.
Hofstadter, Richard, 40 n., 70, 72 n., 73 n., 89, 123
Hogan, D., 289 n.
Hopkinson, Joseph, 83 n.
Horkheimer, Max, 274 n., 277
Horney, Karen, 125, 132 n.
Hsu, Francis, 276 n.
Hudson, Winthrop S., 144 n., 145 n., 151 n.
Hughes, E. C., 251 n.
Humphreys, John H., 310
Hunsberger, Warren S., 25 n.
Hutchinson, John, 189
Hyman, H. H., 220 n.

Inkeles, Alex, 183 n., 276 n., 277–279, 320 n., 346 n.

Jackson, Andrew, 44, 82–84, 101 n., 329
Jacob, Philip E., 150 n.
Jacobs, James R., 93 n.
Jacobs, Paul, 186 n., 193
Jacobson, Dan, 319

James, E., 223 n.
James, J. Franklin, 89 n., 163, 202 n.
Jamison, L., 156 n., 157 n., 159 n.
Jay, John, 26, 33
Jefferson, Thomas, 20, 33–34, 37, 42 n.,
    43 n., 45–46, 48, 65 n., 66, 72, 101 n., 329,
    339; Embargo Act and, 47; on free
    press, 42; in Napoleonic wars, 63–64;
    opposition to "government party," 38;
    rise of national authority under, 45;
    Virginia dynasty of, 44
Jenks, Leland Hamilton, 55, 56 n.
Jensen, Merrill, 30 n., 31 n.
Johnson, F. Ernest, 167 n.
Johnson, John J., 92 n.
Johnson, Richard Mentor, 165 n.
Jones, Maldwyn Allen, 25 n., 26
Jowett, Benjamin, 115

Kaldegg, A., 278 n.
Kalven, Harry, 265 n.
Kann, R. A., 9 n., 26 n., 91 n., 210 n., 344 n.
Karpat, Kemal H., 316 n.
Kautsky, John H., 23 n., 24 n., 69 n.
Kaysen, Carl, 170 n.
Kenworthy, E. W., 332 n.
Kerr, Clark, 181 n., 182 n., 186
Key, V. O., Jr., 301 n.
Killick, A. J., 188 n., 192
Kindleberger, Charles P., 229 n.
King, E. J., 260 n.
Kirchheimer, Otto, 293 n.
Klein, Philip S., 78 n.
Kluckhohn, Clyde, 124, 138–139
Knorr, Klaus, *x*
Komarovsky, Mirra, 181 n.
Korchin, Sheldon J., 178 n.
Kossuth, Lajos, 86 n.
Kristol, Irving, *ix*
Krout, John A., 81 n.
Kuhn, Anne L., 120
Kuznets, Simon, 179 n., 322–323, 324 n.,
    325 n.

La Guardia, Fiorello, 127
Lakeman, Enid, 304 n.
Lambert, James D., 304 n.
Lampman, Robert J., 322–323, 325 n., 335–
    336
Landes, David S., *ix*, 226 n., 249 n.
Landis, Benson Y., 144 n.
Lane, Robert, 284 n.
Lansing, John B., 326 n.
Larrabee, Eric, 1, 60 n.
Laski, Harold, 125 n.
Lavau, G. E., 243 n., 289 n., 297 n.
LeBras, G., 273 n.

Lee, Henry, 18
Lee, M., Jr., 9 n., 26 n., 91 n., 210 n., 344 n.
Lee, Robert, 163 n.
Leiserson, Avery, 306 n.
Leland, L., 280 n.
Lens, Sidney, 189 n.
Lerner, Daniel, 345 n.
Lerner, Max, 1
Lester, Richard, 188 n., 192, 196 n., 202 n.
Leuba, James H., 149 n.
Levinson, Daniel J., 277 n.
Levy, Leonard W., 39 n., 43
Lewis, John L., 181
Lewis, Roy, 221 n., 226 n., 227 n., 241, 242 n.
Lichterman, M., 9 n., 26 n., 91 n., 210 n.,
    344 n.
Lichtheim, George, 8
Lindblad, Ingemar, 192
Lindgren, R. E., 9 n., 26 n., 91 n., 210 n.,
    344 n.
Linton, Ralph, 279 n.
Lipset, Seymour Martin, 8 n., 16 n., 36 n.,
    110 n., 112 n., 129 n., 136 n., 172 n., 181 n.,
    183 n., 190 n., 200 n., 207 n., 213 n., 218 n.,
    223 n., 228 n., 269 n., 282 n., 283 n., 288 n.,
    302 n., 313 n., 345 n.
Lipson, E., 221 n.
Lipson, Leslie, 254, 255 n., 296 n.
Littell, Franklin Hamlin, 148
Lively, Robert A., 54 n.
Livermore, Shaw, Jr., 41 n.
Lloyd George, David, 243 n.
Loewenheim, F. L., 9 n., 26 n., 91 n., 210 n.,
    344 n.
Longfellow, Henry Wadsworth, 72 n.
Loomis, Charles P., 209 n.
Lorwin, Val, 228 n.
Louis XVI, 63 n.
Lowell, E. L., 345 n.
Lowenthal, Leo, *x*, 213 n., 282 n., 283 n.
Lower, A. R. M., 87
Lowie, Robert, 291 n.
Lubell, Samuel, 329 n.
Ludlum, David M., 81 n.
Luethy, Herbert, 228 n.
Lunt, Paul S., 125 n.
Lynd, Robert S., 125
Lydall, Harold, 326 n.
Lynch, William O., 40 n.

McAvoy, Thomas T., 152 n.
McCallum, R. B., 306 n.
McCarthy, Joseph R., 262
McClelland, David, 134–135, 345, 346 n.
McClosky, Herbert, 327 n.
McCready, Benjamin, 114 n.
McGranahan, Donald V., 277, 278 n.
McKean, Thomas, 42

Mackenzie, Jeanne, 202 n., 253 n., 256 n., 262 n., 264 n., 266 n., 267 n., 268 n.
Mackenzie, W. J. M., 315 n.
Mackenzie, Sir William, 250 n.
McKitrick, Eric, 28 n., 30 n.
McLoughlin, William G., 83
MacRae, Duncan, Jr., 301 n.
Madison, James, 20, 29 n., 34, 65 n.; opposition to "government party," 38; Virginia dynasty of, 44
Marshall, T. H., 9 n.
Martin, Kingsley, 219 n.
Martineau, Harriet, 22 n., 59 n., 97, 107–112, 119 n., 120, 141, 142 n., 155
Marvick, Dwaine, 69 n.
Marx, Karl, 272 n.
Matthews, John Pengwerne, 257
Mayer, J. P., 233 n., 242 n., 291 n.
Mead, Margaret, 132 n., 275 n., 280 n., 283 n., 284 n.
Mead, Sidney E., 160 n.
Meany, George, 189 n.
Merton, Robert K., *viii*, 174
Mesick, Jane L., 58 n., 59 n., 108 n., 121
Metraux, Rhoda, 275 n., 280 n., 284 n.
Michels, Robert, 36 n., 208 n., 217, 291
Middleton, Drew, 215 n.
Miller, Daniel R., 137 n.
Miller, Herman, 323, 331 n.
Miller, J. D. B., 254 n., 303 n.
Miller, James Grier, 278 n.
Miller, John C., 39 n.
Miller, Nathan, 53 n.
Miller, William Lee, 40 n., 41 n., 42 n., 159 n.
Millikan, Max F., 24 n.
Mills, C. Wright, 1, 8, 94 n., 115 n., 126 n., 130, 142 n., 156 n., 188 n., 246 n., 316 n.
Mills, Frederick C., 179 n.
Mitchell, William, 213 n., 287 n.
Mitford, Nancy, 244 n.
Mollegen, A. T., 167 n.
Monroe, James, 44, 48, 64 n.
Moore, Barrington, Jr., 8
Morgan, James N., 329 n., 333 n., 335 n., 336 n.
Morison, Elting E., 105 n., 124 n., 139
Morris, Gouverneur, 29 n.
Muirhead, James F., 109, 117, 120 n.
Mulvaney, B. G., 145 n.
Münsterberg, Hugo, 114, 121
Myers, Charles A., 182 n., 186 n.
Myrdal, Gunnar, 97, 191 n., 195, 330

Naegele, Kaspar, 251, 252 n.
Napoleon Bonaparte, 65
Naysmith, Jenny, 218 n.
Nelson, William H., 76 n.

Neufeld, Maurice F., 226 n.
Neumann, Erich Peter, 184
Neumann, Sigmund, 291 n., 305 n., 306 n.
Newcomb, T. M., 346 n.
Nicholas, A. G., 223 n.
Nichols, Roy F., 79 n.
Niebuhr, H. Richard, 157 n., 160 n., 168 n.
Nkrumah, Kwame, 18, 36
Noelle, Elizabeth, 184

Oakeshott, Robert, 173 n., 181 n., 192
Odegard, Peter, 340 n.
O'Dowd, Bernard, 259
Ogle, Charles, 84
Oppenheim, Felix E., 305 n.
Ormsby, Margaret, 302 n.
Orwell, George, 218 n.
Ossowski, Stanislaw, 185 n., 347 n.
Ostrogorski, Moisei Y., 108
Ouseley, William G., 143 n.
Ozanne, Robert, 182 n.

Packard, Vance, 1
Padover, Saul K., 226 n.
Page, Charles, 190 n.
Paine, Tom, 43
Papineau, Louis Joseph, 250 n.
Parrington, V. L., 47 n.
Parsons, Talcott, *viii*, 3–5, 119, 141 n., 209, 210 n., 211 n., 212 n., 213 n., 270, 271 n., 285, 287, 344
Passow, A. Harry, 128
Pelling, Henry, 180 n.
Perkins, Bradford, 45 n., 71 n.
Perlman, Selig, 342 n.
Perry, Stewart E., 279 n., 285 n.
Persons, Stow, 156 n.
Petro, Sylvester, 189 n.
Philips, Irving P., 188 n.
Pierce, Henry, 53 n., 54 n.
Pierson, George W., 155 n.
Pittman, David, 81 n.
Pitts, Jesse R., 229 n.
Pitts, Ruth Ann, *ix*
Plamenatz, John, 93 n.
Plato, 118–119
Platt, Julius W., 64 n.
Pomfret, John D., 332 n.
Potter, David M., 7 n., 179 n., 320–321, 329 n., 348 n.
Price, Leolin, 200 n., 221 n., 264 n.
Priestley, J. B., 262
Primm, James N., 53 n., 54 n.
Pringle, J. D., 268 n.
Probst, George E., 165 n.
Purcell, Richard, 48 n., 49 n.

Raditsa, Bogden, 112 n.
Rasmussen, Albert T., 167 n.
Rawson, D. W., 200 n.
Reder, Melvin W., 181 n.
Renan, Ernest, 16
Renier, G. J., 215 n.
Rezneck, Samuel, 46 n.
Rhys, Ernest, 118 n.
Richardson, Stephen, 221 n.
Richmond, Patricia, 316 n., 317 n.
Riesman, David, 1, 102, 104, 107, 114 n., 119, 122, 126, 128, 130, 132, 135–136, 281–282
Rimlinger, Gustav, 6 n.
Roberts, B. C., 180 n., 189 n., 192, 193 n., 196 n., 198 n.
Robinson, K. E., 315 n.
Roche, John P., 27 n., 28–29
Rokkan, Stein, ix, 192, 344 n.
Rose, Arnold M., 225 n., 252 n.
Rosenberg, Arthur, 233 n.
Ross, Arthur M., 180 n., 196 n., 199 n., 202 n.
Ross, Lloyd M., 201 n.
Rossi, Peter, 183 n., 346 n.
Rossiter, Clinton, 83 n., 85 n., 97
Rosten, Leo, 150 n.
Rostow, Walt W., 59, 105, 124
Rothchild, Donald S., 23 n., 25 n., 27 n.
Rousseau, Jean-Jacques, 226
Rowe, A. P., 254 n.
Runciman, W. G., 37 n.
Rustow, Dankwart, 235 n., 314 n.

Sampson, Anthony, 216 n., 222 n.
Samson, Leon, 178, 341
Sanford, Charles L., 58 n.
Sanford, R. Nevitt, 277 n.
Sangster, Charles, 258
Sanseverino, Luisa R., 186 n.
Sawyer, John E., 226 n.
Schacter, Ruth, 33 n.
Schaff, Philip, 142, 153 n., 163
Schattschneider, E. E., 293, 295 n.
Schlatter, Richard, 95–96
Schlesinger, Arthur, Jr., 80
Schlesinger, Arthur, Sr., 34, 35 n., 90 n., 124–125
Schumpeter, Joseph A., 178, 242 n., 291 n.
Schurmann, Franz, ix
Scott, Robert E., 316 n.
Segal, Harvey, 54 n.
Segerstedt, Torgny, 237
Seidman, Harold, 189 n.
Sellers, Charles, 215 n.
Selznick, Philip, 312
Seward, William, 85
Shannon, Fred A., 48 n.
Shannon, Lyle, 345 n.

Shepard, Benjamin, 49
Shils, Edward, 4 n., 18 n., 23 n., 67–68, 69 n., 70 n., 71 n., 72 n., 91, 92 n., 218 n., 219–220, 242 n., 245 n., 317 n.
Simmel, Georg, 308 n.
Simon, Walter B., 309 n.
Simpson, Hoke S., 179 n., 324 n.
Slichter, Sumner, 198 n.
Smelser, Marshall, 34 n., 39 n., 41 n.
Smelser, Neil, ix, 8, 218 n.
Smith, Alfred E., 340
Smith, Henry Nash, 105
Smith, J. W., 156 n., 159 n.
Smith, James M., 39 n.
Smith, John Cotton, 49 n.
Smith, Timothy L., 146 n., 153, 161 n.
Smith, W. B., 55 n.
Smuts, Robert W., 111 n., 112 n., 171 n., 180
Snyder, Charles R., 81 n.
Sofer, Elaine Graham, 282 n.
Sombart, Werner, 114
Sovani, N. V., 70 n.
Spencer, Herbert, 115 n.
Spiller, Robert E., 60 n., 71 n.
Spindler, G. Dearborn, 276 n.
Sprague, Peleg, 22
Stammer, Otto, ix, 192
Stanton, Alfred H., 279 n., 285 n.
Sternberger, Dolf, 292
Stevens, Thaddeus, 85
Steward, U., 280 n.
Stewart, Rosemary, 221 n., 226 n., 227 n., 241
Stigler, George J., 149, 179 n.
Stiles, Ezra, 19
Stoker, Cleo, xi
Stokes, Anson Phelps, 82 n.
Sturmthal, Adolf, 182 n., 185, 196 n.
Suci, George, 275 n.
Sufrin, Sidney, 198 n.
Sumner, Charles, 72 n., 85
Sumner, William Graham, 89
Sun Yat-sen, 315
Sutton, Francis X., 170 n., 314 n.
Swanson, Guy E., 137 n., 346 n.
Sweet, William W., 157 n.

Taft, Philip, 188 n.
Taft, Ronald, ix, 252 n.
Taine, Hippolyte, 217 n., 218 n.
Thistlethwaite, Frank, 88, 89 n., 97–98
Thomas, Charles M., 63 n.
Thomas, Hugh, 215 n.
Tingsten, Herbert, 310
Titmuss, Richard M., 325 n.
Tobin, James, 170 n.

Tocqueville, Alexis Charles de, 17 n., 80 n., 86 n., 95–96, 102, 108, 110, 112, 114 n., 122, 132 n., 137–138, 141, 154–155, 158, 160, 166, 168, 170 n., 213, 216 n., 226 n., 228–229, 243 n., 253
Tolles, Frederick, 89 n.
Tönnies, Ferdinand, 209
Torrielli, Andrew J., 117 n., 122 n.
Toynbee, Philip, 240 n.
Trevelyan, G. M., 96
Trollope, Anthony, 110, 111 n., 120, 141, 142 n., 156
Trollope, Frances, 110, 111 n., 112
Tropp, Asher, 221 n.
Trow, Martin, *viii*, 36 n., 181 n., 190 n., 207 n.
Truman, David, 301
Truman, Tom, *ix*, 192, 202 n.
Turner, John E., 327 n.
Turner, Ralph, 222
Tyler, Alice, 81 n.
Tyler, John, 84

Ulich, Robert, 244
Underhill, Frank H., *ix*, 16 n., 87, 250, 256, 268 n.
Useem, John, 133 n.
Useem, Ruth Hill, 133 n.

Vaizey, John, 215 n.
Van Buren, Martin, 84
Van Wagenen, R. W., 9 n., 26 n., 91 n., 210 n., 344 n.
Veblen, Thorstein, 114
Verney, Douglas, 235 n.

Walker, Kenneth F., 252 n., 267 n.
Wallace, Edward S., 35 n.

Wallerstein, Immanuel, 18 n., 70 n.
Ward, Russel, 255 n., 256 n., 264, 266 n.
Warner, Charles Dudley, 117
Warner, W. L., 125
Washington, George, 18–19, 37, 42 n., 63 n.; as charismatic leader, 18–23; "Farewell Address," 20, 65; veneration of, 22
Wayne, Ivor, 278 n.
Weber, Max, *viii*, 7, 17, 94, 115, 119, 126, 142, 156, 209 n., 242 n., 246, 316, 291 n.
Webster, Daniel, 84
Wecter, Dixon, 116 n., 119 n., 153 n.
Weems, Mason L., 22 n.
Weiner, Myron, 23, 24 n.
Weinstein, James, 295 n.
Wesley, John, 146
Wheeler, Wayne B., 340 n.
White, Winston, 213 n.
Whitman, Walt, 259
Whyte, William H., 1, 102, 103 n., 104, 107, 119, 122, 126, 128, 132, 135–136, 138
Wildavsky, Aaron, 289 n.
Williams, Daniel D., 160 n.
Williams, Philip, 301 n.
Williams, Raymond, 217 n.
Williams, Robin, 94, 96 n., 140 n., 213 n.
Willis, R. H., 279 n.
Wilson, James, 29 n.
Wilson, Woodrow, 339–340
Wirtz, Willard, 332 n.
Wolfenstein, Martha, 283 n.
Wood, Robert, 138
Wylie, Laurence, 229 n.

Young, Michael, 218 n., 220 n., 224 n.

Zahn, Jane C., 167 n.

Subject Index

abolitionists, 34

abstention, principle of, 65

achievement, equality and, 1–2, 203, 213, 253, 273, 284, 318; gifted child and, 127–129; in Great Britain, 215; and labor unions, 203; legitimacy and, 245; and Old World traditions, 101; other-directedness and, 134–135; Protestant ethic and, 126–127; religion and, 273; school youths' attitude toward, 133; social structure and, 174–175; value system and, 123

achievement-orientation, 132–134

Actors' Equity, 190

address, forms of, 320

"affluent society," 1, 174, 338

AFL-CIO, 189 n.

Africa, kinship with world ideals in, 67–68; mass parties in, 33 n.; nationalism in, 23 n., 24, 35 n.; neutralism in, 62; one-party systems in, 33 n., 36–37; opposition permitted in, 44; party structure in, 31–32, 314; religious nationalism in, 79; rule of law in, 11; unifying functions of parties in, 33 n.

age, education and, 328

Alien and Sedition Acts, 39, 42 n.

America, see United States

American character, changing nature of, 101–139; conformity in, 116–119; continuity of, 106; egalitarianism in, 110; foreign accounts of, 106–122; social barriers and, 113; summary of factors in, 129–139; unchanging nature of, 106–110; values and, 110–122

American history, continuity in, 104; periods in, 106

Americanism, as ideology, 178

American labor movement, 171–173; see also labor unions

American literature, 73–74, 259, 278

American Newspaper Guild, 190

American political system, see political parties; party systems

American Protestantism, fecundity of, 166–167; see also Protestantism; religion

American religion, church–state separation in, 81, 161, 168; competition in, 160; pervasiveness of, 141–151, 155–156; secularity in, 151–159, 166–167; special quality of, 155, 159; value system and, 105, 140–169; voluntarism in, 159–169; see also Protestant ethic; religion

American Revolution, basic values of, 105; effect of in Canada, 87–88; effect of on "lower class," 341; egalitarianism and, 123, 127; legitimacy of authority following, 16–17, 77; national unity and, 26, 30; religion and, 159

American values, 123, 170; see also values; value system

"American way of life," 158, 165, 168

Angola, Portuguese, 24 n.

anti-Americanism, 256

anti-clericalism, 273 n.

anti-Federalists, 30–31

anti-intellectualism, 71–73

anti-Jackson party, 82

anti-Masonic party, 82, 84

Anti-Saloon League, 339 n.

anti-Semitism, 117

anti-Westernism, 35

Arab nations, national unity problem in, 25

aristocracy, collectivity and, 270; equality and, 112; in France, 226, 241; in Germany, 232–233, 242; in Great Britain, 217–218, 243–244, 291; versus labor union leadership, 190–191; versus populism, 76; religion and, 83, 95, 162; secrecy and, 219–220; in Sweden, 235–236

Arminianism, 161–163

army life, 93, 273, 276, 343

Articles of Confederation, 27, 31 n.

ascription, 209–211, 237, 282; achievement and, 245, 249; elitism and, 271

Asia, kinship with world ideals in, 67–68; neutralism in, 62; opposition permitted in, 44; rule of law in, 11

Australia, anti-elitism in, 199; education in, 260–261; as egalitarian society, 199–202, 254–255, 267; frontier in, 255–256; labor unions in, 192, 201, 264–265; law enforcement in, 265; lawyers in,

264; "mateship" in, 252, 266–267; party system in, 303 n.; success ethic in, 253; value differences in, 248–273; wage differentials in, 267
Australian Council of Trade Unions, 201
Australian literature, 258–259
Australian Workers Union, 201, 256 n.
Austria, republic of, 308–309
authoritarianism, 91, 234, 239, 314
authoritarian personality, 127–128, 277–281
authority, in African party structure, 31; decentralized, 197; mistrust of, 121–122; need for, 90; party system and, 313; in post-revolutionary society, 16; revolution and, 11; source of, 313
autonomy, need for, 62–66

Bacongo, 24 n.
bank charters, granting of, 50
bank stock, state investment in, 51–52
Bank of the United States, 48, 51 n.
Baptist Church, 151, 162
Belgian Congo, 24 n.; *see also* Congo
Belgium, party systems in, 305–306
big business, legitimacy of, 127–128
Bonn republic, Germany, 237–239
bounties, state, 49
bourgeoisie, Engels' view of, 5–6; in France, 226, 228; in Great Britain, 240–241; political parties of, 290; rise of, 76
British Amalgamated Engineering Union, 193
British capital, in early American enterprises, 55–56
British Gallup poll, 194 n.
British labor unions, 173, 190
British Labour Party, 194, 217, 219, 324
bureaucracy, college education and, 328; growth of, 282
bureaucratization, fair treatment and, 136; trade unions and, 136; urbanization and, 132, 140
"business unionism," 187

Calvinism, 94, 161–163; capitalism and, 94; decline of, 126; in early U.S., 80; trade unionism and, 294; *see also* Protestant ethic; Puritanism
Canada, anti-Americanism in, 256; conservation in, 250; education in, 260–261; as egalitarian society, 199–202, 251; frontier in, 160; "intellectual superiority" of, 257–258; labor officials in, 201; local autonomy in, 262; parliamentary system of, 301; party systems in, 299–302; as product of counterrevolution, 86; religious change in, 88–89; religious

sects in, 166; "rightist" bias in, 86–87; similarities to U.S., 89; Toryism in, 86–87; value differences in, 248–273
Canadian literature, 258–259
Canadian Protestants, 147
canal-building, state support of, 51–53
cantonal government, Switzerland, 17, 310
capital, foreign, 55–57
capitalism, achievement and, 125; equality and, 175, 178–179; and Protestant ethic, 94, 341; reinforcing of egalitarianism by, 178; revolution and, 175; triumph of, 171; Weber's view of, 7
caste system, British, 115–117, 215–217, 243–244
Catholic Church, American character of, 153; democracy and, 96; in France, 226, 231; growth of, 163; membership in, 145 n., 151
"caution," in American character, 107, 109; in Canadian character, 252
Census Bureau, U.S., 147–149, 323
change, commitment to, 105; materialistic interpretation of, 122–129
character, national, 21, 27, 280; social, 123, 274–278, 285
charismatic leader, defined, 17; role of, 16–23; 315–316
charters, granting of, 50–51
child-rearing, egalitarianism and, 119–120; in France, 283; Germany, 275, 279–280; Great Britain, 220–221; home discipline and, 279; permissiveness in, 124, 274–276
children, democratic character in, 279; early "ripening" of, 119; pampering of, 124; tolerance and equality toward, 119–122
children's stories, as value indicators, 135–136, 345
Chinese Communists, 315
Christian Michelsens Institute, *ix*, 192
Christian Democratic Party, Italy, 308
Christian Democratic Union, Germany, 292
Christianity, democracy and, 94–96; pervasiveness of, 155; *see also* Protestant ethic
Church and State Party, early U.S., 82
church membership, 142–147
Church of England, 88–89
church–state separation, 81, 161, 165, 168
civil liberties, early U.S., 39–41
civil service, under Jackson, 101
Civil War, 91, 106, 112, 165, 341; electoral system and, 309; national authority preceding, 34; Republican Party and, 329

class consciousness, absence of in U.S., 111, 178–179, 214, 342
class differences, early U.S., 92, 341
class system, France, 225–226, 231; Germany, 234, 242, 291; Great Britain, 115–117, 215–217, 243–244; Sweden, 236–237
class values, rise of, 76
clergymen, number of, 148–149
Cold War, new nations and, 62
collective bargaining, 181; American versus European, 198; in Australia and Canada, 200; in France, 227–228
colleges, enrollment figures for, 260, 327; religious belief in, 149–150
Communism and Communists, in Africa and Asia, 314–315; equality and, 262; in France, 229–230, 273 n., 298; in Germany, 233, 291–292; in India, 306; in Italy, 308–309; in new nations, 247; in Poland, 319–320
comparative analysis, methods of, 343–348
conformity, 116–117; versus brotherhood, 138; decline in, 138; equality and, 119; as form of individuality, 137–139; in religion, 139
Congo, national unity problems in, 24–25
Congregationalists, 80–81, 83, 94, 151; and American Revolution, 160; in Nova Scotia, 88
Congress of Industrial Organizations, 181, 185
conscience, religion and, 167
consensus, national unity and, 23–24
conservatism, in Canada, 250; versus democracy, 97; versus liberalism, 343; post-war, 126; religion and, 79; Toryism and, 86–87
constitution, as authority symbol, 312, 314
Constitution, U.S., 34–35, 338
Constitutional Convention, 28–32
contest mobility, 222
Continental Congress, 28
corporation, versus family-owned company, 136; government protection of, 56–57
corruption, decentralization and, 198; in labor unions, 176, 189, 198, 202
crime, in English-speaking nations, 265–266; success and, 176
criticism, sensitivity to, 108–109

decentralization, 198
Declaration of Independence, 70, 97, 225, 338, 341
deference, absence of, 110–112
deism, 80

democracy, conservatism and, 97; minority rights in, 11; odds against in emerging nations, 11; Plato's analysis of, 118; as process, 316; Protestantism and, 157 n. (*see also* Protestant ethic); religion and, 168–169, 204; slow growth of, 316; social distinctions and, 110; stability and, 207–247, 317; turmoil in founding of, 15–16; "tutelary," 315; value systems and, 207–247
Democratic Party, 300, 337; "common man" label of, 330; egalitarian reforms of, 338; labor unions and, 171–173; revival of, 128
democratic personality, versus authoritarian, 277–281
democratic polity, versus revolutionary mood, 10–11; social character and, 274–285; values and, 209–213
democratic process, value and, 268–273
Democratic-Republican Party, 33, 41, 43, 45, 78; anti-elitism of, 85; economic policy of, 62
democratic rights, 39–40
democratic stability, values and, 207–247, 268
democratization, defined, 316
Denmark, labor unions in, 186 n., 187 n., 192
denominationalism, function of, 168
desegregation, 331
diffuseness-specificity, 249, 269, 284
disestablishment, 160–162
dissent, freedom of, 269; *see also* opposition
drama, German versus American, 278
due process, 11

economic development, egalitarianism and, 343; legitimacy and, 246; other-directedness and, 134–135; past rates of, 348; as "payoff," 46; stability and, 290; value system and, 122
economic intervention, forms of, 46–49
education, age and, 328; versus conformity, 138; high-school and college attendance, 327; intellectuals and, 67; number of college students by countries, 260; old-fashioned versus elite, 128; religious, 165
egalitarianism (equalitarianism), 76, 211–213; aggressive, 110–111; in Australia, 254; capitalism and, 178; decline of, 125; economic development and, 343; education and, 127; of frontier, 251; *see also* equality; opportunity; value differences; value systems

Eire, political parties in, 303–304
electoral rules, acceptance of, 44
electoral systems, 301–306; social structure and, 293–295; in two-party system, 314; U.S., 300, 309
elitism, 284; ascription and, 282; diffuseness and, 269; egalitarianism in, 249; European, 226–234, 320; indicators of, 345; political, 208; populism and, 271; schools and, 128, 221–223; social recognition and, 76, 211; stability and, 268; in Sweden, 235–236; values in, 216; in West Germany, 234, 238
embargo, U.S., 47, 59 n., 64
employee, individuality of, 131, 228–231
employer, fear of, 136; loyalty to, 227
England, class lines in, 115–117, 215–217; industrial competition with, 46–47; loans to American industry from, 55; *see also* Great Britain
Englishmen, Americans as, 93
English-speaking democracies, value differences in, 248–273; *see also* Australia; Canada; Great Britain; United States
entrepreneur, 131, 238
Episcopal Church, 151
equality, achievement and, 1–2, 101, 203, 318; anti-elitism and, 84–85; in Australia, 199–202, 252, 254–255, 262; in Canada, 199–202, 251; capitalism and, 175; in child-rearing, 119–121; competition and, 318; conformity and, 116–119; economic development and, 343; gifted child and, 127–129; income and, 321; inequality and, 321–343; labor unions and, 203; opportunity and, 115, 318, 321, 347; other-directedness and, 118–119; political behavior and, 97; religion and, 273; in revolutionary movements, 77; snobbishness and, 117; in social relationships, 112; in Soviet Union, 320; stability and, 268; status-seeking and, 112, 139, 175; success and, 102, 175; wage theories and, 186; "for whites only," 330; *see also* egalitarianism; inequality
Erie Canal, 56
"Establishment," 218, 270, 342
Europe, collective bargaining in, 200; labor leaders in, 172–173, 191–192; labor problems in, 198; school youth attitudes in, 133; social structure in, 181; state church in, 162–164; working-class ideology in, 186; *see also* France; Germany; Great Britain, etc.
evangelism, 6 n., 162
"exclusiveness," stress on, 113 n.

family-owned company, versus corporation, 136
"Farewell Address," Washington's, 20, 65
farm population, 334
fashion, submission to, 115
fatalism, in American character, 108
federal aid, to industry, 46–49
federalism, labor movement and, 196–197; religion and, 80
Federalist, The, 26, 65
Federalists and Federalist Party, 21 n., 73, 329; anti-egalitarianism of, 77; versus anti-Federalists, 30–31; attack on embargo, 47–48; birth of, 32; compared to African parties, 30–33; disappearance of after 1814, 40; economic policy of, 62; fear of organized opposition, 39–40; name adopted by, 31 n.; origin of party, 32; "political suicide" of, 41; resistance to opposition party, 38–40; secession and, 34; in temperance movement, 81; turnover of power to opposition in 1800, 44
feudalism, absence of in U.S., 89, 130
Ford Foundation, *ix*
foreign capital, U.S. need for, 55–57
"foreign entanglements," rejection of, 90
foreign policy, early U.S., 65–66
France, *ancien regime* and aristocracy in, 241; businessmen and capitalism in, 227; child-rearing in, 283; civil service, 231; Communists in, 229–230, 273 n., 298; inner direction in, 283; instability of, 231–233; "modern," 230; political history, 296–298; political parties in, 296–297; pre-industrial values in, 228–229; social structure in, 283–284, 296; two-ballot system in, 300, 314; value systems in, 210, 224–239
franchises, as economic aid, 49–50
fraternal lodges, 138
free press, 42–43
French Revolution, 21, 225, 241; legitimacy of, 228; terror following, 39
frontier, Australia, 255–256; Canada, 250–251; religion and, 160; U.S., 251, 255–258, 338
Fugitive Slave Law, 35
fundamentalists, 151, 339

Gallup poll, British labor, 194 n.
gambling, 49, 82, 176
Gemeinschaft, versus *Gesellschaft*, 209–210
Georgia, state aid to industry in, 52–53

Germany, aristocracy in, 232–233, 242; child-rearing in 275, 279–280; class system in, 291; Communists in, 233, 291–292; dramatic subjects in, 278; military hierarchy of, 276; parent–child relations in, 275; status in, 291; value patterns and systems in, 210, 224–239; white-collar status in, 183–185

Ghana, 18, 36–37, 315

gifted child, 127–129

Gilded Age, 114

God, belief in, 149

"good life," 287

government aid, to industry, 46–49

government ownership, 49–52

government planning, 46

grades, versus popularity, in school, 133–134

Great Britain, achievement in, 215; aristocracy in, 217–218, 244, 291; child-rearing in, 279–280; class system in, 115–117, 215–217, 243–244; collective bargaining in, 200; education in, 260–261; elitism in, 217, 218 n., 219, 224; income distribution in, 325–326; labor leadership in, 190–192; Labour Party, 194, 219, 324; lawyers in, 264; Liberal Party, 294–295, 297; parliamentary history, 240; political secrecy in, 219–220; stability in, 224; values compared to U.S. values, 213–224, 248–273

Great Depression, 106, 125, 157 n., 233, 323, 329, 340

Great Plains, frontier and, 105

hierarchy, rejection of, 76; respect for, 234

high school education, 327

historical analysis, of social systems, 7–10

holidays, national, 75

Homestead Act, 105

identity, establishing of, 16; *see also* national identity

Illinois, church attendance in, 131 n.

ILO Mission Report, 196–197

immigration laws, discrimination in, 338–340

incentives, bases for, 136–137

income, inequality in, 324

income distribution, 322, 325

income tax, 322–323

Independence Day, 75

India, Communists in, 306; languages in, 24 n., national unity problems in, 24; party systems in, 306; religious nationalism in, 79

individuality, versus conformity, 124, 137

Indonesia, national unity problem in, 25; religious nationalism in, 79

industrialism, nationalism and, 46–47; and pre-industrial values, 342

industry, foreign capital and, 55–56; government aid to, 46–49

inequality, versus equality, 340–343; growth of, 125; of Negro, 331–333; in U.S., 321–340

"inner-directed" character, 102–103, 126, 281–285

innovation, crime and, 176–177

intellectual inferiority, sense of, 70, 71 n.; populism and, 68

intellectuals, leadership by, 66–74

interest groups, use of, 26–27

International Ladies Garment Workers Union, 188

International Typographical Union, 190

Ireland, electoral system in, 293; political parties in, 303–304

Israel, party system in, 304; political prestige from leftism in, 74 n., 75 n.

Italy, Communists in, 308–309; wage theories in, 186

Jacksonian Democrats, 83, 300; anti-elitism of, 73, 84

Jamaica, B.W.I., 261

Jay treaty, 33

Jeffersonian Democrats, 20, 33; civil liberties record of, 40–41; "irreligion" of, 80

Jeffersonian Republicans, 21 n.

Jews, as dissenters, 164; immigration of, 152; in motion picture industry, 176 n.; psychic punishment of, 271; snobbishness and, 177

Junkers, 242

jury system, 265

Keynesian economics, 128

Know Nothing Party, 286

Ku Klux Klan, 286, 339–340

labor lawyers, 200

labor leadership, 187–196

labor movement, 171–172

labor parties, 290, 303 n.

labor-saving equipment, 198

labor troubles, equality and, 204

labor unions, American versus British and European, 172–174; and American political system, 196–199; and American value system, 170–204; in Australia and Canada, 199–202; bureaucratization of, 136; corruption in, 176, 189, 198, 202;

criticism as "libel" in, 42–43; equality and, 183, 195; European, 198; and European social structure, 181; France, 227, 231; Germany, 183–185; lack of class-consciousness and self-interest in, 178–179, 342; *laissez faire* in, 181; leadership versus societal values in, 187–196; militancy of, 179–182, 197–198; "more-money" ideology of, 187; number of officials in, 191–196; paradox of, 203; political system and, 196–199; power of, 188; religion and, 203–204; salaries to full-time leaders in, 195; skilled versus unskilled workers in, 185–186; socialist ideologies in, 196; social structure and, 173–178; societal values and, 170–187; wage differentials and, 182–187

Labour Party, Great Britain, 194, 217, 219, 324

laissez faire, versus aid to industry, 48; government ownership and, 52; labor unions and, 181

language, national unity and, 24; in Revolutionary era, 26

Latin America, electoral systems in, 300n.; legitimacy in, 246; underdeveloped status of, 15

law, respect for, 11; rule of, 8–9, 11, 265

lawyers, in English-speaking democracies, 264–265

leader, charismatic, 16–23

leadership, in Great Britain, 215n.; labor unions, 187–196; in political elite, 208–209

leftism, in American political tradition, 85–86; in Canada, 87; of Founding Fathers, 90; in independence struggles, 75–77; in Israel, 74n., 75n.; national identity and, 78; in U.S., 295

legislative supremacy, principle of, 30

legitimacy, achievement and, 245; crisis of, 16–23; and economic development, 246; of French Revolution, 228; of political party, 311; revolution and, 90; stability and, 290; three approaches to, 17

libel, 42–43

Liberal Party, Canada, 306; Great Britain, 294–295, 297; New Zealand, 303

literacy, early U.S., 95

lotteries, state, 48–49

Louisiana Purchase, 59

loyalty, in new political system, 16

Lumpenproletariat, 291

Lutheran Church, 151

McCarthyism, 262n., 263

mail, Sunday delivery of, 81

majority, sovereignty of, 290; tyranny of, 108

Malaya, local rule in, 17

management, bureaucratization and, 136

manual labor, versus white-collar work, 183–185

manufacturing, aid to, 46

manufacturing class, rise of, 57

mass parties, Africa, 33 n.

"mateship," Australia, 252, 266–267

Memorial Day, 75

merchant class, rise of, 57

Methodist Church, 146, 148n., 152, 162

Mexican War, 35, 86n.

Mexico, 316; political systems in, 315–317

military class, 93, 276, 343

minority parties, 312

minority rights, 11, 164

Missouri Compromise, 44

mobility, contest versus sponsored, 222; decrease of, 125; in religion, 167; social, 272

Monroe Doctrine, 65

morality, economic development and, 57–58; and national identity, 80–83, 95–96

Moslem League, 79

Moslem parties, Indonesia, 79

motion picture industry, 176n.

multi-party system, 296, 307–313; failure of, 291

national authority, establishment of, 15–60; versus opposition rights, 36

national celebrations, political creed and, 75

national character, 21, 27, 280

National Council of Churches, 145n., 151

national evolution, comparative studies in, 343–348; historical, 9

national identity, establishing of, 16; formulation of, 61–98; leftist ideology and, 77–78; Puritan tradition and, 94–96; religion and, 78–83; revolution as source of, 74–90

nationalism, and economic independence, 58; economic policy and, 62; industrialism as "payoff" in, 46–47; and intellectual elite, 27, 67–68; versus states' rights, 28–29

National Party, South Africa, 303

national symbols, class values and, 76

national unity, authority and, 36; problem of, 23–35

Nazism, 233–234, 238, 292, 314

Negro, inequality of, 330–333, 337; psychic punishment of, 271; religious affiliation of, 152

"Negro Revolt of 1963," 333
Negro schools, 332
Negro vote, 329, 333
Negro–white relations, 320
neurotic personality, 125–127
neutralism, rise of in Asia and Africa, 62; in U.S., 65–66, 90
neutrality, need for, 62–66
New Brunswick, Canada, 302
New Guinea, language problems in, 24 n.
New Jersey, states' rights stand of (1852), 35
New Jersey Plan, 29
New Jersey Society for Establishing Useful Manufactures, 47 n.
new nation, America as first, 2, 15, *et passim;* charismatic authority in, 18; intellectuals' role in, 69–74; legitimacy in, 246; national unity problem in, 23–26; neutralism and non-alignment in, 62–63; political problems of, 36 n., 37 n.; rule of law in, 11; "socialist" parties in, 85; suppression of opposition rights in, 36–37
New York, church attendance in, 142–143; state aid to industry by, 53
New Zealand, political parties in, 303
Nigeria, autonomy in, 35 n.; national unity problems in, 24 n.; one-party domination in, 37; religious nationalism in, 79
noblesse oblige morality, 241, 270
non-alignment policy, new nations, 62–63
Norway, electoral system in, 293; party systems in, 311; union membership in, 192
Nova Scotia, "inertness" in, 257–258; religious change in, 88
nullification ordinances, 34

occupational mobility, 125
old-age pensions, 337
Old World traditions, achievement and, 101
one-party systems, 16, 33 n., 36–37, 78
opinion, in democratization process, 116, 316; fear of, 108
opportunity, equality of, 2, 115, 318, 321, 347; status-consciousness and, 112; *see also* equality
opposition, Federalists' fear of, 39; rights of, 36–45; as sedition or treason, 39; stability and, 316–317; succession and, 44
"organization man," 103–104
"other-directedness," 102–103, 123, 130, 207; versus achievement-orientation, 135; bureaucratization and, 132; as conformity, 118–119; in Europe, 133; and

"generalized other," 134; versus inner-directedness, 281–285; religion and, 141; urbanization and, 132

Pakistan, national unity problem in, 25 n.
parent–child relationships, 274–275, 283; *see also* child-rearing; children
parent-teacher associations, 221–222
parliamentary systems, 228, 293–294
particularism–universalism, 249, 270, 284
party politics, versus intellectual leadership, 73
party systems, authority and, 313; consequences of, 307–312; social cleavage and, 295–306; social groups and, 286–317; social structure and, 289–295; *see also* political party
patriotism, industrialism and, 47
pattern variables, 209, 270; ranking by country, 249
"payoff," economic development as, 45–60
Pennsylvania, egalitarianism in, 78; state aid to industry in, 52
permissiveness, in child-rearing, 121–122, 274
personal failure, social structure and, 175
personality adjustment, 127
personal responsibility, 163
Philippine Islands, 261
physiocrats, 47
plurality system, 294
Poland, Communists in, 319–320; white-collar workers in, 184
political cleavage, in post-Revolutionary U.S., 26
political elite, 208; *see also* elitism
political party, Constitutional Convention and, 32; first "modern," 33; representation and, 286–289; rise of, 26–27, 34; *see also* party systems
political stability, social change and, 239–247; two-party system and, 309; *see also* stability
populism, excesses of, 271, 285; minority rights and, 11; intellectuals and, 68; rise of, 76, 220, 286; versus rule of law, 11
post-revolutionary society, legitimacy in, 16; rule of law in, 11
poverty, 333–337
predestination, 161
presidential system, U.S., 300–301
primary elections, 300
productivity levels, 348
professions, training of, 72 n.
progressive education, 120, 122, 126–128
Progressive Party, Canada, 302

Prohibition Amendment, 338, 339 n.
property ownership, 326
proportional representation, 293, 299
prostitution, 176
Protestant churches, membership in, 145–147
Protestant ethic, 94, 101, 107, 339; capitalism and, 94, 341; decline of, 126, 136; foreign investment and, 57 n.; versus social ethics, 103; trade unionism and, 204
Protestantism, American, 157–159, 162; crime and, 176; immigration laws favoring, 338–339; minority rights and, 164
provincialism, 27–28
Prussia, 233, 237, 292
psychic energy, conformity and, 138–139
psychic punishment, 271
public opinion, in democratization process, 316
public-opinion polls, 345
public roads and waterways, 49–50
public school system, 2; *see also* education; schools
Puerto Rico, 261
Puritanism, as counter-reformation, 81; effect of, 95–96; labor unions and, 203; significance of, 158–159, 253

Quakers, 152
Quebec, education in, 261

race relations, 214–215
racketeering, success in, 176
radicalism, versus conservatism, 124–125; versus religious innovation or revivalism, 6 n.
railroads, state support of, 50–54
Reader's Digest, 346
religion, achievement and, 273; as adaptive mechanism, 272; American, *see* American religion; church membership, 142–148; church-state separation in, 81, 161, 168; as conduct and good deeds, 156; conformity in, 139; democracy and, 167–169; denominationalism in, 168; in early U.S., 94; equality and, 169, 273; of middle class, 6 n.; mobility in, 167; mutual esteem among competing sects, 154; national identity through, 79–83; Negro and, 272; other-directedness in, 153; pervasiveness of, 156; sects and secularization in, 152–154; "Sunday" versus "weekday" varieties of, 168; trade unions and, 203–205; traditional English, 6; urbanization and, 140; in value systems, 139; voluntarism in, 159–169

religious affiliation, survey of, 147–149
religious education, 165
religious tolerance, 164–165
"Report on Manufactures," Hamilton, 47 n.
representation, social structure and, 287–300
Republican Party, big business and, 127–128; Civil War and, 329; and liberal domination pattern, 329; "popular" appeal of, 38
revolution, American, *see* American Revolution; legitimacy and, 90; national identity through, 74–90; religion and, 95–96; "of rising expectations," 46, 91; value system and, 89
revolutionary groups, equality in, 77
revolutionary ideal, twentieth-century U.S., 97–98
revolutionary intellectual, 67
revolutionary mood, and democratic polity, 10–11
Revolutionary War, *see* American Revolution
rightists, versus conservatism, 97
Rights of Man, doctrine of, 225
rising expectations, revolution of, 46, 91
roads and waterways, state aid through, 49–51
"rules of the game," respect for, 43, 93, 307
rural culture, versus metropolitan, 103

schools, Australia, 254; British versus U.S., 221–223, 327; prayers in, 165; punishment in, 121–122; Sweden, 236; *see also* colleges; education
Scientific American, 324 n.
secession, 34; in Africa, 35 n.
secrecy, in government and politics, 219–220
secret societies, 37
secularity, in American religion, 151–159
Sedition Act, 39, 42 n.
segregation, 331
self-distrust, in American character, 108
self-image, national, *see* national identity
self-interest, lack of in unions, 178–179
self-orientation, versus collectivity-orientation, 270
single-party systems, *see* one-party systems
skilled labor, versus unskilled, 182–187
slavery, U.S., 34, 330–332
small-town ambitions, 131–132
social analysis, monistic approach to, 4–5; patterns in, 137–138

social change, continuity of, 104–105; stability and, 239–247
social character, values and, 123, 274–285
social cleavage, party systems and, 295–306
Social Credit Party, Canada, 302
Social Democratic Party, Germany, 233, 291–292
social distinctions, absence of, 110; capitalism and, 179; *see also* class consciousness; status
social ethic, 103
social groups, party systems and, 286–317
socialism, versus "Americanism," 178
socialist parties, in new states, 85
Socialist Party, France, 231; Germany, 233, 291; Sweden, 237; U.S., 286, 295
socialization process, 133, 275
social mobility, 1; as adaptive mechanism, 272
social recognition, factors in, 76
social science, comparative, 318–348
social stratification, 269 n.
social structure, electoral systems and, 293–295; party systems and, 289–295; unionism and, 173–178
social systems, historical analysis of, 8; hypotheses concerning, 348; value system in, 123
social work agencies, 195
societal values, union leadership and, 187–196; union movement and, 178–187
society, dynamic equilibrium model of, 7–8
South, electoral system in, 309; Negro-white relations in, 214–215, 320; Prohibition and Protestantism in, 339–340; as source of instability, 214–215
South Africa, national unity problem in, 24 n.; party system in, 309; political parties in, 302–303
Southern Baptist Church, 151
Soviet Union, elitism in, 320; income level in, 327; "intellectual inferiority" in, 71 n.
specificity-diffuseness, 209, 213
spoils system, 101 n.
stability, democratic, 207–247, 317; legitimacy and, 290; and social change, 239–247; two-party system and, 309; value system and, 207–247, 268; wealth and, 290
Ständestaat system, Germany, 10, 234
state, aid to industry from, 46–49
state banks, 51–52
state charters, 50–51
state lines, crossing of by political parties, 26–27

"State parties," 312
states' rights, and Democratic-Republican Party, 41; expressions of, 35; versus national authority, 28–29; versus national planning, 48
status and status-seeking, 112–113; books deploring, 138; as conformity, 116; as egalitarianism, 112, 139; in Germany and other countries, 10, 291; inequalities in, 271; in small communities, 132
strikes, 202
subversion, force and, 37–38
"success" ethic, 114, 124; anxiety and, 125; in Australia, 252–253; bureaucracy and, 132; crime and, 176–177; equality and, 102, 175; labor unions and, 174, 189, 204; need for, in U.S., 273; and social structure, 174–175
suffrage, universal, 2, 235
Sunday Blue Laws, 164
Sunday, as day of rest, 81–82
Sunday school, 146
Sweden, aristocracy in, 235–236; electoral system in, 293; old-age pensions in, 337; party system in, 310; union leadership in, 190; union membership in, 192
Swiss Federation, 66
Switzerland, canton system in, 17, 310; multi-party government in, 312

tariff, protective, 48
taxation, as aid to industry, 49 n.
tax changes, U.S., 323
teachers, American versus British, 221–222
temperance movement, 81
theocracy, 82–83
Togoland, British and French, 24 n.
Toryism, 76, 83, 86–87, 92, 160, 250
totalitarianism, 91, 247, 315
Townsend Harris High School, N.Y., 127
trade unions, *see* labor unions
Transport Workers Union, 185
treason, libel and, 42–43
Tunisia, 315
two-ballot system, 300, 307, 314
two-party system, 16, 44, 294–295, 299; in Belgium, 310; in Canada, 302; class conflict and, 290; consequences of, 308; electoral system and, 314; Federalists' view of, 39; national government and, 311; religion and, 82; weaknesses of, 307–308, 312

underdeveloped nations, 246; *see also* new nation
unions, *see* labor unions
Unitarian Church, 151
United Automobile Workers, 185, 188

United Mine Workers, 181

United States, absence of class consciousness in, 214, 342; absence of military class in, 93; aid to industry in early years, 46–48; charismatic authority in, 18; child-rearing in, 119–120, 279–280; church membership in, 143–144; civil liberties in, 39–41; class structure in, 92; compared to Great Britain, 213–224; "democrats" as political leaders in, 85–86; early advantages of, 91; early capitalism, 50–54; early foreign policy, 64–65; economic growth rate, 336; equality in, *see* equality; expansionism of, 59n., 251; family income distribution, 322; fear of by Canada, 251; as first new nation, 2, 15, *et passim*; foreign capital needs, 55–57; frontier in, 255–258; "government party" of Hamilton, 38; Great Britain and, 213–224; identity established, 16; industrial consciousness in, 46; inequality in, 321–340; "international impotence" of, 27; labor movement in, 171–172, 178–187, 192, 196–199; lawyers in, 264; "leftism" in, 75–78, 85–86, 90; legal-rational authority in, 22; legitimacy acquired, 59–60; materialism and love of money in, 58, 122–130; mobility in, 222; as "modern" society, 123; national character formation in, 21; national identity formulated, 61–98; national intellectuals in, 68–69; nationalist leadership in, 30; Negro inequality in, 330–333; "neutralism" of, 62–66, 90; one-party system in, 44; opposition rights in, 37–38; party systems in, 299–300, 307–312; per-capita income in, 333–334; political publicity in, 219–220; poverty in, 333–334; presidential system, 300–301; Puritanism in, 94; rational-legal system of authority, 20; religion in, 94, 140–167; religious materialism, 79–83; school systems, 221; secession threats in first decade, 34; state and local support of industry, 50–54; success ethic in, 114, 124, 132, 174–176, 189, 204, 273; twentieth-century revolutionary ideals of, 97–98; two-party system in, 44 (*see also* two-party system); union membership totals, 192; value cleavages in, 91; value differences in, 213–224, 248–273; *see also* American (adj.)

universalism–particularism, 209, 213

universal suffrage, 235

University of Michigan Survey Research Center, 335–336

unwritten constitution, 269

urbanization, other-directedness and, 132, 140

Uruguay, electoral system in, 300n.

value analysis, 4n., 7

value cleavages, early U.S., 91–92

value conflict, continuity and, 123–124

value differences, in English-speaking democracies, 248–273

value patterns, and democratic polity, 209–213; political process and, 274

values, versus institutions, 2–3, 6; social character and, 274–285

value system, American character and, 110–122; analysis of, 2; Canada, 250–251; as causal factor, 3; central, 4; changes in, 103; character and, 122; and democratic process, 268–273; democratic stability and, 207–247; in dynamic equilibrium model of society, 7–8; foreign capital and, 57; France, 224–239; free choice and, 98; Germany, 224–239; labor unions and, 170–204; national, 209–213; religion and, 139–169; and revolutionary origins, 89; social barriers and, 113; social character and, 123, 274–275; stability and, 268; trade unions and, 170–204

veto groups, 282

violence, in labor unions, 180–181

Virginia, state aid to industry from, 52

Virginia dynasty, 44–45

Virginia Plan, 28–29

voluntarism, religious strength from, 159–169

voluntary associations, egalitarianism and, 195

voting and electoral systems, 293–294, 301–302, 309, 314, 329, 333

wage differentials, labor unions and, 182–187

wage structure, American versus European, 182–187; English-speaking democracies, 267

War of 1812, 44, 47, 58–59, 64–65, 105

wealth, inequality in, 324; per-capita distribution of, 324–325; Protestant ethic and, 341; stability and, 290; striving for, 114–115

Weimar Republic, Germany, 233–235, 291–292, 314

Western world, American patterns for, 130

West Germany, 237–238; *see also* Germany; Weimar Republic

West Indian Federation, 25

Whig Party, 44, 82–85, 240, 300, 329
white-collar worker, 231, 330; wage-pref-
   erence scales for, 183–184
Wisconsin, states' rights stand of 1859 in,
   35
working class, rise of, 76, 104, 227–228;

social status of, 111, 183–184; Sweden,
   237
working-class parties, 290

Yankee peddler, 257
Year Book of American Churches, 148